普通高等教育"十一五"国家级规划教材
中国石油和化学工业优秀教材一等奖

材料科学与工程专业英语
第三版

匡少平　王世颖　顾元香　编

化学工业出版社
·北京·

《材料科学与工程专业英语》为普通高等教育"十一五"国家级规划教材，是根据《大学英语教学大纲》专业阅读部分的要求编写的。全书共分七部分，共 23 个单元，每个单元由一篇课文和一篇阅读材料组成。阅读材料提供与课文相应的背景知识或是课文的续篇；根据课文与阅读材料的内容，配有相应的练习题、注释和词汇表。课文与阅读材料共计 46 篇，其中，第Ⅰ部分为材料科学与工程概论，主要介绍材料科学与工程的历史、材料的分类、材料的特性、材料与化学的关系，以及材料科学的研究进展和发展趋势；第Ⅱ～Ⅶ部分，分别介绍金属材料（包括合金）、陶瓷材料、聚合物材料、复合材料、纳米材料和生物医学材料的化学组成、性质、种类、制造技术和用途等。

　　本书内容丰富、新颖，知识面宽，趣味性强。适于各类材料专业的学生使用，也可作为研究生、教师及相关领域研究人员的学习参考书。

图书在版编目（CIP）数据

材料科学与工程专业英语/匡少平，王世颖，顾元香编．
3 版．—北京：化学工业出版社，2014.12（2025.4重印）
普通高等教育"十一五"国家级规划教材
中国石油和化学工业优秀教材一等奖
ISBN 978-7-122-22031-8

Ⅰ.①材…　Ⅱ.①匡…②王…③顾…　Ⅲ.①材料科学-英语-高等学校-教材　Ⅳ.①H31

中国版本图书馆 CIP 数据核字（2014）第 235798 号

责任编辑：杨　菁　　　　　　　　　　文字编辑：徐雪华
责任校对：王素芹　　　　　　　　　　装帧设计：杨　北

出版发行：化学工业出版社（北京市东城区青年湖南街 13 号　邮政编码 100011）
印　　装：北京天宇星印刷厂
787mm×1092mm　1/16　印张 18½　字数 457 千字　2025 年 4 月北京第 3 版第 17 次印刷

购书咨询：010-64518888　　　　　　　售后服务：010-64518899
网　　址：http://www.cip.com.cn
凡购买本书，如有缺损质量问题，本社销售中心负责调换。

定　　价：49.00 元　　　　　　　　　　　　　　　　　　　　　版权所有　违者必究

前　言

　　出版系列的专业英语教材，是许多院校多年来共同的愿望。在高等教育面向21世纪的改革中，学生的基本素质、知识面及实际工作能力的培养受到空前重视，其中专业英语水平是衡量大学生素质能力的重要指标之一。在此背景下，教育部多次组织会议研究加强外语教学问题，制定有关规范，使外语教学更加受到重视。教材是教学的基本要素之一，与基础英语相比，专业英语教学的教材问题显得尤为突出。

　　国家主管部门的重视和广大院校的呼吁引起了化学工业出版社的关注，他们及时地与原化工部教育主管部门和全国化工类专业教学指导委员会请示协商后，组织全国十余所院校成立了大学英语专业阅读教材编委会。在经过必要的调研后，根据学校需求，编委会优先从各校教学（交流）讲义中确定选题，同时组织力量开展编审工作。本套教材涉及的专业主要包括：化学工程与工艺、石油化工、机械工程、信息工程、工业过程自动化、应用化学、生物工程、环境工程、精细化工及制药工程、材料科学与工程、化工商贸等。

　　《材料科学与工程专业英语》教材第一版于2003年2月由化学工业出版社出版；第二版于2010年1月出版，为普通高等教育"十一五"国家级规划教材。现5年过去了，在材料科学与工程方面出现很多创新理论与技术，因此，有必要将有关新的知识体系对原教材作进一步更新和完善。为此，我们吸收第一版、第二版的出版经验，对教材第二版中的内容进行了重新设计，对部分课文和阅读材料进行更新。

　　教材特点：根据国家"十一五"教材出版规划，按照"全国部分高校化工类及相关专业大学英语专业阅读教材编审委员会"的要求和安排编写的《材料科学与工程专业英语》教材，具有以下特点：(1) 知识面宽：该书囊括了目前与材料科学相关专业的各类知识，金属材料、陶瓷材料、聚合物材料、复合材料、纳米结构材料及生物材料等内容；覆盖范围宽，学科全面。(2) 内容新颖：教材读物均选自国外最新出版的相关学科教材、专著或期刊论文；内容新颖，学科前沿知识丰富，学生和教师都可从中了解材料科学的最新发展趋势。(3) 趣味性强：教材读物在保证学科知识基础性、全面性的前提下，有相当一部分具有很强的趣味性。我们在材料科学类专业英语的教学过程中发现，学生对学科专业以外的知识，如教材中生物材料和纳米材料的功能、应用及其制备表现出极大的兴趣，这样有利于学生拓宽知识面、开拓视野。(4) 读者面宽：《材料科学专业英语》教材适应于各类材料专业的学生使用，也可作为研究生、教师及相关领域研究人员的学习参考书。

　　内容与结构：教材分为7部分（PART），共23个单元（UNIT），每个单元由一篇课文和一篇阅读材料组成。阅读材料提供与课文相应的背景知识或是课文的续篇，以进一步拓展课文的内容。根据课文与阅读材料的内容，配有相应的练习题、注释和词汇表。课文与阅读材料共计46篇，其中：PART Ⅰ 为材料科学与工程概论，共5个单元，包括材料科学与工程的历史、材料的分类、材料的特性、材料与化学的关系，以及材料科学与工程的研究进展和发展趋势；PART Ⅱ～PART Ⅶ，分别介绍金属材料（包括合金）、陶瓷材料、聚合物材料、复合材料、纳米结构材料和生物医学材料的化学组成、性质、种类、制造技术和用途等；教材的最后为附录部分，主要包括自然元素、与材料科学和工程相关的主要国际学术期刊和词汇表。

本教材由匡少平、王世颖、顾元香编写。其中，Unit 1、4、5、6、9、10、11、21、22 和 Appen. 由匡少平编写；Unit 2 由匡少平、王世颖编写；Unit 3、7、8、12、13、14、23 由王世颖编写；Unit 15、16、17、18、19、20 由顾元香编写；教材最后的阅读理解参考答案（Answer to Reading Comprehension）和词汇表（Glossary）由匡少平统一编撰、汇总。全书由匡少平统稿。由于水平所限，教材涉及的内容较广，难免出现疏漏，希望广大读者不吝指正，使本书在使用过程中进一步改进和完善。

致谢：本教材为普通高等教育国家级"十一五"规划教材。在编写过程中得到化学工业出版社大力支持，同时得到青岛科技大学教务处、环境与安全工程学院等大力支持。教材编写过程中，阅读材料选自国际上最新出版的教材、专著、期刊等英文原著。谨致谢忱！

编　者
2014 年 10 月

第一版前言

出版系列的专业英语教材，是许多院校多年来共同的愿望。在高等教育面向21世纪的改革中，学生的基本素质、知识面及实际工作能力的培养受到空前重视，其中专业英语水平是衡量大学生素质能力的重要指标之一。在此背景下，教育部（原国家教委）多次组织会议研究加强外语教学问题，制定有关规范，使外语教学更加受到重视。教材是教学的基本要素之一，与基础英语相比，专业英语教学的教材问题显得尤为突出。

国家主管部门的重视和广大院校的呼吁引起了化学工业出版社的关注，他们及时地与原化工部教育主管部门和全国化工类专业教学指导委员会请示协商后，组织全国十余所院校成立了大学英语专业阅读教材编委会。在经过必要的调研后，根据学校需求，编委会优先从各校教学（交流）讲义中确定选题，同时组织力量开展编审工作。本套教材涉及的专业主要包括：化学工程与工艺、石油化工、机械工程、信息工程、工业过程自动化、应用化学、生物工程、环境工程、精细化工及制药工程、材料科学与工程、化工商贸等。

根据"全国部分高校化工类及相关专业大学英语专业阅读教材编审委员会"的要求和安排编写的《材料科学与工程专业英语》教材，具有以下特点。(1) 知识面宽：该书囊括了目前与材料科学相关专业的各类知识，涉及陶瓷材料、高分子材料、复合材料、纳米材料、金属材料及生物材料等内容；覆盖范围宽，学科全面。(2) 内容新颖：教材读物均选自国外最新出版的相关学科教材、专著或期刊论文；内容新颖，学科前沿知识丰富，学生和教师都可从中了解材料科学的最新发展趋势。(3) 趣味性强：教材读物在保证学科知识基础性、全面性的前提下，有相当一部分具有很强的趣味性。我们在材料科学类专业英语的教学过程中发现，学生对学科专业以外的知识，如教材中生物材料和纳米材料的功能、应用及其制备表现出极大的兴趣，这样有利于学生拓宽知识面、开拓视野。(4) 读者面宽：《材料科学与工程专业英语》教材适应于各类材料专业的学生使用，也可作为研究生、教师及相关领域研究人员的学习参考书。

教材分为7部分（PART），每个部分含3~5个单元（UNIT），共27个单元，每个单元由一篇课文和一篇阅读材料组成。阅读材料提供与课文相应的背景知识或是课文的续篇，以进一步拓展课文的内容。根据课文与阅读材料的内容，配有相应的练习题、注释和词汇表。课文与阅读材料共计54篇，均选自1999年以来出版的原版英文教科书、科技报告、著作及专业期刊等。其中：PART Ⅰ为材料科学与工程概论，包括材料科学与工程的历史、材料的分类、材料的特性、材料与化学的关系以及材料科学的研究进展和发展趋势；PART Ⅱ～PART Ⅶ，分别介绍金属材料（包括合金）、陶瓷材料、高分子材料、复合材料、纳米材料和生物医学材料的化学组成、性质、种类、制造技术和用途等；教材的最后为附录部分，主要包括自然元素（附录1）、与材料科学和工程相关的主要国际学术期刊（附录2）、材料科学和工程的研究团体和协会（附录3）、常用的聚合材料名称（附录4）和词汇表。

本教材在编写过程中得到化学工业出版社的大力支持，同时得到青岛科技大学教务处、化学与分子工程学院、环境与材料科学学院和高分子科学与工程学院等领导的大力支持；另外，教材中许多阅读材料得到 Seeram Ramakrishna，J. R. Jones，F. H.（Sam）Froes 等的大力帮助，有的阅读材料是他们将即将出版的相关教材通过网络发给我们的。在此，我们向他们表示衷心的感谢。

教材由匡少平、张永恒、李旭东三位教师主编（张永恒和李旭东为并列第二主编）。其中，Unit1、2、3、4、6、8、17、23、24、25、26、27 和 Append.1、3 由匡少平同志编写；Unit7、9、10、11、12、20、21、22 由张永恒同志编写；Unit5、13、14、15、16、18、19 和 Append.4 由李旭东同志编写；Append.2 由匡少平同志和张永恒同志完成；教材最后的词汇表（Glossary）由匡少平同志统一编撰、汇总。全书由匡少平同志统稿。张书圣同志审稿。

由于时间所限，教材涉及的内容较广泛，可能出现错漏，希望广大读者不吝指正，使本书在使用过程中不断改进和完善。

编　者
2002 年 12 月

第二版前言

出版系列的专业英语教材，是许多院校多年来共同的愿望。在高等教育面向 21 世纪的改革中，学生的基本素质、知识面及实际工作能力的培养受到空前重视，其中专业英语水平是衡量大学生素质能力的重要指标之一。在此背景下，教育部多次组织会议研究加强外语教学问题，制定有关规范，使外语教学更加受到重视。教材是教学的基本要素之一，与基础英语相比，专业英语教学的教材问题显得尤为突出。

国家主管部门的重视和广大院校的呼吁引起了化学工业出版社的关注，他们及时地与原化工部教育主管部门和全国化工类专业教学指导委员会请示协商后，组织全国十余所院校成立了大学英语专业阅读教材编委会。在经过必要的调研后，根据学校需求，编委会优先从各校教学（交流）讲义中确定选题，同时组织力量开展编审工作。本套教材涉及的专业主要包括：化学工程与工艺、石油化工、机械工程、信息工程、工业过程自动化、应用化学、生物工程、环境工程、精细化工及制药工程、材料科学与工程、化工商贸等。

《材料科学与工程专业英语》教材第一版于 2003 年 2 月由化学工业出版社出版。2002 年 9 月交稿时，其中包括的课文与阅读材料均选自 1999～2002 年的原版英文教材、科技报告、著作及专业期刊。现 6 年多过去了，在材料科学与工程方面出现很多创新理论与技术，因此，有必要将有关新的知识体系对原教材进行更新和完善。2009 年 6 月，该教材第二版被确认为普通高等教育"十一五"国家级规划教材出版。为此，我们吸收第一版时的出版经验，对教材第二版中的内容进行了重新设计，所有课文和阅读材料均选自 2006～2009 年出版的原版英文教科书、科技报告、著作及专业期刊等，并增加了相关的阅读练习。

教材特点：根据国家"十一五"教材出版规划，按照"全国部分高校化工类及相关专业大学英语专业阅读教材编审委员会"的要求和安排编写的《材料科学与工程专业英语》教材，具有以下特点：(1) 知识面宽：该书囊括了目前与材料科学相关专业的各类知识，金属材料、陶瓷材料、聚合物材料、复合材料、纳米结构材料及生物材料等内容，覆盖范围宽，学科全面；(2) 内容新颖：教材读物均选自国外最新出版的相关学科教材、专著或期刊论文，内容新颖，学科前沿知识丰富，学生和教师都可从中了解材料科学的最新发展趋势；(3) 趣味性强：教材读物在保证学科知识基础性、全面性的前提下，有相当一部分具有很强的趣味性。我们在材料科学类专业英语的教学过程中发现，学生对学科专业以外的知识，如教材中生物材料和纳米材料的功能、应用及其制备表现出极大的兴趣，这样有利于学生拓宽知识面、开阔视野；(4) 读者面宽：《材料科学与工程专业英语》教材适用于各类材料专业的学生使用，也可作为研究生、教师及相关领域研究人员的学习参考书。

内容与结构：教材分为 7 部分 (Part)，共 24 个单元，每个单元由一篇课文和一篇阅读材料组成。阅读材料提供与课文相应的背景知识或是课文的续篇，以进一步拓展课文的内容。根据课文与阅读材料的内容，配有相应的练习题、注释和词汇表。课文与阅读材料共计 48 篇，其中：Part I 为材料科学与工程概论，共 6 个单元，包括材料科学与工程的历史、材料的分类、材料的特性、材料与化学的关系，以及材料科学的研究进展和发展趋势；

Part Ⅱ～Part Ⅶ，分别介绍金属材料（包括合金）、陶瓷材料、聚合物材料、复合材料、纳米结构材料和生物医学材料的化学组成、性质、种类、制造技术和用途等；教材的最后为附录部分，主要包括自然元素（附录1）、与材料科学和工程相关的主要国际学术期刊（附录2）和词汇表。

本教材由匡少平、王世颖主编。其中，Unit 1、4～7、10～12、16～23 和 Append. 由匡少平同志编写；Unit 3、8、9、13～15、24 由王世颖同志编写；Unit 2 由匡少平、王世颖编写；教材最后的阅读理解参考答案（Answer to Reading Comprehension）和词汇表（Glossary）由匡少平同志统一编撰、汇总。全书由匡少平同志统稿。

由于水平所限，教材涉及的内容较广，可能出现错漏，希望广大读者不吝指正，使本书在使用过程中不断改进和完善。

致谢：本教材为普通高等教育"十一五"国家级规划教材。在编写过程中得到化学工业出版社的大力支持，同时得到青岛科技大学教务处、化学与分子工程学院等大力支持。教材中部分阅读材料得到德国 Paderborn 大学 Gregor Fels、Sonja Herres-Pawlis 等教授的大力帮助和指导，他们为我们提供了国际上最新出版的化学类教材；在编写过程中得到陈红、王兰兰、赵辉等同志的大力帮助。在此，谨向他们表示衷心感谢。

编 者
2009 年 6 月

Contents

Part I INTRODUCTION TO MATERIALS SCIENCE AND ENGINEERING

Unit 1　Materials Science and Engineering ……………………………………… 1
Unit 2　Classification of Materials and Modern Materials' Needs ………… 12
Unit 3　Atomic Structure of Materials ………………………………………… 23
Unit 4　Physical and Chemical Properties of Materials ……………………… 34
Unit 5　Mechanical Properties of Materials …………………………………… 43

Part II METALLIC MATERIALS AND ALLOYS

Unit 6　Introduction to Metals and Alloys …………………………………… 54
Unit 7　Superalloy ………………………………………………………………… 63
Unit 8　Important Characters of Metallic Materials—Malleability, Ductility & Corrosion …………………………………………………… 74

Part III CERAMICS

Unit 9　Introduction to Ceramic Materials …………………………………… 87
Unit 10　Relationship between Microstructure, Processing, and Applications ……… 98
Unit 11　Bioceramics (Part I) …………………………………………………… 109

Part IV POLYMER

Unit 12　Introduction to Polymer ……………………………………………… 121
Unit 13　Soft Materials: Polymers and Plastics ……………………………… 138
Unit 14　Polymers for Food Packaging and Health Systems ……………… 149

Part V COMPOSITES

Unit 15　Introduction to Composites …………………………………………… 164
Unit 16　Properties of Composite Materials …………………………………… 175
Unit 17　Polymer Nanotechnology: Nanocomposites ………………………… 186

Part VI NANOSTRUCTURED MATERIALS

Unit 18　Nanotechnology and Nanostructured Materials ·· 196
Unit 19　Creation of Nanomaterials ·· 205
Unit 20　Applications of Nanostructured Materials ·· 217

PART VII BIOMATERIALS

Unit 21　Biomaterial: An Introduction ·· 229
Unit 22　Applications of Biocomposites ·· 239
Unit 23　Biocompatible Dental Materials ·· 249

APPENDIXES

Main Journals of Materials Science and Technology ·· 262
Answer to Reading Comprehension ·· 269
Glossary ·· 270
Periodic Table of Elements ·· 286

Part I INTRODUCTION TO MATERIALS SCIENCE AND ENGINEERING

Unit 1 Materials Science and Engineering

Historical Perspective

Materials are properly more deep-seated in our culture than most of us realize. Transportation, housing, clothing, communication, recreation and food production—virtually every segment of our everyday lives is influenced to one degree or another by materials. Historically, the development and advancement of societies have been intimately tied to the members' abilities to produce and manipulate materials to fill their needs. In fact, early civilizations have been designated by the level of their materials development (Stone Age, Bronze Age, Iron Age).

The earliest humans have access to only a very limited number of materials, those that occur naturally stone, wood, clay, skins, and so on. With time they discovered techniques for producing materials that had properties superior to those of the natural ones: these new materials included pottery and various metals. Furthermore, it was discovered that the properties of a material could be altered by heat treatments and by the addition of other substances. At this point, materials utilization was totally a selection process that involved deciding from a given, rather limited set of materials, the one best suited for an application by virtue of its characteristic. It was not until relatively recent times that scientists came to understand the relationships between the structural elements of materials and their properties. This knowledge acquired over approximately the past 100 years has empowered them to fashion, to a large degree, the characteristics of materials. Thus, tens of thousands of different materials have evolved with rather specialized characteristics that meet the needs of our modern and complex society, including metals, plastics, glasses, and fibers.

The development of many technologies that make our existence so comfortable has been intimately associated with the accessibility of suitable materials. An advancement in the understanding of a material type is often the forerunner to the stepwise progression of a technology. For example, automobiles would not have been possible without the availability of inexpensive steel or some other comparable substitutes. In the contemporary era, sophisticated electronic devices rely on components that are made from what are called semiconducting materials.

Materials Science and Engineering

Sometimes it is useful to subdivide the discipline of materials science and engineering into materials science and materials engineering subdisciplines. Strictly speaking, "materials science" involves investigating the relationships that exist between the structures and properties of materials. In contrast, "materials engineering" involves, on the basis of these structure-property correlations, designing or engineering the structure of a material to produce a predetermined set of properties. From a functional perspective, the role of a materials scientist is to develop or synthesize new materials, whereas a materials engineer is called upon to create new products or systems using existing materials and/or to develop techniques for processing materials. Most graduates in materials programs are trained to be both materials scientists and materials engineers.

"Structure" is, at this point, a nebulous term that deserves some explanation. In brief, the structure of a material usually relates to the arrangement of its internal components. Subatomic structure involves electrons within the individual atoms and interactions with their nuclei. On an atomic level, structure encompasses the organization of atoms or molecules relative to one another. The next larger structural realm, which contains large groups of atoms that are normally agglomerated together, is termed "microscopic" meaning that which is subject to direct observation using some type of microscope. Finally, structural elements that can be viewed with the naked eye are termed "macroscopic".

The notion of "property" deserves elaboration. While in service use, all materials are exposed to external stimuli that evoke some type of response. For example, a specimen subject to forces experiences deformation; or a polished metal surface reflects light. A property is a material trait in terms of the kind and magnitude of response to a specific imposed stimulus. Generally, definitions of properties are made independent of material shape and size.

Virtually all important properties of solid materials may be grouped into six different categories: mechanical, electrical, thermal, magnetic, optical, and deteriorative. For each there is a characteristic type of stimulus capable of provoking different responses. Mechanical properties relate deformation to an applied load or force; examples include elastic modulus (stiffness), strength, and toughness. For electrical properties, such as electrical conductivity and dielectric constant, the stimulus is an electric filed. The thermal behavior of solids can be represented in terms of heat capacity and thermal conductivity. Magnetic properties demonstrate the response of a material to the application of a magnetic field. For optical properties, the stimulus is electromagnetic or light radiation; index of refraction and reflectivity are representative optical properties. Finally, deteriorative characteristics relate to the chemical reactivity of materials.

In addition to structure and properties, two other important components are involved in the science and engineering of materials—namely "processing" and "performance". With regard to the relationships of these four components, the structure of a material depends on how it is processed. Furthermore, a material's performance is a function of its properties. Thus, the interrelationship among processing, structure, properties, and performance is as depicted as follows:

Processing→Structure→Properties→Performance

Why Study Materials Science and Engineering?

Why do we study materials? Many an applied scientist or engineer, whether mechanical, civil, chemical, or electrical, is at one time or another exposed to a design problem involving materials, such as a transmission gear, the superstructure for a building, an oil refinery component, or an integrated circuit chip. Of course, materials scientists and engineers are specialists who are totally involved in the investigation and design of materials.

Many times, a materials problem is one of selecting the right material from thousands available. The final decision is normally based on several criteria. First, the in-service conditions must be characterized, for these dictate the properties required of material. On only rare occasions does a material possess the maximum or ideal combination of properties. Thus, it may be necessary to trade one characteristic for another. The classic example involves strength and ductility; normally, a material having a high strength has only a limited ductility. In such cases a reasonable compromise between two or more properties may be necessary.

A second selection consideration is any deterioration of material properties that may occur during service operation. For example, significant reductions in mechanical strength may result from exposure to elevated temperatures or corrosive environments.

Finally, probably the overriding consideration is that of economics. What will the finished product cost? A material may be found that has the ideal set of properties but is prohibitively expensive. Here again, some compromise is inevitable. The cost of a finished piece also includes any expense incurred during fabrication to produce the desired shape.

The more familiar an engineer or scientist is with the various characteristics and structure-property relationships, as well as processing techniques of materials, the more proficient and confident he or she will be in making judicious materials choices based on these criteria.

(*Selected from William D. Callister, Jr, and David G. Rethwisch, Materials Science and Engineering: An Introduction. 9th ed. John Wiley & Sons, 2014*)

New Words and Expressions

Pottery　*n*. 陶瓷
by virtue of　依靠（……力量），凭借，由于，因为
empower　*v*. 授权，准许，使能够
empower sb. to do sth.　授权某人做某事
forerunner　*n*. 先驱（者），预兆
stepwise　*a*. 逐步地，分阶段地
interdisciplinary　*a*. 交叉学科的
metallurgy　*n*. 冶金学
nebulous　*a*. 星云的，云雾状的，模糊的，朦胧的

agglomerate　　*n*. 大团，大块；*a*. 成块的，凝聚的
elaboration　　*n*. 详尽的细节，解释，阐述
elastic modulus　　弹性模量
stiffness　　*n*. 刚度
toughness　　*n*. 韧性
electrical conductivity　　电导性，电导率
dielectric constant　　介电常数
thermal conductivity　　热导性，热导率
heat capacity　　热容
processing　　*v*.（材料的）加工，处理
structure　　*n*.（材料的）结构，构造
property　　*n*.（材料的）特征，性质
performance　　*n*.（材料的）性能
refraction　　*n*. 折射
reflectivity　　*n*. 反射
strength　　*n*. 强度
ductility　　*n*. 延展性
corrosive　　*a*. 腐蚀的，蚀坏的，腐蚀性的；*n*. 腐蚀物，腐蚀剂
overriding　　*a*. 最重要的，高于一切的
prohibitive　　*a*. 禁止的，抑制的
judicious　　*a*. 明智的
criterion　　*n*.（pl. criteria）标准，准则，尺度

Notes

① It was not until relatively recent times that scientists came to understand the relationships between the structural elements of materials and their properties. 这是一个强调句，强调时间。came to+不定式，译为"终于……"，"开始……"。参考译文：直到最近，科学家才终于了解材料的结构要素与其特性之间的关系。

② The notion of "property" deserves elaboration. deserve，应受，值得；elaboration，详尽阐述。参考译文："property"一词的概念值得详细阐述。

③ The thermal behavior of solids can be represented in terms of heat capacity and thermal conductivity. 句中 represent 的意思是"表现"、"表示"、"描绘"，term 是指"术语"。本句的意思是：固体材料的热行为可用热容和热导等术语来描述。

④ In addition to structure and properties, two other important components are involved in the science and engineering of materials—namely "processing" and "performance". component，原指"组成"、"成分"，该句中指材料科学与工程研究的主要内容；namely，译为"即"。参考译文：除结构与特征外，材料科学与工程还包括另外两项重要的研究内容，即（材料的）加工与性能。

⑤ Many an applied scientist or engineer, …, is at one time or another exposed to a design problem involving materials. many a (an, another)+单数名词，许多的，多的，一

个接一个的，例如：many a person，许多人。be exposed to，暴露，面临，处于……境地。参考译文：许多应用科学家或工程师，……，在某个时候都将面临着涉及材料的设计问题。

⑥ On only rare occasions does a material possess the maximum or ideal combination of properties. 这是一个倒装强调句，其原句为：A material possesses the maximum or ideal combination of properties on only rare occasions. 句中的 on only rare occasions，可翻译为"只有在极少数情况下"，注意"occasions"用的是复数；possess 是"具有"的意思。

Exercises

1. Question for discussion
(1) What is materials science? What is materials engineering?
(2) What are the main components of materials science and engineering?
(3) Give the important properties of solid materials.
(4) Please elaborate the relationships of processing, structure, properties and performance.
(5) Why do we study materials science and engineering?
(6) Give some example about the problem of materials science and engineering.

2. Translate the following into Chinese

materials science	Stone Age
naked eye	Bronze age
elastic modulus	stiffness and toughness
optical property	integrated circuit
mechanical strength	thermal conductivity

• "Materials science" involves investigating the relationships that exist between the structures and properties of materials. In contrast, "Materials engineering" involves, on the basis of these structure-property correlations, designing or engineering the structure of a material to produce a predetermined set of properties.

• Virtually all important properties of solid materials may be grouped into six different categories: mechanical, electrical, thermal, magnetic, optical, and deteriorative.

• In addition to structure and properties, two other important components are involved in the science and engineering of materials—namely "processing" and "performance".

• The more familiar an engineer or scientist is with the various characteristics and structure-property relationships, as well as processing techniques of materials, the more proficient and confident he or she will be in making judicious materials choices based on these criteria.

• On only rare occasions does a material possess the maximum or ideal combination of properties. Thus, it may be necessary to trade one characteristic for another.

3. Translate the following into English

交叉学科   介电常数

固体材料   热容

力学性质   电磁辐射

材料加工   弹性系数（模数）

- 直到最近，科学家才终于了解材料的结构要素与其特性之间的关系。
- 材料工程学主要解决材料的制造问题和材料的应用问题。
- 材料的加工过程不但决定了材料的结构，同时决定了材料的特征和性能。
- 材料的力学性能与其所受的外力或负荷而导致的变形有关。

4. Reading comprehension

(1) Which material does not occur in nature? _____

(A) pottery   (B) wood   (C) clay   (D) stone

(2) According to the text, all the following statements are true EXCEPT _____ .

(A) The earliest humans have access to only a very limited number of materials.

(B) The properties of a material could be altered by heat treatments.

(C) The properties of a material could be altered by the addition of other substances.

(D) The human beings in Bronze Age came to understand the relationships between the structural elements of materials and their properties.

(3) In the sentence "The thermal behavior of solids can be represented in terms of heat capacity and thermal conductivity", the word "represented" means _____ .

(A) replaced   (B) described   (C) stood for   (D) delegated

(4) According to the author, which of the following properties are important for solid materials?

(A) mechanical and deteriorative   (B) electric and magnetic

(C) thermal and optical   (D) A, B and C

(5) According to the interrelationship of processing, structure, properties, and performance of solid materials indicated in the text, which of the following statements is TRUE? _____

(A) The structure of a solid material depends on its performance.

(B) The processing of a solid material can result in the alteration of its structure, but can not change its properties and performance.

(C) Ultimately, the processing of a solid material determines its structure, properties, and performance.

(D) The properties of a solid material are derived from its performance.

(6) Why do we study materials science and engineering? _____

(A) Because we will be exposed to a design problem involving materials at one time or another.

(B) Because any deterioration of material properties may occur during service operation.

(C) Because the economic consideration for a material is also inevitable.

(D) A, B and C.

Reading Materials

The Development of Materials Science

Materials science and engineering is an interdisciplinary field involving the properties of matter and its applications to various areas of science and engineering. This science investigates the relationship between the structure of materials at atomic or molecular scale and their macroscopic properties. It includes elements of applied physics and chemistry, as well as chemical, mechanical, civil and electrical engineering. With significant media attention to nanoscience and nanotechnology in recent years, materials science has been propelled to the forefront at many universities. It is also an important part of forensic engineering and forensic materials engineering, the study of failed products and components.

History

The material of choice of a given era is often its defining point; the Stone Age, Bronze Age, and Steel Age are examples of this. Materials science is one of the oldest forms of engineering and applied science, deriving from the manufacture of ceramics. Modern materials science evolved directly from metallurgy, which itself evolved from mining. A major breakthrough in the understanding of materials occurred in the late 19th century, when Willard Gibbs demonstrated that thermodynamic properties relating to atomic structure in various phases are related to the physical properties of a material. Important elements of modern materials science are a product of the space race: the understanding and engineering of the metallic alloys, and silica and carbon materials, used in the construction of space vehicles enabling the exploration of space. Materials science has driven, and been driven by, the development of revolutionary technologies such as plastics, semiconductors, and biomaterials.

Before the 1960s (and in some cases decades after), many *materials science* departments were named *metallurgy* departments, from a 19th and early 20th century emphasis on metals. The field has since broadened to include every class of materials, including: ceramics, polymers, semiconductors, magnetic materials, medical implant materials and biological materials.

Fundamentals of Materials Science

In materials science, rather than haphazardly looking for and discovering materials and exploiting their properties, one instead aims to understand materials fundamentally so that new materials with the desired properties can be created.

The basis of all materials science involves relating the desired properties and relative performance of a material in a certain application to the structure of the atoms and phases in that material through characterization. The major determinants of the structure of a material and thus of its properties are its constituent chemical elements and the way in which it has been processed into its final form. These, taken together and related through the laws of thermodynamics, govern a material's microstructure, and thus its properties.

An old adage in materials science says: "materials are like people; it is the defects that make them interesting". The manufacture of a perfect crystal of a material is currently physically impossible. Instead materials scientists manipulate the defects in crystalline materials such as precipitates, grain boundaries (Hall-Petch relationship), interstitial atoms, vacancies or substitutional atoms, to create materials with the desired properties.

Not all materials have a regular crystal structure. Polymers display varying degrees of crystallinity, and many are completely non-crystalline. Glasses, some ceramics, and many natural materials are amorphous, not possessing any long-range order in their atomic arrangements. The study of polymers combines elements of chemical and statistical thermodynamics to give thermodynamic, as well as mechanical, descriptions of physical properties.

In addition to industrial interest, materials science has gradually developed into a field which provides tests for condensed matter or solid state theories. New physics emerge because of the diverse new material properties which need to be explained.

Materials in Industry

Radical materials advances can drive the creation of new products or even new industries, but stable industries also employ materials scientists to make incremental improvements and troubleshoot issues with currently used materials. Industrial applications of materials science include materials design, cost-benefit tradeoffs in industrial production of materials, processing techniques (casting, rolling, welding, ion implantation, crystal growth, thin-film deposition, sintering, glassblowing, etc.), and analytical techniques (characterization techniques such as electron microscopy, X-ray diffraction, calorimetry, nuclear microscopy (HEFIB), Rutherford backscattering, neutron diffraction, etc.).

Besides material characterization, the material scientist/engineer also deals with the extraction of materials and their conversion into useful forms. Thus ingot casting, foundry techniques, blast furnace extraction, and electrolytic extraction are all part of the required knowledge of a metallurgist/engineer. Often the presence, absence or variation of minute quantities of secondary elements and compounds in a bulk material will have a great impact on the final properties of the materials produced, for instance, steels are classified based on 1/10th and 1/100 weight percentages of the carbon and other alloying elements they contain. Thus, the extraction and purification techniques employed in the extraction of iron in the blast furnace will have an impact of the quality of steel that may be produced.

The overlap between physics and materials science has led to the offshoot field of *materials physics*, which is concerned with the physical properties of materials. The approach is generally more macroscopic and applied than in condensed matter physics.

The study of metal alloys is a significant part of materials science. Of all the metallic alloys in use today, the alloys of iron (steel, stainless steel, cast iron, tool steel, alloy steels) make up the largest proportion both by quantity and commercial value. Iron alloyed with various proportions of carbon gives low, mid and high carbon steels. For the steels, the hardness and tensile strength of the steel is directly related to the amount of carbon present, with increasing carbon levels also leading to lower ductility and toughness. The addition of silicon and graphitization will produce cast irons (although some cast irons are made precisely with no graphitization). The addition of chromium, nickel and molybdenum to carbon steels (more than 10%) gives us stainless steels.

Other significant metallic alloys are those of aluminium, titanium, copper and magnesium. Copper alloys have been known for a long time (since the Bronze Age), while the alloys of the other three metals have been relatively recently developed. Due to the chemical reactivity of these metals, the electrolytic extraction processes required were only developed relatively recently. The alloys of aluminium, titanium and magnesium are also known and valued for their high strength-to-weight ratios and, in the case of magnesium, their ability to provide electromagnetic shielding. These materials are ideal for situations where high strength-to-weight ratios are more important than bulk cost, such as in the aerospace industry and certain automotive engineering applications.

Other than metals, polymers and ceramics are also an important part of materials science. Polymers are the raw materials (the resins) used to make what we commonly call plastics. Plastics are really the final product, created after one or more polymers or additives have been added to a resin during processing, which is then shaped into a final form. Polymers which have been around, and which are in current widespread use, include polyethylene, polypropylene, PVC, polystyrene, nylons, polyesters, acrylics, polyurethanes, and polycarbonates. Plastics are generally classified as "commodity", "specialty" and "engineering" plastics.

PVC (polyvinyl-chloride) is widely used, inexpensive, and annual production quantities are large. It lends itself to an incredible array of applications, from artificial leather to electrical insulation and cabling, packaging and containers. Its fabrication and processing are simple and well-established. The versatility of PVC is due to the wide range of plasticisers and other additives that it accepts. The term "additives" in polymer science refers to the chemicals and compounds added to the polymer base to modify its material properties.

Polycarbonate would be normally considered an engineering plastic (other examples include PEEK, ABS). Engineering plastics are valued for their superior strengths and other special material properties. They are usually not used for disposable applications, unlike commodity plastics.

Specialty plastics are materials with unique characteristics, such as ultra-high strength, electrical conductivity, electro-fluorescence, high thermal stability, and so on.

It should be noted here that the dividing line between the various types of plastics is not based on material but rather on their properties and applications. For instance, polyethylene (PE) is a cheap, low friction polymer commonly used to make disposable shopping bags and trash bags, and is considered a commodity plastic, whereas Medium-Density Polyethylene MDPE is used for underground gas and water pipes, and another variety called Ultra-high

Molecular Weight Polyethylene UHMWPE is an engineering plastic which is used extensively as the glide rails for industrial equipment and the low-friction socket in implanted hip joints.

Another application of material science in industry is the making of composite materials. Composite materials are structured materials composed of two or more macroscopic phases. An example would be steel-reinforced concrete; another can be seen in the "plastic" casings of television sets, cell-phones and so on. These plastic casings are usually a composite material made up of a thermoplastic matrix such as acrylonitrile-butadiene-styrene (ABS) in which calcium carbonate chalk, talc, glass fibres or carbon fibres have been added for added strength, bulk, or electro-static dispersion. These additions may be referred to as reinforcing fibres, or dispersants, depending on their purpose.

(Selected from http://en.wikipedia.org/wiki/Materials_science, 2014)

New Words and Expressions

ceramic　n. 陶器；a. 陶器的
metallurgy　n. 冶金学
plastic　a. 塑料的；n. 塑料，（外科）整形的
semiconductor　n. 半导体
biomaterial　a. 生物材料的；n. 生物材料
polymer　n. 聚合体，聚合物
implant　v. & n. 深植，嵌入
crystalline　a. 晶体的，结晶的
thermodynamics　n. 热力学
foundry　n. 铸造，铸造场，铸造类
electrolytic　a. 电解的，由电解产生的
extraction　n. 抽出，取出，抽出物
purification　n. 净化，纯化，提纯
chromium　n. 铬
nickel　n. 镍
molybdenum　n. 钼
aluminium　n. 铝
titanium　n. 钛
copper　n. 铜
magnesium　n. 镁
resin　n. 树脂（松香，树脂状沉淀物，树脂制品）
additives　n. 添加剂，助剂
fluorescence　n. 发荧光，荧光
polyethylene　n. 聚乙烯
composite　a. 合成的，复合的；n. 合成物，复合材料
calcium carbonate　碳酸钙

glass fibres 玻璃纤维
carbon fibres 碳纤维

Notes

① An old adage in materials science says: "materials are like people; it is the defects that make them interesting". adage 是指"格言"、"谚语"。"it is the defects that…",这是一个强调句,意思是"正是材料本身存在的缺陷,……"

② The study of polymers combines elements of chemical and statistical thermodynamics to give thermodynamic, as well as mechanical, descriptions of physical properties. 句中的 elements 是指化学和热力学的"原理"或"基础"。该句的意思是指:通过对聚合物材料的研究,结合化学和热力学原理,不但可以确定其热力学性质,还可以确定其力学性质,并对其物理特性进行描述。

③ For the steels, the hardness and tensile strength of the steel is directly related to the amount of carbon present, with increasing carbon levels also leading to lower ductility and toughness. tensile strength 指"拉伸强度",carbon levels 是指钢材中的含碳量的多少。参考译文:对钢材而言,其硬度和拉伸强度与钢材中碳含量有着直接的关系,随着含碳量的增加,可导致钢材的延展性和强度降低。

④ Polymers are the raw materials (the resins) used to make what we commonly call plastics. Plastics are really the final product, created after one or more polymers or additives have been added to a resin during processing, which is then shaped into a final form. which is then shaped into a final form, 意思是"然后将之加工成最终的形状"。参考译文:聚合物是用来制造我们经常所说的塑料的原材料(树脂);塑料才是最终产品,它是由一种或多种聚合物以及助剂加入到一种树脂中,通过加工成型而制造的。

⑤ It should be noted here that the dividing line between the various types of plastics is not based on material but rather on their properties and applications. the dividing line 指"分界"或"分界线"。参考译文:在这里应该指出的是,不同类型塑料之间的分界不是根据材料本身来确定,而是根据材料的性质和应用来划分的。

⑥ Composite materials are structured materials composed of two or more macroscopic phases. structured material 是"结构材料";phase 是"相"或"相位"。参考译文:复合材料是由两个或多个宏观相组成的结构材料。

Reading Comprehension

(1) According to the reading material, which of statements about Willard Gibbs is NOT TRUE? _____
(A) He had great achieve in the late 19th century.
(B) He was the father of materials science and invented many structured materials.
(C) He found that the thermodynamics is related to the physic properties of a material.
(D) He interpreted the thermodynamic properties relating to atomic structure.

(2) The fundamentals of materials science are related to _____ of a material.

(A) the desired properties   (B) the relative performance
(C) the perfect structure   (D) both A and B

(3) About the crystallinity of materials, all the following statements are false EXCEPT _____.

(A) Not all materials have a regular crystal structure.
(B) All polymers show the fine crystallinity.
(C) All ceramics are not amorphous.
(D) Most glasses possess long-range order in their atomic arrangements.

(4) Industrial applications of materials science include _____ besides materials design.

(A) processing techniques   (B) cost-benefit tradeoffs
(C) analytical techniques   (D) A, B and C

(5) About the steel, which of the following statements is NOT TRUE? _____
(A) The steel is kind of alloy of iron.
(B) The tensile strength of the steel is directly related to the amount of carbon present.
(C) The ductility of the steel will increase with the increase of the carbon levels.
(D) The toughness of the steel will decrease with the increase of the carbon levels.

(6) According to the passage, the author implies that _____.
(A) with significant media attention to nanoscience and nanotechnology in recent years, materials science has been propelled to the forefront at many universities.
(B) the industrial interests are very important for the development of materials science.
(C) the study of metal alloys is a significant part of materials science.
(D) radical materials advances can drive the creation of new products or even new industries.

Unit 2 Classification of Materials and Modern Materials' Needs

Classification of Materials

Solid materials have been conveniently grouped into three basic categories: metals, ceramics, and polymers, a scheme based primarily on chemical makeup and atomic structure. Most materials fall into one distinct grouping or another. In addition, there are the composites that are engineered combinations of two or more materials. Another category is advanced materials—those used in high-technology applications, such as semiconductors, biomaterials, smart materials, and nanoengineered materials.

Metals Metals are composed of one or more metallic elements (such as iron, aluminum, copper, titanium, gold, and nickel), and often also nonmetallic elements (for example, carbon, nitrogen, and oxygen) in relatively small amounts. Atoms in metals and their alloys are arranged in a very orderly manner, and are relatively dense in comparison to the ceramics and polymers. With regard to mechanical characteristics, these materials are relatively stiff and strong, yet are ductile (i. e. , capable of large amounts of deformation without fracture), and are resistant to fracture, which accounts for their widespread use in structural applications. Metallic materials have large numbers of nonlocalized electrons; that is, these electrons are not bound to particular atoms. Many properties of metals are directly attributable to these electrons. For example, metals are extremely good conductors of electricity and heat, and are not transparent to visible light; a polished metal surface has a lustrous appearance. In addition, some of the metals (such as Fe, Co, and Ni) have desirable magnetic properties.

Ceramics Ceramics are compounds between metallic and nonmetallic elements; they are most frequently oxides, nitrides, and carbides. For example, some of the common ceramic materials include aluminum oxide (or alumina, Al_2O_3), silicon dioxide (or silica, SiO_2), silicon carbide (SiC), silicon nitride (Si_3N_4), and, in addition, what some refer to as the *traditional ceramics*—those composed of clay minerals (i. e. , porcelain), as well as cement, and glass. With regard to mechanical behavior, ceramic materials are relatively stiff and strong—stiffnesses and strengths are comparable to those of the metals. In addition, ceramics are typically very hard. On the other hand, they are extremely brittle (lack ductility), and are highly susceptible to fracture. These materials are typically insulative to the passage of heat and electricity (i. e. , have low electrical conductivities), and are more resistant to high temperatures and harsh environments than metals and polymers. With regard to optical characteristics, ceramics may be transparent, translucent, or opaque, and some of the oxide ceramics (e. g. , Fe_3O_4) exhibit magnetic behavior.

Polymers Polymers include the familiar plastic and rubber materials. Many of them are organic compounds that are chemically based on carbon, hydrogen, and other nonmetallic elements (viz. O, N, and Si) . Furthermore, they have very large molecular structures, often chain-like in nature that have a backbone of carbon atoms. Some of the common and familiar polymers are polyethylene (PE), nylon, poly (vinyl chloride) (PVC), polycarbonate (PC), polystyrene (PS), and silicone rubber. These materials typically have low densities, whereas their mechanical characteristics are generally dissimilar to the metallic and ceramic materials—they are not as stiff nor as strong as these other material types. However, on the basis of their low densities, many times their stiffnesses and strengths on a per mass basis are comparable to the metals and ceramics. In addition, many of the polymers are extremely ductile and pliable (i. e. , plastic), which means they are easily formed into complex shapes. In general, they are relatively inert chemically and unreactive in a large number of environments. One major drawback to the polymers is their tendency to soften and/or decompose at modest temperatures, which, in some instances, limits their use. Furthermore, they have low electrical conductivities and are nonmagnetic.

Composites A composite is composed of two (or more) individual materials that come from the categories discussed above—metals, ceramics, and polymers. The design goal of a composite is to achieve a combination of properties that is not displayed by any single material, and also to incorporate the best characteristics of each of the component materials. A large number of composite types are represented by different combinations of metals, ceramics, and polymers. Furthermore, some naturally-occurring materials are also composites—for example, wood and bone. However, most of those are synthetic (or man-made) composites.

One of the most common and familiar composites is fiberglass, in which small glass fibers are embedded within a polymeric material (normally an epoxy or polyester). The glass fibers are relatively strong and stiff (but also brittle), whereas the polymer is more flexible. Thus, fiberglass is relatively stiff, strong, and flexible. In addition, it has a low density.

Another technologically important material is the carbon fiber-reinforced polymer (CFRB) composite—carbon fibers that are embedded within a polymer. These materials are stiffer and stronger than glass fiber-reinforced materials but more expensive. CFRP composites are used in some aircraft and aerospace applications, as well as in high-tech sporting equipment (e.g., bicycles, golf clubs, tennis rackets, skis/snowboards) and recently in automobile humpers. The new Boeing 787 fuselage is primarily made from such CFRP composites.

Modern Materials' Needs

In spite of the tremendous progress that has been made in the discipline of materials science and engineering within the past few years, technological challenges remain, including the development of even more sophisticated and specialized materials, as well as consideration of the environmental impact of materials production. Some comment is appropriate relative to these issues so as to round out this perspective.

Nuclear energy holds some promise, but the solutions to the many problems that remain necessarily involve materials, such as fuels, containment structures, and facilities for the disposal of radioactive waste.

Significant quantities of energy are involved in transportation. Reducing the weight of transportation vehicles (automobiles, aircraft, trains, etc.), as well as increasing engine operating temperatures, will enhance fuel efficiency. New high-strength, low-density structural materials remain to be developed, as well as materials that have higher-temperature capabilities, for use in engine components.

Furthermore, there is a recognized need to find new, economical sources of energy and to use present resources more efficiently. Materials will undoubtedly play a significant role in these developments. For example, the direct conversion of solar power into electrical energy has been demonstrated. Solar cells employ some rather complex and expensive materials. To ensure a viable technology, materials that are highly efficient in this conversion process yet less costly must be developed.

The hydrogen fuel cell is another very attractive and feasible energy-conversion technology that has the advantage of being nonpolluting. It is just beginning to be implemented in batteries for electronic devices and holds promise as the power plant for automobiles. New materials still need to be developed for more efficient fuel cells and also for better catalysts to be used in the production of hydrogen.

Furthermore, environmental quality depends on our ability to control air and water pollution. Pollution control techniques employ various materials. In addition, materials processing and refinement methods need to be improved so that they produce less environmental degradation—that is, less pollution and less despoilage of the landscape from the mining of raw materials. Also, in some materials manufacturing processes, toxic substances are produced, and the ecological impact of their disposal must be considered.

Many materials that we use are derived from resources that are nonrenewable—that is, not capable of being regenerated, including polymers, for which the prime raw material is oil, and some metals. These nonrenewable resources are gradually becoming depleted, which necessitates: (1) the discovery of additional reserves, (2) the development of new materials having comparable properties with less adverse environmental impact, and/or (3) increased recycling efforts and the development of new recycling technologies. As a consequence of the economics of not only production but also environmental impact and ecological factors, it is becoming increasingly important to consider the "cradle-to-grave" life cycle of materials relative to the overall manufacturing process.

(Selected from William D. Callister, Jr, and David G. Rethwisch, Materials Science and Engineering: An Introduction. 9th ed. John Wiley & Sons, 2014)

New Words and Expressions

classification   *n*. 分类，类别
ceramic   *n*. 陶瓷，陶瓷制品
polymer   *n*. 聚合物，聚合体，聚合材料
chemical makeup   化学组成
atomic structure   原子结构
nonlocalized electrons   游离电子
composite   *n*. 复合物，复合体，复合材料
semiconductor   *n*. 半导体，半导体材料
biomaterial   *n*. 生物材料
nanoengineered   *a*. 纳米工程的
attributable   *a*. 可归功于……的
transparent   *a*. 透明的，显然的，明晰的
visible light   可见光
polished   *a*. 抛光的，擦亮的
lustrous   *a*. 有光泽的，光辉的
oxide   *n*. 氧化物
nitride   *n*. 氮化物
carbide   *n*. 碳化物
brittle   *a*. 易脆的，易碎的

mechanical behavior　力学行为
inert　*a*. 惰性的，不活泼的
flexible　*a*. 灵活的，易弯曲的，柔韧的
flexibility　*n*. 灵活性，柔韧性
decompose　*v*. 分解，腐烂
fiberglass　*n*. 纤维玻璃
radioactive waste　放射性废弃物
transportation vehicle　交通工具
fuel efficiency　燃烧效率
solar cell　太阳能电池
hydrogen fuel cell　氢燃料电池
catalyst　*n*. 催化剂
environmental degradation　环境退化
nonrenewable　*a*. 不可再生的
nonrenewable resource　不可再生资源

Notes

① …, a scheme based primarily on chemical makeup and atomic structure. a scheme 指本句中材料的分类方案；chemical makeup，化学组成（构成）。参考译文：……，一种主要基于化学构成和原子结构的材料分类方案。

② Metals are composed of one or more metallic elements (such as iron, aluminum, copper, titanium, gold, and nickel), and often also nonmetallic elements (for example, carbon, nitrogen, and oxygen) in relatively small amounts. Be composed of，由……组成；relatively small amounts，极少量的。参考译文：金属材料由一种或多种金属元素（如铁、铝、铜、钛、金和镍）组成，且通常含有极少量的非金属元素（例如，碳、氮和氧）。

③ Metallic materials have large numbers of nonlocalized electrons; that is, these electrons are not bound to particular atoms. nonlocalized，游离的；that is，即；be bound to，被束缚的。参考译文：金属材料有大量的游离电子，即：这些电子不属于特定的原子。

④ A composite is composed of two (or more) individual materials that come from the categories discussed above—metals, ceramics, and polymers. 参考译文：复合材料是由两种或两种以上的不同材料构成，这些材料是上面讨论的基本材料类型，即金属材料、陶瓷材料和聚合材料。

⑤ Nuclear energy holds some promise. Hold promise，有希望的，可望。这是一种习惯用法。又如：Geothermal exploration holds promise in combating the energy crisis，探勘地热可望缓解能源危机。

⑥ …, it is becoming increasingly important to consider the "cradle-to-grave" life cycle of materials relative to the overall manufacturing process. "cradle-to-grave" life cycle of materials，指材料"从摇篮到坟墓"的整个生命周期，亦即，材料从制造到废弃的整个生命周期。

Exercises

1. Question for discussion

(1) Give the basic classifications of materials based on chemical makeup and atomic structure.

(2) What are nonlocalized electrons?

(3) What are polymers? Please give some examples.

(4) Why do we design composite materials?

(5) Please explain nonrenewable resource.

(6) Please tell the relationship between materials production and environment.

2. Translate the following into Chinese

composite materials   nonlocalized electrons

advanced materials   nonrenewable resource

semiconductors   biomaterials

smart materials   nanoengineered materials

• Solid materials have been conveniently grouped into three basic categories: metals, ceramics, and polymers, a scheme based primarily on chemical makeup and atomic structure.

• Metals are composed of one or more metallic elements (such as iron, aluminum, copper, titanium, gold, and nickel), and often also nonmetallic elements (for example, carbon, nitrogen, and oxygen) in relatively small amounts.

• Polymers include the familiar plastic and rubber materials. Many of them are organic compounds that are chemically based on carbon, hydrogen, and other nonmetallic elements (viz. O, N, and Si).

• A composite is composed of two (or more) individual materials that come from metals, ceramics, and polymers.

• Nuclear energy holds some promise, but the solutions to the many problems that remain necessarily involve materials, such as fuels, containment structures, and facilities for the disposal of radioactive waste.

• It is becoming increasingly important to consider the "cradle-to-grave" life cycle of materials relative to the overall manufacturing process.

3. Translate the following into English

先进材料   陶瓷材料

高性能材料   黏土矿物

合金   太阳能电池

玻璃纤维   氢燃料电池

• 金属元素有许多游离电子，金属材料的许多性质可直接归功于这些电子。

• 金属材料由一种或多种金属元素组成，且通常含有极少量的非金属元素。

• 许多聚合物材料是有机化合物，并具有大的分子结构。

- 复合材料是由两种或两种以上的不同材料构成。

4. Reading comprehension

(1) Why are metals extremely good conductors of electricity? _____
(A) Because metals are quite strong, yet deformable.
(B) Because metals are not transparent to visible light.
(C) Because metals have large numbers of nonlocalized electrons.
(D) Because the electrons of metals are bound to particular atoms.

(2) All statements about ceramics are true EXCEPT _____ .
(A) Ceramics consist mainly of clay minerals, cement, and glass.
(B) Ceramics are generally insulators of electricity and heat.
(C) Ceramics are less resistant to harsh environments than metals and polymers.
(D) Ceramics are hard but very brittle

(3) Polymers have some important characteristics EXCEPT _____ .
(A) typically low densities
(B) relatively inert chemically
(C) low electrical conductivities
(D) magnetic

(4) Which statement about composite is NOT TRUE according to the tex? _____
(A) A composite is composed of two or more individual materials.
(B) A composite combines the properties not displayed by any single material.
(C) A Composite incorporates the best characteristics of each of the component materials.
(D) Naturally-occurring materials such as wood and bone are not composites.

(5) In the sentence "Another technologically important material is the carbon fiber-reinforced polymer (CFRB) composite—carbon fibers that are embedded within a polymer", the word "embedded" means _____ .
(A) replaced   (B) implanted   (C) involved   (D) characterized

(6) The nonrenewable resources are becoming depleted, according to the text which necessitates EXCEPT _____ :
(A) the discovery of additional reserves
(B) the development of new materials with less adverse environmental impact
(C) the increase of recycling efforts and the development of new recycling technologies
(D) the decrease of manufacturing process

Reading Material

Advanced Materials

Materials utilized in high-technology (or high-tech) applications are sometimes termed *advanced materials*. By high technology, we mean a device or product that operates or functions using relatively intricate and sophisticated principles, including electronic equipment (camcorders, CD/DVD players), computers, fiber-optic systems, spacecraft, aircraft, and military rocketry. These advanced materials are typically traditional materials whose properties have been enhanced and also newly developed, high-performance materials. Furthermore, they may be of all material types (e. g., metals, ceramics, polymers), and are normally expensive. Advanced materials include semiconductors, biomaterials, and what we may term "materials of the future" (that is, smart materials and nanoengineered materials).

Semiconductors

Semiconductors have electrical properties that are intermediate between the electrical conductors (i. e., metals and metal alloys) and insulators (i. e., ceramics and polymers). Furthermore, the electrical characteristics of these materials are extremely sensitive to the presence of minute concentrations of impurity atoms, for which the concentrations may be controlled over very small spatial regions. Semiconductors have made possible the advent of integrated circuitry that has totally revolutionized the electronics and computer industries (not to mention our lives) over the past three decades.

Biomaterials

Biomaterials are employed in components implanted into the human body to replace diseased or damaged body parts. These materials must not produce toxic substances and must be compatible with body tissues (i. e., must not cause adverse biological reactions). All of the above materials—metals, ceramics, polymers, composites, and semiconductors — may be used as biomaterials.

Smart Materials

Smart (or intelligent) materials are a group of new and state-of-the-art materials now being developed that will have a significant influence on many of our technologies. The adjective "smart" implies that these materials are able to sense changes in their environments and then respond to these changes in predetermined manners—traits that are also found in living organisms. In addition, this "smart" concept is being extended to rather sophisticated systems that consist of both smart and traditional materials.

Components of a smart material (or system) include some type of sensor (which detects an input signal) and an actuator (which performs a responsive and adaptive function). Actuators may be called upon to change shape, position, natural frequency, or mechanical characteristics in response to changes in temperature, electric fields, and/or magnetic fields.

Four types of materials are commonly used for actuators: shape memory alloys, piezoelectric ceramics, magnetostrictive materials, and electroheological/magnetorheological fluids. Shape memory alloys are metals that, after having been deformed, revert back to their original shape when temperature is changed. Piezoelectric ceramics expand and contract in response to an applied electric field (or voltage); conversely, they also generate an electric field when their dimensions are altered. The behavior of magnetostrictive materials is analogous to that of the piezoelectrics, except that they are responsive to magnetic fields. Also, electrorheological and magnetorheological fluids are liquids that experience dramatic changes in viscosity upon the application of electric and magnetic fields, respectively.

Materials/devices employed as sensors include optical fibers, piezoelectric materials (including some polymers), and microelectromechanical systems.

For example, one type of smart system is used in helicopters to reduce aerodynamic cockpit noise created by the rotating rotor blades. Piezoelectric sensors inserted into the blades monitor blade stresses and deformations; feedback signals from these sensors are fed into a computer-controlled adaptive device that generates noise-canceling antinoise.

Nanomaterials

One new material class that has fascinating properties and tremendous technological promise is the nanomaterials, which may be any one of the four basic types—metals, ceramics, polymers, or composites. However unlike these other materials, they are not distinguished on the basis of their chemistry but rather their size; the nano prefix denotes that the dimensions of these structural entities are on the order of a nanometer (10^{-9} m) as a rule, less than 100 nanometers (nm, equivalent to the diameter of approximately 500 atoms).

Prior to the advent of nanomaterials, the general procedure scientists used to understand the chemistry and physics of materials was to begin by studying large and complex structures and then investigate the fundamental building blocks of these structures that are smaller and simpler. This approach is sometimes termed top-down science. However, with the development of scanning probe microscopes, which permit observation of individual atoms and molecules, it has become possible to design and build new structures from their atomic-level constituents, one atom or molecule at a time (i.e. "materials by design"). This ability to arrange atoms carefully provides opportunities to develop mechanical, electrical, magnetic, and other properties that are not otherwise possible. We call this the bottom-up approach and the study of the properties of these materials is termed nanotechnology.

Some of the physical and chemical characteristics exhibited by matter may experience dramatic changes as particle size approaches atomic dimensions. For example, materials that are opaque in the macroscopic domain may become transparent on the nanoscale; some solids become liquids, chemically stable materials become combustible, and electrical insulators become conductors. Furthermore, properties may depend on size in this nanoscale domain. Some of these effects are quantum mechanical in origin, whereas others are related to surface phenomena—the proportion of atoms located on surface sites of a particle increase dramatically as its size decreases.

Because of these unique and unusual properties, nanomaterials are finding niches in electronic, biomedical, sporting, energy production, and other industrial applications. For examples, catalytic converter for automobiles; nanocarbons-fullerenes, carbon nanotubes, and grapheme; particles of carbon black as reinforcement for automobile tires; nanocomposites;

magnetic nanosize grains that are used for hard disk drives; and magnetic particles that store data on magnetic tapes, and so on.

Whenever a new material is developed, its potential for harmful and toxicological interactions with humans and animals must be considered. Small nanoparticles have exceedingly large surface area-to-volume ratios, which can lead to high chemical reactivities. Although the safety of nanomaterials is relatively unexplored, there are concerns that they may be absorbed into the body through the skin, lungs, and digestive tract at relatively high rates, and that some, if present in sufficient concentrations, will pose health risks—such as damage to DNA or promotion of lung cancer.

(Selected from William D. Callister, Jr, and David G. Rethwisch, *Materials Science and Engineering: An Introduction*. 9th ed. John Wiley & Sons, 2014)

New Words and Expressions

fiber-optic   *a*. 光纤的，光纤材料的
insulator   *n*. 绝缘体，绝热器
insulative   *a*. 绝缘的
implant   *n*. 移植，植入
sensor   *n*. 传感器，传感材料
piezoelectric ceramics   压电陶瓷
aerodynamic   *a*. 空气动力学的
antinoise   *a*. 抗噪声的，减少噪声的
nanomaterial   *n*. 纳米材料；*a*. 纳米材料的
prefix   *n*. 前缀，词首，前加成分
scanning probe microscope   扫描探针显微镜
nanotube   *n*. 纳米管
carbon nanotube   碳纳米管
grapheme   *n*. 石墨

Notes

① Advanced materials include semiconductors, biomaterials, and what we may term "materials of the future"(that is, smart materials and nanoengineered materials). term, 把……叫做，把……称为。参考译文：先进材料包括半导体材料、生物材料以及我们所说的"未来材料"（即智能材料和纳米工程材料）。

② These materials must not produce toxic substances and must be compatible with body tissue (i. e. must not cause adverse biological reactions). compatible 是指植入人体内的 biomaterials（生物材料）必须与 body tissue（人体组织）相互兼容，即两者之间不产生排异反应；must not cause adverse biological reactions 意思是"一定不能产生不利的生物学反应", adverse 是指"不利的"、"相反的"、"逆的"。

③ The adjective "smart" implies that these materials are able to sense changes in their environments and then respond to these changes in predetermined manners. 参考译文：形容

词"smart"（智能）暗示，这些材料能够感知环境的变化，然后以预定的方式对这些变化做出反应。

④ The "nano" prefix denotes that the dimensions of these structural entities are on the order of a nanometer (10^{-9} m)。prefix，前缀；the order of，……的级，指数量的级次。参考译文：前缀"nano"代表的是这些结构体的大小为纳米（10^{-9} m）级。

⑤ …others are related to surface phenomena—the proportion of atoms located on surface sites of a particle increase dramatically as its size decreases. 该句描述的是纳米材料的一个重要特性："表面现象"，或称为"表面效应"；即随着颗粒尺寸变小，颗粒表面原子的比例急剧增加。

⑥ Small nanoparticles have exceedingly large surface area-to-volume ratios, which can lead to high chemical reactivities. surface area-to-volume ratio，表面积与体积的比值。参考译文：小的纳米粒子具有极大的表面积体积比，这可导致高的化学反应性。

Reading Comprehension

(1) Advanced materials are typically _____?
(A) traditional materials whose properties have been enhanced.
(B) newly developed, high-performance materials.
(C) inexpensive materials.
(D) both A and B.

(2) Which statement about smart materials is NOT TRUE according to the text? _____
(A) Smart (or intelligent) materials are a group of new and state-of-the-art materials now being developed that will have a significant influence on many of our technologies.
(B) Smart materials are able to sense changes in their environments and then respond to these changes in predetermined manners.
(C) As a kind of smart materials, shape memory alloys after having been deformed can revert back to their original shapes when temperature is changed.
(D) "Smart" concept is being extended to much more sophisticated systems than traditional materials.

(3) Which materials are not described as intelligent materials in the text? _____
(A) shape memory alloys (B) piezoelectric ceramics
(C) carbon nanotubes (D) magnetostrictive materials

(4) According to the text, what are the difference between "top-down" and "bottom-up" approaches? _____
(A) Top-down is from microscopic to macroscopic.
(B) Bottom-up is from microscopic to macroscopic.
(C) Both of them are from microscopic to macroscopic.
(D) Both of them are from macroscopic to microscopic.

(5) Materials may experience the following changes EXCEPT _____ as particle size

decreases.

(A) Opaque in the macroscopic domain may become transparent on the nanoscale.

(B) Some liquids become solids.

(C) Chemically stable materials become combustible.

(D) Electrical insulators become conductors.

(6) The sentence "the safety of nanomaterials is relatively unexplored" means _____ .

(A) Nanomaterials should be fast developed.

(B) The particle sizes should be further decreased.

(C) The harmful and toxicological interactions should be investigated in detail.

(D) The rates of materials into the body should be promoted.

Unit 3　Atomic Structure of Materials

It should be clear that all matter is made of atoms. From the periodic table (Figure 1.1), it can be seen that there are only about 100 different kinds of atoms in the entire Universe. These same 100 atoms form thousands of different substances ranging from the air we breathe to the metal used to support tall buildings. Metals behave differently than ceramics, and ceramics behave differently than polymers. The properties of matter depend on which atoms are used and how they are bonded together.

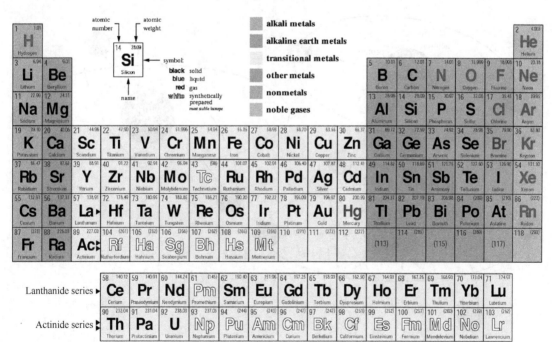

Figure 1.1　The periodic table

The structure of materials can be classified by the general magnitude of various features being considered. The three most common major classification of structural, listed generally in increasing size, are:

Atomic structure, which includes features that cannot be seen, such as the types of bonding between the atoms, and the way the atoms are arranged.

Microstructure, which includes features that cannot be seen with the naked eye, but using a microscope.

Macrostructure includes features that can be seen with the naked eye.

The atomic structure primarily affects the chemical, physical, thermal, electrical, magnetic, and optical properties. The microstructure and macrostructure can also affect these properties but they generally have a larger effect on mechanical properties and on the rate of chemical reaction. The properties of a material offer clues as to the structure of the material. The strength of metals suggests that these atoms are held together by strong bonds. However, these bonds must also allow atoms to move since metals are also usually formable. To understand the structure of a material, the type of atoms present, and how the atoms are arranged and bonded must be known.

From elementary chemistry it is known that the atomic structure (Figure 1.2) of any element is made up of a positively charged nucleus surrounded by electrons revolving around it. An element's atomic number indicates the number of positively charged protons in the nucleus. The atomic weight of an atom indicates how many protons and neutrons in the nucleus. To determine the number of neutrons in an atom, the atomic number is simply subtracted from the atomic weight.

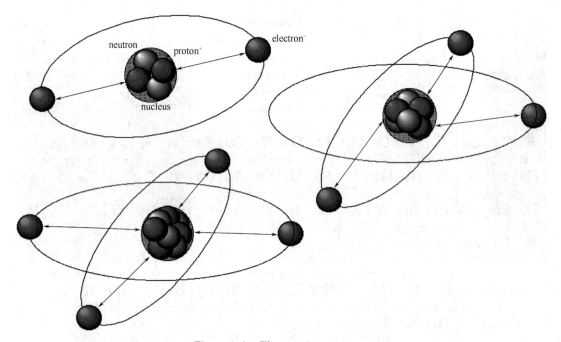

Figure 1.2 The atomic structure.

Atoms like to have a balanced electrical charge. Therefore, they usually have negatively charged electrons surrounding the nucleus in numbers equal to the number of protons. It is also known that electrons are present with different energies and it is convenient to consider these electrons surrounding the nucleus in energy "shells." For example, magnesium, with an atomic number of 12, has two electrons in the inner shell, eight in the second shell and two in the outer shell.

All chemical bonds involve electrons. Atoms will stay close together if they have a shared interest in one or more electrons. Atoms are at their most stable when they have no partially-filled electron shells. If an atom has only a few electrons in a shell, it will tend to lose them to empty the shell. These elements are metals. When metal atoms bond, a metallic bond occurs. When an atom has a nearly full electron shell, it will try to find electrons from another atom so that it can fill its outer shell. These elements are usually described as non-metals. The bond between two nonmetal atoms is usually a covalent bond. Where metal and nonmetal atom come together an ionic bond occurs. Additionally, there are also other types of bonds such as the metallic, covalent and ionic bonds, and so on.

(*Selected from http://www.ndt-ed.org/EducationResources/ CommunityCollege/Materials/cc_mat_index.htm*, 2014)

New Words and Expressions

atomic structure　原子结构
ceramic　*n.* 制陶术，制陶业，陶瓷
magnitude　*n.* 大小，数量，巨大，广大，量级
microstructure　*n.* 微观结构，显微结构
macrostructure　*n.* 宏观结构
magnetic　*a.* 磁的，有磁性的，有吸引力的
optical　*a.* 眼的，视力的，光学的
nuclear　*a.* 核子的，原子能的，核的，中心的［复数 nucleus］；*n.* 核子
proton　*n.* 质子
magnesium　*n.* 镁

Notes

① From the periodic table below, it can be seen that there are only about 100 different kinds of atoms in the entire Universe. periodic table = periodic table of elements 即：（元素）周期表。参考译文：从下面的元素周期表中可以看出：整个宇宙仅仅有大约 100 种不同的原子。

② The properties of matter depend on which atoms are used and how they are bonded together. 参考译文：物质的性质依赖于原子的组成和成键情况。

③ To understand the structure of a material, the type of atoms present, and how the atoms are arranged and bonded must be known. To ＋…，表示目的，the type of atoms present, and how the atoms are arranged and bonded 做并列主语，根据中文语序可翻译成宾语。参考译文：为了了解材料的结构，必须知道原子的类型以及原子是如何排列的、如何键合的。

④ To determine the number of neutrons in an atom, the atomic number is simply subtracted from the atomic weight. 为了确定原子中中子的数目，因此，把 To determine…提到

句首。科技英语中常见此种句式。

⑤ Therefore, they usually have negatively charged electrons surrounding the nucleus in numbers equal to the number of protons. "they" 指的是上一句中的 atom, proton 是质子。本句的意思是：因此，原子中围绕原子核旋转的带负电的电子的数目一般等于质子的数目。

⑥ For example, magnesium, with an atomic number of 12, has two electrons in the inner shell, eight in the second shell and two in the outer shell. in the inner shell 是指原子的最内层，即靠近原子核的一层；the outer shell 是指原子结构的最外一层。参考译文：例如镁，原子序数是 12，最内层有 2 个电子，第二层有 8 个电子，最外层有 2 个电子。

Exercises

1. Question for discussion
（1）What are the three most common major classifications of structural materials?
（2）What are the important features of atomic structure? What about other structures?
（3）Which properties does atomic structure primarily affect?
（4）What are the main differences between microstructure and macrostructure?
（5）What indicates the atomic weight of an atom?
（6）What will 12 electrons distribute in the shell of magnesium atom?

2. Translate the following into Chinese

naked eye   transition elements
mechanical property   atomic number
elementary chemistry   positively charged protons

- Metals behave differently than ceramics, and ceramics behave differently than polymers.
- The atomic structure primarily affects the chemical, physical, thermal, electrical, magnetic, and optical properties. The microstructure and macrostructure can also affect these properties but they generally have a larger effect on mechanical properties and on the rate of chemical reaction.
- The strength of metals suggests that these atoms are held together by strong bonds.
- An element's atomic number indicates the number of positively charged protons in the nucleus. The atomic weight of an atom indicates how many protons and neutrons in the nucleus.

3. Translate the following into English

微观结构   宏观结构
化学反应   原子量
电荷平衡   带正电子的原子核

- 从我们呼吸的空气到各种各样性质迥异的金属，成千上万种物质是由 100 多种原子组成的。
- 事实证明金属原子是通过很强的键结合在一起的。
- 微观结构是指能够通过显微镜观察到的而不是用肉眼直接观察到的结构；宏观结构是指可以直接用肉眼观察到的结构。
- 原子核中质子和中子的量的总和就是原子量。

4. Reading Comprehension

(1) According to the passage, which properties does atomic structure primarily affect? _____

(A) Chemical and physical properties　　(B) Thermal and electrical properties

(C) Magnetic and optical properties　　(D) A, B and C

(2) According to the text, which of statements is NOT TRUE? _____

(A) Microstructure means that structures can be seen by a microscope.

(B) Microstructure means that structures can be seen with the naked eye.

(C) Macrostructure includes features that can be seen with the naked eye.

(D) The microstructure and macrostructure can also affect these properties such as chemical, physical, thermal, electrical, magnetic, and optical properties.

(3) Which bonds will allow atoms to move since metals are also usually formable? _____

(A) Metallic bond　　(B) Ionic bond

(C) Covalent bond　　(D) Not mentioned in the text.

(4) An element's atomic number indicates the number of _____ in the nucleus.

(A) positively charged protons

(B) negatively charged electrons

(C) positively charged protons and negatively charged electrons

(D) none of the above

(5) About the atoms, all the following statements are true EXCEPT _____.

(A) Electrons in atoms are present with different energies.

(B) The atomic weight of an atom indicates how many protons in the nucleus.

(C) Atoms usually have negatively charged electrons surrounding the nucleus in numbers equal to the number of protons.

(D) Atoms like to have a balanced electrical charge.

(6) _____ will be discussed in the next pages according to the text.

(A) Metallic Bonding in Materials

(B) Hydrogen bonding in Materials

(C) Covalent Bonding in Materials and Ionic Bonding in Materials

(D) Metallic, Covalent and Ionic Bonds in Materials

Reading Material

Metallic, Covalent and Ionic Bonds in Materials

All chemical bonds involve electrons. Atoms will stay close together if they have a shared interest in one or more electrons. Atoms are at their most stable when they have no partially-filled electron shells. If an atom has only a few electrons in a shell, it will tend to lose them to empty the shell. These elements are metals. When metal atoms bond, a metallic bond occurs. When an atom has a nearly full electron shell, it will try to find electrons from another atom so that it can fill its outer shell. These elements are usually described as nonmetals. The bond between two nonmetal atoms is usually a covalent bond. Where metal and nonmetal atom come together an ionic bond occurs. There are also other, less common, types of bond but the details are beyond the scope of this material. On the next few pages, the Metallic, Covalent and Ionic bonds will be covered in more detail.

Ionic Bonding

Ionic bonding occurs between charged particles. These may be atoms or groups of atoms. Ionic bonding occurs between metal atoms and nonmetal atoms. Metals usually have 1, 2, or 3 electrons in their outermost shell. Nonmetals have 5, 6, or 7 electrons in their outer shell. Atoms with outer shells that are only partially filled are unstable. To become stable, the metal atom wants to get rid of one or more electrons in its outer shell. Losing electrons will either result in an empty outer shell or get it closer to having an empty outer shell. It would like to have an empty outer shell because the next lower energy shell is a stable shell with eight electrons.

Since electrons have a negative charge, the atom that gains electrons becomes a negatively charged ion (i.e. anion) because it now has more electrons than protons. Alternately, an atom that loses electrons becomes a positively charged ion (i.e. cation). The particles in an ionic compound are held together because there are oppositely charged particles that are attracted to one another.

Figure 1.3 schematically shows the process that takes place during the formation of an i-

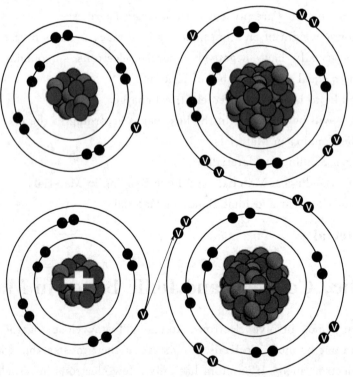

Figure 1.3 The formation of an ionic bond between sodium and chlorine atoms

onic bond between sodium and chlorine atoms. Note that sodium has one valence electron that it would like to give up so that it would become stable with a full outer shell of eight. Also note that chlorine has seven valence electrons and it would like to gain an electron in order to have a full shell of eight. The transfer of the electron causes the previously neutral sodium atom to become a positively charged ion (cation), and the previously neutral chlorine atom to become a negatively charged ion (anion). The attraction for the cation and the anion is called the ionic bond.

Some common features of materials with ionic bonds:
- Hard
- Good insulators
- Transparent
- Brittle or cleave rather than deform

Covalent Bonding

Where a compound only contains nonmetal atoms, a covalent bond is formed by atoms sharing two or more electrons. Nonmetals have 4 or more electrons in their outer shells (except boron). With this many electrons in the outer shell, it would require more energy to remove the electrons than would be gained by making new bonds. Therefore, both the atoms involved share a pair of electrons. Each atom gives one of its outer electrons to the electron pair, which then spends some time with each atom. Consequently, both atoms are held near each other since both atoms have a share in the electrons (Figure 1.4).

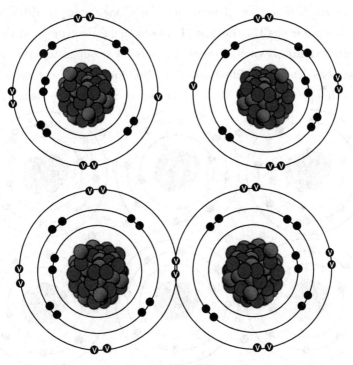

Figure 1.4 The formation of a covalent bond

More than one electron pair can be formed with half of the electrons coming from one atom and the rest from the other atom. An important feature of this bond is that the electrons are tightly held and equally shared by the participating atoms. The atoms can be of the same element or different elements. In each molecule, the bonds between the atoms are strong but the bonds between molecules are usually weak. This makes many solid materials with covalent bonds brittle. Many ceramic materials have covalent bonds.

Compounds with covalent bonds may be solid, liquid or gas at room temperature depending on the number of atoms in the compound. The more atoms in each molecule, the higher a compound's melting and boiling temperature will be. Since most covalent compounds contain only a few atoms and the forces between molecules are weak, most covalent compounds have low melting and boiling points. However, some, like carbon compounds, can be very large. An example is the diamond in which carbon atoms each share four electrons to form giant lattices.

Some common features of materials with covalent bonds:
- Hard
- Good insulators
- Transparent
- Brittle or cleave rather than deform

Metallic Bonding

A common characteristic of metallic elements is that they contain only one to three electrons in the outer shell. When an element has only one, two or three valence electrons (i.e. electrons in the outer shell), the bond between these electrons and the nucleus is relatively weak. So, for example, when aluminum atoms are grouped together in a block of metal, the outer electrons leave individual atoms to become part of common "electron cloud" (Figure 1.5). In this arrangement, the valence electrons have considerable mobility and are

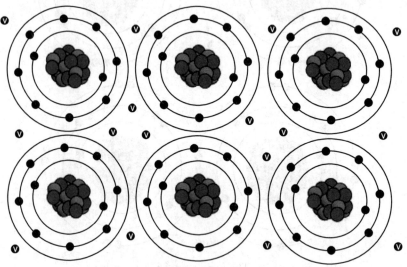

Figure 1.5 The metallic bond of aluminum

able to conduct heat and electricity easily. Also, the delocalized nature of the bonds, make it possible for the atoms to slide past each other when the metal is deformed instead of fracturing like glass or other brittle material.

Since the aluminum atoms lose 3 electrons, they end up having a positive charge and are designated Al^{3+} ions (cations). These ions repel each other but are held together in the block because the negative electrons are attracted to the positively charged ions. A result of the sharing of electrons is the cations arrange themselves in a regular pattern. This regular pattern of atoms is the crystalline structure of metals. In the crystal lattice, atoms are packed closely together to maximize the strength of the bonds. An actual piece of metal consists of many tiny crystals called grains that touch at grain boundaries.

Some common features of materials with metallic bonds:
- Good electrical and thermal conductors due to their free valence electrons
- Opaque
- Relatively ductile

Van der Waals Bonding

The van der Waals bonds occur to some extent in all materials but are particularly important in plastics and polymers. These materials are made up of a long string molecules consisting of carbon atoms covalently bonded with other atoms, such as hydrogen, nitrogen, oxygen, fluorine. The covalent bonds within the molecules are very strong and rupture only under extreme conditions. The bonds between the molecules that allow sliding and rupture to occur are called van der Waals forces.

When ionic and covalent bonds are present, there is some imbalance in the electrical charge of the molecule. Take water (Figure 1.6) as an example. Research has determined the hydrogen atoms are bonded to the oxygen atoms at an angle of 104.5°. This angle produces a positive polarity at the hydrogen-rich end of the molecule and a negative polarity at the other end. A result of this charge imbalance is that water molecules are attracted to each

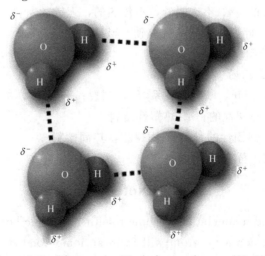

Figure 1.6 The van der Waals forces of water (H_2O)

other. This is the force that holds the molecules together in a drop of water.

This same concept can be carried on to plastics, except that as molecules become larger, the van der Waals forces between molecules also increase. For example, in polyethylene the molecules are composed of hydrogen and carbon atoms in the same ratio as ethylene gas. But there are more of each type of atom in the polyethylene molecules and as the number of atoms in a molecule increases, the matter passes from a gas to a liquid and finally to a solid. Polymers are often classified as being either a thermoplastic or a thermosetting material.

(*Selected from http：//www.ndt-ed.org/EducationResources/ CommunityCollege/Materials/cc_mat_index.htm*, 2014)

New Words and Expressions

outermost *a.* 最外面的，最远的
anion *n.* 阴离子
cation *n.* 阳离子
get rid of *v.* 摆脱，除去
oppositely *adv.* 相对地，对立地
schematic *a.* 示意性的
formation *n.* 形成，构成
sodium *n.* 钠
chlorine *n.* 氯
previously *adv.* 先前，以前
transparent *a.* 透明的，显然的，明晰的
brittle *a.* 易碎的，脆弱的
cleave *v.* 劈，劈开，裂开，黏着，坚持
deform *v.* （使）变形
boron *n.* 硼
aluminum *n.* 铝
opaque *n.* 不透明的；*a.* 不透明的，不传热的，迟钝的
fracture *n.* 破裂，碎裂，龟裂；*v.* （使）破碎，（使）破裂
repel *v.* 击退，抵制
polyethylene *n.* 聚乙烯
rupture *v.* 破裂，裂开，断绝（关系等），割裂；*n.* 破裂，决裂，割裂
thermoplastic *a.* 热塑性的；*n.* 热塑性塑料
thermosetting *a.* 热固性的；*n.* 热固树脂，热固塑料
remelt *v.* 再融化，再熔化

Notes

① Where metal and nonmetal atom come together an ionic bond occurs. = The combination of a metal and a nonmetal atom will form an ionic bond = Ionic bonding occurs between metal atoms and nonmetal atoms. 参考译文：金属和非金属原子结合在一起形成离

子键。

② These may be atoms or groups of atoms. These 是指上面所提到的 charged particles。参考译文：这些带电的粒子可以是原子或原子团。

③ Note that sodium has one valence electron that it would like to give up so that it would become stable with a full outer shell of eight. Note，注意，根据上下文意思，句中是指（人们）注意到……，科技英语中常常把作为主语的人省略，翻译时可根据中文习惯加以调整。"give up"是指放弃，停止，抛弃，把……送交等，这里是指可以供给的、失掉的。参考译文：我们注意到钠原子有一个可以失掉的价电子，这样就可以达到最外层是8个电子的稳定结构。

④ The transfer of the electron causes the previously neutral sodium atom to become a positively charged ion (cation), and the previously neutral chlorine atom to become a negatively charged ion (anion). neutral，是指中性的或不带电荷的；positively，是指肯定的或带正电的；negatively，是指否定的或带负电的。参考译文：电子的转移使原来中性的钠原子变成了带正电荷的离子（阳离子），使原来中性的氯原子变成带负电荷的离子（阴离子）。

⑤ A common characteristic of metallic elements is they contain only one to three electrons in the outer shell. 句中… is they …实际是that引导的从句做宾语，省略了that。参考译文：金属元素的一个基本特性是：它们的最外层只有1~3个电子。

⑥ When ionic and covalent bonds are present, there is some imbalance in the electrical charge of the molecule. imbalance, "im"表示否定，不平衡，不均衡。参考译文：当离子键和共价键共存时，分子间就存在一些电荷的不平衡。

Reading Comprehension

(1) At room temperature, which factor will affect the states of a compound with covalent bonds? _____
(A) The number of atoms (B) Thermal properties
(C) Magnetic and optical properties (D) The forces between molecules

(2) According to the reading material, which of statements about bonds is NOT TRUE? _____
(A) All chemical bonds involve electrons.
(B) Atoms are at their most stable when they have no partially-filled electron shells. These elements are nonmetals.
(C) The bond between two nonmetal atoms is usually a covalent bond.
(D) The bond between a metal and a nonmetal atom is usually an ionic bond.

(3) The feature of _____ is not the common feature of materials of covalent bonds.
(A) Hardness (B) Transparence
(C) Good electrical conductors (D) Brittleness

(4) Polymers are often classified as _____ and _____ materials. _____ materials can be easily remelted for forming or recycling and _____ material cannot be easily remelted.

(A) plastics; rubber; Plastics; rubber
(B) rubber; plastics; Rubber; plastics
(C) thermoplastic; thermosetting; Thermoplastic; thermosetting
(D) thermosetting; thermoplastic; Thermosetting; thermoplastic
(5) About the metallic bonding, all the following statements are true EXCEPT _____.
(A) Metallic bonding made materials with metallic bonds good electrical and thermal conductors due to their free valence electrons.
(B) When an element has only one, two or three valence electrons, the bond between these electrons and the nucleus is relatively weak.
(C) A common characteristic of metallic elements is they contain only one to three electrons in the outer shell.
(D) In the crystal lattice, atoms are packed closely together to minimize the strength of the bonds.
(6) _____ will be discussed in the next pages according to the passage.
(A) Which bond is the strongest bond
(B) Hydrogen bonding
(C) The common features of metallic bonds and ionic bonds
(D) The different features of covalent bonds and ionic bonds

Unit 4　Physical and Chemical Properties of Materials

Physical properties are those that can be observed without changing the identity of the substance. The general properties of matter such as color, density, hardness, are examples of physical properties. Properties that describe how a substance changes into a completely different substance are called chemical properties. Flammability and corrosion/ oxidation resistance are examples of chemical properties.

The difference between a physical and chemical property is straightforward until the phase of the material is considered. When a material changes from a solid to a liquid to a vapor it seems like them become a difference substance. However, when a material melts, solidifies, vaporizes, condenses or sublimes, only the state of the substance changes. Consider ice, liquid water, and water vapor, they are all simply H_2O. Phase is a physical property of matter and matter can exist in four phases: solid, liquid, gas and plasma.

In general, some of the more important physical and chemical properties from an engineering material standpoint include phase transformation temperatures, density, specific gravity, thermal conductivity, linear coefficient of thermal expansion, electrical conductivity and resistivity, magnetic permeability, and corrosion resistance, and so on.

Phase Transformation Temperatures

When temperature rises and pressure is held constant, a typical substance changes from solid to liquid and then to vapor. Transitions from solid to liquid, from liquid to vapor, from vapor to solid and visa versa are called phase transformations or transitions. Since some substances have several crystal forms, technically there can also be solid to another solid form phase transformation.

Phase transitions from solid to liquid, and from liquid to vapor absorb heat. The phase transition temperature where a solid changes to a liquid is called the *melting point*. The temperature at which the vapor pressure of a liquid equals 1 atm (101.3 kPa) is called the *boiling point*. Some materials, such as many polymers, do not go simply from a solid to a liquid with increasing temperature. Instead, at some temperature below the melting point, they start to lose their crystalline structure but the molecules remain linked in chains, which results in a soft and pliable material. The temperature at which a solid, glassy material begins to soften and flow is called the glass transition temperature.

Density

Mass can be thinly distributed as in a pillow, or tightly packed as in a block of lead. The space the mass occupies is its volume, and the mass per unit of volume is its density.

Mass (m) is a fundamental measure of the amount of matter. Weight (w) is a measure of the force exerted by a mass and this force is produced by the acceleration of gravity. Therefore, on the surface of the earth, the mass of an object is determined by dividing the weight of an object by 9.8 m/s² (the acceleration of gravity on the surface of the earth). Since we are typically comparing things on the surface of the earth, the weight of an object is commonly used rather than calculating its mass.

The density (r) of a material depends on the phase it is in and the temperature. (The density of liquids and gases is very temperature dependent) Water in the liquid state has a density of $1 g/cm^3 = 1000 g/m^3$ at 4℃. Ice has a density of 0.917 g/cm^3 at 0℃, and it should be noted that this decrease in density for the solid phase is unusual. For almost all other substances, the density of the solid phase is greater than that of the liquid phase. Water vapor (vapor saturated air) has a density of 0.051 g/cm^3.

Some common units used for expressing density are grams/cubic centimeter, kilograms/cubic meter, grams/milliliter, grams/liter, pounds for cubic inch and pounds per cubic foot; but it should be obvious that any unit of mass per any unit of volume can be used.

Specific Gravity

Specific gravity is the ratio of density of a substance compared to the density of fresh water at 4℃ (39℉). At this temperature the density of water is at its greatest value and equal 1 g/mL. Since specific gravity is a ratio, so it has no units. An object will float in water if its density is less than the density of water and sink if its density is greater that that of water. Similarly, an object with specific gravity less than 1 will float and those with a specific gravity greater than one will sink. Specific gravity values for a few common substances are: Au, 19.3; mercury, 13.6; alcohol, 0.7893; benzene, 0.8786. Note that since water has a density of 1 g/cm³, the specific gravity is the same as the density of the material measured in g/cm³.

Magnetic Permeability

Magnetic permeability or simply permeability is the ease with which a material can be magnetized. It is a constant of proportionality that exists between magnetic induction and magnetic field intensity. This constant is equal to approximately 1.257×10^{-6} Henry per meter (H/m) in free space (a vacuum). In other materials it can be much different, often substantially greater than the free-space value, which is symbolized μ_0.

Materials that cause the lines of flux to move farther apart, resulting in a decrease in magnetic flux density compared with a vacuum, are called diamagnetic. Materials that concentrate magnetic flux by a factor of more than one but less than or equal to ten are called paramagnetic; materials that concentrate the flux by a factor of more than ten are called ferromagnetic. The permeability factors of some substances change with rising or falling temperature, or with the intensity of the applied magnetic field.

In engineering applications, permeability is often expressed in relative, rather than in absolute, terms. If μ_0 represents the permeability of free space (that is, 1.257×10^{-6} H/m) and μ represents the permeability of the substance in question (also specified in henrys per meter), then the relative permeability, μ_r, is given by:

$$\mu_r = \mu / \mu_0$$

For non-ferrous metals such as copper, brass, aluminum etc., the permeability is the same as that of "free space", i.e. the relative permeability is one. For ferrous metals however the value of μ_r may be several hundred. Certain ferromagnetic materials, especially powdered or laminated iron, steel, or nickel alloys, have μ_r that can range up to about 1,000,000. Diamagnetic materials have μ_r less than one, but no known substance has relative permeability much less than one. In addition, permeability can vary greatly within a metal part due to localized stresses, heating effects, etc.

When a paramagnetic or ferromagnetic core is inserted into a coil, the inductance is multiplied by μ_r compared with the inductance of the same coil with an air core. This effect is useful in the design of transformers and eddy current probes.

(*Selected from http://www.ndt-ed.org/EducationResources/ CommunityCollege/Materials/cc_mat_index.htm*, 2014)

New Words and Expressions

density　*n.* 密度
flammability　*n.* 易燃的，可燃性的
corrosion　*n.* 侵蚀（腐蚀，锈）
oxidation　*n.* 氧化，氧化作用，生锈
condense　*v.* 升华
phase　*n.* 相，相位，时期，阶段

plasma   *n*. 等离子体
coefficient   *n*. 系数
pliable   *a*. 易曲折的，柔软的，柔顺的
mercury   *n*. 汞，水银
vacuum   *n*. 真空，空间
paramagnetic   *a*. 顺磁性的；*n*. 顺磁性体
diamagnetic   *a*. 反磁性的；*n*. 反磁性体
ferromagnetic   *a*. 铁磁的，铁磁体的；*n*. 铁磁体
brass   *n*. 黄铜
inductance   *n*. 感应系数，自感应

Notes

① Instead, at some temperature below the melting point, they start to lose their crystalline structure but the molecules remain linked in chains, which results in a soft and pliable material. 参考译文：当温度低于熔点时，聚合物的晶体结构破坏，但其分子仍然连接在分子链上，从而形成一种柔软和柔顺性材料。

② Mass can be thinly distributed as in a pillow, or tightly packed as in a block of lead. pillow，枕头，用作枕头的东西；lead，铅。参考译文：质量可以像枕头似的稀疏地分布，也可以像铅那样紧紧地堆积在一起。

③ Therefore, on the surface of the earth, the mass of an object is determined by dividing the weight of an object by 9.8 m/s^2 (the acceleration of gravity on the surface of the earth). 物理上，地球表面的重力加速度 $g=9.8$ m/s^2。参考译文：因此，在地球表面，物体的质量由物体的重量和重力加速度所决定。

④ In other materials it can be much different, often substantially greater than the free-space value, which is symbolized…. free-space，真空。参考译文：其他材料却截然不同，通常远远大于真空值……。

⑤ Materials that cause the lines of flux to move farther apart, resulting in a decrease in magnetic flux density compared with a vacuum, are called diamagnetic. magnetic flux density，磁通量密度。参考译文：由于互相排斥而往相反的方向移动，导致磁通量密度比真空中小，这种材料为反磁性材料。

⑥ In engineering applications, permeability is often expressed in relative, rather than in absolute, terms. relative，相对的；absolute，绝对的。参考译文：在工程应用中，渗透率通常用相对值而不是绝对值来表示。

Exercises

1. Question for discussion

(1) What are physical and chemical properties of materials according to this article? Can you take some examples?

(2) What do some of the more important physical and chemical properties from an engi-

neering material standpoint include?

(3) Which phases can matter exist in?

(4) What is the melting point, the boiling point, the glass transition temperature?

(5) What is the relationship between mass and weight?

(6) What is diamagnetic, paramagnetic and ferromagnetic?

2. Translate the following into Chinese

phase transformation temperatures   specific gravity
thermal conductivity   the melting point
the acceleration of gravity   magnetic permeability

- An object will float in water if its density is less than the density of water and sink if its density is greater that that of water. Similarly, an object with specific gravity less than 1 will float and those with a specific gravity greater than one will sink.

- Materials that cause the lines of flux to move farther apart, resulting in a decrease in magnetic flux density compared with a vacuum, are called diamagnetic. Materials that concentrate magnetic flux by a factor of more than one but less than or equal to ten are called paramagnetic; materials that concentrate the flux by a factor of more than ten are called ferromagnetic.

- Certain ferromagnetic materials, especially powdered or laminated iron, steel, or nickel alloys, have μ_r that can range up to about 1,000,000. Diamagnetic materials have μ_r less than one, but no known substance has relative permeability much less than one.

- When a paramagnetic or ferromagnetic core is inserted into a coil, the inductance is multiplied by μ_r compared with the inductance of the same coil with an air core.

3. Translate the following into English

密度   沸点   磁感应
热导率   玻璃转变温度   有色金属
线性热膨胀系数   单位体积质量

- 化学性质是用来描述一种物质是怎样变成另外一种完全不同的物质的。
- 相变是一种物理性质，并且物质存在四种相：固相，液相，气相和等离子体。
- 当温度低于熔点时，聚合物的晶体结构破坏，但其分子仍然连接在分子链上，从而形成一种柔软和柔顺性材料。
- 在工程应用中，渗透率通常用相对值而不是绝对值来表示。

4. Reading comprehension

(1) Which of the following is TRUE according to the text? _____

(A) When matter changes from a solid to a liquid to a vapor, this change is a chemical property of water.

(B) When a material melts, solidifies, vaporizes, condenses or sublimes, this change is a physical property of matter.

(C) Phase transitions from liquid to solid, and from vapor to liquid absorb heat.

(D) Many polymers go simply from a solid to a liquid with increasing temperature.

(2) Some common units used for expressing density are the following except _____.

(A) grams/cubic centimeter (B) kilograms/square meter
(C) grams /milliliter (D) pounds for cubic inch
(3) We learn from the ten paragraph that _____ .
(A) An object will float in water if its density is greater than the density of water and sink if its density is less than that of water.
(B) An object with specific gravity greater than 1 will float and those with a specific gravity less than 1 will sink.
(C) Alcohol will float in water and Au will sink in water.
(D) Mercury will float in water and benzene will sink in water.
(4) From the Magnetic permeability which of the following is not true? _____
(A) Materials that cause the lines of flux to move farther apart, resulting in a decrease in magnetic flux density compared with a vacuum, are called diamagnetic.
(B) Materials that concentrate magnetic flux by a factor of 10 are called paramagnetic.
(C) Materials that concentrate the flux by a factor of 8 are called ferromagnetic.
(D) For aluminum, the relative permeability is one.
(5) Which is useful in the design of transformers and eddy current prokes? _____
(A) When a paramagnetic or ferromagnetic core is inserted into a coil, the inductance is multiplied by μ_r compared with the inductance of the same coil with an air core.
(B) Permeability can vary greatly with in a metal part due to localized stresses, heating effects, etc.
(C) The permeability factors of some substance change with rising or falling temperature, or with the intensity of the applied magnetic field.
(D) Diamagnetic materials have μ_r less than one, but no known substance has relative permeability much less than one.
(6) If $\mu = 2.514 \times 10^{-4}$ H/m, then relative permeability is _____ .
(A) 0.005 (B) 200 (C) 0.2 (D) 0.5

Reading Materials

Conductivity Properties of Materials

Electrical Conductivity and Resistivity

It is well known that one of the subatomic particles of an atom is the electron. The electrons carry a negative electrostatic charge and under certain conditions can move from atom to atom. The direction of movement between atoms is random unless a force causes the electrons to move in one direction. This directional movement of electrons due to an electromotive force is what is known as electricity.

Electrical conductivity

Electrical conductivity is a measure of how well a material accommodates the movement of an electric charge. It is the ratio of the current density to the electric field strength. Its SI derived unit is the Siemens per meter, but conductivity values are often reported as percent IACS. IACS is an acronym for International Annealed Copper Standard or the material that was used to make traditional copper-wire. The conductivity of the annealed copper (5.8108×10^7 S/m) is defined to be 100% IACS at 20℃. All other conductivity values are related back to this conductivity of annealed copper. Therefore, iron with a conductivity value of 1.044×10^7 S/m, has a conductivity of approximately 18% of that of annealed copper and this is reported as 18% IACS. An interesting side note is that commercially pure copper products now often have IACS conductivity values greater than 100% because processing techniques have improved since the adoption of the standard in 1913 and more impurities can now be removed from the metal.

Conductivity values in Siemens/meter can be converted to % IACS by multiplying the conductivity value by 1.724×10^{-6}. When conductivity values are reported in microsiemens/centimeter, the conductivity value is multiplied by 172.41 to convert to the % IACS value.

Electrical conductivity is a very useful property since values are affected by such things as a substances chemical composition and the stress state of crystalline structures. Therefore, electrical conductivity information can be used for measuring the purity of water, sorting materials, checking for proper heat treatment of metals, and inspecting for heat damage in some materials.

Electrical resistivity

Electrical resistivity is the reciprocal of conductivity. It is the opposition of a body or substance to the flow of electrical current through it, resulting in a change of electrical energy into heat, light, or other forms of energy. The amount of resistance depends on the type of material. Materials with low resistivity are good conductors of electricity and materials with high resistivity are good insulators.

The SI unit for electrical resistivity is the ohm meter. Resistivity values are more commonly reported in micro ohm centimeters units. As mentioned above resistivity values are simply the reciprocal of conductivity so conversion between the two is straightforward. For example, a material with two micro ohm centimeter of resistivity will have 1/2 microsiemens/centimeter of conductivity. Resistivity values in microhm centimeters units can be converted to % IACS conductivity values with the following formula:

$$172.41/\text{resistivity} = \% \text{ IACS}$$

Thermal Conductivity

Thermal conductivity (λ) is the intrinsic property of a material which relates its ability to conduct heat. Heat transfer by conduction involves transfer of energy within a material without any motion of the material as a whole. Conduction takes place when a temperature gradient exists in a solid (or stationary fluid) medium. Conductive heat flow occurs in the direction of decreasing temperature because higher temperature equates to higher molecular energy or more molecular movement. Energy is transferred from the more energetic to the less energetic molecules when neighboring molecules collide.

Thermal conductivity is defined as the quantity of heat (Q) transmitted through a unit thickness (L) in a direction normal to a surface of unit area (A) due to a unit temperature gradient (ΔT) under steady state conditions and when the heat transfer is dependent only on the temperature gradient. In equation form this becomes the following:

Thermal Conductivity = heat × distance / (area × temperature gradient)
$$\lambda = Q \times L / (A \times \Delta T)$$

Linear Coefficient of Thermal Expansion

When heat is added to most materials, the average amplitude of the atoms' vibrating within the material increases. This, in turn, increases the separation between the atoms causing the material to expand. If the material does not go through a phase change, the expansion can be easily related to the temperature change. The linear coefficient of thermal expansion (α) describes the relative change in length of a material per degree temperature change. As shown in the following equation, α is the ratio of change in length (Δl) to the total starting length (l_i) and change in temperature (ΔT).

$$\alpha = \frac{\Delta l}{l_i \Delta T}$$

By rearranging this equation, it can be seen that if the linear coefficient of thermal expansion is known, the change in components length can be calculated for each degree of temperature change. This effect also works in reverse. That is to say, if energy is removed from a material then the object's temperature will decrease causing the object to contract.

Thermal expansion (and contraction) must be taken into account when designing products with close tolerance fits as these tolerances will change as temperature changes if the materials used in the design have different coefficients of thermal expansion. It should also be understood that thermal expansion can cause significant stress in a component if the design does not allow for expansion and contraction of components. The phenomena of thermal expansion can be challenging when designing bridges, buildings, aircraft and spacecraft, but it can be put to beneficial uses. For example, thermostats and other heat-sensitive sensors make use of the property of linear expansion.

(*Selected from* http://www.ndt-ed.org/EducationResources/ CommunityCollege/Materials/cc_mat_index.htm, 2014)

New Words and Expressions

electromotive force 电动势
electrical conductivity 电导率，导电性
resistivity *n.* 抵抗力，电阻系数
acronym *n.* 缩写字，字头语
impurity *n.* 不纯，杂质

inspect　*v.* 检查，调查，监查，检阅
reciprocal　*n.* 倒数
insulator　*n.* 绝缘体，绝热器
temperature gradient　温度梯度
collide　*v.* 碰撞，互撞，抵触
gradient　*n.* 倾斜度，坡度，梯度
amplitude　*n.* 振幅
vibrating　*n.* 振动，振荡
be calculated for　为适合……而设计的，适合于
close tolerance　紧公差，严格的容限
thermostat　*n.* 恒温器

Notes

① It is well known that one of the subatomic particles of an atom is the electron. subatomic，原子内的。参考译文：众所周知，原子中存在一种粒子叫做电子。

② It is the ratio of the current density to the electric field strength. the current density，电流密度；the electric field strength，电场强度。参考译文：电导率是电流密度与电场强度的比值。

③ As mentioned above resistivity values are simply the reciprocal of conductivity so conversion between the two is straightforward. conversion，换算；straightforward，简单的，易懂的。参考译文：因为电阻率是电导率的倒数，因此它们之间的换算也非常简单。

④ Energy is transferred from the more energetic to the less energetic molecules when neighboring molecules collide. 参考译文：当相邻的分子碰撞时，能量从高能量的分子向低能量的分子转移。

⑤ When heat is added to most materials, the average amplitude of the atoms' vibrating within the materials increases. 参考译文：当加热时，大多数材料中原子振荡的振幅会增大。

⑥ By rearranging this equation, it can be seen that if the linear coefficient of thermal expansion is known, the change in components length can be calculated for each degree of temperature change. rearrange，重新安排，重新整理；the linear coefficient of thermal expansion，线性热膨胀系数。参考译文：将公式重新换算，可以发现如果线性热膨胀系数已知，温度每变化一度，则组分长度的变化即可求得。

Reading Comprehension

(1) We learn from the first paragraph that _____ .
(A) the electrons carry a negative electrostatic and always can move from atom to atom.
(B) the direction of movement between atoms is random even though a force the electrons are given.
(C) electricity is the directional movement of electrons.
(D) an atom only has one subatomic particle.

(2) _____ causes the directional movement of electrons.

(A) The electrons carrying a negative electrostatic charge

(B) An electromotive force

(C) Electrical conductivity

(D) The movement of an electric charge

(3) If electrical conductivity value is 1.044×10^7, then electrical resistivity is _____ .

(A) 9.6×10^{-8} (B) 9.6×10^{-6} (C) 2.088×10^{-7} (D) 0.522×10^7

(4) From Electrical resistivity, which of the following is TURE? _____

(A) If materials have low resistivity, they are good insulators.

(B) The micro ohm centimeter also is the SI unit for electrical resistivity.

(C) A material with two microsiemens/centimeter of conductivity will have 1/2 micro ohm centimeter of resistivity.

(D) All resistivity values can be converted to %IACS conductivity values with the following formula: 172.41/ resistivity = %IACS.

(5) In thermal conductivity equation form, which of the following is not included? _____

(A) the quantity of heat   (B) a surface of unit area

(C) distance   (D) the temperature of environment

(6) We learn from the last paragraph that _____ .

(A) Thermal expansion must be taken into account when designing every product.

(B) The tolerance is in equation form of the linear coefficient of thermal expansion.

(C) When designing bridges, buildings, aircraft and spacecraft, the phenomena of thermal expansion must avoid.

(D) We can make good use of the property of linear expansion when designing bridges, building, thermostats, and other heat-sensitive sensors.

Unit 5   Mechanical Properties of Materials

The mechanical properties of a material are those properties that involve a reaction to an applied load. The mechanical properties of metals determine the range of usefulness of a material and establish the service life that can be expected. Mechanical properties are also used to help classify and identify material. The most common properties considered are strength, ductility, hardness, impact resistance, and fracture toughness.

Most structural materials are anisotropic, which means that their material properties vary with orientation. The variation in properties can be due to directionality in the microstructure (texture) from forming or cold working operation, the controlled alignment of fiber reinforcement and a variety of other causes. Mechanical properties are generally specific to product form such as sheet, plate, extrusion, casting, forging, and etc. Additionally, it is common to see mechanical property listed by the directional grain structure of the material. In products such as sheet and plate, the rolling direction is called the longitudinal direction, the width of the product is called the transverse direction, and the thickness is called the short transverse direction. The grain orientations in standard wrought forms of metallic products are shown the image.

The mechanical properties of a material are not constants and often change as a function of temperature, rate of loading, and other conditions. For example, temperatures below room temperature generally cause an increase in strength properties of metallic alloys; while ductility, fracture toughness, and elongation usually decrease. Temperatures above room temperature usually cause a decrease in the strength properties of metallic alloys. Ductility may increase or decrease with increasing temperature depending on the same variables.

It should also be noted that there is often significant variability in the values obtained when measuring mechanical properties. Seemingly identical test specimen from the same lot of material will often produce considerable different results. Therefore, multiple tests are commonly conducted to determine mechanical properties and values reported can be an average value or calculated statistical minimum value. Also, a range of values are sometimes reported in order to show variability.

Loading

The application of a force to an object is known as loading. Materials can be subjected to many different loading scenarios and a material's performance is dependant on the loading conditions. There are five fundamental loading conditions; tension, compression, bending, shear, and torsion. Tension is the type of loading in which the two sections of material on either side of a plane tend to be pulled apart or elongated. Compression is the reverse of tensile loading and involves pressing the material together. Loading by bending involves applying a load in a manner that causes a material to curve and results in compressing the material on one side and stretching it on the other. Shear involves applying a load parallel to a plane which caused the material on one side of the plane to want to slide across the material on the other side of the plane. Torsion is the application of a force that causes twisting in a material.

If a material is subjected to a constant force, it is called static loading. If the loading of the material is not constant but instead fluctuates, it is called dynamic or cyclic loading. The way a material is loaded greatly affects its mechanical properties and largely determines how, or if, a component will fail; and whether it will show warning signs before failure actually occurs.

Stress

The term stress (s) is used to express the loading in terms of force applied to a certain cross-sectional area of an object. From the perspective of loading, stress is the applied force or system of forces that tends to deform a body. From the perspective of what is happening within a material, stress is the internal distribution of forces within a body that balance and react to the loads applied to it. The stress distribution may or may not be uniform, depending on the nature of the loading condition. For example, a bar loaded in pure tension will essentially have a uniform tensile stress distribution. However, a bar loaded in bending will have a stress distribution that changes with distance perpendicular to the normal axis.

Strain

Strain is the response of a system to an applied stress. When a material is loaded with a force, it produces a stress, which then causes a material to deform. Engineering strain is defined as the amount of deformation in the direction of the applied force divided by the initial length of the material. This results in a unitless number, although it is often left in the unsimplified form, such as inches per inch or meters per meter. For example, the strain in a bar that is being stretched in tension is the amount of elongation or change in length divided by its original length. As in the case of stress, the strain distribution may or may not be uniform in a complex structural element, depending on the nature of the loading condition.

If the stress is small, the material may only strain a small amount and the material will return to its original size after the stress is released. This is called elastic deformation, because like elastic it returns to its unstressed state. Elastic deformation only occurs in a material when stresses are lower than a critical stress called the yield strength. If a material is loaded beyond it elastic limit, the material will remain in a deformed condition after the load is removed. This is called plastic deformation.

Tensile Properties

Tensile properties indicate how the material will react to forces being applied in tension. A tensile test is a fundamental mechanical test where a carefully prepared specimen is loaded in a very controlled manner while measuring the applied load and the elongation of the specimen over some distance. Tensile tests are used to determine the modulus of elasticity, elastic limit, elongation, proportional limit, reduction in area, tensile strength, yield point, yield strength and other tensile properties.

Hardness

Hardness is the resistance of a material to localized deformation. The term can apply to deformation from indentation, scratching, cutting or bending. In metals, ceramics and most polymers, the deformation considered is plastic deformation of the surface. For elastomers and some polymers, hardness is defined at the resistance to elastic deformation of the surface. The lack of a fundamental definition indicates that hardness is not be a basic property of a material, but rather a composite one with contributions from the yield strength, work hardening, true tensile strength, modulus, and others factors. Hardness measurements are widely used for the quality control of materials because they are quick and considered to be nondestructive tests when the marks or indentations produced by the test are in low stress areas.

Toughness

The ability of a metal to deform plastically and to absorb energy in the process before fracture is termed toughness. The emphasis of this definition should be placed on the ability to absorb energy before fracture. Recall that ductility is a measure of how much something deforms plastically before fracture, but just because a material is ductile does not make it tough. The key to toughness is a good combination of strength and ductility. A material with high strength and high ductility will have more toughness than a material with low strength and high ductility. Therefore, one way to measure toughness is by calculating the area under the stress strain curve from a tensile test. This value is simply called "material toughness" and it has units of energy per volume. Material toughness equates to a slow absorption of energy by the material.

(Selected from http://www.ndt-ed.org/EducationResources/CommunityCollege/Materials/cc_mat_index.htm, 2014)

New Words and Expressions

strength   n. 强度
ductility   n. 可延展性,延伸度,可锻性,韧性
hardness   n. 硬度,硬性
toughness   n. 强硬,韧性,黏性
toughness test 韧性试验,韧度试验
anisotropic a. 各向异性的（非均质）
orientation n. 定位,适应,定向,方位
directionality n. 方向,方向性
alignment   n. 调整（成直线,准线,定向,直线性）,对准,校直,对齐
forging   n. 锻件,锻造（法）
constant   a. 经常的,不变的; n. 常数,恒量
tension   n. 张力,拉力
compression n. 压缩,缩小
shear   n. 剪切,切变,扭曲
torsion   n. 扭力,扭转,扭曲
fluctuate   v. 波动,变动,起伏
stress   n. 应力,压力
perpendicular n. 垂直线,垂直的位置
normal axis 垂直轴,法线轴
strain   n. 应变,拉紧
specimen   n. 样本,标本,试样,样品
modulus   n. 模数,模量,系数

Notes

① The mechanical properties of a material are not constants and often change as a function of temperature, rate of loading, and other conditions. constant, 不变的; as…, 随着……; a function of temperature, 温度条件。参考译文：材料的力学性能不是固定不变的,

它随着温度条件、负载率和其他条件的变化而发生改变。

② Materials can be subjected to many different loading scenarios and a material's performance is dependant on the loading conditions. be subjected to，遭受，经历，遭遇；be dependant on，依赖，依靠，取决于。

③ From the perspective of what is happening within a material, stress is the internal distribution of forces within a body that balance and react to the loads applied to it. "what" 引导一个名词从句；internal，内在的；react to，与……起反应，起作用；"that" 引导表语从句，用来修饰 "the internal distribution of forces"。

④ Engineering strain is defined as the amount of deformation in the direction of the applied force divided by the initial length of the material. divided by，用……除尽；… be defined as…，……定义为……。参考译文：工程应变可定义为：所施加力方向上的材料的改变量与材料原始长度的比值。

⑤ A tensile test is a fundamental mechanical test where a carefully prepared specimen is loaded in a very controlled manner while measuring the applied load and the elongation of the specimen over some distance. "where" 引导一个表语从句，修饰 "mechanical test"。参考译文：拉伸试验是一种基本的力学测试，它是对所制备好的样品施加一种可以控制的负荷，来测量所施加的负荷和在一段距离内样品的拉长。

⑥ …but rather a composite one with contributions from the yield strength, work hardening, true tensile strength, modulus, and others factors. the yield strength，屈服强度；work hardening，加工硬化（金属晶体结构永久变形所致），加工强化；true tensile strength，纯拉伸强度。

Exercises

1. Question for discussion

(1) Please give some examples to explain the application of the mechanical properties of materials.

(2) What are the longitudinal direction, the transverse direction, and the short transverse direction?

(3) Because of the variability in the values obtaining, what should we usually do when measuring mechanical properties of materials?

(4) Explain the following notions: tension, compression, bending, shear, and torsion.

(5) What are the differences between elastic deformation and plastic deformation?

(6) How to distinguish toughness and ductility?

2. Translate the following into Chinese

the service life	the longitudinal direction	the transverse direction
dynamic or cyclic loading	the initial length of the material	elastic deformation
plastic deformation	localized deformation	

• The mechanical properties of metals determine the range of usefulness of a material and establish the service life that can be expected.

- Therefore, multiple tests are commonly conducted to determine mechanical properties and values reported can be an average value or calculated statistical minimum value.
- The way a material is loaded greatly affects its mechanical properties and largely determines how, or if, a component will fail; and whether it will show warning signs before failure actually occurs.
- However, a bar loaded in bending will have a stress distribution that changes with distance perpendicular to the normal axis.
- Elastic deformation only occurs in a material when stresses are lower than a critical stress called the yield strength.

3. Translate the following into English

实验样品　　　　静负荷　　　　作用力　　　　垂直轴
工程应变　　　　临界应力　　　屈服强度　　　应力面积　　　应力-应变曲线

- 通常，温度低于室温时，金属合金的强度性质降低，而延展性、破碎韧度和拉伸性能增强。
- 从材料的角度来说，应力是一种在材料内部所分布的力，它起到平衡所施加的负荷并与其发生相互作用。
- 工程应变可定义为：所施加力方向上的材料的改变量与材料原始长度的比值。
- 高强度和高延展性的材料比低强度和低延展性的材料的韧性高。

4. Reading comprehension

(1) When temperatures below room temperature, all of the following decrease except _____.

(A) ductility　　　(B) strength　　　(C) fracture toughness　　　(D) elongation

(2) In paragraph 4 the author illustrates _____.

(A) the mechanical properties of materials are not constants and often change as conditions

(B) there is significant variability in the values obtained when measuring mechanical properties

(C) the application of the mechanical properties of materials

(D) how to measure the mechanical properties of materials

(3) _____ is the type of loading which caused the material on one side of the plane to want to slide across the material on the other side of the plane.

(A) Tension　　　(B) Shear　　　(C) Compression　　　(D) Torsion

(4) Elastic deformation only occurs in a material when _____.

(A) stresses are lower than the yield strength

(B) stresses are higher than a critical stress

(C) the stress is big

(D) a material is loaded beyond its elastic limit

(5) Hardness measurements are widely used for the quality control of materials because _____.

(A) they have marks or indentations in the materials

(B) they are tested in low stress areas

(C) they are simple to do

(D) hardness is a basic property of a material

(6) According to this article, which property has the ability to absorb energy before fracture? _____.

(A) tensile properties　　(B) hardness　　(C) toughness　　(D) strain

Reading Materials

Fatigue Properties of Materials

Fatigue cracking is one of the primary damage mechanisms of structural components. Fatigue cracking results from cyclic stresses that are below the ultimate tensile stress, or even the yield stress of the material. The name "fatigue" is based on the concept that a material becomes "tired" and fails at a stress level below the nominal strength of the material. The facts that the original bulk design strengths are not exceeded and the only warning sign of an impending fracture is an often hard to see crack, makes fatigue damage especially dangerous.

The fatigue life of a component can be expressed as the number of loading cycles required to initiate a fatigue crack and to propagate the crack to critical size. Therefore, it can be said that fatigue failure occurs in three stages—crack initiation; slow, stable crack growth; and rapid fracture.

Dislocations play a major role in the fatigue crack initiation phase. In the first stage, dislocations accumulate near surface stress concentrations and form structures called persistent slip bands (PSB) after a large number of loading cycles. PSBs are areas that rise above (extrusion) or fall below (intrusion) the surface of the component due to movement of material along slip planes. This leaves tiny steps in the surface that serve as stress risers where tiny cracks can initiate. These tiny crack (called microcracks) nucleate along planes of high shear stress which is often 45° to the loading direction.

In the second stage of fatigue, some of the tiny microcracks join together and begin to propagate through the material in a direction that is perpendicular to the maximum tensile stress. Eventually, the growth of one or a few crack of the larger cracks will dominate over the rest of the cracks. With continued cyclic loading, the growth of the dominate crack or cracks will continue until the remaining uncracked section of the component can no longer support the load. At this point, the fracture toughness is exceeded and the remaining cross-section of the material experiences rapid fracture. This rapid overload fracture is the third stage of fatigue failure.

Factors Affecting Fatigue Life

In order for fatigue cracks to initiate, three basic factors are necessary. First, the loading pattern must contain minimum and maximum peak values with large enough variation or fluctuation. The peak values may be in tension or compression and may change over time but the reverse loading cycle must be sufficiently great for fatigue crack initiation. Secondly, the peak stress levels must be of sufficiently high value. If the peak stresses are too low, no crack initiation will occur. Thirdly, the material must experience a sufficiently large number of cycles of the applied stress. The number of cycles required to initiate and grow a crack is largely dependant on the first to factors.

In addition to these three basic factors, there are a host of other variables, such as stress concentration, corrosion, temperature, overload, metallurgical structure, and residual stresses which can affect the propensity for fatigue. Since fatigue cracks generally initiate at a surface, the surface condition of the component being loaded will have an effect on its fatigue life. Surface roughness is important because it is directly related to the level and number of stress concentrations on the surface. The higher the stress concentration the more likely a crack is to nucleate. Smooth surfaces increase the time to nucleation. Notches, scratches, and other stress risers decrease fatigue life. Surface residual stress will also have a significant effect on fatigue life. Compressive residual stresses from machining, cold working, heat treating will oppose a tensile load and thus lower the amplitude of cyclic loading.

S-N Fatigue Properties

There are two general types of fatigue tests conducted. One test focuses on the nominal stress required to cause a fatigue failure in some number of cycles. This test results in data presented as a plot of stress (S) against the number of cycles to failure (N), which is known as an *S-N* curve. A log scale is almost always used for N.

The data is obtained by cycling smooth or notched specimens until failure. The usual procedure is to test the first specimen at a high peak stress where failure is expected in a fairly short number of cycles. The test stress is decreased for each succeeding specimen until one or two specimens do not fail in the specified numbers of cycles, which is usually at least 10^7 cycles. The highest stress at which a run out (non-failure) occurs is taken as the fatigue threshold. Not all materials have a fatigue threshold (most nonferrous metallic alloys do not) and for these materials the test is usually terminated after about 10^8 or 5×10^8 cycles.

Since the amplitude of the cyclic loading has a major effect on the fatigue performance, the *S-N* relationship is determined for specific loading amplitude. The amplitude is express as the R ratio value, which is the minimum peak stress divided by the maximum peak stress. ($R = \sigma_{min}/\sigma_{max}$). It is most common to test at an R ratio of 0.1 but families of curves, with each curve at a different R ratio, are often developed.

A variation to the cyclic stress controlled fatigue test is the cyclic strain controlled test. In this test, the strain amplitude is held constant during cycling. Strain controlled cyclic loading is more representative of the loading found in thermal cycling, where a component expands and contracts in response to fluctuations in the operating temperature.

It should be noted that there are several short comings of *S-N* fatigue data. First, the conditions of the test specimens do not always represent actual service conditions. For example, components with surface conditions, such as pitting from corrosion, which differs from the condition of the test specimens will have significantly different fatigue performance. Furthermore, there is often a considerable amount of scatter in fatigue data even when carefully machined standard specimens out of the same lot of material are used. Since there is considerable scatter in the data, a reduction factor is often applied to the S-N curves to provide conservative values for the design of components.

(*Selected from http：//www.ndt-ed.org/EducationResources/ CommunityCollege/Materials/cc_mat_index.htm*，2014)

New Words and Expressions

fatigue *n.* 疲乏，疲劳，软化
propagate *v.* 传播，传送，传输
dislocation *n.* 位错，错位，断层
persistent slip bands（PSB） 稳定滑移带
extrusion *n.* 挤出，推出，挤压
intrusion *n.* 凹陷
nucleate *v.* 成核，形成晶核
shear stress 剪切应力
peak *n.* 高峰，峰值
metallurgical *a.* 冶金的，冶金学的
residual *a.* 残余的，剩余的
propensity *n.* 倾向，习性，倾向性
notch *n.* 刻痕
succeeding *a.* 接连的（随后的）
the fatigue threshold 疲劳极限
terminate *v.* 结束，终止
thermal cycling 热循环，热交变
contract *v.* 缩短，缩小，收缩
pitting *n.* 金属点状腐蚀（小孔，烧熔边缘，软化）
scatter *n.* 散布，分散
reduction factor 换算系数，简缩因数
conservative values 守恒值

Notes

① PSBs are areas that rise above (extrusion) or fall below (intrusion) the surface of the component due to movement of material along slip planes. extrusion，突出；intrusion，凹陷。参考译文：由于材料沿滑动平面移动，在组分表面形成一些突起或凹陷的区域，这些区域叫做稳定滑移带。

② With continued cyclic loading, the growth of the dominate crack or cracks will continue until the remaining uncracked section of the component can no longer support the load. remaining, 残余的。参考译文：随着循环负荷的持续施加，占支配地位的裂纹继续增加，直到残余的没有发生裂纹的部分不能支持所施加的负荷。

③ Compressive residual stresses from machining, cold working, heat treating will oppose a tensile load and thus lower the amplitude of cyclic loading. cold working, 冷加工。参考译文：在加工、冷加工、热处理过程中产生的压缩残余应力对拉伸负荷起抵制作用，因此可以降低循环负荷的振幅。

④ The test stress is decreased for each succeeding specimen until one or two specimens do not fail in the specified numbers of cycles, which is usually at least 10^7 cycles. succeeding, 随后的; specified, 指定的，特定的。参考译文：在接下来的实验样品，应力逐渐减少，直到在特定的循环次数下（通常至少为 10^7 循环次）有一个或两个样品不再出现疲劳现象。

⑤ The amplitude is express as the R ratio value, which is the minimum peak stress divided by the maximum peak stress $(R=\sigma_{min}/\sigma_{max})$. 参考译文：振幅用比值 R 来表示，即最低峰处的应力比最高峰处的应力 $(R=\sigma_{min}/\sigma_{max})$。

⑥ Strain controlled cyclic loading is more representative of the loading found in thermal cycling, where a component expands and contracts in response to fluctuations in the operating temperature. thermal cycling, 热循环，热交变。参考译文：比较有代表性的循环负荷应变存在于热循环中，在这个过程中，组分随着操作温度的起伏变化而扩张或压缩。

Reading Comprehension

(1) Fatigue cracking occurs because of _____.
(A) cyclic stresses   (B) the ulimate tensile stress
(C) the nominal strength of the material   (D) crack initiation

(2) Paragraphs 3 and 4 explain _____.
(A) why dislocations play a major role in the fatigue crack initiation phase
(B) that fatigue failure occurs in three stages
(C) the reasons for dislocations
(D) factors affecting fatigue cracking

(3) All of the following are factors for fatigue cracks to initiate, except _____.
(A) the peak values with large enough variation or fluctuation
(B) the peak stress levels with sufficiently high value
(C) dislocations accumulating near surface stress concentrations
(D) a sufficiently large number of cycles of the applied stress

(4) Surface roughness will have an effect on fatigue life of material because _____.
(A) the peak values may be intension or compression and may change over time
(B) it is directly related to the level and number of stress concentrations on the surface
(C) the shear stress is often 45° to the loading direction
(D) the tiny microcracks join together and begin to propagate through the material

(5) From S-N Fatigue Properties, which of the following is true? _____.

(A) The test stress is increased for each following specimen
(B) The test is always terminated after about 10^8 or 5×10^8 cycles
(C) The amplitude is express as the R ratio value, which is dimensionless
(D) The strain amplitude is not held constant during cycling in the cyclic strain controlled test
(6) All of the following are disadvantage of S-N fatigue data except _____.
(A) the conditions of the test specimens do not always represent actual service conditions
(B) there is often a considerable amount of scatter in fatigue data
(C) surface conditions of components could affect S-N fatigue data, such as pitting from corrosion
(D) conservation values are used in the design of components

Part II METALLIC MATERIALS AND ALLOYS

Unit 6 Introduction to Metals and Alloys

Definition

In chemistry, a metal (Greek: *Metallon*) is defined as an element that readily loses electrons to form positive ions (cations) and forms metallic bonds between other metal atoms (forming ionic bonds with non-metals).

The metals of the periodic table are formally defined as lithium, beryllium, sodium, magnesium, aluminium, potassium, calcium, scandium, titanium, vanadium, chromium, manganese, iron, cobalt, nickel, copper, zinc, gallium, rubidium, strontium, yttrium, zirconium, niobium, molybdenum, technetium, ruthenium, rhodium, palladium, silver, cadmium, indium, tin, antimony, caesium, barium, lanthanum, hafnium, tantalum, tungsten, rhenium, osmium, iridium, platinum, gold, mercury, thallium, lead, and bismuth. Metals are sometimes described as a lattice of positive ions surrounded by a cloud of delocalized electrons. Metals are one of the three groups of elements as distinguished by their ionization and bonding properties, along with the metalloids and nonmetals. On the periodic table, a diagonal line drawn from boron (B) to polonium (Po) separates the metals from the nonmetals. Most elements on this line are metalloids, sometimes called semi-metals; elements to the lower left are metals; elements to the upper right are nonmetals.

An alternative definition of metals is that they have overlapping conduction bands and valence bands in their electronic structure. This definition opens up the category for metallic polymers and other organic metals, which have been made by researchers and employed in high-tech devices. These synthetic materials often have the characteristic silvery-grey reflectiveness (luster) of elemental metals.

Chemical Properties

Metals are usually inclined to form cations through electron loss, reacting with oxygen in the air to form oxides over changing timescales (iron rusts over years, while potassium burns in seconds). The alkali metals are the most volatile, followed by the alkaline earth metals, found in the leftmost two groups of the periodic table. Examples:

$$4Na + O_2 \longrightarrow 2Na_2O \text{ (sodium oxide)}$$

$$2Ca + O_2 \longrightarrow 2CaO \text{ (calcium oxide)}$$

$$4Al + 3O_2 \longrightarrow 2Al_2O_3 \text{ (aluminium oxide)}$$

The transition metals (such as iron, copper, zinc, and nickel) take much longer to oxidize. Others, like palladium, platinum and gold, do not react with the atmosphere at all. Some metals form a barrier layer of oxide on their surface which cannot be penetrated by further oxygen molecules and thus retain their shiny appearance and good conductivity for many decades (like aluminium, some steels, and titanium). The oxides of metals are basic (as opposed to those of nonmetals, which are acidic), although this may be considered a rule of thumb, rather than a fact.

Painting, anodising or plating metals are good ways to prevent their corrosion. However, a more reactive metal in the electrochemical series must be chosen for coating, especially when chipping of the coating is expected. Water and the two metals form an electrochemical cell, and if the coating is less reactive than the coatee, the coating actually *promotes* corrosion.

Physical Properties

Metals in general have superior electric and thermal conductivity, high luster and density, and the ability to be deformed under stress without cleaving. While there are several metals that have low density, hardness, and melting points, these (the alkali and alkaline earth metals) are extremely reactive, and are rarely encountered in their elemental, metallic form.

Density: The majority of metals have higher densities than the majority of nonmetals. Nonetheless, there is wide variation in the densities of metals; lithium is the least dense solid element and osmium is the densest. The metals of groups ⅠA and ⅡA are referred to as the light metals because they are exceptions to this generalization. The high density of most metals is due to the tightly-packed crystal lattice of the metallic structure. The strength of metallic bonds for different metals reaches a maximum around the center of the transition series, as those elements have large amounts of delocalized electrons in a metallic bond. However, other factors (such as atomic radius, nuclear charge, number of bonding orbitals, overlap of orbital energies, and crystal form) are involved as well.

Malleability: The nondirectional nature of metallic bonding is thought to be the primary reason for the malleability of metal. Planes of atoms in a metal are able to slide across one another under stress, accounting for the ability of a crystal to deform without shattering.

When the planes of an ionic bond is slid past one another, the resultant change in location shifts ions of the same charge into close proximity, resulting in the cleavage of the crystal. Covalently bonded crystals can only be deformed by breaking the bonds between atoms, thereby resulting in fragmentation of the crystal.

Conductivity: The electrical and thermal conductivity of metals originate from the fact that in the metallic bond, the outer electrons of the metal atoms form a gas of nearly free electrons, moving as an electron gas in a background of positive charge formed by the ion cores. Good mathematical predictions for electrical conductivity, as well as the electrons' contribution to the heat capacity and heat conductivity of metals can be calculated from the free electron model, which does not take the detailed structure of the ion lattice into account.

Electric charge: When considering the exact band structure and binding energy of a metal, it is necessary to take into account the positive potential caused by the specific arrangement of the ion cores—which is periodic in crystals. The most important consequence of the periodic potential is the formation of a small band gap at the boundary of the brillouin zone. Mathematically, the potential of the ion cores is treated in the nearly-free electron model.

Alloys

An alloy is a mixture of two or more elements in solid solution in which the major component is a metal. Most pure metals are either too soft, brittle or chemically reactive for practical use. Combining different ratios of metals as alloys modifies the properties of pure metals to produce desirable characteristics. The aim of making alloys is generally to make them less brittle, harder, resistant to corrosion, or have a more desirable color and luster. Examples of alloys are steel (iron and carbon), brass (copper and zinc), bronze (copper and tin), and duralumin (aluminium and copper). Alloys specially designed for highly demanding applications, such as jet engines, may contain more than ten elements.

(*Selected from http://en.wikipedia.org/wiki/Metal*, 2014)

New Words and Expressions

lattice   *n.* 晶格
distinguished by   以……为特征
valence bands   价带
cation   *n.* 正离子，阳离子
oxide   *n.* 氧化物
anodising   阳极处理
plating   *v.* 镀；*n.* 电解法分离，电镀
corrosion   *n.* 侵蚀，腐蚀（锈）
luster   *n.* 光泽；*v.* 有光泽，发亮，使……发光
cleaving   劈开，裂开
encountered   *n.* 遇到
malleability   *n.* 可锻性，延展性，柔韧性
shattering   破碎，震动，震裂
covalent   *a.* 共有原子价的，共价的

Notes

① The oxides of metals are basic (as opposed to those of nonmetals, which are acidic), although this may be considered a rule of thumb, rather than a fact. basic, 碱性的。参考译文：非金属氧化物呈酸性，相反地，金属氧化物呈碱性，尽管这可能只是个经验法则，并没有事实来证明。

② The strength of metallic bonds for different metals reaches a maximum around the center of the transition series, as those elements have large amounts of delocalized electrons in a metallic bond. "those"指代"the transition series", as 引导一个原因状语从句。参考译文：因为过渡族元素的金属键中存在大量游离电子，所以不同金属的金属键的强度在过渡族元素中心周围达到最大值。

③ Covalently bonded crystals can only be deformed by breaking the bonds between atoms, thereby resulting in fragmentation of the crystal. 参考译文：只有破坏原子之间的共价键，共价键晶体才会变形，从而导致晶体的破碎。

④ The electrical and thermal conductivity of metals originate from the fact that in the metallic bond, the outer electrons of the metal atoms form a gas of nearly free electrons, moving as an electron gas in a background of positive charge formed by the ion cores. "that"引导同位语从句，是对"the fact"的解释说明。参考译文：金属的导电性和导热性来源于金属键中金属原子外的电子形成的自由电子云在由离子核形成的正电荷的背景下像电子云一样移动。

⑤ Good mathematical predictions for electrical conductivity, as well as the electrons' contribution to the heat capacity and heat conductivity of metals can be calculated from the free electron model, which does not take the detailed structure of the ion lattice into account. 本句结构为… can be calculated from…, which 引导一个定语从句修饰"the free electron model"。参考译文：良好的电导率数学预测与电子对金属热容和热导性的影响，可以在不考虑离子格架的具体结构的情况下由自由电子模型计算出来。

Exercises

1. Question for discussion

(1) What are the differences among metals, metalloids and nonmetals?

(2) Which chemical properties do metals have? And which physical properties do metals have?

(3) Why do the majority of metals have high densities?

(4) What do the electrical and thermal conductivity of metals originate from?

(5) What is the aim of making alloys? Please give some examples of alloys.

2. Translate the following into Chinese

conduction bands　　　　　alkali metals
atomic radius　　　　　　　overlap of orbital energies
the ion lattice　　　　　　　solid solution

• In chemistry, a metal is defined as an element that readily loses electrons to form positive ions and forms metallic bonds between other metal atoms.

• The nondirectional nature of metallic bonding is thought to be the primary reason for the malleability of metal.

• Covalently bonded crystals can only be deformed by breaking the bonds between atoms, thereby resulting in fragmentation of the crystal.

- Alloys specially designed for highly demanding applications, such as jet engines, may contain more than ten elements.

3. Translate the following into English

离域电子　　　　　　　　电子结构

碱土金属　　　　　　　　化学电池

核电荷　　　　　　　　　导电性

- 金属有时被描述为由游离电子团包围的正离子晶格。
- 通常地，金属具有良好的导电性和导热性，具有金属光泽，密度较大，并且具有在压力下变形而不会断裂的能力。
- 合金是指两种或两种以上的元素形成的固溶体混合物，其中主要组分为金属。
- 不同比率的金属结合成为合金可以改变纯金属的性质从而产生所需要的性能。

4. Reading comprehension

(1) Which of the following is TRUE according to the text? _____.

(A) An element which can form positive ions is metal.

(B) Metals can readily obtain electrons to form positive ions and forms metallic bonds between other metal atoms.

(C) Elements to the lower left of the diagonal line drawn from boron (B) to polonium (Po) are metals.

(D) Elements to the upper right of the diagonal line drawn from boron (B) to polonium (Po) are metals.

(2) The most volatile metals in chemical properties are _____.

(A) alkaline earth metals　　　　(B) alkali metals

(C) aluminium　　　　　　　　(D) rare earth metals

(3) According to the passage, the high density of most metals is because of _____.

(A) the tightly-packed crystal lattice of the metallic structure

(B) the overlapping conduction bands and valence bands in their electronic structure

(C) large amounts of delocalized electrons in a metallic bond

(D) large atomic radius

(4) All of the following is factors why the strength of metallic bonds for different metals reaches a maximum around the center of the transition series EXCEPT _____.

(A) large amounts of delocalized electrons in a metallic bond

(B) atomic radius and nuclear charge

(C) number of bonding orbitals and overlap of orbital energies

(D) crystal lattice of the metallic structure

(5) The primary reason for the malleability of metal is _____.

(A) the nondirectional nature of metallic bonding

(B) the slide ability of planes of atoms in a metal under stress

(C) the bonds between atoms breaking of covalently bonded crystals

(D) a gas of nearly free electrons formed by the outer electrons of the metal atoms

Reading Material

Metals and Their Applications

Categories

Base metal: In chemistry, the term *"base metal"* is used informally to refer to a metal that oxidizes or corrodes relatively easily, and reacts variably with dilute hydrochloric acid (HCl) to form hydrogen. Examples include iron, nickel, lead and zinc. Copper is considered a base metal as it oxidizes relatively easily, although it does not react with HCl. It is commonly used in opposition to noble metal.

In alchemy, a base metal was a common and inexpensive metal, as opposed to precious metals, mainly gold and silver. A longtime goal of the alchemists was the transmutation of base metals into precious metals.

In numismatics, coins used to derive their value primarily from the precious metal content. Most modern currencies are fiat currency, allowing the coins to be made of base metal.

Ferrous metal: The term "ferrous" is derived from the latin word meaning "containing iron". This can include pure iron, such as wrought iron, or an alloy such as steel. Ferrous metals are often magnetic, but not exclusively.

Noble metal: Noble metals are metals that are resistant to corrosion or oxidation, unlike most base metals. They tend to be precious metals, often due to perceived rarity. Examples include tantalum, gold, platinum, and rhodium.

Precious metal: A precious metal is a rare metallic chemical element of high economic value. Chemically, the precious metals are less reactive than most elements, have high luster and high electrical conductivity. Historically, precious metals were important as currency, but are now regarded mainly as investment and industrial commodities. Gold, silver, platinum and palladium each have an ISO 4217 currency code. The best-known precious metals are gold and silver. While both have industrial uses, they are better known for their uses in art, jewelry, and coinage. Other precious metals include the platinum group metals: ruthenium, rhodium, palladium, osmium, iridium, and platinum, of which platinum is the most widely traded. Plutonium and uranium could also be considered precious metals.

The demand for precious metals is driven not only by their practical use, but also by their role as investments and a store of value. Palladium was, as of summer 2006, valued at a little under half the price of gold, and platinum at around twice that of gold. Silver is substantially less expensive than these metals, but is often traditionally considered a precious metal for its role in coinage and jewelry.

Extraction

Metals are often extracted from the Earth by means of mining, resulting in ores that are relatively rich sources of the requisite elements. Ore is located by prospecting techniques, followed by the exploration and examination of deposits. Mineral sources are generally divided into surface mines, which are mined by excavation using heavy equipment, and subsurface mines.

Once the ore is mined, the metals must be extracted, usually by chemical or electrolytic reduction. Pyrometallurgy uses high temperatures to convert ore into raw metals, while hydrometallurgy employs aqueous chemistry for the same purpose. The methods used depend on the metal and their contaminants.

Applications

Some metals and metal alloys possess high structural strength per unit mass, making them useful materials for carrying large loads or resisting impact damage. Metal alloys can be engineered to have high resistance to shear, torque and deformation. However the same metal can also be vulnerable to fatigue damage through repeated use, or from sudden stress failure when a load capacity is exceeded. The strength and resilience of metals has led to their frequent use in high-rise building and bridge construction, as well as most vehicles, many appliances, tools, pipes, non-illuminated signs and railroad tracks.

The two most commonly used structural metals, iron and aluminium, are also the most abundant metals in the Earth's crust.

Metals are good conductors, making them valuable in electrical appliances and for carrying an electric current over a distance with little energy lost. Electrical power grids rely on metal cables to distribute electricity. Home electrical systems, for the most part, are wired with copper wire for its good conducting properties.

The thermal conductivity of metal is useful for containers to heat materials over a flame. Metal is also used for heat sinks to protect sensitive equipment from overheating.

The high reflectivity of some metals is important in the construction of mirrors, including precision astronomical instruments. This last property can also make metallic jewelry aesthetically appealing.

Some metals have specialized uses; Radioactive metals such as Uranium and Plutonium are used in nuclear power plants to produce energy via nuclear fission. Mercury is a liquid at room temperature and is used in switches to complete a circuit when it flows over the switch contacts. Shape memory alloy is used for applications such as pipes, fasteners and vascular stents. However they are very good at conducting electricity and heat.

Astronomy

In the specialized usage of astronomy and astrophysics, the term "metal" is often used to refer to any element other than hydrogen or helium, including substances as chemically non-metallic as neon, fluorine, and oxygen. Nearly all the hydrogen and helium in the Universe was created in Big Bang nucleosynthesis, whereas all the "metals" were produced by nucleosynthesis in stars or supernovae. The Sun and the Milky Way Galaxy are composed of roughly 70% hydrogen, 30% helium, and 2% "metals" by mass.

(*Selected from* http://en.wikipedia.org/wiki/Metal, 2014)

New Words and Expressions

oxidize $v.$ 氧化，生锈
corrode $v.$ 使腐蚀，侵蚀
dilute $v.$ 冲淡，稀释
alchemy $n.$ 炼金术
transmutation $n.$ 变形，变化
numismatics $n.$ 货币学，古币
currency $n.$ 货币
ferrous $a.$ 含铁的
magnetic $a.$ 有磁性的
rarity $n.$ 稀薄（稀有，珍品）
pyrometallurgy $n.$ 火法冶金学（热冶学，火冶学）
aqueous chemistry   液相化学
possess $v.$ 持有，占有，拥有
unit mass   单位质量，质量单位
resilience $n.$ 弹力，弹性，弹性变形
astronomy $n.$ 天文学
astrophysics $n.$ 天体物理学
nucleosynthesis $n.$ 核合成，核聚变

Notes

① In chemistry, the term '*base metal*' is used informally to refer to a metal that oxidizes or corrodes relatively easily, and reacts variably with dilute hydrochloric acid (HCl) to form hydrogen. dilute hydrochloric acid，稀盐酸。参考译文：化学上对贱金属的非正式定义为，一种比较易氧化或腐蚀，并且容易与稀盐酸发生反应释放出氢气的金属。

② Ore is located by prospecting techniques, followed by the exploration and examination of deposits. prospecting，勘探，探矿。参考译文：通过勘探技术确定矿石的位置，然后再对矿床进行开发和探测。

③ Mineral sources are generally divided into surface mines, which are mined by excavation using heavy equipment, and subsurface mines. which 引导一个定语从句，修饰 surface mines。参考译文：一般而言，矿产资源分为露天矿和地下矿，其中露天矿是用重型挖掘设备开采的。

④ Some metals and metal alloys possess high structural strength per unit mass, making them useful materials for carrying large loads or resisting impact damage. structural strength，结构强度。参考译文：一些金属和金属合金具有很高的单位质量结构强度，使得它们成为承载大负荷或抗撞击损伤的有效材料。

⑤ The two most commonly used structural metals, iron and aluminium, are also the most abundant metals in the Earth's crust. the Earth's crust，地壳。参考译文：铁和铝是两种最常用的结构材料，也是地壳中含量最丰富的金属。

⑥ In the specialized usage of astronomy and astrophysics, the term "metal" is often used to refer to any element other than hydrogen or helium, including substances as chemically non-metallic as neon, fluorine, and oxygen. 参考译文：在天文学和天体物理学的专业化应用中，金属是指除氢、氦以外的，像氖、氟和氧这些在化学上为非金属的其他元素。

Reading Comprehension

(1) All of the following are properties of the base metal EXCEPT _____.

(A) it oxidizes or corrodes relatively easily

(B) it reacts variably with dilute hydrochloric acid (HCl) to form hydrogen

(C) copper is considered a base metal as it oxidizes relatively easily and reacts with HCl

(D) a base metal was a common and inexpensive metal in alchemy as opposed to precious metals

(2) According to the categories of metals we can see that _____ have the highest economic value.

(A) base metals　　(B) ferrous metals　　(C) noble metals　　(D) precious metals

(3) Some metal and metal alloy materials can be used to carry large loads or resisting impact damage due to _____.

(A) high structural strength per unit mass they possessing

(B) vulnerability to fatigue damage through repeated use

(C) The resilience of metals

(D) high resistance to shear, torque and deformation of metal alloys

(4) Which of the following is NOT true about "the metal applications"? _____.

(A) Iron and aluminium are the most commonly used structural metals which are also the most abundant metals in the Earth's crust

(B) Metals are valuable in electrical appliances because of their good conducting properties

(C) The thermal conductivity of metal is useful for containers to heat sensitive equipment

(D) The high reflectivity of some metals is important in the construction of mirrors, including precision astronomical instruments

(5) It can be learned from the last paragraph that _____.

(A) the term "metal" is often used to refer to any element other than hydrogen, helium, neon, fluorine, and oxygen in astronomy and astrophysics

(B) all the hydrogen and helium in the Universe was created in Big Bang nucleosynthesis

(C) the "metal" in astronomy and astrophysics are neon, fluorine, and oxygen which are non-metallic in chemistry

(D) the Sun and the Milky Way Galaxy are composed of roughly 70% hydrogen, 30% helium, and 2% "metals" by volume

Unit 7　Superalloy

A superalloy, or high-performance alloy, is an alloy that exhibits excellent mechanical strength and creep resistance at high temperatures, good surface stability, and corrosion and oxidation resistance. Superalloys typically have an austenitic face-centered cubic crystal structure. A superalloy's base alloying element is usually nickel, cobalt, or nickel-iron. Superalloy development has relied heavily on both chemical and process innovations and has been driven primarily by the aerospace and power industries. Typical applications are in the aerospace, industrial gas turbine and marine turbine industry, e. g. for turbine blades for hot sections of jet engines. Examples of superalloys are Hastelloy, Inconel, Waspaloy, Rene alloys (e. g. Rene 41, Rene 80, Rene 95), Haynes alloys, Incoloy, MP98T, TMS alloys, and CMSX single crystal alloys.

Introduction

Superalloys are metallic materials for service at high temperatures, particularly in the hot zones of gas turbines. Such materials allow the turbine to operate more efficiently by withstanding higher temperatures. Turbine Inlet Temperature (TIT), which is a direct indicator of the efficiency of a gas turbine engine, depends on the temperature capability of 1st stage high pressure turbine blade made of Ni base superalloys exclusively.

One of the most important superalloy properties is high temperature creep resistance. Other crucial material properties are fatigue life, phase stability, as well as oxidation and corrosion resistance.

Superalloys develop high temperature strength through solid solution strengthening. Oxidation and corrosion resistance is provided by the formation of a protective oxide layer which is formed when the metal is exposed to oxygen and encapsulates the material, and thus protecting the rest of the component. Oxidation or corrosion resistance is provided by elements such as aluminium and chromium. By far the most important strengthening mechanism is through the formation of secondary phase precipitates such as gamma prime and carbides through precipitation strengthening.

Chemical development

Creep resistance is dependent on slowing the speed of dislocations within the crystal structure. The gamma prime phase [$Ni_3(Al, Ti)$] present in nickel and nickel-iron superalloys presents a barrier to dislocations. Chemical additions such as aluminum and titanium promote the creation of the gamma prime phase. The gamma prime phase size can be precisely controlled by careful precipitation hardening heat treatments. Cobalt base superalloys do not have a strengthening secondary phase like gamma prime. Many other elements, both common and exotic, (including not only metals, but also metalloids and nonmetals) can be present; chromium, cobalt, molybdenum, tungsten, tantalum, aluminium, titanium, zirconium, niobium, rhenium, carbon, boron and hafnium are just a few examples.

Process development

The historical developments in superalloy processing have brought about considerable increases in superalloy operating temperatures. Superalloys were originally iron based and cold wrought prior to the 1940s. In the 1940s investment casting of cobalt base alloys significantly raised operating temperatures. The development of vacuum melting in the 1950s allowed for very fine control of the chemical composition of superalloys and reduction in contamination and in turn led to a revolution in processing techniques such as directional solidification of alloys and single crystal superalloys.

Single-crystal superalloys (SC superalloys) are formed as a single crystal using a modified version of the directional solidification technique, so there are no grain boundaries in the material. The mechanical properties of most other alloys depend on the presence of grain boundaries, but at high temperatures, they would participate in creep and must be replaced by other mechanisms. In many such alloys, islands of an ordered intermetallic phase sit in a matrix of disordered phase, all with the same crystalline lattice. This approximates the dislocation-pinning behavior of grain boundaries, without introducing any amorphous solid into the structure.

Applications

Superalloys are used where there is a need for high temperature strength and corrosion/oxidation resistance.

The largest applications of superalloys are the following: aircraft and industrial gas turbines; rocket engines; space vehicles; submarines; nuclear reactors; military electric motors, chemical processing vessels, and heat exchanger tubing.

Many of the industrial nickel-based superalloys contain alloying elements, including chromium, aluminium, and titanium, also molybdenum, tungsten, niobium, tantalum and cobalt.

Metallurgy of superalloys

The superalloys of the first generation were intended for operation up to 700 ℃ (973 K). The up-to-date superalloys of the fourth generation are used as single or monocrystals and are extra alloyed, especially with ruthenium. They can operate up to 1100 ℃ (1373 K).

The structure of most precipitation strengthened nickel-base superalloys consists of the gamma matrix, and of intermetallic γ' precipitates. The γ-phase is a solid solution with a face-centered crystal lattice and randomly distributed different species of atoms.

By contrast, the γ'-phase has an ordered crystalline lattice of type L_12. In pure Ni_3Al phase atoms of aluminium are placed at the vertices of the cubic cell and form the sublattice A. Atoms of nickel are located at centers of the faces and form the sublattice B. The phase is not strictly stoichiometric. There may exist an excess of vacancies in one of the sublattices, which leads to deviations from stoichiometry. Sublattices A and B of the γ'-phase can solute a considerable proportion of other elements. The alloying elements are dissolved in the γ-phase as well. The γ'-phase hardens the alloy through an unusual mechanism called the yield stress anomaly. Dislocations dissociate in the γ'-phase, leading to the formation of an anti-phase boundary. It turns out that at elevated temperature, the free energy associated with the anti-phase boundary (APB) is considerably reduced if it lies on a particular plane, which by coincidence is not a permitted slip plane. One set of partial dislocations bounding the APB cross-slips so that the APB lies on the low-energy plane, and, since this low-energy plane is not a permitted slip plane, the dissociated dislocation is now effectively locked. By this mechanism, the yield strength of γ'-phase Ni_3Al actually increases with temperature up to about 1000 ℃, giving superalloys their currently unrivalled high-temperature strength.

In addition, it is often beneficial for a grain boundary containing nickel-base alloy to contain carbides for improvements in creep strength. Where the carbides (e. g. MC where M is a metal and C is a carbon atom) are precipitated at the grain boundaries, they act to pin the grain boundaries and improve the resistance to sliding and migration that would occur during creep diffusion. However the fracture toughness of the alloy is reduced, together with the ductility and rupture strength, if they precipitate within a grain, or if they form as a continuous grain boundary film.

Coating of superalloys

Products from superalloys, which are subjected to high working temperatures and corrosive atmosphere (like first stages of turbine blades of the jet engines) are coated with various kinds of coatings. Mainly, two kinds of coating processes are applied: pack cementation process and gas phase coating. Both of them are CVD coatings. In most cases, after the coating process, near-surface regions of parts are enriched with aluminum, the matrix of the coating is nickel aluminide.

Pack cementation process

The pack cementation process is carried out at lower temperatures (about 750℃). The parts are loaded into boxes, which contain a mixture of powders: active coating material, containing aluminum, activator (chloride or fluoride) and thermal ballast (like aluminum oxide). At high temperatures the gaseous aluminum chloride (or fluoride) is transferred to the surface of part and diffuses inside (mostly, inward diffusion). After the end of the process the so-called "green coating" is produced, which is too thin and brittle for direct use. A subsequent diffusion heat treatment (several hours at temperatures about 1080℃) leads to the further inward diffusion and formation of the desired coating.

Gas phase coating

This process is carried out at higher temperatures: about 1080℃. The coating material is usually loaded on special trays without physical contact with parts. The coating mixture contains active coating material and activator, but, usually does not contain thermal ballast. Like in the pack cementation process, the gaseous aluminum chloride (or fluoride) is transferred to the surface of the part. However, in this case, the diffusion is outwards. This kind of coating also requires diffusion heat treatment.

Superalloys in the future

The availability of superalloys during past decades has led to a steady increase in the turbine entry temperatures and the trend is expected to continue. Sandia National Laboratories is studying a new method for making superalloys, known as radiolysis. It introduces an entirely new area of research into creating alloys and superalloys through nanoparticle synthesis. "This process holds promise as a universal method of nanoparticle formation. By developing our understanding of the basic material science behind these nanoparticle formations, we'll then be able to expand our research into other aspects of superalloys, like nickel-based alloys." Tina Nenoff says.

(*Selected from http://en.wikipedia.org/wiki/Superalloy*, 2014)

New Words and Expressions

superalloy　*n.* 超耐热合金
creep corrosion　裂隙腐蚀
creep resistance　蠕变阻力，蠕滑阻力，抗蠕变力，蠕变强度，蠕爬极限
austenitic　*a.* 奥氏体的
austenitic alloy steel　奥氏合金钢（高锰钢）
aerospace　*n.* 大气圈及其以外的宇宙空间；*a.* 宇宙空间的，宇宙航行的
gas turbine　*n.* 燃气涡轮
marine turbine　船用汽轮机
blade　*n.* 刀刃，刀片
Hastelloy　哈司特镍合金，镍基合金（耐盐酸，耐蚀，耐热）
Waspaloy　沃斯帕洛伊合金，一种耐高热镍基合金
Rene alloys　雷内（男子名）合金
Haynes alloys　海恩斯（姓氏）合金
indicator　*n.* 指示器，指示剂
exclusively　*adv.* 排外地，专有地
crucial　*a.* 至关紧要的
fatigue　*n.* 疲乏，疲劳，累活；*v.* 使疲劳，使心智衰弱，疲劳
encapsulate　*v.* 装入胶囊，压缩，形成胶囊
aluminium　*n.* 铝；*a.* 铝的
chromium　*n.* 铬
precipitate　*n.* 沉淀物；*v.* 猛抛，使陷入，促成，使沉淀，猛地落下
yield stress　屈服应力，屈服点

carbide   *n.* 碳化物
dislocation   *n.* 混乱，断层，脱臼
titanium   *n.* 钛
cobalt   *n.* 钴
metalloid   *n.* 非金属；*a.* 非金属的
molybdenum   *n.* 钼
tungsten   *n.* 钨
tantalum   *n.* 钽
zirconium   *n.* 锆
niobium   *n.* 铌
rhenium   *n.* 铼
boron   *n.* 硼
hafnium   *n.* 铪
contamination   *n.* 玷污，污染，污染物
solidification   *n.* 凝固
ruthenium   *n.* 钌
sublattice   *n.* 子格
stoichiometric number   化学计算（数）值
fracture   *n.* 破裂，骨折；*v.* （使）破碎，（使）破裂
rupture strength   断裂强度
cementation   *n.* 黏固
activator   *n.* 催化剂，触媒
ballast   *n.* 压舱物，沙囊
radiolysis   *n.* 射解（作用），辐解（作用）

Notes

① Such materials allow the turbine to operate more efficiently by withstanding higher temperatures. withstand：经受住。allow…to do…允许……做……，by 表示途径。参考译文：由于这种材料耐高温，由这种材料制成的涡轮就可以在高温下得到更有效的应用。

② Oxidation and corrosion resistance is provided by the formation of a protective oxide layer which is formed when the metal is exposed to oxygen and encapsulates the material, and thus protecting the rest of the component. 这个句子较长，which 引导了一个定语从句，该定语从句中还有一个由 when 引导的时间状语从句。参考译文：当金属暴露在氧气或者压缩成材料时，形成的氧化层能够保护化合物未被氧化或腐蚀的其他部分（即氧化膜可以保护其内层金属），这就是金属的抗氧化抗腐蚀性质。

③ Many other elements, both common and exotic, (including not only metals, but also metalloids and nonmetals) can be present; chromium, cobalt, molybdenum, tungsten, tantalum, aluminium, titanium, zirconium, niobium, rhenium, carbon, boron or hafnium are just a few examples. common：共同的，公共的，公有的，普通的，常见的；exotic：外来的，奇异的，稀有的。参考译文：许多其他元素无论是常见的还是稀有的（包括金属、类金

属和非金属元素）也可以加入（到超耐热合金中），例如：铬、钴、钼、钨、钽、铝、钛、锆、铌、铼、碳、硼和铪等。

④ Many of the industrial nickel-based superalloys contain alloying elements, including chromium, aluminium, and titanium, also molybdenum, tungsten, niobium, tantalum and cobalt. many of 大多数，很多。参考译文：很多工业上使用的超耐热镍合金都含有铬、铝、钛、钼、钨、铌、钽和钴等元素。

⑤ The up-to-date superalloys of the fourth generation are used as single or monocrystals and are extra alloyed, especially with ruthenium. up-to-date：直到最近的，最新的；ruthenium：钌。本句的意思是：第四代超耐热合金是目前最新的合金，可以制成单晶使用，加工过程很特殊，尤其是含钌的超合金更为特殊。

⑥ The availability of superalloys during past decades has led to a steady increase in the turbine entry temperatures and the trend is expected to continue. lead to：导致，通向。参考译文：在过去的十几年中，超耐热合金已用于制造涡轮，这使涡轮的进口温度不断提高，而且这种发展趋势仍在继续。

Exercises

1. Question for discussion

(1) What are superalloys? Give some examples.
(2) What is Turbine Inlet Temperature (TIT)?
(3) Where have superalloys been used? Give some applications.
(4) Try to describe the pack cementation process.
(5) Try to describe the metallurgy of superalloys in brief.
(6) Discuss the future of superalloys.

2. Translate the following into Chinese

high-performance alloy　　　　　　mechanical strength
single crystal alloys　　　　　　　　oxidation and corrosion resistance
precipitation strengthening　　　　crystalline lattice

• Superalloy development has relied heavily on both chemical and process innovations and has been driven primarily by the aerospace and power industries.

• Creep resistance is dependent on slowing the speed of dislocations within the crystal structure.

• The historical developments in superalloy processing have brought about considerable increases in superalloy operating temperatures.

• Single-crystal superalloys (SC superalloys) are formed as a single crystal using a modified version of the directional solidification technique, so there are no grain boundaries in the material.

3. Translate the following into English

面心立方晶体结构　　　　　　　　涡轮入口温度
金属材料　　　　　　　　　　　　相稳定性
核反应堆　　　　　　　　　　　　纳米粒子的合成

- 典型的超耐热合金具有奥氏体的面心立方晶体结构。
- 根据超耐热合金的性质，超耐热合金的产品可以在高温和腐蚀环境中得到应用。
- 超耐热合金主要用于航空工业、潜水、核反应堆、军用发动机等方面。
- 高温下气态的氯化铝或氟化铝可以从超耐热合金内部转移到表面。

4. Reading comprehension

（1）According to the passage, why do single-crystal superalloys have no grain boundaries in the materials? _____

(A) Because they are formed as a single crystal using a directional solidification technique.

(B) Because of a single crystal using a modified version of the directional solidification technique.

(C) Because they are formed as a single crystal using a modified version of the directional solidification technique.

(D) A, B and C

（2）The important superalloy properties are _____ .

(A) high temperature creep resistance (B) fatigue life, phase stability

(C) oxidation and corrosion resistance (D) All of the above

（3）What's the γ-phase of nickel-base superalloys? _____

(A) It is a solid solution with a face-centered crystal lattice and sameness species of atoms.

(B) It is a solid solution with a body-centered crystal lattice and different species of atoms.

(C) It is a solid solution with a body-centered crystal lattice and randomly species of atoms.

(D) It is a solid solution with a face-centered crystal lattice and randomly distributed atoms.

（4）In the pack cementation process, a subsequent diffusion heat treatment about _____ ℃ leads to the further inward diffusion and formation of the desired coating.

(A) 1080℃　　　　　　　　　　(B) 750℃

(C) 750～1080℃　　　　　　　　(D) not mentioned in the text

（5）About gas phase coating, all the following statements are true EXCEPT _____ .

(A) The process is carried out at higher temperatures: about 1080℃.

(B) The coating material is usually loaded on special trays with physical contact with parts.

(C) The coating mixture contains active coating material and activator.

(D) This kind of coating also requires diffusion heat treatment.

（6）What did Sandia National Laboratories study according to the passage? _____

(A) Radiolysis for making superalloys.

(B) A new method for nanoparticle synthesis.

(C) New area of research into creating alloys.

(D) New area of research into superalloys

Reading Material

Metallurgy

Metallurgy is a domain of materials science that studies the physical and chemical behavior of metallic elements, their intermetallic compounds, and their compounds, which are called alloys. It is also the technology of metals: the way in which science is applied to their practical use. Metallurgy is commonly used in the craft of metalworking.

Extractive metallurgy

Extractive metallurgy is the practice of removing valuable metals from an ore and refining the extracted raw metals into a purer form. In order to convert a metal oxide or sulfide to a purer metal, the ore must be reduced physically, chemically, or electrolytically.

Extractive metallurgists are interested in three primary streams: feed, concentrate (valuable metal oxide/sulfide), and tailings (waste). After mining, large pieces of the ore feed are broken through crushing and/or grinding in order to obtain particles small enough where each particle is either mostly valuable or mostly waste. Concentrating the particles of a value in a form supporting separation enables the desired metal to be removed from waste products.

Mining may not be necessary if the ore body and physical environment are conducive to leaching. Leaching dissolves minerals in an ore body and results in an enriched solution. The solution is collected and processed to extract valuable metals.

Ore bodies often contain more than one valuable metal. Tailings of a previous process may be used as a feed in another process to extract a secondary product from the original ore. Additionally, a concentrate may contain more than one valuable metal. That concentrate would then be processed to separate the valuable metals into individual constituents.

Important common alloy systems

Common engineering metals include aluminium, chromium, copper, iron, magnesium, nickel, titanium and zinc. These are most often used as alloys. Much effort has been placed on understanding the iron-carbon alloy system, which includes steels and cast irons. Plain carbon steels are used in low cost, high strength applications where weight and corrosion are not a problem. Cast irons, including ductile iron are also part of the iron-carbon system.

Stainless steel or galvanized steel are used where resistance to corrosion is important. Aluminium alloys and magnesium alloys are used for applications where strength and lightness are required.

Cupro-nickel alloys such as Monel are used in highly corrosive environments and for non-magnetic applications. Nickel-based superalloys like Inconel are used in high temperature applications such as turbochargers, pressure vessels, and heat exchangers. For extremely high temperatures, single crystal alloys are used to minimize creep.

Production engineering of metals

In production engineering, metallurgy is concerned with the production of metallic components for use in consumer or engineering products. This involves the production of alloys, the shaping, the heat treatment and the surface treatment of the product. The task of the metallurgist is to achieve balance between material properties such as cost, weight, strength, toughness, hardness, corrosion and fatigue resistance, and cost. To achieve this goal, the operating environment must be carefully considered. In a saltwater environment, ferrous metals and some aluminium alloys corrode quickly. Metals exposed to cold or cryogenic conditions may endure a ductile to brittle transition and lose their toughness, becoming more brittle and prone to cracking. Metals under continual cyclic loading can suffer from metal fatigue. Metals under constant stress at elevated temperatures can creep.

Metal working processes

Metals are shaped by processes such as casting, forging, flow forming, rolling, extrusion, sintering, metalworking, machining and fabrication. With casting, molten metal is poured into a shaped mould. With forging, a red-hot billet is hammered into shape. With rolling, a billet is passed through successively narrower rollers to create a sheet. With extrusion, a hot and malleable metal is forced under pressure through a die, which shapes it before it cools. With sintering, a powdered metal is compressed into a die at high temperature. With machining, lathes, milling machines, and drills cut the cold metal to shape. With fabrication, sheets of metal are cut with guillotines or gas cutters and bent into shape.

"Cold working" processes, where the product's shape is altered by rolling, fabrication or other processes while the product is cold, can increase the strength of the product by a process called work hardening. Work hardening creates microscopic defects in the metal, which resist further changes of shape.

Various forms of casting exist in industry and academia. These include sand casting, investment casting (also called the "lost wax process"), die casting and continuous casting.

Joining

Welding: Welding is a technique for joining metal components by melting the base material. A filler material of similar composition may also be melted into the joint.

Brazing: Brazing is a technique for joining metals at a temperature below their melting point. A filler with a melting point below that of the base metal is used, and is drawn into the joint by capillary action. Brazing results in a mechanical and metallurgical bond between work pieces.

Soldering: Soldering is a method of joining metals below their melting points using a filler metal. Soldering results in a mechanical joint and occurs at lower temperatures than brazing.

Heat treatment: Metals can be heat treated to alter the properties of strength, ductility, toughness, hardness or resistance to corrosion. Common heat treatment processes include annealing, precipitation strengthening, quenching, and tempering. The annealing process softens the metal by allowing recovery of cold work and grain growth. Quenching can be used to harden alloy steels, or in precipitation hardenable alloys, to trap dissolved solute atoms in solution. Tempering will cause the dissolved alloying elements to precipitate, or in the case of quenched steels, improve impact strength and ductile properties.

Surface treatment

Plating: Electroplating is a common surface-treatment technique. It involves bonding a thin layer of another metal such as gold, silver, chromium or zinc to the surface of the product. It is used to reduce corrosion as well as to improve the product's aesthetic appearance.

Thermal spray: Thermal spraying techniques are another popular finishing option, and often have better high temperature properties than electroplated coatings.

Case hardening: Case hardening is a process in which an alloying element, most commonly carbon or nitrogen, diffuses into the surface of a monolithic metal. The resulting interstitial solid solution is harder than the base material, which improves wear resistance without sacrificing toughness.

Electrical and electronic engineering: Metallurgy is also applied to electrical and electronic materials where metals such as aluminium, copper, tin, silver, and gold are used in power lines, wires, printed circuit boards and integrated circuits

(*Selected from http://en.wikipedia.org/wiki/Metallurgy*, 2014)

New Words and Expressions

metallurgy　*n*. 冶金，冶金术
metallurgist　*n*. 冶金家，冶金学者
domain　*n*. 领土，领地，范围，领域
craft　*n*. 工艺，手艺
metalworking　*n*. 金属加工术，金属工
extractive　*a*. 引得出的，抽取的，萃取的；*n*. 抽出物，精，熬汁
tailing　*n*. 残渣，尾料，屑
ore　*n*. 矿石，含有金属的岩石
crush　*v*. 压碎，碾碎，压服，压垮，粉碎，（使）变形
grind　*v*. 磨（碎），碾（碎），折磨
leach　*v*. 滤去
enrich　*v*. 使富足，使肥沃，装饰，加料于，浓缩
cupro-nickel alloys　铜镍合金
Monel　*n*. 蒙乃尔铜-镍合金
turbocharger　*n*. 涡轮增压器
prone　*a*. 倾向于

continual　*a.* 连续的，频繁的，持续不断的
fatigue　*n.* 疲乏，疲劳，累活；*v.* 使疲劳，使心智衰弱，疲劳
cast　*n.* 投掷，铸件，脱落物；*v.* 投，抛，投射，浇铸
forge　*v.* 稳步前进，铸造，伪造
cryogenic　*a.* 低温学的
roll　*a.* 滚动，滚转，（使）摇摆，（使）摇晃，卷起，卷拢；*v.* 辗，轧
extrusion　*n.* 挤出，推出，喷出的，突出的，赶出
sinter　*n.* 烧结物，熔渣；*v.* 使烧结
molten　*v.* 熔化；*a.* 熔铸的
mould　*n.* ［亦作 mold］霉，模具；*v.* 用土覆盖，发霉，铸造
malleable　*a.* 有延展性的，可锻的
lathe　*n.* 车床；*v.* 用车床加工
guillotine　*n.* 断头台，（切纸的）闸刀；*v.* 处斩刑，切（纸）
wax　*n.* 蜡，蜡状物，增加，月亮由亏转盈；*v.* 变大，增大，月亮渐满，上蜡于
quench　*v.* 结束，熄灭，淬火，熄灭，平息
anneal　*n.* 退火，焖火，锻炼，磨练（意志）
plating　*n.* 电镀，被覆金属
monolithic　*n.* 单片电路，单块集成电路
sacrifice　*n.* 牺牲，献身，祭品，供奉；*v.* 牺牲，献出，献祭，供奉

Notes

① Metallurgy is a domain of materials science that studies the physical and chemical behavior of metallic elements, their intermetallic compounds, and their compounds, which are called alloys. domain：领土，领地，（活动、学问等的）范围，领域；intermetallic：金属间（化合）的。参考译文：冶金学属于材料科学的范畴，研究的是金属元素、金属间化合物及其混合物即合金的物理化学行为。

② Extractive metallurgy is the practice of removing valuable metals from an ore and refining the extracted raw metals into a purer form. refine…into…由……精炼成……。参考译文：萃取冶金是从矿石中提取贵金属，然后把提取的金属进一步提纯的过程。

③ The solution is collected and processed to extract valuable metals. the solution 指的是上句中的 an enriched solution，是浓缩的溶液；extract：萃取。参考译文：收集浓缩溶液，萃取贵金属。

④ Plain carbon steels are used in low cost, high strength applications where weight and corrosion are not a problem. plain carbon steel：普通碳钢。参考译文：普通碳钢适合于低成本高强度的应用领域，且不需要考虑负荷和腐蚀问题。

⑤ The task of the metallurgist is to achieve balance between material properties such as weight, strength, toughness, hardness, corrosion and fatigue resistance, and cost. 参考译文：冶金学家的任务是从材料的性质与成本中达到平衡，例如：负荷、强度、韧性、硬度、抗腐蚀和疲劳。

⑥ Welding is a technique for joining metal components by melting the base material.

welding：焊接法，定位焊接。参考译文：焊接法是通过熔化基本材料使金属组分连接在一起的技术。

Reading Comprehension

(1) Extractive metallurgists are interested in three primary streams: _____ .

(A) feed, concentrate, and tailings

(B) physics, chemicals, or electrolytical materials

(C) gas, liquid, and solid

(D) not mentioned in the text

(2) Stainless steel or galvanized steel are used where _____ is important.

(A) weight and corrosion   (B) resistance to oxidation

(C) strength and lightness   (D) resistance to corrosion

(3) About alloys, all the following statements are true EXCEPT _____ .

(A) Aluminium alloys and magnesium alloys are used for applications where strength and lightness are required.

(B) Both aluminium alloys and magnesium alloys have the same properties.

(C) Cupro-nickel alloys such as Monel are used in highly corrosive environments and for non-magnetic applications.

(D) Nickel-based superalloys like Inconel are used in high temperature applications such as turbochargers, pressure vessels, and heat exchangers.

(4) According to the text, which of the following statements is true? _____

(A) In a saltwater environment, all of ferrous metals and aluminium alloys corrode quickly.

(B) Metals exposed to hot conditions may endure a ductile to brittle transition and lose their toughness, becoming more brittle and prone to cracking.

(C) Metals under continual cyclic loading cannot suffer from metal fatigue.

(D) Metals under constant stress at elevated temperatures can creep.

(5) With _____ , molten metal is poured into a shaped mould.

(A) forging   (B) rolling   (C) casting   (D) sintering

(6) _____ is used to reduce corrosion as well as to improve the product's aesthetic appearance.

(A) Thermal spraying   (B) Case hardening

(C) Surface treatment   (D) Electroplating

Unit 8　Important Characters of Metallic Materials
—Malleability, Ductility & Corrosion

Malleability: Malleability refers to metals which can be hammered into different shapes. The non-directional nature of metallic bonding is thought to be the primary reason for the malleability of metal. Planes of atoms in a metal are able to slide across one another under stress, accounting for the ability of a crystal to deform without shattering.

When the planes of an ionic bond is slid past one another, the resultant change in location shifts ions of the same charge into close proximity, resulting in the cleavage of the crystal. Covalently bonded crystals can only be deformed by breaking the bonds between atoms, thereby resulting in fragmentation of the crystal.

Ductility: Ductility refers to metals which can be drawn into wires. Not all metals are malleable or ductile. Cast iron, for example, is quite hard but brittle. But most metals are malleable or ductile because of the way in which atoms are arranged. In a metal the atoms lie close together and, while they strongly attract one another, may be able to "flow" past each other whilst maintaining their proximity and the metal's shape can be changed. In metals, the valence (outermost) electrons of the metal atoms are in fact not bound to their parent atoms, but in fact roam relatively freely between atoms, in a "sea" of sorts (in the simplest picture). This allows them to travel around, carrying electrical current with minimal resistance.

This sea of electrons model also helps to explain malleability and ductility. Since the bonds between metal atoms are not forced into specific orientations (such as in organic molecules) the metal atoms can flow past each other without breaking and remain bound to each other. This confers malleability and ductility.

A characteristic of metals is being very malleable and ductile. However, mercury is liquid at room temperature, and being liquid, it cannot be changed. There are probably a few exceptions to this, but most metals are malleable and ductile. Most of the d-block elements are ductile and malleable as, Iron, Copper, Silver, and Gold and so on. Among which gold is the most malleable and ductile metal.

Corrosion: Corrosion involves the deterioration of a material as it reacts with its environment. Corrosion is the primary means by which metals deteriorate. Corrosion literally consumes the material reducing load carrying capability and causing stress concentrations. Corrosion is often a major part of maintenance cost and corrosion prevention is vital in many designs. Corrosion is not expressed in terms of a design property value like other properties but rather in more qualitative terms such as a material is immune, resistant, susceptible or very susceptible to corrosion.

The corrosion process is usually electrochemical in nature, having the essential features of a battery. Corrosion is a natural process that commonly occurs because unstable materials, such as refined metals want to return to a more stable compound. For example, some metals, such as gold and silver, can be found in the earth in their natural, metallic state, and they have little tendency to corrode. Iron is a moderately active metal and corrodes readily in the presence of water. The natural state of iron is iron oxide and the most common iron ore is Hematite with a chemical composition of Fe_2O_3. Rust, the most common corrosion product of iron, also has a chemical composition of Fe_2O_3.

The difficulty in terms of energy required to extract metals from their ores is directly related to the ensuing tendency to corrode and release this energy. The electromotive force series (See Table 2.1) is a ranking of metals with respect to their inherent reactivity. The most noble metal is at the top and has the highest positive electrochemical potential. The most active metal is at the bottom and has the most negative electrochemical potential.

Table 2.1 Partial Electromotive Force Series

Standard Potential	Electrode Reaction (at 25℃), V-SHE	Standard Potential	Electrode Reaction (at 25℃), V-SHE
$Au^{3+} + 3e \longrightarrow Au$	1.498	$Cd^{2+} + 2e \longrightarrow Cd$	−0.403
$Pd^{2+} + 2e \longrightarrow Pd$	0.987	$Fe^{2+} + 2e \longrightarrow Fe$	−0.440
$Hg^{2+} + 2e \longrightarrow Hg$	0.854	$Cr^{3+} + 3e \longrightarrow Cr$	−0.744
$Ag^{+} + e \longrightarrow Au$	0.799	$Cr^{2+} + 2e \longrightarrow Cr$	−0.910
$Cu^{+} + e \longrightarrow Cu$	0.521	$Zn^{2+} + 2e \longrightarrow Zn$	−0.763
$Cu^{2+} + 2e \longrightarrow Cu$	0.337	$Mn^{2+} + 2e \longrightarrow Mn$	−1.180
$2H^{+} + 2e \longrightarrow H_2$	0.000(Ref.)	$Ti^{2+} + 2e \longrightarrow Ti$	−1.630
$Pb^{2+} + 2e \longrightarrow Pb$	−0.126	$Al^{3+} + 3e \longrightarrow Al$	−1.662
$Sn^{2+} + 2e \longrightarrow Sn$	−0.136	$Be^{2+} + 2e \longrightarrow Be$	−1.850
$Ni^{2+} + 2e \longrightarrow Ni$	−0.250	$Mg^{2+} + 2e \longrightarrow Mg$	−2.363
$Co^{2+} + 2e \longrightarrow Co$	−0.277	$Li^{+} + e \longrightarrow Li$	−3.050

Note that aluminum, as indicated by its position in the series, is a relatively reactive metal; among structural metals, only beryllium and magnesium are more reactive. Aluminum owes its excellent corrosion resistance to the barrier oxide film that is bonded strongly to the surface and if damaged reforms immediately in most environments. On a surface freshly abraded and exposed to air, the protective film is only 10 Angstroms thick but highly effective at protecting the metal from corrosion.

Corrosion involves two chemical processes, oxidation and reduction. Oxidation is the process of stripping electrons from an atom and reduction occurs when an electron is added to an atom. The oxidation process takes place at an area known as the anode. At the anode, positively charged atoms leave the solid surface and enter into an electrolyte as ions. The ions leave their corresponding negative charge in the form of electrons in the metal which travel to the location of the cathode through a conductive path. At the cathode, the corresponding reduction reaction takes place and consumes the free electrons. The electrical balance of the circuit is restored at the cathode when the electrons react with neutralizing positive ions, such as hydrogen ions, in the electrolyte. From this description, it can be seen that there are four essential components that are needed for a corrosion reaction to proceed. These components are an anode, a cathode, an electrolyte with oxidizing species, and some direct electrical connection between the anode and cathode. Although atmospheric air is the most common environmental electrolyte, natural waters, such as seawater rain, as well as man-made solutions, are the environments most frequently associated with corrosion problems.

A typical situation might involve a piece of metal that has anodic and cathodic regions on the same surface. If the surface becomes wet, corrosion may take place through ionic exchange in the surface water layer between the anode and cathode. Electron exchange will take place through the bulk metal. Corrosion will proceed at the anodic site according to a reaction

such as:
$$M \longrightarrow M^{2+} + 2e$$

Where M is a metal atom. The resulting metal cations (M^{2+}) are available at the metal surface to become corrosion products such as oxides, hydroxides, etc. The liberated electrons travel through the bulk metal (or another low resistance electrical connection) to the cathode, where they are consumed by cathodic reactions such as

$$2H^+ + 2e \longrightarrow H_2$$

The basic principles of corrosion that were just covered, generally apply to all corrosion situation except certain types of high temperature corrosion. However, the process of corrosion can be very straightforward but is often very complex due to variety of variable that can contribute to the process. A few of these variable are the composition of the material acting in the corrosion cell, the heat treatment and stress state of the materials, the composition of the electrolyte, the distance between the anode and the cathode, temperature, protective oxides and coating, and so on.

Types of Corrosion

Corrosion is commonly classified based on the appearance of the corroded material. The classifications used vary slightly from reference to reference but there is generally considered to be eight different forms of corrosion. There forms are:

Uniform or general. Corrosion that is distributed more or less uniformly over a surface.

Localized. Corrosion that is confined to small area. Localized corrosion often occurs due to a concentrated cell. A concentrated cell is an electrolytic cell in which the electromotive force is caused by a concentration of some components in the electrolyte. This difference leads to the formation of distinct anode and cathode regions.

- Pitting—corrosion that is confined to small areas and take the form of cavities on a surface.
- Crevice—corrosion occurring at locations where easy access to the bulk environment is prevented, such as the mating surfaces of two components.
- Filiform—Corrosion that occurs under some coatings in the form of randomly distributed threadlike filaments.

Inter-granular. Preferential corrosion at or along the grain boundaries of a metal.

- Exfoliation—a specific form of corrosion that travels along grain boundaries parallel to the surface of the part causing lifting and flaking at the surface. The corrosion products expand between the uncorroded layers of metal to produce a look that resembles pages of a book. Exfoliation corrosion is associated with sheet, plate and extruded products and usually initiates at unpainted or unsealed edges or holes of susceptible metals.
- **Galvanic**—corrosion associated primarily with the electrical coupling of materials with significantly different electrochemical potentials.
- **Environmental Cracking**—brittle fracture of a normally ductile material that occurs partially due to the corrosive effect of an environment.

• Corrosion fatigue—fatigue cracking that is characterized by uncharacteristically short initiation time and/or growth rate due to the damage of corrosion or buildup of corrosion products.

• High temperature hydrogen attack—the loss of strength and ductility of steel due to a high temperature reaction of absorbed hydrogen with carbides. The result of the reaction is decarburization and internal fissuring.

• Hydrogen Embrittlement—the loss of ductility of a metal resulting from absorption of hydrogen.

• Liquid metal cracking—cracking caused by contact with a liquid metal.

• Stress corrosion—cracking of a metal due to the combined action of corrosion and a residual or applied tensile stress.

Erosion corrosion—a corrosion reaction accelerated by the relative movement of a corrosive fluid and a metal surface.

Fretting corrosion—damage at the interface of two contacting surfaces under load but capable of some relative motion. The damage is accelerated by movement at the interface that mechanically abraded the surface and exposes fresh material to corrosive attack.

Dealloying—the selective corrosion of one or more components of a solid solution alloy.

Dezincification—corrosion resulting in the selective removal of zinc from copper-zinc alloys.

(*selected from http：//www.ndt-ed.org/EducationResources/CommunityCollege/Materials.htm*，2014 and *www.answers.com/chemistry*，2014)

New Words and Expressions

ductility　　*n*. 延展性，柔软性，顺从
corrosion　　*n*. 侵蚀，腐蚀状态
deteriorate　　*v*. （使）恶化
immune　　*a*. 免疫的
susceptible　　*a*. 易受影响的，易感动的，容许……的；*n*. （因缺乏免疫力而）易得病的人
hematite　　*n*. 赤铁矿
rust　　*n*. 铁锈；*v*. （使）生锈
electromotive　　*a*. 电测的
noble　　*a*. 高尚的，贵族的，高贵的；*n*. 贵族
beryllium　　*n*. 铍
abrade　　*v*. 磨损，摩擦，折磨
angstrom　　*n*. 埃（长度单位）
anode　　*n*. 阳极，正极
cathode　　*n*. 阴极
pitting　　蚀损斑
crevice　　*n*. （墙壁，岩石等的）裂缝
filiform　　*a*. 丝状的，纤维状的

intergranular   晶粒间的，粒间的
preferential   *a*. 先取的，优先的，特惠的
exfoliation   *n*. 脱落，脱落物
unpainted   无复层的；未上漆的
unsealed   未密封的，打开的
galvanic   *a*. 流电的，抽搐的，以流电所产的
dealloying   脱合金成分腐蚀
dezincification   脱锌

Notes

① Corrosion is often a major part of maintenance cost and corrosion prevention is vital in many designs. 参考译文：维护费用中主要部分是由腐蚀引起的，腐蚀防护在很多设计中也是至关重要的。

② The corrosion process is usually electrochemical in nature, having the essential features of a battery. 参考译文：腐蚀过程是自然状态下的电化学过程，与电池的原理类似。

③ On a surface freshly abraded and exposed to air, the protective film is only 10 Angstroms thick but highly effective at protecting the metal from corrosion. 参考译文：新磨损的界面暴露在空气中时，会迅速生成厚约10Å的保护膜，这种保护膜可以有效地防止金属被腐蚀。

④ The ions leave their corresponding negative charge in the form of electrons in the metal which travel to the location of the cathode through a conductive path. 参考译文：生成金属离子后，金属中就产生了带有等价负电荷的电子，电子会流经外电路到达正极。

⑤ The basic principles of corrosion that were just covered, generally apply to all corrosion situation except certain types of high temperature corrosion. 参考译文：腐蚀的基本原理几乎可以涵盖所有情况下的腐蚀反应，但不包括高温下发生的某些腐蚀反应。

⑥ The classifications used vary slightly from reference to reference but there is generally considered to be eight different forms of corrosion. 参考译文：在不同的文献资料中分类方法也略有不同，但通常情况下将腐蚀划分为八类。

Exercises

1. Questions for discussion

(1) Why are metals ductile malleable and conduct electricity?
(2) Are all metals ductile and malleable?
(3) What metals are ductile and malleable? Which is most malleable and ductile metal?
(4) Why did the author say corrosion is a natural process?
(5) Which kinds of metals want to be a more stable compound? Give some examples.
(6) In nature, iron is likely to turn into Fe_2O_3. Is it a process of corrosion?
(7) How many forms of corrosion are there according to the passage? What are they?
(8) What is an erosion corrosion?

(9) Try to describe the fretting corrosion.

2. Translate the following into Chinese

electromotive force series   electrochemical potential
oxidation process   electrical balance
basic principle   Fretting corrosion

- The corrosion process is usually electrochemical in nature, having the essential features of a battery.
- The difficulty in terms of energy required to extract metals from their ores is directly related to the ensuing tendency to corrode and release this energy.
- The electrical balance of the circuit is restored at the cathode when the electrons react with neutralizing positive ions, such as hydrogen ions, in the electrolyte.

3. Translate the following into English

保护膜   电路
自由电子   电子转移
金属离子   正极反应

- 金和银这类金属在自然界中是以金属状态存在的，在环境中它们不容易被腐蚀。
- 氧化过程中从金属中夺取电子，而还原过程中金属得到电子。
- 当金属表面处于湿润状态之后，在表面上的水层中会发生正负极之间的粒子转移，这就是腐蚀。
- 通常情况下腐蚀的种类是根据被腐蚀后金属的外观来进行划分的。

4. Reading comprehension

(1) What is the most common corrosion product of iron? _____
  (A) Fe_2O_3 (B) Fe   (C) Fe_3O_4 (D) A, B and C

(2) Which metal is the most active in the following four metals? _____
  (A) Pt   (B) Hg   (C) Co   (D) Ni

(3) Why does aluminum owe its excellent corrosion resistance? _____
  (A) The presence of the barrier oxide film.
  (B) Aluminum is stable in its metallic state.
  (C) Its high positive electrochemical potential.
  (D) A, B and C

(4) Which of the following process does not take place at the anode? _____
  (A) Oxidation process
  (B) Reduction process
  (C) The process of stripping electrons from an atom
  (D) Chemical process

(5) _____ is not associated with corrosion problems of the metals exposed in the air.
  (A) Natural waters   (B) Man-made solutions
  (C) Seawater rain   (D) Air

(6) _____ is not essential for a corrosion reaction to proceed.
  (A) An anode

(B) Water
(C) Electrical connection between the anode and cathode
(D) An electrolyte

(7) Which is most malleable and ductile metal?
(A) Copper　　　　　(B) Silver　　　　　(C) Iron　　　　　(D) Gold

Reading Material

The Effect of Nanostructuring on Physical and Mechanical Properties of Metallic Materials

Modern technologies allow altering significantly the structure of polycrystalline materials. In particular, nanocrystalline metals and alloys are becoming more widely used. Metallic materials with a similar structure are characterized by large length of the grain boundaries. This feature of the structure leads to the fact that many of the properties of these materials may significantly differ from those of conventional polycrystalline materials. This paper presents the results of experimental studies related with the study of the influence of nanostructuring on the specific strength, wear resistance, corrosion resistance and thermal diffusivity of bulk metallic materials having a structural application.

Experimental

As the objects of comparative tests we examined conventional and nanostructured samples of primary aluminum (Aluminium1100), copper C11000, titanium, purified by iodide method, aluminum-magnesium alloy 518.0, casting bronze C95200, and also experimental alloy, what inclusive 60.67% (mass fraction) of the titanium and 39.33% of the aluminum. The formation of nanostructure of metallic materials was performed by the current treatment of the corresponding melts. Availability of the nanostructuring we determined by

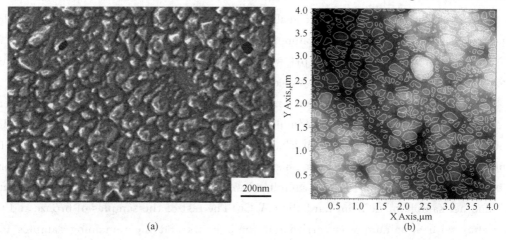

(a)　　　　　　　　　　　　　　　　(b)

Figure 2.1　Photos of the bronze structure. (a) SEM images (ZEISS Cross Beam AURIGA microscope),
(b) segmented image of the structure (atomic force microscope NEXT)

the atomic force microscopy and electronic microscopy. As an example, Figure 2.1 shows the images of the bronze structure, and Figure 2.2 shows the histogram of the distribution of grain sizes. The values of specific strength and corrosion resistance (corrosion rate) were calculated as the arithmetic mean of the relevant tests of three samples of a metal or an alloy. Each sample was obtained from different initial cast work pieces. The specific strength of metals and alloys was determined by the compression of cylindrical shaped samples. For the samples loading we used the compression machine MC-1000 with a device for the testing of the samples. The measurement error of the load on the sample was $\pm 1\%$. Geometrical sizes of the samples were determined with a precision ± 0.01 mm. The density of the samples of metals and alloys needed to calculate the specific resistance was determined by hydrostatic weighing. To determine the mass of the samples we used the electronic laboratory scales with accuracy $\pm 1 \times 10^{-4}$ g, equipped with a device for the hydrostatic weighing.

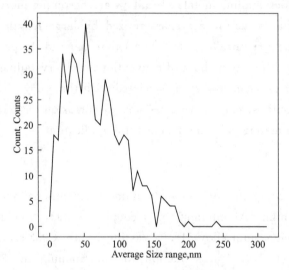

Figure 2.2 The histogram of the distribution of grain sizes (middle size of a grain is 84 nm)

The corrosion resistance of metals and alloys was determined by the mass loss of the cylindrical shaped samples, placed at room temperature for 144 hours in a model solution containing 30 g/L of NaCl and acidified with acetic acid to a pH = 4.0. The maximum error in determining of the estimated value of the corrosion rate in the experiments did not exceed 5%.

The determination of the wear resistance of the samples (the mass loss in friction per unit of the contact surface area) was conducted at the Institute of Engineering Science (Ural Branch of the Academy of Sciences in Ekaterinburg, Russia) at the friction machine ChMT-1, equipped with a special knot friction. This assembly provides a standardized reproduction of shaped axial impact load on the test sample of annular shape, constituting a pair of friction with another sample made from hard alloy W-Co. The test of the samples of bronze and titanium alloy with aluminum was carried out for 5 hours and the remaining samples for 3 hours. The estimated error of determining the durability of this method amounts to no more than 3%. Additionally, in this paper the studies of thermal diffusivity of titanium in the temperature range 1000~1600 K were conducted. The measurements were performed by dynamic-sky plane temperature waves with automated measuring complex providing error not exceeding 3%. The results of comparative experiments are viewed in Table 2.2 and in following text.

Table 2.2 The influence of the nanostructuring to the properties of metallic materials

Metal/alloy	Nanostructured	Specific strength σ, m²/s²	Durability ε, g/m²	Corrosion rate V, g/(m² · h)
Cu	−	25.5×10³	242.0	0.2023
Cu	+	30.4×10³	213.1	0.1819
Bronze	−	55.0×10³	323.4	0.0758
Bronze	+	72.3×10³	277.8	0.0677
Al-Mg alloy	−	107×10³	1405.5	0.8213
Al-Mg alloy	+	134×10³	1065.9	0.7303
Ti-Al alloy	−	203×10³	128.7	0.0183
Ti-Al alloy	+	264×10³	87.5	0.0163
Al	−	29.3×10³	840.2	0.1355
Al	+	35.2×10³	602.9	0.1230

The results of experiments confirm the influence of nanostructuring on the properties of metallic materials and allow us to estimate the extent of this influence. Thus, in the framework of the reference of the study the samples of nanostructured metals and alloys have increased values of specific strength to 19%~31%, increased to 11%~32% values of wear resistance and lower to about 11% the rate of corrosion. The change of the thermal diffusivity of nanostructured titanium also lay in marked limits of change of properties. For example, at 1000 K this value is corresponding to 5.6×10⁻⁶ m²/s at 1260 K ~7.6×10⁻⁶ m²/s, which is 1.2 times lower than for conventional polycrystalline titanium at the same temperatures. The observed change in thermal diffusivity of the titanium confirms that the properties of nanostructured materials due to the peculiarities of their structure, that primarily characterized by great length of grain boundaries / fragments. It is known that the thermal diffusivity of the material α related to its thermal conductivity λ, and heat capacity C_p and density ρ with ratio $\alpha = \lambda/(C_p \cdot \rho)$. Nanocrystalline substances have greater capacity than the coarse-grained materials. Despite the fact that the coefficients of linear thermal expansion of materials with nanostructure exceed these ratios for conventional polycrystalline, their density differs insignificantly. Given that nanocrystalline materials must possess of reduced thermal conductivity, from the above relationship for a is follows the fact that their thermal diffusivity must also be smaller than the conventional structure of substances.

Conclusions

Comparative tests performed in this study showed that nanocrystalline structure formed in the studied metallic materials has a significant impact to their properties. It is found that the experimental samples of nanostructured metals and alloys exhibit the values of specific strength increased to 18%~31%, the values of durability increased to 11%~32% and the values of the corrosion rate smaller to about 11%. It is noted that the temperature conductivity of the nanostructured titanium at 1000 K at 1.2 times lower than in a conventional polycrystalline state. Given the results of measurements of the thermal diffusivity of titanium the set of changes in properties can be primarily due to the high extent of inter-grain boundaries in nanostructured metallic materials.

(*selected from Advanced Materials Research* 2014, 905: 47-50)

New Words and Expressions

polycrystalline   *adj*. [晶体] 多晶的
nanocrystalline   *n*. 纳米晶体，奈米晶
grain boundary   [晶体学] 晶界
iodide method   碘化法
aluminum   *n*. [化学] 铝（金属元素）
titanium   *n*. [化学] 钛（金属元素）
casting   *n*. 铸造，铸件，投掷，角色分配；*v*. 铸造，投掷，投向，选派演员，扔掉（cast 的 ing 形式）
inclusive   *a*. 包括的，包含的
mass fraction   *n*. 质量分数
melts   *n*. [冶] 熔体（melt 的复数）；*v*. 熔化（melt 的第三人称单数形式）
atomic force microscopy   原子力显微镜
histogram   *n*. [统计] 直方图，柱状图，频率曲线
corrosion resistance   [化学] 耐蚀性，抗腐蚀性
hydrostatic weighing   流体静力称重，水下皮脂测定法
arithmetic   *n*. 算术，计算，演算，估算；*a*. 算术（上）的，运算的，根据算术法则的
cylindrical   *a*. 呈圆筒形的，圆柱体的 [亦作 cylindric]
specific strength   [力] 比强度，强度系数
durability test   耐久性试验，施工测量，寿命试验，疲劳试验
coarse-grained   *a*. 纹理粗糙的，粗鲁的，粗鄙的

Notes

① Availability of the nanostructuring we determined by the atomic force microscopy and electronic microscopy. 亦可写作：We determined the availability of nanostructure of metallic materials by the atomic force microscopy and electronic microscopy. 参考译文：我们通过原子力显微镜和电子显微镜测量了金属材料纳米结构的可得性。

② The corrosion resistance of metals and alloys was determined by the mass loss of the cylindrical shaped samples, placed at room temperature for 144 hours in a model solution containing 30 g/L of NaCl and acidified with acetic acid to a pH = 4.0. 参考译文：在30 g/L 的 NaCl 标准溶液中加入醋酸，调节溶液的 pH = 4.0，将柱形的样品置于该溶液中，室温下浸泡 144h，通过测定放置前后样品的质量变化，即可测定金属及合金的抗腐蚀性。

③ Ural Branch of the Academy of Sciences in Ekaterinburg, Russia 通常写作：Ural Branch of the Russian Academy of Sciences (Ekaterinburg, Russia). 参考译文：俄罗斯科学院的乌拉尔分院（叶卡捷琳堡，俄罗斯）。

Exercises

1. Questions for discussion
(1) Try to describe the properties of metallic materials.
(2) What are nanocrystalline metals and alloys?
(3) What could we learn from Figure 2.1?
(4) What could influent the properties of metallic materials?

2. Translate the following into Chinese
specific strength   wear resistance
corrosion resistance   geometrical sizes
thermal diffusivity   hydrostatic weighing

• Metallic materials with a similar structure are characterized by large length of the grain boundaries.

• The formation of nanostructure of metallic materials was performed by the current treatment of the corresponding melts.

• This paper presents the results of experimental studies related with the study of the influence of nanostructuring on the specific strength, wear resistance, corrosion resistance and thermal diffusivity of bulk metallic materials having a structural application.

• The values of specific strength and corrosion resistance (corrosion rate) were calculated as the arithmetic mean of the relevant tests of three samples of a metal or an alloy.

• To determine the mass of the samples we used the electronic laboratory scales with accuracy $\pm 1 \times 10^{-4}$ g, equipped with a device for the hydrostatic weighing.

3. Translate the following into English
抗腐蚀性   质量分数
铸造青铜   质量损失
强度系数   疲劳试验

• 通过电流处理（电弧放电），使金属熔化（成为烟尘状态）从而形成合金或金属单质纳米材料。

• 纳米合金材料由于其粒径尺寸及结构不同于块状合金材料，因而在电、磁、抗蚀性、催化等方面表现出良好且独特的性质。

• 纳米晶体物质比粗粒的普通材料具有更好的吸附性能。

4. Reading comprehension
(1) Which is WRONG about the preparation method of nanomaterial? _____
(A) Wide attention was received on using porous anodic alumina membrane as a template to prepare nanostructured materials.

(B) We can prepare nanomaterial by colloid chemical methods.

(C) The author prepared nanomaterial by electrochemical methods in the text.

(D) The author prepared titanium nanomaterial by iodide methods in the text.

(2) How many nanostructured samples are examined in the text? _____

(A) 7　　　　　　(B) 6　　　　　　(C) 5　　　　　　(D) 4

(3) What can we see from Figure 2.2? _____

(A) The middle size of a grain is 84 nm in the histogram of the distribution of grain sizes.

(B) The measurement error of the load on the sample was $\pm 1\%$.

(C) Geometrical sizes of the samples were determined with a precision ± 0.01 mm.

(D) The density of the samples of metals and alloys needed to calculate the specific resistance was determined by hydrostatic weighing.

(4) Which of the following does NOT take place in the text? _____

(A) The thermal diffusivity of nanostructured titanium is changed as the reaction temperature changed.

(B) The samples of nanostructured metals and alloys have increased values of specific strength to $19\% \sim 31\%$.

(C) The thermal diffusivity of nanostructured titanium is corresponding to 5.6×10^{-6} m²/s at 1000 K and to 7.6×10^{-6} m²/s at 1260K.

(D) The thermal diffusivity of nanostructured titanium is 1.2 times lower than for conventional polycrystalline titanium at 1260K.

(5) It is found that the values of _____ are increased in the experimental samples of nanostructured metals and alloys in the text.

(A) specific strength and corrosion rate　　(B) thermal diffusivity and durability

(C) specific strength and durability　　　　(D) temperature conductivity and corrosion rate

(6) The author give us the conclusions that _____ .

(A) nanocrystalline structure formed in the studied materials has a significant impact to their properties.

(B) the experimental samples exhibit the values of specific strength increased to $18\% \sim 31\%$, the values of durability increased to $11\% \sim 32\%$ and the values of the corrosion rate smaller to about 11%.

(C) the temperature conductivity of the nanostructured titanium at 1000 K at 1.2 times lower than in a conventional polycrystalline state.

(D) the results of measurements of titanium are due to the high extent of inter-grain boundaries in nanostructured materials.

Part III CERAMICS

Unit 9 Introduction to Ceramic Materials

The word ceramic is derived from the Greek *keramos*, which means "potter's clay" or "pottery." Its origin is a Sanskrit term meaning "to burn." So the early Greeks used "keramos" when describing products obtained by heating clay-containing materials. The term has long included all products made from fired clay, for example, bricks, fireclay refractories, sanitaryware, and tableware.

In 1822, silica refractories were first made. Although they contained no clay, the traditional ceramic process of shaping, drying, and firing was used to make them. So the term "ceramic," while retaining its original sense of a product made from clay, began to include other products made by the same manufacturing process. The field of ceramics (broader than the materials themselves) can be defined as the art and science of making and using solid articles that contain as their essential component a ceramic. This definition covers the purification of raw materials, the study and production of the chemical compounds concerned, their formation into components, and the study of structure, composition, and properties.

Ceramics are usually associated with "mixed" bonding—a combination of covalent, ionic, and sometimes metallic. They consist of arrays of interconnected atoms; there are no discrete molecules. This characteristic distinguishes ceramics from molecular solids such as iodine crystals (composed of discrete I_2 molecules) and paraffin wax (composed of long-chain alkane molecules). It also excludes ice, which is composed of discrete H_2O molecules and often behaves just like many ceramics. The majority of ceramics are compounds of metals or metalloids and nonmetals. Most frequently they are oxides, nitrides, and carbides. However, diamond and graphite are also classified as ceramics. These forms of carbon are inorganic in the most basic meaning of the term: they were not prepared from the living organism.

General Properties

Ceramics generally have specific properties associated with them. We will look at some properties and see how closely they match our expectations of what constitutes a ceramic.

Brittleness. This probably comes from personal experiences such as dropping a glass beaker or a dinner plate. The reason that the majority of ceramics are brittle is the mixed ionic-covalent bonding that holds the constituent atoms together. At high temperatures (above the glass transition temperature) glass no longer behaves in a brittle manner; it behaves as a viscous liquid. That is why it is easy to form glass into intricate shapes. So what we can say is that most ceramics are brittle at room temperature but not necessarily at elevated temperatures.

Poor electrical and thermal conduction. The valence electrons are tied up in bonds, and are not free as they are in metals. In metals it is the free electrons—the electron gas—that determines many of their electrical and thermal properties. Diamond, which is classified as a ceramic, has the highest thermal conductivity of any known material. The conduction mechanism is due to phonons, not electrons. Ceramics can also have high electrical conductivity: (1) the oxide ceramic, ReO_3, has an electrical conductivity at room temperature similar to that of Cu; (2) the mixed oxide $YBa_2Cu_3O_7$ is an HTSC; it has zero resistivity below 92 K. These are two examples that contradict the conventional wisdom when it comes to ceramics.

Compressive strength. Ceramics are stronger in compression than in tension, whereas metals have comparable tensile and compressive strengths. This difference is important when we use ceramic components for load-bearing applications. It is necessary to consider the stress distributions in the ceramic to ensure that they are compressive. An important example is in the design of concrete bridges—the concrete, a CMC, must be kept in compression. Ceramics generally have low toughness, although combining them in composites can dramatically improve this property.

Chemical insensitivity. A large number of ceramics are stable in both harsh chemical and thermal environments. Pyrex glass is used widely in chemistry laboratories specifically because it is resistant to many corrosive chemicals, stable at high temperatures (it does not soften until 1100 K), and is resistant to thermal shock because of its low coefficient of thermal expansion (33×10^{-7} K^{-1}). It is also widely used in bakeware.

Transparent. Many ceramics are transparent because they have a large E_g. Examples include sapphire watch covers, precious stones, and optical fibers. Glass optical fibers have a percent transmission $>96\%$ km^{-1}. Metals are transparent to visible light only when they are very thin, typically less than 0.1 μm.

Although it is always possible to find at least one ceramic that shows a typical behavior, the properties mentioned above are in many cases different from those shown by metals and polymers.

Types of Ceramic and Their Applications

Large numbers of materials are ceramics. The applications for these materials are diverse, from bricks and tiles to electronic and magnetic components. These applications use the wide range of properties exhibited by ceramics. Some of these properties are listed in Table 3.1 together with examples of specific ceramics and applications. The functions of ceramic products are dependent on their chemical composition and microstructure, which determines their properties. It is the interrelationship between structure and properties that is a key element of materials science and engineering.

Table 3.1 Properties and Applications for Ceramics

Property	Example	Application
Electrical	$Bi_2Ru_2O_7$	Conductive component in thick film resistors
	Doped ZrO_2	Electrolyte in solid-oxide fuel cells
	Indium tin oxide (ITO)	Transparent electrode
	SiC	Furnace elements for resistive heating
	$YBaCuO_7$	Superconducting quantum interference devices (SQUIDs)
	SnO_2	Electrodes for electric glass melting furnaces
Dielectric	Al_2O_3	Spark plug insulator
	$PbZr_{0.5}Ti_{0.5}O_3$ (PZT)	Micropumps
	SiO_2	Furnace bricks
	$(Ba,Sr)TiO_3$	Dynamic random access memories (DRAMs)
	Lead magnesium	Chip capacitors
Magnetic	γ-Fe_2O_3	Recording tapes
	$Mn_{0.4}Zn_{0.6}Fe_2O_4$	Transformer cores in touch tone telephones
	$BaFe_{12}O_{19}$	Permanent magnets in loudspeakers
	$Y_{2.66}Gd_{0.34}Fe_{4.22}Al_{0.68}Mn_{0.09}O_{12}$	Radar phase shifters
Optical	Doped SiO_2	Optical fibers
	α-Al_2O_3	Transparent envelopes in street lamps
	Doped $ZrSiO_4$	Ceramic colors
	Doped $(Zn,Cd)S$	Fluorescent screens for electron microscopes
	$Pb_{1-x}La_x(Zr_zTi_{1-z})_{1-x/4}O_3$ (PLZT)	Thin-film optical switches
	Nd doped $Y_3Al_5O_{12}$	Solid-state lasers
Mechanical	TiN	Wear-resistant coatings
	SiC	Abrasives for polishing
	Diamond	Cutting tools
	Si_3N_4	Engine components
	Al_2O_3	Hip implants
Thermal	SiO_2	Space shuttle insulation tiles
	Al_2O_3 and AlN	Packages for integrated circuits
	Lithium-aluminosilicate glass ceramics	Supports for telescope mirrors
	Pyrex glass	Laboratory glassware and cookware

You may find that, in addition to dividing ceramics according to their properties and applications, it is common to class them as *traditional* or *advanced*. Traditional ceramics include high-volume items such bricks and tiles, toilet bowls (whitewares), and pottery. Advanced ceramics include newer materials such as laser host materials, piezoelectric ceramics, ceramics for dynamic random access memories (DRAMs), and so on, often produced in small quantities with higher prices. There are other characteristics that separate these categories.

Traditional ceramics are usually based on clay and silica. There is sometimes a tendency to equate traditional ceramics with low technology, however, advanced manufacturing techniques are often used. Competition among producers has caused processing to become more efficient and cost effective. Complex tooling and machinery is often used and may be coupled with computer-assisted process control.

Advanced ceramics are also referred to as "special," "technical," or "engineering" ceramics. They exhibit superior mechanical properties, corrosion/oxidation resistance, or electrical, optical, and/or magnetic properties. While traditional clay-based ceramics have been used for over 25,000 years, advanced ceramics have generally been developed within the last 100 years.

Table 3.2 compares traditional and advanced ceramics in terms of the type of raw materials used, the forming and shaping processes, and the methods used for characterization.

Table 3.2 A comparison of different aspects of traditional and advanced ceramics

comparison aspects	traditional ceramics	advanced ceramics
raw materials preparation	raw minerals clay silica	chemically prepared powders - precipitation - spray dry - freeze dry - vapor phase - sol-gel
forming	potters wheel slip casting	slip casting injection molding sol-gel hot pressing hiping rapid prototyping
high-temperature processing	flame kiln	electric furnace hot press reaction sinter vapor deposition plasma spraying microwave furnace
finishing process	erosion glazing	erosion laser machining plasma spraying ion implantation coating
characterization	visible examination light microscopy	light microscopy X-ray diffraction electron microscopy scanned probe microscopy neutron diffraction surface analytical methods

(*Selected from Carter C. Barry, Norton M. Grant, Ceramic Materials: Science and Engineering, 2ed, Springer, 2013*)

New Words and Expressions

pottery　*n.* 陶器

refractories　耐火材料

sanitaryware　*n.* 卫生洁具，卫生陶器

tableware　*n.* 餐具

discrete　*a.* 不连续的，离散的

viscous　*a*. 黏的，有黏性的，黏性的
intricate　*a*. 复杂的，错综的
pyrex　*n*. 耐热玻璃
bakeware　*n*. 烘焙用具，烘烤器皿
sapphire　*n*. 蓝宝石，宝石蓝；*a*. 蓝宝石色的
tiles　*n*. 瓷砖
electrode　*n*. 电极
capacitor　*n*. 电容器
radar　*n*. 雷达
fluorescent　*n*. 荧光灯；*a*. 荧光的
abrasives　研磨剂，研磨材料
aluminosilicate　*n*. 铝硅酸盐（硅酸铝）
lithium-aluminosilicate　锂铝硅酸盐
piezoelectric　*a*. 压电的

Notes

① Ceramics are usually associated with "mixed" bonding—a combination of covalent, ionic, and sometimes metallic. 参考译文：通常，陶瓷的化合键为共价-离子混合键，有时是共价-离子-金属混合键。

② This characteristic distinguishes ceramics from molecular solids such as iodine crystals (composed of discrete I_2 molecules) and paraffin wax (composed of long-chain alkane molecules). distinguish…from…，把……与……区别开。参考译文：这种特征（指上文提到的陶瓷由互相连接的原子组成）将陶瓷与分子固体，例如由离散碘分子构成的碘单晶和由长链烷烃分子组成的固体石蜡，区分开来。

③ The reason that the majority of ceramics are brittle is the mixed ionic-covalent bonding that holds the constituent atoms together. 本句结构为"the reason is …"，第一个 that 引导一个同位语从句，第二个 that 引导一个定语从句。参考译文：大部分陶瓷之所以易碎的原因是陶瓷是通过离子-共价混合键将组成原子结合在一起的。

④ Although it is always possible to find at least one ceramic that shows a typical behavior, the properties mentioned above are in many cases different from those shown by metals and polymers. 参考译文：尽管可能至少发现一种陶瓷具有以上所述的典型特征，但是在许多情况下，这些特征与金属和陶瓷表现的性能不同。

⑤ The functions of ceramic products are dependent on their chemical composition and microstructure, which determines their properties. 参考译文：陶瓷产品的功能取决于它们的化学组成和微结构，正是这些化学组成与微结构决定着它们的性能。

⑥ You may find that, in addition to dividing ceramics according to their properties and applications, it is common to class them as traditional or advanced. 参考译文：你可以发现，除了通过它们的性能和应用来区分陶瓷之外，通常还可以将其分为传统陶瓷和先进陶瓷。

Exercises

1. Question for discussion

(1) Where is the word "ceramic" derived from?
(2) Why is it easy to form glass into intricate shapes?
(3) Please give the basic properties of ceramic materaials.
(4) Please give some application examples of ceramic materaials.
(5) What are traditional ceramics? And what are advanced ceramics? Please give some examples.
(6) What are the differences between traditional ceramics and advanced ceramics?

2. Translate the following into Chinese

the purification of raw materials   long-chain alkane molecules
glass beaker   viscous liquid
spark plug insulator   glass ceramics
computer-assisted process control   surface analytical methods

• We will look at some properties and see how closely they match our expectations of what constitutes a ceramic.

• At high temperatures (above the glass transition temperature) glass no longer behaves in a brittle manner; it behaves as a viscous liquid.

• They exhibit superior mechanical properties, corrosion/oxidation resistance, or electrical, optical, and/or magnetic properties.

• While traditional clay-based ceramics have been used for over 25,000 years, advanced ceramics have generally been developed within the last 100 years.

3. Translate the following into English

玻璃转变温度   离子共价键
应力分布   热膨胀系数
玻璃光纤   材料科学与工程
固体氧化物燃料电池 电子显微镜

• 作为陶瓷的金刚石是所知的材料中,具有最高导热性的材料。

• 陶瓷的压缩强度大于拉伸强度,而金属的压缩强度与拉伸强度相当。

• 尽管陶瓷与复合材料结合可以显著地改善陶瓷的韧性,但是在通常情况下陶瓷的韧性比较差。

• 陶瓷产品的功能取决于它们的化学组成和微结构,正是这些化学组成与微结构决定着它们的性能。

4. Reading comprehension

(1) The majority of ceramics are brittle because _____ .
(A) ceramics behaves in a brittle manner at room temperature
(B) the mixed ionic-covalent bonding holds the constituent atoms together
(C) ceramics behaves as a viscous liquid at high temperatures
(D) ceramics are composed of discrete molecules

(2) The conduction mechanism of diamond which has the highest thermal conductivity due to _____ .

(A) free electrons   (B) the electron gas   (C) phonons   (D) electrons

(3) Which of the following is NOT true according to the poor electrical and thermal conduction property of ceramics? _____ .

(A) The valence electrons are tied up in bonds and are not free in ceramics

(B) Diamond which is classified as a ceramic has the highest thermal conductivity of any known material

(C) the oxide ceramic ReO_3 has an electrical conductivity at room temperature similar to that of Cu

(D) the mixed oxide $YBa_2Cu_3O_7$ has zero resistivity below 92 ℃

(4) The functions of ceramic products are dependent on _____ , which determines their properties.

(A) the interrelationship between structure and properties

(B) their chemical composition and microstructure

(C) the forming and shaping processes

(D) the methods used for characterization

(5) _____ is a key element of materials science and engineering according to the applications of ceramics.

(A) Considering the stress distributions in the materials

(B) The interrelationship between structure and properties

(C) Chemical composition and microstructure of materials

(D) Market and future for materials

(6) According to the classification of ceramics, which of the following is NOT true? _____ .

(A) Low technologies are used without any advanced manufacturing techniques in traditional ceramics

(B) Advanced ceramics are often produced in small quantities with higher prices

(C) Advanced ceramics exhibit superior mechanical properties, corrosion/oxidation resistance, or electrical, optical, and/or magnetic properties

(D) The applying time of traditional clay-based ceramics is far longer than that of advanced ceramics

Reading Material

The Market and Future for Ceramics

Market

Ceramics is a multibillion dollar industry. Worldwide sales are about $100 billion ($ 10^{11}) per year; the U. S. market alone is over $35 billion ($ 3.5×10^{10}) annually. As with all economic data there will be variations from year to year. The *Ceramic Industry* (CI)

is one organization that provides regular updates of sales through its annual *Giants in Ceramics survey*.

The general distribution of industry sales is as follows: 55% glass, 17% advanced ceramics, 10% whiteware, 9% porcelain enamel, 7% refractories, and 2% structural clay.

In the United States, sales of structural clay in the form of bricks are valued at $160 M per month. However, financially, the ceramics market is clearly dominated by glass. The major application for glass is windows. World demand for flat glass is about 40 billion square feet—worth over $40 billion. Overall market distribution in the United States is as follows: 32% flat glass, 18% lighting, 17% containers, 17% fiber glass, 9% TV tubes (CRTs), 5% consumer glassware, 1% technical/ laboratory, and 1% others.

Advanced ceramics form the second largest sector of the industry. More than half of this sector is electrical and electronic ceramics and ceramic packages: 36% capacitors/substrates/packages, 23% other electrical/electronic ceramics, 13% other, 12% electrical porcelain, 8% engineering ceramics, and 8% optical fibers.

High-temperature ceramic superconductors, which would fall into the category of advanced ceramics, are not presently a major market area. They constitute less than 1% of the advanced ceramics market. Significant growth has been predicted because of their increased use in microwave filters and resonators, with particular application in the area of cell phones.

Engineering ceramics, also called structural ceramics, include wear-resistant components such as dies, nozzles, and bearings. Bioceramics such as ceramic and glassceramic implants and dental crowns account for about 20% of this market. Dental crowns are made of porcelain and over 30 million are made in the United States each year.

Whiteware sales, which include sanitaryware (toilet bowls, basins, etc.) and dinnerware (plates, cups), account for about 10% of the total market for ceramics. The largest segment of the whiteware market, accounting for about 40%, is floor and wall tiles. In the United States we use about 2.5 billion (2.5×10^9) square feet of ceramic tiles per year. Annual sales of sanitaryware in the United States total more than 30 million pieces.

Porcelain enamel is the ceramic coating applied to many steel appliances such as kitchen stoves, washers, and dryers. Porcelain enamels have much wider applications as both interior and exterior paneling in buildings, for example, in subway stations. Because of these widespread applications it is perhaps not surprising that the porcelain enameling industry accounts for more than $3 billion per year.

More than 50% of refractories are consumed by the steel industry. The major steelmaking countries are China, Japan, and the United States. Structural clay products include bricks, sewer pipes, and roofing tiles. These are high-volume low-unit-cost items. Each year about 8 billion bricks are produced in the United States with a market value of over $1.5 billion.

Critical Issues for the Future

Although glass dominates the global ceramics market, the most significant growth is in advanced ceramics. There are many key issues that need to be addressed to maintain this growth and expand the applications and uses of advanced ceramics. It is in these areas that there will be increasing employment opportunities for ceramic engineers and materials scientists.

Structural ceramics include silicon nitride (Si_3N_4), silicon carbide (SiC), zirconia (ZrO_2), boron carbide (B_4C), and alumina (Al_2O_3). They are used in applications such as cutting tools, wear components, heat exchangers, and engine parts. Their relevant properties are high hardness, low density, high-temperature mechanical strength, creep resistance, corrosion resistance, and chemical inertness. There are three key issues to solve in order to expand the use of structural ceramics: reducing cost of the final product, improving reliability, and improving reproducibility.

Electronic ceramics include barium titanate ($BaTiO_3$), zinc oxide (ZnO), lead zirconate titanate [$Pb(Zr_x Ti_{1-x})O_3$], aluminum nitride (AlN), and HTSCs. They are used in applications as diverse as capacitor dielectrics, varistors, microelectromechanical systems (MEMS), substrates, and packages for integrated circuits. There are many challenges for the future: integrating with existing semiconductor technology, improving processing, and enhancing compatibility with other materials.

Bioceramics are used in the human body. The response of these materials varies from nearly inert to bioactive to resorbable. Nearly inert bioceramics include alumina (Al_2O_3) and zirconia (ZrO_2). Bioactive ceramics include hydroxyapatite and some special glass and glass-ceramic formulations. Tricalcium phosphate is an example of a resorbable bioceramic; it dissolves in the body. Three issues will determine future progress: matching mechanical properties to human tissues, increasing reliability, and improving processing methods.

Coatings and films are generally used to modify the surface properties of a material, for example, a bioactive coating deposited onto the surface of a bioinert implant. They may also be used for economic reasons; we may want to apply a coating of an expensive material to a lower cost substrate rather than make the component entirely from the more expensive material. An example of this situation would be applying a diamond coating on a cutting tool. In some cases we use films or coatings simply because the material performs better in this form. An example is the transport properties of thin films of HTSCs, which are improved over those of the material in bulk form. Some issues need to be addressed: understanding film deposition and growth, improving film/substrate adhesion, and increasing reproducibility.

Composites may use ceramics as the matrix phase and/or the reinforcing phase. The purpose of a composite is to display a combination of the preferred characteristics of each of the components. In CMCs one of the principal goals has been to increase fracture toughness through reinforcement with whiskers or fibers. When ceramics are the reinforcement phase in, for example, metal matrix composites the result is usually an increase in strength, enhanced creep resistance, and greater wear resistance. Three issues must be solved: reducing processing costs, developing compatible combinations of materials (e.g., matching coefficients of thermal expansion), and understanding interfaces.

Nanoceramics can be either well established or at an early stage in their development. They are widely used in cosmetic products such as sunscreens, and we know they are critical in many applications of catalysis, but their use in fuel cells, coatings, and devices, for example, is often quite new. There are three main challenges: making them, integrating them into devices, and ensuring that they do not have a negative impact on society.

(*Selected from Carter C. Barry, Norton M. Grant, Ceramic Materials: Science and Engineering, 2ed, Springer, 2013*)

New Words and Expressions

porcelain *a.* 瓷制的，精美的，脆的
enamel *n.* 珐琅，瓷釉
microwave *n.* 微波
resonator *n.* 共鸣器，共振器
nozzle *n.* 喷嘴，接管
bearing *n.* 轴承
bioceramics 生物陶瓷
glassceramic 微晶玻璃
basin *n.* 盆，脸盆
sewer *n.* 下水道，污水管
creep resistance 蠕滑阻力，抗蠕变力
varistor *n.* 压敏电阻
microelectromechanical systems 微机电系统
inert *a.* 惰性的，迟钝的
hydroxyapatite *n.* 羟磷灰石
dissolve *v.* 溶解，解散
deposition *n.* 沉积作用（沉积物，矿床）
principal *a.* 主要的，最重要的
fracture toughness 断裂韧度
cosmetic *a.* 化妆用的
sunscreen *n.* （防晒油中的）遮光剂

Notes

① High-temperature ceramic superconductors, which would fall into the category of advanced ceramics, are not presently a major market area. 参考译文：目前，被归类为先进陶瓷的高温陶瓷超导体不占有主要市场。

② Because of these widespread applications it is perhaps not surprising that the porcelain enameling industry accounts for more than $3 billion per year. 参考译文：因为搪瓷的应用非常广泛，所以对于搪瓷上釉工业每年产值占 30 多亿美元，我们对此并不感到吃惊。

③ There are many key issues that need to be addressed to maintain this growth and expand the applications and uses of advanced ceramics. that 引导一个定语从句，修饰 "issues"，本句结构为：There are many key issues；第二个动词不定式 to 后面跟着两个动词短语 "maintain this growth" 和 "expand the applications and uses of advanced ceramics"。参考译文：在保持增长和扩大先进陶瓷的应用和用途方面有许多重要的问题需要阐明。

④ They are used in applications as diverse as capacitor dielectrics, varistors, microelectromechanical systems (MEMS), substrates, and packages for integrated circuits. they 指代 "electronic ceramics"。参考译文：电子陶瓷材料在电容器电介质、压敏电阻、微机电系统、基片和集成电路的包裹方面都有比较广泛的应用。

⑤ Coatings and films are generally used to modify the surface properties of a material, for example, a bioactive coating deposited onto the surface of a bioinert implant. the surface properties, 表面性能。参考译文：通常，运用涂层和薄膜可以修饰材料的表面性能，例如，一种沉积在生物惰性移植体表面的生物活性涂层。

⑥ We may want to apply a coating of an expensive material to a lower cost substrate rather than make the component entirely from the more expensive material. 参考译文：我们可能会在低成本的基底材料上运用比较昂贵的涂层材料，而不是所有的组成成分都要用比较昂贵的材料。

Reading Comprehension

(1) Financially, the ceramics market is clearly dominated by _____ according to the text.

(A) advanced ceramics (B) glass
(C) whiteware (D) porcelain enamel

(2) It has been predicted that high-temperature ceramic superconductors may have significant growth because of _____.

(A) they falling into the category of advanced ceramics
(B) they being a major market area presently
(C) their increased use in microwave filters and resonators with particular application in the area of cell phones
(D) their good properties in applications

(3) Which of the following is TRUE according to the text? _____.

(A) More than half of the glass application is flat glass
(B) High-temperature ceramic superconductors form the third largest sector of the ceramics market
(C) High-temperature ceramic superconductors, engineering ceramics and whiteware all belong to the category of advanced ceramics
(D) The steel industry consume more than 50% of refractories which account for about 7% of the total market for ceramics

(4) All of the following are key issues to solve in order to expand the use of structural ceramics EXCEPT _____.

(A) reducing cost of the final product
(B) improving reliability
(C) improving high-temperature mechanical strength
(D) improving reproducibility
(5) Which of the following is NOT the challenge of electronic ceramics for the future? _____.
(A) integrating with existing semiconductor technology
(B) improving reproducibility
(C) improving processing
(D) enhancing compatibility with other materials
(6) All of the following issues will determine future progress of bioceramics EXCEPT _____.
(A) reducing cost of the final product
(B) matching mechanical properties to human tissues
(C) increasing reliability
(D) improving processing methods
(7) Compatible property is important in all of the following materials except for _____.

(A) structural ceramics   (B) electronic ceramics
(C) bioceramics   (D) composites

Unit 10   Relationship between Microstructure, Processing, and Applications

Relationship between Microstructure, Processing, and Applications

The field of materials science and engineering is often defined by the interrelationship between four topics—synthesis and processing, structure and composition, properties, and performance. To understand the behavior and properties of any material, it is essential to understand its structure. Structure can be considered on several levels, all of which influence final behavior. At the finest level is the electron configuration, which affects properties such as color, electrical conductivity, and magnetic behavior.

The arrangement of electrons in an atom influences how it will bond to another atom and this, in turn, impacts the crystal structure. The arrangement of the atoms or ions in the material also needs to be considered. Crystalline ceramics have a very regular atomic arrangement whereas in noncrystalline or amorphous ceramics (e.g., oxide glasses) there is no long-range order, although locally we may identify similar polyhedra. Such materials often behave differently relative to their crystalline counterparts. Not only perfect lattices and ideal structures have to be considered but also the presence of structural defects that are unavoidable in all materials, even the amorphous ones. Examples of such defects include impurity atoms and dislocations.

Polycrystalline ceramics have a structure consisting of many grains. The size, shape, and orientation of the grains play a key role in many of the macroscopic properties of these materials, for example, mechanical strength. In most ceramics, more than one phase is present, with each phase having its own structure, composition, and properties. Control of the type, size, distribution, and amount of these phases within the material provides a means to control properties. The microstructure of a ceramic is often a result of the way it was processed. For example, hotpressed ceramics often have very few pores. This may not be the case in sintered materials.

The interrelationship between the structure, processing, and properties will be evident throughout this text but are illustrated here by five examples.

1. The strength of polycrystalline ceramics depends on the grain size through the Hall-Petch equation. In general, as the grain size decreases the strength increases. The grain size is determined by the size of the initial powder particles and the way in which they were consolidated. The grain boundaries in a polycrystalline ceramic are also important. The strength then depends on whether or not the material is pure, contains a second phase or pores, or just contains glass at the grain boundaries. The relationship is not always obvious for nanoceramics.

2. Transparent or translucent ceramics require that we limit the scattering of light by pores and second-phase particles. Reduction in porosity may be achieved by hot pressing to ensure a high-density product. This approach has been used to make transparent PLZT ceramics for electrooptical applications such as the flash-blindness goggles.

3. Thermal conductivity of commercially available polycrystalline AlN is usually lower than that predicted by theory because of the presence of impurities, mainly oxygen, which scatter phonons. Adding rare earth or alkaline metal oxides (such as Y_2O_3 and CaO, respectively) can reduce the oxygen content by acting as a getter. These oxides are mixed in with the AlN powder before it is shaped. The second phase, formed between the oxide additive and the oxide coating on the AlN grains, segregates to triple points.

4. Soft ferrites such as $Mn_{1-\delta}Zn_\delta Fe_2O_4$ are used in a range of different devices, for example, as the yoke that moves the electron beam in a television tube. The permeability of soft ferrites is a function of grain size. Large defect-free grains are preferred because we need to have very mobile domain walls. Defects and grain boundaries pin the domain walls and make it more difficult to achieve saturation magnetization.

5. Alumina ceramics are used as electrical insulators because of their high electrical resistivity and low dielectric constant. For most applications pure alumina is not used. Instead we blend the alumina with silicates to reduce the sintering temperature. These materials are known as debased aluminas and contain a glassy silicate phase between alumina grains. Debased aluminas are generally more conductive (lower resistivity) than pure aluminas, and are used in spark plugs.

Safety

When working with any material, safety considerations should be uppermost. There are several important precautions to take when working with ceramics.

Toxicity of powders containing, for example, Pb or Cd or fluorides should be known. When shipping the material, the manufacturer supplies information on the hazards associated with their product. It is important to read this information and keep it accessible. Some standard resources that provide information about the toxicity of powders and the "acceptable" exposure levels are given in the References.

Small particles should not be inhaled. The effects have been well known, documented, and often ignored since the 1860s. Proper ventilation, improved cleanliness, and protective clothing have significantly reduced many of the industrial risks. Care should be taken when handling any powders (of both toxic and nontoxic materials). The most injurious response is believed to be when the particle size is $<1\mu m$; larger particles either do not remain suspended in the air sufficiently long to be inhaled or, if inhaled, cannot negotiate the tortuous passage of the upper respiratory tract. The toxicity and environmental impact of nanopowders have not been clearly addressed, but are the subject of various studies such as a recent report by the Royal Society (2004).

High temperatures are used in much of ceramic processing. The effects of high temperatures on the human body are obvious. What is not so obvious is how hot something actually is. Table 3.3 gives the color scale for temperature. From this tabulation you can see that an alumina tube at 400℃ will not show a change in color but it will still burn skin.

Table 3.3 The Color Scale of Temperature

Color	Corresponding T	Color	Corresponding T
Barely visible red	525℃	Orange	1100℃
Dark red	700℃	Orange-white	1200℃
Cherry red just beginning to appear	800℃	Dull white	1300℃
Clear red	900℃	Bright white	1400℃
Bright red, beginning orange	1000℃		

Organics are used as solvents and binders during processing. Traditionally, organic materials played little role in ceramic processing. Now they are widely used in many forms of processing. Again, manufacturers will provide safety data sheets on any product they ship. This information is important and should always be read carefully.

As a rule, the material safety data sheets (MSDS) should be readily accessible for all the materials you are using; many states require that they are kept in the laboratory.

(*Selected from Carter C. Barry, Norton M. Grant, Ceramic Materials: Science and Engineering, 2ed, Springer, 2013*)

New Words and Expressions

configuration *n.* 结构，布局，形态
polyhedra *n.* 多面体
impurity *n.* 不纯，杂质
sintered *v.* 烧结；*a.* 烧结的（熔结的，黏结的）

porosity　*n*. 多孔性，有孔性
electrooptical　*a*. 电光的
goggles　*n*. 护目镜，眼罩
rare earth　*n*. 稀土元素，稀土
getter　*n*. 吸气剂
segregate　*a*. 分离的，被隔离的；*v*. 分离，隔离，分凝
ferrites　*n*. 陶铁磁体
soft ferrites　软性铁氧体
yoke　*n*. 轭，轭状物
permeability　*n*. 渗透性，磁导率，渗透率
pin　*v*. 将……用针别住，钉住，压住
uppermost　*a*. 最高的，至上的；*adv*. 最初，首先
precaution　*n*. 注意事项，预防措施
inhale　*v*. 吸入
ventilation　*n*. 通风，换气
injurious　*a*. 有害的，伤害的

Notes

① At the finest level is the electron configuration, which affects properties such as color, electrical conductivity, and magnetic behavior. finest, 原意为"好的，出色的"，在这里的意思是"最精细的"。参考译文：能够对材料的颜色、导电性和磁性产生影响的电子形态是材料的最精细的水平。

② Crystalline ceramics have a very regular atomic arrangement whereas in noncrystalline or amorphous ceramics (e.g., oxide glasses) there is no long-range order, although locally we may identify similar polyhedra. long-range order, 长程有序性。参考译文：结晶陶瓷具有非常规则的原子排列，然而，这种长程有序性排列在非晶体和无定形陶瓷中却不存在，尽管在局部我们可以看到相似的多面体结构。

③ Thermal conductivity of commercially available polycrystalline AlN is usually lower than that predicted by theory because of the presence of impurities, mainly oxygen, which scatter phonons. that 指代 "thermal conductivity"，which 引导定语从句修饰 "oxygen"。参考译文：因为杂质的存在，主要是能够散播声子的氧气的存在，导致商业上应用的多晶体AlN的热导性通常比预计的理论值要低。

④ Some standard resources that provide information about the toxicity of powders and the "acceptable" exposure levels are given in the References. 本句结构为 "Some standard resources are given in the References"，that 引导一个定语从句。

⑤ The toxicity and environmental impact of nanopowders have not been clearly addressed, but are the subject of various studies such as a recent report by the Royal Society (2004). but 后省略主语 "the toxicity and environmental impact of nanopowders"，address，本义为"发表演说，讨论"，在文中为"提出"的意思。参考译文：目前纳米粉体的毒性与环境影响还没有被明确提出，但它却是许多研究的主题，2004年英国皇家科学院的研究报告就是其中一例。

Exercises

1. Question for discussion

(1) Which interrelationship is the field of materials science and engineering often defined by?

(2) What are the differences between crystalline ceramics and noncrystalline or amorphous ceramics?

(3) What is the grain size determined by?

(4) Why alumina ceramics can be used as electrical insulators?

(5) Please enumerate some important precautions when working with ceramics.

2. Translate the following into Chinese

the electron configuration   polycrystalline ceramics
the oxygen content   the oxide coating
the electron beam   electrical insulators
the industrial risks   upper respiratory tract

- The field of materials science and engineering is often defined by the interrelationship between four topics—synthesis and processing, structure and composition, properties, and performance.

- Not only perfect lattices and ideal structures have to be considered but also the presence of structural defects that are unavoidable in all materials, even the amorphous ones.

- Reduction in porosity may be achieved by hot pressing to ensure a high-density product.

- When shipping the material, the manufacturer supplies information on the hazards associated with their product.

3. Translate the following into English

结晶陶瓷   晶粒边界
碱性金属氧化物   氧化物添加剂
三相点   饱和磁化强度
电视显像管   颜色标度

- 想要了解任一材料的行为与性能，有必要先了解它的结构。
- 晶粒尺寸是由初始粉体颗粒的大小和它们的凝结方式所决定的。
- 透明与半透明陶瓷需要限制由气孔和二相粒子引起的光的散射。
- 因为氧化铝陶瓷具有高电阻率和低介电常数，所以它可以用作电的绝缘体。

4. Reading comprehension

(1) We can learn from the first paragraph that _____ .

(A) the field of materials science and engineering is often defined by the interrelationship between structure and processing

(B) it is essential to understand the behavior and properties of any material to understand its structure

(C) the electron configuration can affect color, electrical conductivity, and magnetic behavior properties of materials

(D) the arrangement of electrons in an atom can impacts its crystal structure

(2) According to the description of the crystalline ceramics, which of the following is NOT true? _____ .

(A) Crystalline ceramics have a very regular atomic arrangement whereas in noncrystalline or amorphous ceramics there is no long-range order

(B) Crystalline ceramics have perfect lattices and ideal structures without any structural defects

(C) The arrangement of electrons in an atom influences how it will bond to another atom

(D) The size, shape, and orientation of the grains play a key role in many of the macroscopic properties of polycrystalline ceramics

(3) All of the following are what the strength of polycrystalline ceramics depends on EXCEPT _____ .

(A) the grain size through the Hall-Petch equation

(B) the size of the initial powder particles and the way in which they were consolidated

(C) whether or not the material is pure

(D) whether or not the material contains a second phase or pores, or just contains glass at the grain boundaries

(4) According to the fifth example in this text, alumina ceramics are used as electrical insulators because of _____ .

(A) their high electrical resistivity and low dielectric constant

(B) their high electrical resistivity and high dielectric constant

(C) their low electrical resistivity and low dielectric constant

(D) their low electrical resistivity and high dielectric constant

(5) We can learn from the important safety precautions when working with any material that _____ .

(A) people will have the most injurious response when the particle size is $>1\mu m$

(B) larger particles can remain suspended in the air sufficiently long

(C) the toxicity and environmental impact of nanopowders have been clearly addressed by the Royal Society

(D) it is important to read the information of toxicity of powders and keep it accessible when shipping the material

Reading Material

Advanced Ceramics

The topic of advanced ceramics is exciting as technologies developed in research laboratories and universities become adopted by industry. This market segment shows continued growth offering good employment opportunities for MS&E graduates. In advanced materials, three areas are emerging: ceramic nanopowders, high-temperature superconductors, and ceramic-matrix composites.

Ceramic Nanopowders

Nanotechnology is a "hot" research topic. The field is trendy, popular, and high-tech. Although silica and iron oxide nanoparticles have a commercial history spanning half a century or more it is really only within the last 15~20 years that technologies have been developed for producing ultrapure nanosized powders of a range of ceramics. The global nanoparticle market, which is dominated by ceramics, is now around $1 billion. Current applications for ceramic nanoparticles are:

Electronic, magnetic, and optoelectronic applications account for 70%. The largest single use is slurries of abrasive silica particles (50~70 nm) for chemical/mechanical polishing (CMP).

Biomedical, pharmaceutical, and cosmetic applications account for 18%. Sunscreens use nanosized powders of TiO_2 or ZnO.

Energy, catalytic, and structural applications account for the remaining 12%. Uses include catalyst supports (e.g., for low-temperature H_2 production), ceramic membranes, fuel cells, and scratch-resistant coatings.

A recent example of the potential of nanosized ceramic powders in medicine is the demonstration that 5 nm cerium oxide (CeO_2) nanoparticles can prolong the life of brain cells. Usually these cells live for around 25 days in the laboratory, but after a low dose of the nanoparticles they have been shown to survive and function normally for 6 months. The hope is that this approach might one day be used to treat age-related disorders such as Alzheimer's disease. It was also found that the treated cells had increased protection against damage from ultraviolet (UV) radiation. The implication is that the nanoparticles mop up free radicals—reactive molecules that damage cells and are known to be involved in aging and inflammation.

An energy-related application undergoing extensive testing is the use of 10 nm CeO_2 particles as additives to diesel fuel. The CeO_2 nanoparticles catalyze the combustion of the fuel. The claim is that they release oxygen to oxidize carbon monoxide and hydrocarbon gases to carbon dioxide, and also reduce quantities of harmful nitrogen oxides. The result is a cleaner burning fuel that converts more fuel to carbon dioxide, produces less noxious exhaust, and deposits less carbon on the engine walls.

The market for nanosized powders is much smaller than for conventional ceramic powders, but the cost per kilogram is much higher. Despite progress in scaling up production and reducing costs, nanosized powders remain relatively expensive (often 100 times more than conventional ceramic powders).

There are growing concerns about the impact of nanoparticles on human health and the environment. Inhaling fine quartz particles is known to cause silicosis, a potentially fatal scarring of delicate lung tissue. Fine particles shed from hip and knee replacements as they wear cause inflammation of the surrounding tissues and may result in the implant having to be replaced. Studies in which carbon nanotubes were placed directly into the lungs of mice showed that there was significant damage to the lung tissue. Because many of the potential applications for nanoparticles are in the human body it is important to determine their safety. It is also necessary to evaluate their environmental impact.

High-Temperature Superconductors

One of the benefits of increasing T_c above 77K is that liquid nitrogen rather than liquid helium can be used as the coolant. Liquid nitrogen is both cheaper and more readily available than liquid helium. You will find the cost of liquid nitrogen described as either less than milk or less than cheap beer! The cost of liquid helium is often likened to fine champagne.

Soon after the discovery of high-temperature superconductors (HTSC) and, in particular, the YBCO compound there were grand predictions that these materials would revolutionize areas such as a high-speed transportation and power transmission. The applications to date have been a little more modest. Magnetic levitation (maglev) for high-speed transportation has not been achieved with HTSC, but continues to a limited extent with the use of low-temperature materials. The other major application proposed for HTSC was in power transmission. However, due to the high cost and impracticality of cooling miles of superconducting wire, this has happened only with short "test runs." In May 2001 about 150,000 residents of Copenhagen, Denmark began receiving their electricity through superconducting cables. The superconductor chosen for this application was BSCCO in the form of a tape wrapped around a flexible duct that carries the liquid N_2. The remainder of the cable consists of thermal and electrical insulation. In November 2001 commercial power was delivered to about 30,000 homes in Detroit, Michigan using a similar approach.

One area in which HTSC is poised to make a significant impact is in filters that improve network performance between wireless (cellular) devices and cell sites. Superconductivity avoids a typical trade-off by filtering out interference from adjacent signal bands without hindering the base station's ability to pick up weak signals. This market could be a $10 billion business by 2011.

According to estimates by the European Conectus consortium the worldwide market for HTSC products is projected to grow to about $5 billion by 2010 and to almost $40 billion by 2020.

Ceramic-Matrix Composites

Ceramic-matrix composites (CMCs) are being developed to provide an alternative to single-phase ceramic components because of the possibility of designing with higher toughness. The most important CMCs will probably be those with continuous fiber reinforcement. Ceramic-matrix composites are at a relatively early stage of development compared to polymer-matrix composites (PMCs) and metal-matrix composites (MMCs) and significant research is needed if they are to meet their full potential.

Cost: Nonoxide fibers cost thousands of dollars per kilogram. Oxide fibers, even those that have been commercially available for years, sell for hundreds of dollars per kilogram. The main reason is that production volumes are small. Most fiber-reinforced CMCs utilize a layer between the fiber and matrix to optimize mechanical properties. The methods used for depositing this layer tend to be expensive and difficult to scale up for production.

Understanding failure modes: We generally want a weak fiber-matrix interface in CMCs. A propagating crack is deflected around the fibers and does not propagate through the fibers. This situation is opposite to that in PMCs where we often want a strong interface so that the load is transferred to the stronger fibers.

Increase temperature stability: Fiber-reinforced CMCs have been demonstrated to survive in the severe environment of a gas turbine engine for 2500 hours at temperatures up to 1200°C. The use of environmental barrier coatings (EBCs) such as oxide layers on SiC appears to help extend durability, but more research is needed to determine whether they present a long-term solution.

Scale-up: The high price of finished components made from fiber-reinforced CMCs is a major limitation. Reducing materials costs and increasing production volume would reduce costs substantially. One of the requirements for large-scale manufacturing of CMCs is the development of quick and inexpensive quality control procedures that can be used during production. The main processing defects are voids, density variations, and cracks. X-ray computed tomography (CT) is a powerful technique for this type of investigation and high-resolution detectors can detect defects and resolve features as small as 5 μm. But the technique remains expensive and slow and is not suitable at the present time for in-line process control.

Ceramics as the Enabling Materials

As you have realized from the discussion of capacitors, glass, data storage, etc., ceramic materials are often the critical part of a program or product even if the consumer never sees them.

Sapphire single crystals are grown for use in substrates, as windows, as IR-transparent domes, in jewel bearings, and as the "glass" on your best watch, but there are other applications of these and other single crystals that most of us never see. Large sapphire crystals are being tested for use in the LIGO Fabry-Perot interferometer. The aim of LIGO (laser interferometer gravitational wave observatory) is to study astrophysical gravitational waves. There are two LIGO sites, one in eastern Washington and one in Louisiana. Sapphire should reduce the thermal noise compared to the fused silica that was initially used. The LIGO requires the crystals to be 35 cm in diameter and 12 cm long and uses 5N-pure alumina powder. The factors studied in assessing the sapphire mirrors for future generations of LIGO include all aspects of the influence of temperature on mechanical properties and the results are compared with the current fused-silica mirrors. In either case, the ceramic is the enabling material and is the topic of very focused research.

(Selected from Carter C. Barry, Norton M. Grant, *Ceramic Materials*: *Science and Engineering*, 2ed, Springer, 2013)

New Words and Expressions

ceramic-matrix composites 陶瓷基复合材料
ultrapure *a*. 超高纯的
slurry *n*. 浆体，研磨液
abrasive *n*. 研磨剂
chemical/mechanical polishing 化学机械抛光
pharmaceutical *a*. 药物的（医药的）
Alzheimer 老年痴呆症，阿兹海默氏症
ultraviolet *a*. 紫外线的
free radicals 自由基
inflammation *n*. 发炎，红肿，炎症
diesel *n*. 柴油机，内燃机
combustion *n*. 燃烧
silicosis *n*. 矽肺病（硅肺）
magnetic levitation 磁悬浮
coolant *n*. 冷冻剂
consortium *n*. 联合，合伙
optimize *v*. 优化，使……完善
propagate *v*. 传播，传送
tomography *n*. 断层摄影术
resolution *n*. 分辨率，清晰度
capacitor *n*. 电容器
interferometer *n*. 干涉计，干涉仪

Notes

① The topic of advanced ceramics is exciting as technologies developed in research laboratories and universities become adopted by industry. 参考译文：当研究型实验室与大学所发明的技术实际应用到工业中时，先进陶瓷就逐渐变成一个热门话题。

② Although silica and iron oxide nanoparticles have a commercial history spanning half a century or more it is really only within the last 15～20 years that technologies have been developed for producing ultrapure nanosized powders of a range of ceramics. it is … that … 为一个强调句，强调时间。参考译文：尽管二氧化硅和铁氧化物纳米粒子有跨越半个多世纪的商业史，但在陶瓷中生产超高纯度纳米级粉体的技术是在最近的 15 到 20 年才发展起来。

③ The implication is that the nanoparticles mop up free radicals—reactive molecules that damage cells and are known to be involved in aging and inflammation. 第一个"that"引导一个表语从

句，第二个"that"引导一个定语从句。free radicals—reactive molecules，自由基活性分子。参考译文：纳米微粒可以将损坏细胞并且导致老化和炎症的自由基活性分子扫除。

④ The claim is that they release oxygen to oxidize carbon monoxide and hydrocarbon gases to carbon dioxide, and also reduce quantities of harmful nitrogen oxides. hydrocarbon，碳氢化合物。that 引导一个表语从句，they 指代"the combustion of the fuel"。参考译文：燃料燃烧释放出的氧气将一氧化碳和碳氢化合物气体氧化成二氧化碳，并且也减少了有害氮氧化物的释放量。

⑤ Fine particles shed from hip and knee replacements as they wear cause inflammation of the surrounding tissues and may result in the implant having to be replaced. 本句结构"Fine particles cause…and may result in…"。参考译文：由于移植的髋膝关节的磨损而脱落的微细颗粒可以导致周围组织的发炎，并且可能导致需要新的移植体来代替原来的移植关节。

⑥ Studies in which carbon nanotubes were placed directly into the lungs of mice showed that there was significant damage to the lung tissue. "in which carbon nanotubes were placed directly into the lungs of mice"为"study"的同位语。参考译文：将碳纳米管直接放入老鼠肺部的研究表明它对肺部组织会产生极大的损害。

Reading Comprehension

(1) Current applications for ceramic nanoparticles are clearly dominated by _____ according to the text.

(A) electronic, magnetic, and optoelectronic applications

(B) biomedical, pharmaceutical, and cosmetic applications

(C) energy, catalytic, and structural applications

(D) high-temperature superconductor applications

(2) Why the treated cells have increased protection against damage from ultraviolet radiation? _____.

(A) 5 nm cerium oxide nanoparticles can prolong the life of brain cells

(B) The nanoparticles mop up free radicals—reactive molecules that damage cells and are known to be involved in aging and inflammation

(C) The cells which are after a low dose of the nanoparticles live longer than that of usual cells

(D) Nanosized ceramic powders in medicine might one day be used to treat age-related disorders such as Alzheimer's disease

(3) Which of the following is NOT an advantage of the use of 10nm CeO_2 particles as additives to diesel fuel? _____.

(A) Reducing quantities of harmful nitrogen oxides

(B) Producing less noxious exhaust

(C) Depositing less carbon on the engine walls

(D) Converting more fuel to carbon monoxide

(4) According to the application of High-Temperature Superconductors, which of the

following is NOT true? _____ .

 (A) The use of HTSC in power transmission has happened only with short "test runs" due to the high cost and impracticality of cooling miles of superconducting wire

 (B) Magnetic levitation for high-speed transportation has been achieved with HTSC, although a majority of them continues to a limited extent with the use of low-temperature materials

 (C) Superconductivity avoids a typical trade-off by filtering out interference from adjacent signal bands without hindering the base station's ability to pick up weak signals

 (D) The worldwide market for HTSC products is projected to grow to about $5 billion by 2010 and to almost $40 billion by 2020

(5) Ceramic-matrix composites are being developed to provide an alternative to single-phase ceramic components because of _____ .

 (A) their higher toughness   (B) their higher electrical conductivity

 (C) their higher thermal conductivity   (D) their higher hardness

(6) Which of the following are at a relatively early stage of development? _____ .

 (A) Polymer-matrix composites   (B) Metal-matrix composites

 (C) Ceramic-matrix composites   (D) Fiber-matrix composites

Unit 11 Bioceramics (Part I)

 Biomaterial is a non-viable material used in a medical device intended to interact with biological systems. The field of bioceramics is relatively new; it did not exist until the 1970s. However, many bioceramics are not new materials. One of the most important is Al_2O_3, a constituent of many traditional ceramic products.

 If a nearly inert material is implanted into the body it initiates a protective response that leads to encapsulation by a non adherent fibrous coating about $1\mu m$ thick. Over time this leads to complete isolation of the implant. A similar response occurs when metals and polymers are implanted. In the case of bioactive ceramics a bond forms across the implant-tissue interface that mimics the bodies natural repair process. Bioactive ceramics such as HA can be used in bulk form or as part of a composite or as a coating. Resorbable bioceramics, such as tricalcium phosphate (TCP), actually dissolve in the body and are replaced by the surrounding tissue. It is an important requirement, of course, that the dissolution products are not toxic. As in the case of HA, TCP is often used as a coating rather than in bulk form. It is also used in powder form, e. g., for filling space in bone.

 There are a number of clinical uses of bioceramics. The uses go from head to toe and include repairs to bones, joints, and teeth. These repairs become necessary when the existing part becomes diseased, damaged, or just simply wears out. There are many other applications of bioceramics including pyrolytic carbon coatings for heart valves and special radioactive glass formulations for the treatment of certain tumors.

Advantages and Disadvantages of Ceramics

In the selection of a material for a particular application we always have a choice. Materials selection is a critical part of any component design process and is especially important for implants and other medical devices.

The three main classes of material from which we can select for a load-bearing application are metals, polymers, and ceramics. The main advantage of ceramics over other implant materials is their biocompatibility: some are inert in the physiological environment while others have a controlled reaction in the body. The main disadvantages of most bioceramics are low toughness (which can affect reliability), and high E (which can lead to stress shielding).

One of the main ways of increasing the toughness of ceramics is to form a composite. The ceramic may be the reinforcement phase, the matrix, or both. An example of a polymer-matrix composite (PMC) reinforced with a bioceramic is polyethylene (PE) reinforced with HA particles. The toughness of the composite is greater than that of HA and, E is more closely matched to that of bone. Bioceramics are also used as coatings on metal substrates. An example is a bioactive glass coating on stainless steel, which utilizes the strength and toughness of steel and the surface-active properties of the glass.

Ceramic Implants

The requirements for a ceramic implant depend on what its role in the body will be. For example, the requirements for a total hip prosthesis (THP) will be different from those for a middle ear implant. However, there are two basic criteria: (1) The ceramic should be compatible with the physiological environment; (2) Its mechanical properties should match those of the tissue being replaced.

Most bioceramic implants are in contact with bone. Bone is a living material composed of cells and a blood supply encased in a strong composite structure. The composite consists of collagen, which is flexible and very tough, and crystals of an apatite of calcium and phosphate, resembling calcium hydroxyapatite; we will proceed as if it is HA. It is the HA component that gives bone its hardness. The acicular apatite crystals are 20~40 nm in length and 1.5~3 nm wide in the collagen fiber matrix. Two of the various types of bone that are of most concern in the use of bioceramics are cancellous (spongy bone) and cortical (compact bone).

Cancellous bone is less dense than cortical bone. Every bone of the skeleton has a dense outer layer of compact bone covering the spongy bone, which is in the form of a honeycomb of small needle-like or flat pieces called trabeculae. Because of its lower density, cancellous bone has a lower E and higher strain-to-failure ratio than cortical bone. Both types of bone have higher E than soft connective tissues, such as tendons and ligaments. The difference in E between the various types of connective tissues ensures a smooth gradient in mechanical stress across a bone, between bones, and between muscles and bones.

The mechanical properties of the implant are clearly very important. If the implant has a much higher E than the bone it is replacing then a problem called stress shielding can occur. Stress shielding weakens bone in the region at which the applied load is lowest or is in compression. (Bone must be loaded in tension to remain healthy.) Bone that is unloaded or is loaded in compression will undergo a biological change that leads to resorption. Eliminating stress shielding, by reducing E, is one of the primary motivations for the development of bioceramic composites.

Alumina and Zirconia

Al_2O and ZrO_2 are two nearly inert bioceramics. They undergo little or no chemical change during long-term exposure to body fluids. High-density, high-purity ($>$99.5%) alumina is used in a number of implants, particularly as load-bearing hip prostheses and dental implants. By 2006, $>10^6$ hip prostheses used an alumina ball for the femoral-head component.

Although some alumina dental implants are made from single crystals, most alumina implants are very fine-grained polycrystalline Al_2O_3. These are usually made by pressing followed by sintering at temperatures in the range of 1600~1800℃. A small amount of MgO ($<$0.5%) is added, which acts as a grain growth inhibitor and allows a high-density product to be achieved by sintering without pressure.

An important requirement for any implant material is that it should outlast the patient. Because of the probabilistic nature of failure in ceramics it is not possible to provide specific and definite lifetime predictions for each individual implant. Studies show, as you might expect, that increased loads and longer times increase the probability of failure. Results from aging and fatigue studies show that it is essential that Al_2O_3 implants be produced with the highest possible standards of quality assurance, especially if they are to be used as orthopedic prostheses in younger patients.

Although alumina ceramics combine excellent biocompatibility and outstanding wear resistance they have only moderate flexural strength and low toughness. This limits the diameter of most alumina femoral head prostheses to 32mm. Zirconia ceramics have higher fracture toughness, higher flexural strength, and lower E than alumina ceramics. However, there are some concerns with ZrO_2: (1) There is a slight decrease in flexural strength and toughness of zirconia ceramics exposed to bodily fluids. The reason is associated with the martensitic transformation from the tetragonal to the monoclinic phase. A similar transformation has been observed to occur in aqueous environments. (2) The wear resistance of zirconia is inferior to that of alumina. In ceramic/ceramic combinations the wear rate of zirconia can be significantly higher than that of alumina. In combination with ultrahigh-molecular weight polyethylene (UHMWPE) excessive wear of the polymer occurs. (3) Zirconia may contain low concentrations of long half life radioactive elements such as Th and U, which are difficult and expensive to separate out. The main concern is that they emit α-particles (He nuclei) that can destroy both soft and hard tissue. Although the activity is small, there are questions concerning the long-term effect of α radiation emission from zirconia ceramics.

(Selected from Carter C. Barry, Norton M. Grant, Ceramic Materials:
Science and Engineering, 2ed, Springer, 2013)

New Words and Expressions

encapsulation *n.* 封装，封装性，密封
mimic *v.* 模仿
HA 透明质酸
tumor *n.* 肿块，肿瘤
pyrolytic *a.* 热解的（高温分解的）
physiological *a.* 生理的，生理学的
encase *v.* 包围，包住，包裹
collagen *n.* 胶原，骨胶原
apatite *n.* 磷灰石
calcium hydroxyapatite 羟基磷灰石
acicular *a.* 针状的
cancellous *a.* 多孔的，网眼状的，网状骨质的
cortical *a.* 皮层的，皮质的，有关脑皮层的
skeleton *n.* 骨架，骨骼
trabeculae *n.* 骨小梁
tendon *n.* 腱，肌腱
ligaments *n.* 韧带
body fluids 体液
femoral-head 股骨头
inhibitor *n.* 抑止剂
probabilistic *n.* 概率的，概率性的
orthopedic *a.* 整形外科的
tetragonal *a.* 四角形的，正方晶系的，四方的
monoclinic *a.* 单斜的

Notes

① If a nearly inert material is implanted into the body it initiates a protective response that leads to encapsulation by a non adherent fibrous coating about 1μm thick. 参考译文：如果一种接近惰性的材料被植入体内将会引起一种保护性反应，这种反应可引起非黏着性纤维层的包裹，厚度大约 1μm。

② An example is a bioactive glass coating on stainless steel, which utilizes the strength and toughness of steel and the surface-active properties of the glass. bioactive glass coating，生物活性玻璃涂层；stainless steel，不锈钢；which 引导一个定语从句。参考译文：不锈钢生物活性玻璃涂层就是一个例子，它主要利用钢的强度和韧性以及玻璃的表面活性特征。

③ The composite consists of collagen, which is flexible and very tough, and crystals of an apatite of calcium and phosphate, resembling calcium hydroxyapatite. which 引导一个定语从句修饰"collagen"。参考译文：这种复合物是由非常有弹性以及韧性的骨胶原和与钙羟基磷灰石极为相似的钙磷灰石晶体组成的。

④ The difference in E between the various types of connective tissues ensures a smooth gradient in mechanical stress across a bone, between bones, and between muscles and bones. gradient, 梯度；mechanical stress, 机械应力。参考译文：不同种类的连接组织其弹性模量不同，这种不同能够保证在骨、骨与骨之间以及肌肉与骨之间存在一个机械应力光滑梯度。

⑤ Studies show, as you might expect, that increased loads and longer times increase the probability of failure. that 引导一个宾语从句。参考译文：研究表明，可能像你期待的一样，负荷的增加以及时间的延长会增加失效的概率。

⑥ Results from aging and fatigue studies show that it is essential that Al_2O_3 implants be produced with the highest possible standards of quality assurance, especially if they are to be used as orthopedic prostheses in younger patients. 第一个 that 引导一个宾语从句，第二个 that 引导一个主语从句，作宾语从句的主语。参考译文：老化与疲劳的研究结果表明，Al_2O_3 植入物要具有可能最高标准的质量保障，尤其是它们用于年轻患者的矫正假肢上。

Exercises

1. Question for discussion
（1）Which three classes of materials can we select for a load-bearing application?
（2）What is the main advantage of ceramics over other implant materials? What are the main disadvantages of most bioceramics?
（3）What are the basic criteria for a ceramic implant?
（4）What are the differences between cancellous bone and cortical bone?
（5）Why is it not possible to provide specific and definite lifetime predictions for each individual implant?
（6）Briefly state the differences between alumina ceramics and zirconia ceramics.

2. Translate the following into Chinese
protective response　　　　　　　bioactive ceramics
pyrolytic carbon coatings　　　　　the reinforcement phase
a grain growth inhibitor　　　　　ultrahigh-molecular weight polyethylene

• Materials selection is a critical part of any component design process and is especially important for implants and other medical devices.

• The three main classes of material from which we can select for a load-bearing application are metals, polymers, and ceramics.

• High-density, high-purity （>99.5%) alumina is used in a number of implants, particularly as load-bearing hip prostheses and dental implants.

• In ceramic/ceramic combinations the wear rate of zirconia can be significantly higher than that of alumina.

3. Translate the following into English
控制反应　　　　　　　　　　　应力屏蔽
全髋关节置换术　　　　　　　　断裂应变率
断裂应变率　　　　　　　　　　机械应力
弯曲强度　　　　　　　　　　　马氏体相变

• 生物材料是应用到医疗器械中并与生物系统发生相互作用的一种非活性材料。

- 当现有的机体部分发生病变、损坏或只是简单的磨损时,这些修复就会变得很有必要。
- 因为骨松质的密度低,所以它的弹性模量比骨皮质低,断裂应变率比骨皮质高。
- 利用降低弹性模量的方法来排除应力屏蔽是生物陶瓷复合材料发展的一个主要目的。
- 这里有许多关于氧化锆陶瓷 α 辐射排放的长期效应问题,尽管这种作用很小。

4. Reading comprehension

(1) We can learn from the second paragraph that _____.
(A) a protective response will lead to encapsulation by a adherent fibrous coating
(B) a nearly inert material implanted into the bodycan lead to complete isolation of the implant
(C) a protective response also occurs when metals and polymers are implanted
(D) the dissolution products of tricalcium phosphate are noxious in the body

(2) The main advantage of ceramics over other implant materials is _____ according to the text.
(A) high toughness   (B) biocompatibility
(C) high stress shielding (D) low toughness

(3) which component gives bone its hardness? _____
(A) the collagen   (B) the acicular apatite crystals
(C) the HA   (D) the calcium hydroxyapatite

(4) All of the following are the characteristics of cancellous bone EXCEPT _____.
(A) having lower density than cortical bone
(B) having a lower E than cortical bone
(C) having higher strain-to-failure ratio than cortical bone
(D) having a lower E than tendons and ligaments

(5) According to the last paragraph, which of the following is NOT true? _____.
(A) Zirconia ceramics have higher fracture toughness, higher flexural strength, and lower E than alumina ceramics
(B) A slight decrease in flexural strength and toughness of zirconia ceramics only occurs in bodily fluids
(C) In ceramic combinations the wear rate of zirconia can be significantly higher than that of alumina
(D) Long half-life radioactive elements which exist in Zirconia are difficult and expensive to separate out

Reading Material

Bioceramics (Part II)

Bioactive Glasses

Bioactive materials form an interfacial bond with surrounding tissue. The first and most thoroughly studied bioactive glass is known as Bioglass 45S5 and was developed at the University of Florida. Bioglass 45S5 is a multicomponent oxide glass with the following composition (in wt%): 45% SiO_2, 24.5% Na_2O, 24.4% CaO, and 6% P_2O_5.

The majority of bioactive glasses are based on the same four components and all current bioactive glasses are silicates. Bioactive glasses have a random, two-dimensional sheet-like structure with a low density. This is a result of the relatively low SiO_2 content. Bioglass is mechanically weak and has low fracture toughness. Both these properties are related to the glass structure.

Bioactive glasses can readily be made using the processes developed for other silicate glasses. The constituent oxides, or compounds that can be decomposed to oxides, are mixed in the right proportions and melted at high temperatures to produce a homogeneous melt. On cooling a glass is produced. Because bioactive glasses are going to be used inside the body it is necessary to use high-purity starting materials and often the melting is performed in Pt or Pt alloy crucibles to minimize contamination.

Bioactive glasses have certain properties that are relevant to their application in the body.

Advantages: There is a relatively rapid surface reaction that leads to fast tissue bonding. There are five reaction stages on the glass side of the interface. The reaction rates and mechanisms at each of the five stages have been determined by Fourier transform infrared (FTIR) spectroscopy. Bonding to tissue requires a further series of reactions that are at present not as well defined. But the bonding process starts when biological moieties are adsorbed onto the SiO_2-hydroxycarbon-apatite layer. In addition, E is in the range $30 \sim 35$ GPa, close to that of cortical bone.

Disadvantages: They are mechanically weak. Tensile bending strengths are typically $40 \sim 60$ MPa. In addition, the fracture toughness is low.

As a result of this combination of properties bioactive glasses are not found in load-bearing applications, rather they are used as coatings on metals, in low-loaded or compressively loaded devices, in the form of powders, and in composites. The first successful use of Bioglass 45S5 was as a replacement for the ossicles (tiny bones) in the middle ear.

Cone-shaped plugs of bioactive glasses have been used in oral surgery to fill the defect in the jaw created when a tooth is removed. Bioactive glass implants have also been used to repair the one that supports the eye (the orbital socket).

In powder form, bioactive glasses have been used in the treatment of periodontal disease and for the treatment of patients with paralysis of one of the vocal cords. When mixed with autologous bone they have been used in maxillofacial reconstruction (i.e., mixed with natural bone to rebuild a jaw).

Glass-ceramics are produced by ceramming a glass: converting it to a largely crystalline form by heat treatment. Several glass-ceramic compositions are bioactive. Their behavior in the body is very similar to that of the bioactive glasses, i.e., they form a strong interfacial bond with tissue.

Bioceramics in Composites

The main reason for forming composites is to improve the mechanical properties, most often toughness, above that of the stand-alone ceramic. For bioceramic composites we often are trying to increase K_{IC} and decrease E.

The first bioceramic composite was a stainless-steel fiber/bioactive glass composite made of Bioglass 45S5 and AISI 316L stainless steel. The composite was made by first forming a preform of the discontinuous metal fibers, then impregnating it with molten glass, and finally heat treating the composite to develop the desired mechanical properties.

For effective stress transfer between the glass matrix and the reinforcing metal fibers when the composite is under load, there must be a strong glass-metal bond. This requires that the glass wet the metal surface during processing. Wetting is achieved by oxidizing the metal fibers before they are immersed in the glass. Chemical analysis across the glass-metal interface showed that there is Fe diffusion from the oxide into the glass and Si diffusion from the glass into the oxide. The composition gradient across the interface indicates chemical interaction between the two phases, which leads to improved adhesion.

Other current bioceramic composites of interest are Ti-fiber-reinforced bioactive glass, ZrO_2-reinforced A-W glass, TCP-reinforced PE, and HA-reinforced PE. Hydroxyapatite-reinforced PE is a good illustration of a composite that can have properties that are not available in a single material. These composites were developed as a bone replacement that would have a matched modulus, be ductile, and bioactive.

Bioceramic Coatings

Applying a glass or ceramic coating onto the surface of a substrate allows us to have the best of both worlds. We have the bulk properties of the substrate and the surface properties of the coating. There are three main reasons for applying a coating: (1) Protect the substrate against corrosion, (2) Make the implant biocompatible, and (3) Turn a nonbioactive surface into a bioactive one. There are four substrate-coating combinations: polycrystalline ceramic on ceramic, glass on ceramic, polycrystalline ceramic on metal, and glass on metal.

Bioceramic coatings are often used on metallic substrates in which the fracture toughness of the metal is combined with the ability of the coating to present a bioactive surface to the surrounding tissue. The use of a bioceramic coating on a metal implant can lead to earlier stabilization of the implant in the surrounding bone and extend the functional life of the prosthesis. Under the proper conditions a cementless prosthesis should remain functional longer than a cemented device in which stability is threatened by fracture of the bone cement.

Pyrolytic Carbon Heart Valves

Carbon is an important bioceramic. It combines outstanding biocompatibility and chemical inertness. Carbon exists in many forms, the most important form of carbon for biomedical applications is a type of pyrolytic graphite known as the low temperature isotropic form (LTI carbon).

Low-temperature isotropic carbon is an example of what are referred to as turbostratic carbons. These have a disordered structure based on graphite (and thus are also called turbostratic graphite). In turbostratic carbon the ABABA stacking sequence is disrupted through random rotations or displacement of the layers relative to each other. The individual LTI carbon crystallites are only ~10 nm in size and are arranged randomly in the bulk material. This microstructure leads to the material having isotropic mechanical and physical properties, unlike graphite in which the properties are highly anisotropic. The density and mechanical properties of LTI are influenced by the number of carbon vacancies in each of the layers and distortions within each plane. The densities range from 1400 kg/m^3 up to a theoretical maximum of 2200 kg/m^3.

High-density LTI carbons are the strongest bulk form of turbostratic carbon; their strengths can be increased further by adding Si. The material then consists of discrete submicrometer β-SiC particles randomly dispersed in a matrix of roughly spherical micrometer-sized subgrains of pyrolytic carbon; the carbon itself has a "subcrystalline" turbostratic structure, with a crystallite size typically <10 nm. This is analogous to the microstructure produced during precipitation hardening of metals.

Nanobioceramics

By 2012, there will be books on the uses of nanoparticles and there are already hundreds of research papers. There may also be books discussing the toxicity of these materials. The asbestos fibers linked to respiratory illness have widths <250nm; amphibole (red or blue asbestos) fibers are about 75~240 nm wide, therefore definitely counting as nanoparticles.

TiO_2 nanoparticles are used in sunscreen to protect the skin from UV radiation. The particles used for this application are typically 10~100 nm in diameter and block both UVA (320~400 nm) and UVB (290~320 nm) irradiation.

There is some concern that these nanoparticles (and those of ZnO) are so active that they might catalyze the breakdown of DNA, but they do not appear to penetrate the outer layers of the skin. The positive aspect of this is the potential for using these same TiO_2 nanoparticles for photo-killing of malignant cells—known as photodynamic therapy. TiO_2 and ZnO particles are actually being coated with silica so that the particle surface is more inert. (A use for core-shell nanoparticles.)

Dental Ceramics

The felspathic porcelains (porcelain's based on feldspar) are used as the veneer to "cap" the front of a tooth for cosmetic reasons; these veneers are ~500μm thick. Today, this material is mainly replaced by glass, although the name may not have changed. Leucite is added to modify the thermal expansion coefficient. Dicor is the glass-ceramic developed by Corning for construction of replacement teeth.

The tooth is cast as a glass using a lost-wax mold and then cerammed. Alumina has also been used to form the tooth, although porosity causes failure during "use". One way to improve this is to infiltrate the alumina with a lanthanum-containing glass (known commercially as In-Ceram).

(*Selected from Carter C. Barry, Norton M. Grant, Ceramic Materials:*
Science and Engineering, 2ed, Springer, 2013)

New Words and Expressions

fracture toughness　断裂韧性
homogeneous　*a.* 均质的
crucible　*n.* 坩埚
Fourier transform infrared spectroscopy　傅里叶变换红外光谱
moieties　*n.* 基团
ossicle　*n.* 听小骨
orbital　*a.* 眼窝的
periodontal　*a.* 牙周的
paralysis　*n.* 瘫痪
vocal cords　声带
autologous　*a.* 自体的，自身的
maxillofacial　*a.* 颌面部的
impregnate　*v.* 浸渍，饱和
composition gradient　成分梯度
pyrolytic　*a.* 热解的（高温分解的）
disrupt　*v.* 使……分裂，使……分散
rotation　*n.* 旋转
precipitation　*n.* 沉淀，凝结，析出
irradiation　*n.* 照射，辐射
malignant　*a.* 恶性的，有害的
photodynamic therapy　光动力学疗法
felspathic　*a.* 长石质的

Notes

① The constituent oxides, or compounds that can be decomposed to oxides, are mixed in the right proportions and melted at high temperatures to produce a homogeneous melt. that 引导的定语从句修饰 "compounds"。参考译文：这些氧化物或能够分解成氧化物的化合物组分以合理的配比混合在一起，然后在高温下熔化成一种均质熔体。

② Because bioactive glasses are going to be used inside the body it is necessary to use high-purity starting materials and often the melting is performed in Pt or Pt alloy crucibles to minimize contamination. 本句为 and 连接的两个并列句，because 引导一个原因状语从句。参考译文：因为要将生物活性玻璃用于体内，所以有必要采用高纯度原始材料，而且为减少污染物的生成，熔解过程通常在铂或铂合金坩埚中进行。

③ As a result of this combination of properties bioactive glasses are not found in load-bearing applications, rather they are used as coatings on metals, in low-loaded or compressively loaded devices, in the form of powders, and in composites. load-bearing, 承载; rather, 宁愿, 宁可。参考译文：综合生物活性玻璃的这些性能，由此可见，生物活性玻璃不能应用在受载条件下，而是在低负荷或压缩负荷装置中以粉体和复合材料的形式被用作金属涂层。

④ The composition gradient across the interface indicates chemical interaction between the two phases, which leads to improved adhesion. 参考译文：（玻璃与金属）界面的成分梯度特征表明在两相之间发生了相互化学作用，这种作用可以改善黏附性。

⑤ In turbostratic carbon the ABABA stacking sequence is disrupted through random rotations or displacement of the layers relative to each other. 参考译文：在乱层碳结构中，由于层与层之间的任意旋转或移动导致这种 ABABA 铺层顺序被破坏。

⑥ The density and mechanical properties of LTI are influenced by the number of carbon vacancies in each of the layers and distortions within each plane. the number of 后面连接两个并列的宾语 "carbon vacancies" 和 "distortions"。参考译文：各层的碳空穴数和各平面内的扭曲变形数可以影响 LTI 的密度和机械性能。

Reading Comprehension

(1) Which of the following is true according to the bioactive glasses? _____ .
(A) All current bioactive glasses are based on the same four components
(B) Bioactive glasses have a random, two-dimensional sheet-like structure with a high density
(C) The use of high-purity starting materials is necessary because bioactive glasses are going to be used inside the body
(D) The low fracture toughness is an advantage of bioactive glasses

(2) _____ have been used in oral surgery to fill the defect in the jaw created when a tooth is removed.
(A) Glass-ceramic compositions   (B) Cone-shaped plugs of bioactive glasses
(C) Bioactive glasses in powder form   (D) Bioceramic composites

(3) The main reason for forming bioceramic composites is to _____ .
(A) improve the mechanical properties   (B) increase K_{IC}
(C) decrease E (D) A, B and C

(4) All of the following are the main reasons for applying a coating EXCEPT _____ .
(A) protecting the substrate against corrosion
(B) making the implant biocompatible
(C) improving surface properties of the coating
(D) turning a nonbioactive surface into a bioactive one

(5) Which of the following is NOT true according to the low-temperature isotropic carbon? _____ .

(A) They have a disordered structure because of random rotations or displacement of the layers relative to each other
(B) This microstructure of LTI carbon crystallites leads to the material having isotropic mechanical and physical properties
(C) Strengths of the high-density LTI carbons can be decreased further by adding Si
(D) High-density LTI carbons are the strongest bulk form of turbostratic carbon

(6) One way to improve the porosity of alumina using which causes failure during "use" is _____ .
(A) to "cap" the front of a tooth using the felspathic porcelains
(B) to infiltrate the alumina with a lanthanum-containing glass
(C) to modify the thermal expansion coefficient
(D) to infiltrate the alumina with a actinium-containing glass

Part IV POLYMER

Unit 12 Introduction to Polymer

A polymer is a large molecule (macromolecule) composed of repeating structural units connected by covalent chemical bonds. The word is derived from the Greek words πολυ (poly), meaning "many"; and μέρος (meros), meaning "part".

The growth of polymers

Polymers are studied in the fields of polymer chemistry, polymer physics, and polymer science. Polymers, or materials composed of long molecular chains, are now well-accepted for a wide variety of applications, both structural and non-structural, and for mass-manufactured as well as one-off speciality products. The growth in their use has continued in the last two decades or more, despite the effects of several recessions in industrial activity (Figure 4.1). In the same period the demand for traditional materials like metals, ceramics and glasses has remained static or even fallen. Steel usage in the UK, for example, has fallen from about 14 million tonnes in the 1970s to about 12 million tonnes in the 1990s, while that of aluminium has stayed at about 600 000 tonnes. The growth in use of polymers is forecast to continue into the next millennium, with consumption approaching 4 million tonnes in the UK. In one of the most active areas, that of thermoplastic polymers, consumption is divided between packaging, building, and a wide range of other applications (Figure 4.2).

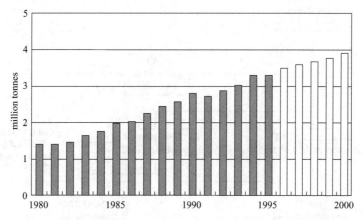

Figure 4.1 Growth in demand for polymers in the UK, 1980~2000.

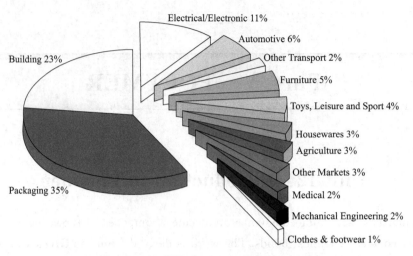

Figure 4.2 UK plastics applications 1995

Polymer types

Traditionally, the industry has produced two main types of synthetic polymer - plastics and rubbers (Figure 4.3). The distinction is that plastics are, by and large, rigid materials at service temperatures while rubbers are flexible, low modulus materials which exhibit long-range elasticity. Plastics are further subdivided into thermoplastics and thermosets, the latter type being materials where the long chains are linked together by crosslinks, a feature they share with conventional vulcanized rubbers. As Figure 3 shows, however, the distinction in terms of stiffness has become blurred by the development of thermoplastic elastomers (TPEs). Moreover, all polymers, irrespective of their nature, can be reinforced by a very wide range of fillers to produce composite materials.

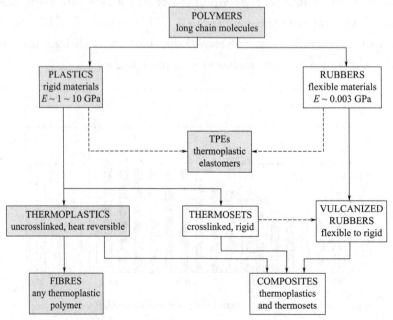

Figure 4.3 Classification of polymers by property

Another way of classifying polymers is in terms of their form or function, varying from additives to other bulk materials (e. g. viscosity modifiers in plaster), coatings to products (e. g. paints), film and membranes to fibres (e. g. textiles) and bulk products such as pipe, containers and mouldings (Figure 4. 4). Some of these materials are of course used as products in their own right, or manipulated further into finished products. This does not always happen, however, some polymers being a disposable intermediary in certain industrial processes. Thus photoresists are used to create the circuit patterns on semiconductor chips through controlled degradation, and are entirely absent in the final product.

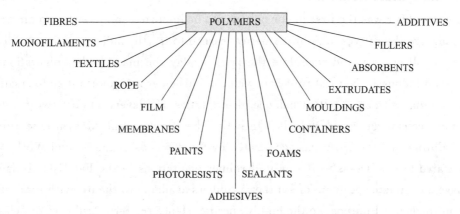

Figure 4. 4   Classification of polymers by design function

The first polymeric materials to be used were entirely natural in origin and required relatively little modification to be adapted for useful purposes. Such materials included wood from various species of tree, fibres for rope and textile fabrics, and amber adhesive for attaching stone and metal tools to wooden handles. Rubber was used by the early Americans for containers, shoes and balls. Ways of processing them to shape and improving their properties were developed during the Victorian era, but it was not until the growth of the organic chemical industry that the first synthetic polymers were made. The true molecular nature of materials like natural rubber and synthetics like Bakelite was not understood until about the 1920s when Hermann Staudinger recognized their chain-like structure. That period saw the growth of polymer chemistry, by which monomers could be synthesized and polymerized in a controlled way to give macromolecular materials. Some of today's major polymers were discovered in this period and were commercialized in the 1930s and 1940s. They included materials like polychloroprene (*Neoprene* rubber), nylon, polyester (*Terylene* or *Dacron*) and polyethylene (*Polythene*- note that trademarks for polymers are shown as proper names).

The raw materials for making the monomers had at first been based on coal tar derivatives but, with the rise of the petrochemical industry based on oil and natural gas, a much wider range of basic chemical building blocks became available. Fundamental advances in the understanding of catalysis led to the discovery of many new polymers in the post-1945 period—variations on simple polymers like polyethylene as well as entirely new stereo regular polymers like polypropylene. That progress has continued at an increasing rate up to the present. Novel polymers, like aromatic polyamides and polyimides which were discovered only in the 1960s, have been developed, while speciality, high temperature materials like polysulphones have penetrated new markets hitherto inaccessible to the traditional range of commercial polymers. The achievement has been a direct result of pioneering scientific research closely linked to development by industry.

Natural and synthetic rubbers

Natural rubber was the first major polymer to be imported and used for commercial purposes. Long ago the natives of South America learned to tap the indigenous *Hevea Brasiliensis* trees to collect, dry and coagulate the latex. Today the main rubber plantations are in Malaysia and Indonesia. Natural rubber is well established as an important and versatile engineering material with an excellent balance of properties. However, almost two-thirds of the rubber now consumed world-wide is synthetic. The development of synthetic rubbers in Western Europe and the USA was accelerated by the demands of the Second World War and the associated loss of access to the natural rubber plantations in the Far East. Today's engineers have a complete spectrum of synthetic rubbers available to them, with properties ranging from the general-purpose to the highly specific. Hence the term 'rubber' or 'elastomer' is more properly the generic name for a class of polymeric materials of widely varying properties. The properties and common uses of a selection of both general-purpose and speciality rubbers are shown in Table 4.1.

Table 4.1 General-purpose and speciality rubbers: properties and uses

Rubber		General properties	Typical uses
BR	butadiene (polybutadiene)	Special-purpose rubbers of density 0.93 Mg/m^3. Good low-temperature properties and abrasion resistance. High resilience (low damping) and therefore low heat build-up at ordinary temperature. Poor resistance to oils and hydrocarbons.	Resilient mounts, tyre sidewalls (blended with NR)
CR	Chloroprene (*Neoprene*)	Versatile special-purpose rubbers of density 1.20 Mg/m^3 and good mechanical and electrical properties. Very good resistance to ozone oxidation, heat and flame.	Car radiator hose, gaskets, seals, conveyor belts, bridge bearings
EPM, EPDM	ethylene-propylene copolymer and terpolymer	The copolymer (EPM) and terpolymers (EPDM) are general-purpose rubbers of density about 0.85 Mg/m^3 Good mechanical properties and resilience. Can accept very high loadings of oils and fillers. Very good resistance to ozone, oxidation, chemical, weathering and high and low temperatures.	Conveyor belts, hose, general goods
NR	natural rubber (*cis*-polyisoprene)	An excellent general-purpose rubber of density 0.93 Mg/m^3 High resistance to tearing and abrasion. High resilience at 20℃ and therefore low heat build-up under the action of dynamic stresses. Swells in mineral oils and degreasing solvents.	Tyres, suspension systems, bushes, bridge bearings

Rubber		General properties	Typical uses
NBR	nitrile (acrylonitrile-butadiene copolymer)	Special-purpose rubbers of density 1.0 Mg/m^3 and moderate mechanical properties. Poor cold resistance. Excellent resistance to swelling in hydrocarbons and alcohols. The greatest oil and alcohol resistance occurs in rubbers with a high acrylonitrile content.	Fuel lines and linings
SBR	styrene-butadiene copolymer	A good general-purpose rubber of density 0.94 Mg/m^3, competitive in properties with NR when reinforced with carbon black. Very good abrasion resistance. Swelling and adhesion properties similar to NR, ageing resistance better than NR.	Tyres, often in direct competition with NR

Thermoplastics and thermosets

As already stated, polymers including rigid plastics were first developed in the last century from natural precursors. The sealing wax employed by the Victorians, for example, was usually based on the natural polymer shellac, an exudate of the Indian lac insect. Shellac is an early natural thermoplastic - defined as a material which softens and hardens reversibly on heating and cooling. In theory these reversible physical changes will take place without a corresponding change in the chemical structure of the material. This is why scrap thermoplastic can be reused. In practice, some thermal and oxidative degradation occurs and recycling must be done only with an understanding of the effect that it has upon the properties of the final moulding.

Thermosets can be defined as those polymers which become irreversibly hard on heating or by addition of special chemicals. This hardening involves a chemical change (curing) and hence scrap thermoset cannot be recycled except as a filler material. The curing process invariably involves a chemical reaction which connects the linear molecules together to form a single macromolecule. These connections are known as crosslinks.

Scrap rubbers cannot be recycled easily, because of vulcanization which crosslinks the chains during moulding. It will be seen later that rubbers at the early stages of their processing can be considered to fit the definition of thermoplastics, but in their final moulded state they are properly defined as thermosets.

As with rubbers, the impetus for the development of new and better synthetic plastics followed supply and demand. Initially the demand was for cheaper substitutes for traditional materials, but today no plastic is cheap and some are extremely expensive with unique properties designed to satisfy the stringent requirements of sophisticated products. Table 4.2 lists the names and acronyms of the bulk-use commodity plastics and some of the more specialized and expensive materials, and comments on their important properties and uses.

Table 4.2 General-purpose and speciality plastics

	Plastic	Comments
PMMA	acrylic, poly(methyl methacrylate)	Thermoplastic. A transparent rigid polymer.
ABS	acrylonitrile-butadiene-styrene	Based on SAN resin modified with polybutadiene rubber.
EP	epoxy	Thermoset. Resins used for encapsulation, adhesives, surface coatings and high-strength fibre-reinforced composites.
GRP	glass-reinforced plastic (mainly polyester)	Thermoset. Reinforced with glass fibre in various forms, such as chopped strand mat (CSM) and woven rovings (WR). Used for pipes, tanks, boat hulls, etc. May be applied as SMC or DMC.
HDPE	high density polyethylene	Thermoplastic. Linear polyolefin widely used in blow moulding.
HIPS	high impact polystyrene	Thermoplastic. A polystyrene modified by copolymerization with butadiene to improve its toughness.
LDPE	low density polyethylene	Thermoplastic. Branched polyolefin used for film and as electrical insulator, made at high pressures.
MF	melamine formaldehyde	Thermoset. Used in domestic ware, switches, plugs, etc.
PA	nylon, polyamide	Thermoplastic. Used in bearings, gears, mouldings, wall plugs, etc.
PF	phenolic, phenol formaldehyde	Thermoset. Moulding material and laminating resin. Sometimes known as *Bakelite*.
PAN	polyacrylonitrile	A fibre-forming thermoplastic polymer. One of the base polymers used to make carbon fibre.
UPR	polyester (unsaturated polyester resin)	Thermoset. A solution of polyester containing unsaturated groups in styrene or other polymerizable solvent. Matrix resin for GRP.
PET	poly(ethylene terephthalate)	Thermoplastic. A major fibre-forming polymer and a moulding material for beer bottles, etc. In competition with poly(butylene terephthalate)(PBT), a related thermoplastic polyester.
PVC	poly(vinyl chloride)	Thermoplastic. Can be plasticized to produce a leathery material. Unplasticized PVC (UPVC) used for rainwater goods, pipes, etc.
SAN	styrene-acrylonitrile	Thermoplastic. Rigid transparent material used for water jugs and beakers, etc.
SMC	sheet moulding compound	Thermoset. Sheets of glass fibre impregnated with polyester resin(td)

(*Selected from http://www.open.edu/openlearn/science-maths-technology/science/chemistry/introduction-polymers/content-section-0*, 2014; *Figure 1 is from British Plastics Federation and Figure 2 is from BPF Statistics*)

New Words and Expressions

macromolecule *n.* 巨大分子，高分子

speciality *n.* 专业，专长，特性，特制品，同 specialty

recession   n. 经济衰退，不景气，后退，撤退，凹处，退场
tonnes   n. 吨，公吨（tonne 的名词复数）
aluminium   n. 铝；a. 铝的
flexible   a. 灵活的，易弯曲的，柔韧的，易被说服的，柔性，灵活，弹性的，多变的
modulus   n. 系数，模数，模，模量
latter   a. 后者的，末了的，较后的，后者，次序或时间在后，后面的
vulcanized rubbers   硫化橡胶，橡皮，硬橡皮
blur   vt. & vi. 涂污，弄脏，（使）变模糊，（使）难以区分，疾驰残影，模糊，污点，
          污迹，n. 污迹，污斑，模糊不清的事物，暧昧不明
irrespective   a. 不考虑的，不顾的，无关的，不顾的，不论，不考虑的
disposable   a. 一次性的，可任意处理的，用后就抛弃的，免洗的，可供使用的，n.
          使用后随即抛掉的东西（尤指容器等），一次性用品，一次性，一次性手套
intermediary   a. 中间人的，调解的，居间的，媒介的，n. 中间人，媒介，调解人，
          中间阶段，中介，中间的，仲裁者，中间人
photoresists   n. 光阻剂，光产酸剂，碱溶性聚酯
amber   n. 琥珀，琥珀色，a. 琥珀色的，琥珀制的 v. 使成琥珀色，钙铝榴石
bakelite   n. 酚醛树脂，电木，酚醛塑料，电胶木
polychloroprene   n. 聚氯丁烯，氯丁橡胶，聚氯丁二烯
neoprene rubber   n. 氯丁（二烯）橡胶，氯丁橡胶，药水糊
terylene   n. 涤纶
dacron   涤纶，聚酯纤维，涤纶织物
hitherto   adv. 到目前为止，迄今，至今
hevea Brasiliensis trees 巴西橡胶树
coagulate   vt. & vi. 凝固，使结块，使变稠，a. [废语] 凝固的，凝结的，凝聚的
latex   n. 胶乳，（尤指橡胶树的）橡浆，人工合成胶乳（用以制作油漆、黏合剂和织物）
plantations   n. 种植园，大农场（plantation 的名词复数）
the Far East   n. 远东地区，远东
abrasion resistance   抗磨损性
high resilience   高弹性
low damping   弱阻尼
resilient mounts   a. 能复原的，弹回的，有弹性的，能立刻恢复精神的，n. 坚韧，弹性
tyre sidewalls   轮胎侧壁
ozone oxidation 臭氧氧化，臭氧氧化法，臭氧法，臭氧的氧化
radiator hose   散热器软管，水箱橡皮管，水箱软管，侧散热器软管
gaskets   n. 垫圈，衬垫（gasket 的名词复数）密合垫，材料垫片
seals   n. 密封件 v. 密封（seal 的第三人称单数），决定，确定，封上（信封）
conveyor belts   输送带
bridge bearings   桥梁支座
copolymer   n. 共聚物，共多聚体
terpolymer   n. 三元共聚物
impetus   n. 动力，促进，势头；声势
acronyms   n. 首字母缩略词（acronym 的名词复数）

Notes

① The word is derived from the Greek words πολυ (poly), meaning "many"; and μέρος (mer), meaning "part". derive from…, 由……衍生。The word 指的是 polymer。参考译文：这个单词是由希腊字母衍生出来的，poly 意思是很多，mer 表示部分的。

② Polymers are studied in the fields of polymer chemistry, polymer physics, and polymer science. in the fields of：领域。参考译文：人们通常研究聚合物的领域是聚合物化学、聚合物物理和聚合物科学。

③ Traditionally, the industry has produced two main types of synthetic polymer—plastics and rubbers. 参考译文：通常，工业上主要生产两种类型的合成高分子化合物，分别是塑料和橡胶。

④ Plastics are further subdivided into thermoplastics and thermosets, the latter type being materials where the long chains are linked together by crosslinks, a feature they share with conventional vulcanized rubbers. share with：与……分享，意思是：与……共有，与……一样。参考译文：塑料可以进一步细分为热塑性塑料和热固性塑料，后者是材料在长链的交联连接在一起，这一特点与传统硫化橡胶类似。

⑤ The true molecular nature of materials like natural rubber and synthetics like Bakelite was not understood until about the 1920s when Hermann Staudinger recognized their chain-like structure. Hermann Staudinger 人名，赫尔曼·施陶丁格，1881 年 3 月 23 日～1965 年 9 月 8 日，德国化学家，在大分子化学领域作出了开拓性贡献，因对高分子研究以及确立高分子概念获得 1953 年诺贝尔化学奖。

⑥ However, almost two-thirds of the rubber now consumed world-wide is synthetic. two-thirds：三分之二；以此类推，one third：三分之一。four fifths：五分之四。参考译文：然而，目前世界上使用的橡胶有三分之二是合成橡胶。

Exercises

1. Question for discussion

(1) What is a polymer?

(2) Where are polymers widely used?

(3) What is a plastic?

(4) What is a rubber?

(5) What is the distinct of thermoplastics and thermosets?

2. Translate the following into Chinese

polymer synthesis   low damping
abrasion resistance   biological synthesis
high resilience   ozone oxidation

- Polymers, or materials composed of long molecular chains, are now well-accepted for a wide variety of applications, both structural and non-structural, and for mass-manufactured as well as one-off speciality products.

• The distinction is that plastics are, by and large, rigid materials at service temperatures while rubbers are flexible, low modulus materials which exhibit long-range elasticity.

• Thus photoresists are used to create the circuit patterns on semiconductor chips through controlled degradation, and are entirely absent in the final product.

• Thermosets can be defined as those polymers which become irreversibly hard on heating or by addition of special chemicals.

3. Translate the following into English

热塑性塑料　　　　　　　　酚醛树脂
氯丁橡胶　　　　　　　　　输送带
聚合反应　　　　　　　　　共聚物

• 塑料主要被分为热塑性塑料和热固性塑料两种类型，橡胶主要分为天然橡胶和人工合成橡胶两种类型。

热塑性塑料是应用最广的塑料，它最大的特点是在一定的温度下可以熔融成任意形状，冷却后形状不变，而且这种变化是可以反复进行的。

• 人们对于高分子化合物的需求一直在不断增长，而对于传统材料，如金属、陶瓷和玻璃的需求一直保持不变或者处于下降趋势。

• 热固性化合物在受热时会发生化学变化，因此，它和热塑性化合物的特点是不一样的。

4. Reading Comprehension

(1) We can see from figure 1 that _____ in the 1970s to 1990.
(A) steel usage has fallen　　(B) aluminium usage has stayed
(C) polymers usage has increased　　(D) all of the above

(2) Traditionally, the industry has produced two main types of synthetic polymer _____.
(A) thermoplastics and thermosets　　(B) elastomers and vulcanized rubbers
(C) rigid and low modulus materials　　(D) plastics and rubbers

(3) What is CR?
(A) CR is a versatile special-purpose rubber and have very good mechanical and electrical properties.
(B) CR has a very good resistance to ozone oxidation, heat and flame. It can be used to make Car radiator hose, gaskets, seals, conveyor belts, bridge bearings.
(C) Both A and B
(D) Not mentioned in the text.

(4) When did the first synthetic polymers be made?
(A) Before Victorian era
(B) During the growth of the organic chemical industry
(C) Victorian era
(D) Not mentioned in the text

(5) The author may discuss _____ first in the following paragraphs?
(A) consumption of plastics

(B) polymer properties
(C) product interaction
(D) product design and manufacture

(6) Which is true according to the author? _____
(A) A polymer is a mixture of monomers.
(B) PVC is a thermoplastic. And it cannot be plasticized to produce a leathery material.
(C) PET is a thermoset. It is a major fibre-forming polymer and a moulding material for beer bottles, etc.
(D) PMMA is a thermoplastic. And it also a transparent rigid polymer.

Reading Material

Polymer Structure and Synthesis

Polymers include natural materials such as rubber and synthetic materials such as plastics and elastomers. Polymers are very useful materials because their structures can be altered and tailored to produce materials (1) with a range of mechanical properties, (2) in a wide spectrum of colors and (3) with different transparent properties.

A polymer is composed of many simple molecules that are repeating structural units called monomers. A single polymer molecule may consist of hundreds to a million monomers and may have a linear, branched, or network structure. Covalent bonds hold the atoms in the polymer molecules together and secondary bonds then hold groups of polymer chains together to form the polymeric material. Copolymers are polymers composed of two or more different types of monomers.

Polymer Chains (Thermoplastics and Thermosets)

A polymer is an organic material and the backbone of every organic material is a chain of carbon atoms. The carbon atom has four electrons in the outer shell. Each of these valence electrons can form a covalent bond to another carbon atom or to a foreign atom. The key to the polymer structure is that two carbon atoms can have up to three common bonds and still bond with other atoms. The elements found most frequently in polymers and their valence numbers are: H, F, Cl, and I with 1 valence electron; O and S with 2 valence electrons; N with 3 valence electrons and C and Si with 4 valence electrons.

The ability for molecules to form long chains is a vital to producing polymers. Consider the material polyethylene (Figure 4.5), which is made from ethane gas, C_2H_6. Ethane gas has a two carbon atoms in the chain and each of the two carbon atoms share two valence electrons with the other. If two molecules of ethane are brought together, one of the carbon bonds in each molecule can be broken and the two molecules can be joined with a carbon to carbon bond. After the two are joined, there are still two free valence electrons at each end of the chain for joining other or polymer chains. The process can continue liking more mole-

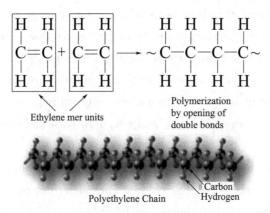

Figure 4.5 Polyethylene structure

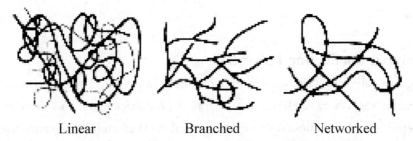

Figure 4.6 Different types of carbon backbone structures

cules and polymers together until it is stopped by the addition of anther chemical (a terminator), that fills the available bond at each end of the molecule. This is called a linear polymer and is building block for thermoplastic polymers (Figure 4.6).

The polymer chain is often shown in two dimensions, but it should be noted that they have a three dimensional structure. Each bond is at 109° to the next and, therefore, the carbon backbone extends through space like a twisted chain of Tinker Toys. When stress is applied, these chains stretch and the elongation of polymers can be thousands of times greater than it is in crystalline structures.

The length of the polymer chain is very important. As the number of carbon atoms in the chain is increased to beyond several hundred, the material will pass through the liquid state and become a waxy solid. When the number of carbon atoms in the chain is over 1000, the solid material polyethylene, with its characteristics of strength, flexibility and toughness, is obtained. The change in state occurs because as the length of the molecules increases, the total binding forces between molecules also increases.

It should also be noted that the molecules are not generally straight but are a tangled mass. Thermoplastic materials, such as polyethylene, can be pictured as a mass of intertwined worms randomly thrown into a pail. The binding forces are the result of van der Waals forces between molecules and mechanical entanglement between the chains. When thermoplastics are heated, there is more molecular movement and the bonds between molecules can be easily broken. This is why thermoplastic materials can be remelted.

There is another group of polymers in which a single large network, instead of many molecules is formed during polymerization. Since polymerization is initially accomplished by heating the raw materials and brining them together, this group is called thermosetting polymers or plastics. For this type of network structure to form, the molecules must have more than two places for boning to occur; otherwise, only a linear structure is possible. These chains form jointed structures and rings, and may fold back and forth to take on a partially crystalline structure.

Since these materials are essentially comprised of one giant molecule, there is no movement between molecules once the mass has set. Thermosetting polymers are more rigid and generally have higher strength than thermoplastic polymers. Also, since there is no opportunity for motion between molecules in a thermosetting polymer, they will not become plastic when heated.

Nanostructured Conducting Polymers

Conducting polymers (CPs) were first produced in the late 1970s as a novel generation of organic materials that have electrical and optical properties similar to those of metals and inorganic semiconductors; these polymers also exhibit other useful properties such as ease of synthesis and flexibility in processing. Ps have highly conjugated chains, meaning their chemical, physical and electrochemical properties are reversible and can be controlled by doping/dedoping processes. Typical conducting polymers include polypyrrole (PPy), polyaniline (PANi), polythiophene (Pth), poly (3,4-ethylenedioxythiophene)(PEDOT), and PEDOT derivatives. To date, conducting polymers have been widely studied for their applications in electroluminescence, solar batteries, electromagnetic shielding, rechargeable batteries, material corrosion protection, neural probes, artificial muscles or actuators and drug delivery devices (Table 4.3).

Table 4.3 Biomedical applications of conducting polymers

Nanostructured conducting polymers	Chemical formula	Commonly used synthetic method	Biomedical applications
Polyaniline	[structure]	In-situ synthesis Hard-template method	Neural electrode coatings
		Emulsion polymerization	Biosensors
		Soft-template method Electrochemical synthesis	Artificial muscles and actuators
		Enzymatic method	Drug delivery
Polypyrrole	[structure]	Soft-template method	Neural electrode coatings
		Electrochemical synthesis	Biosensors
		In-situ synthesis	Artificial muscles and actuators
		Enzymatic synthesis	Drug delivery

续表

Nanostructured conducting polymers	Chemical formula	Commonly used synthetic method	Biomedical applications
Polythiophene		Hard-template method	Neural electrode coatings
		Electrical Deposition method	Artificial muscles and actuators
		Soft-template method	Drug delivery
Poly(3,4-ethylene-dioxythiophene)		Soft-template method	Neural probes
		Electrochemical synthesis	Biosensors
		Lithography method In-situ synthesis	Artificial muscles and actuators
		Template-free method	Drug delivery

Conducting polymers usually have nanostructures, which may be composed of nanoparticles, nanowires, nanofibers or nanotubes. Studies have shown that the surface area, surface roughness and surface area to volume ratio can dramatically increase on the nanoscale, leading to superior physicochemical properties, including mechanical, electrical, optical, catalytic, and magnetic properties. In recent years, many studies have focused on the development of inorganic semiconductor and metallic nanostructures. Nanostructured conducting polymers, however, have not garnered much attention.

Nanostructured conducting polymers have shown many advantages over conventional counterparts, including high electrical conductivity, efficient charge transport and good biocompatibility. Their applications in biomedical fields may include neural probes, biosensors and drug delivery systems because of these properties.

Synthesis of nanostructured conducting polymers

The methods for preparation of conducting polymers include chemical oxidative polymerization, electrochemical polymerization and physical methodologies (e.g., electro-spinning). Nanostructures of conducting polymers, such as nanotubes, nanowires, and nanoparticles, were successfully fabricated in this study. At present, a number of methods, including hard-template, soft-template, and template-free methodologies, have been used to synthesize nanostructured conducting polymers.

Hard-Template Method

Hard-template synthesis employs a physical template with a special morphology as a scaffold to fabricate target materials with the same morphology. The hard-template scaffolds usually include an insoluble porous membrane, zeolite and templates with nanosized channels, which are made of materials such as anodized alumina oxide. For example, poly (3,4-ethylenedioxythiophene)(PEDOT) nanotubes and nanorods were synthesized using anodized alumina oxide as the hard template. Nanomaterials made from inorganic or biological materials can be used as templates or seeds to direct the growth of conducting polymer nanofibers, wires and tubes. Figure 4.7 shows a schematic of the preparation of different nanostructured conducting polymers using the hard-template method. In addition to chemical polymerization, nanostructured conducting polymers prepared by the hard-template method can be obtained by electrochemical polymerization. For electrochemical polymerization, a lm is usually needed to coat the surface of the membrane. Electrochemical polymerization is more complex, expensive and inef cient than chemical polymerization, but it is highly controllable. The surface morphology of the film was characterized, and the electrochemical properties were measured using the Cyclic Voltammetry (CV) technique.

Soft-Template Method

Soft-template synthesis is a method of fabricating nanotubes or nanofibers by adding amphiphilic molecules, such as surfactants, micelles or liquid crystals, to a chemical polymerization bath. It is a self-assembly process; the amphiphilic molecules self-assemble to form ordered aggregates through hydrophilic-hydrophobic interactions, hydrogen bonds, Van der Waals forces, etc. when the concentration of the molecules is above the critical micelle concentration. The soft-template method has many advantages including the following:

(i) the geometric dimensions of the prepared 1-D structures can be controlled by changing the surfactant to monomer molar ratio, reaction temperature and time or other conditions;

(ii) the method is simple, cheap and effective; and

(iii) the template is easily removed from the product.

Figure 4.8 depicts the mechanisms for the syntheses of different nanostructured conducting polymers using the soft-template method.

The soft-template method has some disadvantages. For example, it requires post-processing to remove the template, which complicates the preparation process and often destroys or disorders the formed nanostructures. These disadvantages lead to low productive efficiency, limiting the large-scale production of nanostructured conducting polymers.

Template-Free Method

In this fabrication method, polyaniline nanofibers first form at the interface between an aqueous acidic solution including an oxidant and an organic solution of aniline. Once the polyaniline forms, it immediately diffuses into the aqueous phase; secondary growth and polyaniline agglomeration are thus suppressed. Therefore, pure polyaniline nanofibers are obtained. The average diameter of polyaniline nanofibers can range from 30 nm to 120 nm depending on which doping acid is used.

(*Selected from https: //www. nde-ed. org/EducationResources/CommunityCollege/ Materials/Structure/polymer. htm*, 2014 *and http: //www. aspbs. com/jnn/ Journal of Nanoscience & Nanotechnology*, 2014; *Figure*4.8 *and* 4.9 *are reprinted from L. Xia, et al., J. Colloid Interface Sci.* 341, 1 (2010). © 2010, *Elsevier Ltd.*)

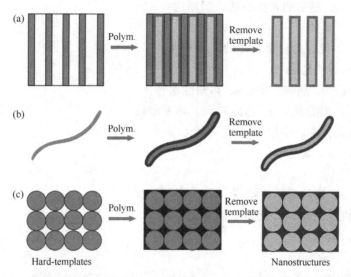

Figure 4.7 Schematic of the hard-template synthesis of different conducting polymers with nanostructure: (a) Porous membrane as the hard-template to produce conducting polymer nanotubes and nanowires; (b) nanofibers as the hard-template to produce conducting polymer nanotubes; (c) colloidal particles as the hard-template to produce nanoporous membranes.

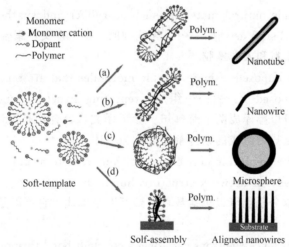

Figure 4.8 Schematic of the mechanism of the soft-template synthesis of different conducting polymers with nanostructure. (a) Micelles acted as soft-templates in the formation of nanotubes. Micelles were formed by the self-assembly of dopants, and the polymerization were carried out on the surface of the micelles; (b) nanowires formed by the protection of dopants. The polymerization were carried out inside the micelles; (c) monomer droplets acted as soft-templates in the formation of micro-sphere; and (d) polymerization on the substrate producing aligned nanowire arrays.

New Words and Expressions

elastomer   *n.* 弹性体，人造橡胶
spectrum   *n.* 光，光谱，型谱，频谱

transparent　*a*．透明的，显然的，明晰的
monomer　*n*．单体
polymeric　*a*．聚合的，聚合体的
copolymer　*n*．共聚物
thermoplastic　*a*．热塑性的；*n*．热塑性塑料
thermoset　*a*．热固的；*n*．热固树脂，热固塑料
backbone　*n*．脊椎，中枢
polyethylene　*n*．聚乙烯
ethane　*n*．乙烷
terminator　*n*．终结者，终结器
tangle　*n*．混乱状态；*v*．处于混乱状态
pail　*n*．桶，提桶
entanglement　*n*．纠缠
giant　*a*．庞大的，巨大的；*n*．巨人，大力士，巨大的动物或植物
In-situ synthesis　原位合成
methodology　*n*．方法学，方法论

Notes

① Polymers include natural materials such as rubber and synthetic materials such as plastics and elastomers. such as 例如……，像这种的。参考译文：聚合物包括天然材料例如橡胶和合成材料例如塑料和人造橡胶。

② A polymer is composed of many simple molecules that are repeating structural units called monomers. composed of：由……组成；repeating structural unit：重复的结构单元。这是一个定语从句，可以翻译成两个简单句。参考译文：聚合物是由许多简单分子构成的，这些简单分子通过重复排列组成的结构单元被称为单体。

③ A single polymer molecule may consist of hundreds to a million monomers and may have a linear, branched, or network structure. hundreds to a million：数百个到百万个。参考译文：一个单聚合物分子也可以包括数百个到百万个单体，它可以是线状的、枝状的或者是网状的。

④ Each of these valence electrons can form a covalent bond to another carbon atom or to a foreign atom. valence electron：价电子；foreign：外国的，外交的，外来的，不相关的；foreign atom：指的是除了碳原子之外的杂原子。本句的意思是：每一个价电子都能与另一个碳原子或其他原子形成一个共价键。

⑤ The elements found most frequently in polymers and their valence numbers are：H，F，Cl，and I with 1 valence electron；O and S with 2 valence electrons；N with 3 valence electrons and C and Si with 4 valence electrons. valence number：价数。valence electron：价电子。本句的意思是：聚合物中常见元素及其价数分别是：H，F，Cl 和 I 有 1 个价电子，O 和 S 有 2 个价电子，N 有 3 个价电子，C 和 Si 有 4 个价电子。

⑥ The polymer chain is often shown in two dimensions，but it should be noted that they have a three dimensional structure. 这是一个被动句，科技英文中，通常会把作为主语

的人省略掉，而采用被动语态。参考译文：聚合物的链通常表现为二维的，但是需要注意的是它们具有三维结构。

Reading Comprehension

(1) _____ are polymers composed of two or more different types of monomers.

(A) Copolymers (B) Polymers

(C) Polymeric material (D) thermosetting polymer

(2) According to the passage, which of the following is NOT TRUE? _____

(A) Polymers are very useful materials because their structures cannot be altered and tailored to produce materials.

(B) Polymers are very useful materials because they have a wide spectrum of colors.

(C) Polymers are very useful materials because they have different transparent properties.

(D) Polymers are very useful materials because they have a range of mechanical properties.

(3) The carbon backbone extends through space like a twisted chain of Tinker Toys as each bond is at _____ to the next carbon atom.

(A) over 1000℃ (B) 109°

(C) 1000℃ (D) over 109°

(4) Which characteristic is not belonging to the solid material polyethylene when the number of carbon atoms in the chain is over 1000?

(A) Improving strength

(B) The material will pass through the liquid state and become a waxy solid

(C) The length of the molecules increases

(D) The total binding forces between molecules increases

(5) There is no opportunity for motion between molecules in a _____ polymer, they will not become plastic when heated.

(A) thermosetting (B) thermoplastic

(C) thermoset (D) thermoplastic and thermosetting

(6) According to the thermosetting polymers, which of the following is NOT TRUE?

(A) In fact thermosetting polymers are plastics.

(B) During polymerization, there is also another group of polymers formed.

(C) The molecules must have more than two places for boning to occur to form the network structure.

(D) A linear structure is to form when the molecules have more than two places for boning.

(7) Which method can be used for preparation of conducting polymers?

(A) chemical oxidative polymerization (B) electrochemical polymerization

(C) physical methodologies (D) A, B, and C

(8) At present, which methods have been used to synthesize nanostructured conducting polymers according to the author?

(A) hard-template (B) template-free
(C) soft-template (D) A, B, and C

Unit 13 Soft Materials: Polymers and Plastics

For a long time humans processed naturally occurring polymers, such as wool, leather, silk, and natural rubber, into usable materials. During the past 70 years or so, chemists have learned to form synthetic polymers by polymerizing monomers through controlled chemical reactions. A great many of these synthetic polymers have a backbone of carbon-carbon bonds because carbon atoms have an exceptional ability to form strong stable bonds with one another.

Plastics are materials that can be formed into various shapes, usually by the application of heat and pressure. Thermoplastic materials can be reshaped. For example, plastic milk containers are made from a polymer known as polyethylene that has a high molecular mass. These containers can be melted down and the polymer recycled for some other use. In contrast, a thermosetting plastic is shaped through irreversible chemical processes and therefore cannot be reshaped readily.

An elastomer is a material that exhibits rubbery or elastic behavior. When subjected to stretching or bending, it regains its original shape upon removal of the distorting force, provided that it has not been distorted beyond some elastic limit. Some polymers, such as nylon and polyesters, can also be formed into fibers that, like hair, are very long relative to their cross-sectional area and are not elastic. These fibers can be woven into fabrics and cords and fashioned into clothing, tire cord, and other useful objects.

Making Polymers

The simplest example of a polymerization reaction is the formation of polyethylene from ethylene molecules. In this reaction the double bond in each ethylene molecule "opens up", and two of the electrons originally in this bond are used to form new C—C single bonds with two other ethylene molecules:

Polymerization that occurs by the coupling of monomers through their multiple bonds is called addition polymerization.

We can write the equation for the polymerization reaction as follows:

$$n\mathrm{CH_2}=\mathrm{CH_2} \longrightarrow \left[\begin{array}{c} \mathrm{H} \;\; \mathrm{H} \\ |\;\;\;\; | \\ -\mathrm{C}-\mathrm{C}- \\ |\;\;\;\; | \\ \mathrm{H} \;\; \mathrm{H} \end{array}\right]_n$$

Here n represents the large number—ranging from hundreds to many thousands—of monomer molecules (ethylene in this case) that react to form one large polymer molecule. Within the polymer a repeat unit (the unit shown in brackets in Equation above) appears along the entire chain. The ends of the chain are capped by carbon-hydrogen bonds or by some other bond, so that the end carbons have four bonds.

Polyethylene is a very important material; more than 20 billion pounds are produced in the United States each year. Although its composition is simple, the polymer is not easy to make. Only after many years of research were the right conditions identified for manufacturing this commercially useful polymer. Today many different forms of polyethylene, varying widely in physical properties, are known. Polymers of other chemical compositions provide still greater variety in physical and chemical properties.

A second general kind of reaction used to synthesize commercially important polymers is condensation polymerization. In a condensation reaction two molecules are joined to form a larger molecule by elimination of a small molecule such as H_2O. For example, an amine (a compound containing the —NH_2 group) will react with a carboxylic acid (a compound containing the —COOH group) to form a bond between N and C along with the formation of H_2O.

In the formation of many nylons a diamine, a compound with an —NH_2 group at each end, is reacted with a diacid, a compound with a —COOH group at each end. For example, nylon 6, 6 is formed when a diamine that has six carbon atoms and an amino group on each end is reacted with adipic acid, which also has six carbon atoms.

A condensation reaction occurs on each end of the diamine and the acid. The components of H_2O are split out, and N—C bonds are formed between molecules.

Would it be possible to make a condensation polymer out of this molecule alone?

Structure and Physical Properties of Polymers

The simple structural formulas given for polyethylene and other polymers are deceptive. Because each carbon atom in polyethylene is surrounded by four bonds, the atoms are arranged in a tetrahedral fashion, so that the chain is not straight. Furthermore, the atoms are relatively free to rotate around the C—C single bonds. Rather than being straight and rigid, therefore, the chains are very flexible (Figure 4.9), folding readily. The flexibility in the molecular chains causes the entire polymer material to be very flexible.

Figure 4.9 The structural chain of polyethylene

Both synthetic and naturally occurring polymers commonly consist of a collection of macromolecules (large molecules) of different molecular weights. Depending on the conditions of formation, the molecular weights may be distributed over a wide range or be closely clustered around an average value. In part because of this distribution in molecular weights, polymers are largely amorphous (noncrystalline) materials. Rather than exhibiting a well-defined crystalline phase with a sharp melting point, they soften over a range of temperatures.

There are side chains off the main chain of the polymer. These branches inhibit the formation of crystalline regions, reducing the density of the material. High-density polyethylene (HDPE) is used to form bottles, drums, and pipes. This form has less branching and thus a higher degree of crystallinity. The properties of polyethylene can be "tuned" by varying the average length, crystallinity, and branching of the chains, making it a very versatile material.

Various substances may be added to polymers to provide protection against the effects of sunlight or against degradation by oxidation. In addition, the physical properties of polymeric materials can be modified extensively by adding substances with lower molecular mass, called plasticizers, to reduce the extent of interactions between chains and thus to make the polymer more pliable. Polyvinyl chloride (PVC), for example, is a hard, rigid material of high molecular mass that is used to manufacture home drainpipes. When blended with a suitable substance of lower molecular mass, however, it forms a flexible polymer that can be used to make rain boots and doll parts. In some applications the plasticizer in a plastic object may be lost over time because of evaporation. As this happens, the plastic loses its flexibility and becomes subject to cracking.

Polymers can be made stiffer by introducing chemical bonds between the polymer chains. Forming bonds between chains is called cross-linking. The greater the number of cross-links in a polymer, the more rigid the material will be. Whereas thermoplastic materials consist of independent polymer chains, thermosetting ones become cross-linked when heated, and it is the cross-links that allow them to hold their shapes.

An important example of cross-linking is the vulcanization of natural rubber, a process discovered by Charles Goodyear in 1839. Natural rubber is formed from a liquid resin derived from the inner bark of the Hevea brasiliensis tree (Figure 4.10). Chemically, it is a polymer of isoprene, C_5H_8. Because rotation about the carbon-carbon double bond does not readily occur, the orientation of the groups bound to the carbons is rigid. In naturally occurring rubber, the chain extensions are on the same side of the double bond. Natural rubber is not a useful polymer because it is too soft and too chemically reactive. Goodyear accidentally discovered that adding sulfur to rubber and then heating the mixture makes the rubber harder and reduces its susceptibility to oxidation or other chemical attack. Cross-linking of about 5%

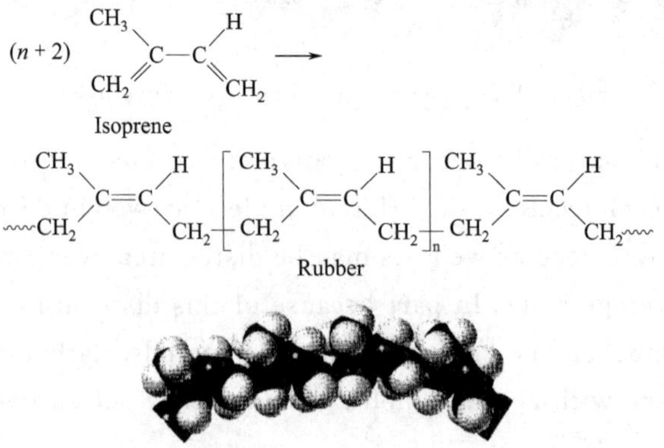

Figure 4.10 Natural rubber derived from the inner bark of the Hevea brasiliensis tree

of the double bonds creates a flexible, resilient rubber. When the rubber is stretched, the cross-links help prevent the chains from slipping, so that the rubber retains its elasticity.

(Selected from Theodore L. Brom, H. Eugene LeMay, Jr., and Bruce E. Bursten, Chemistry: The Central Science, 13th Edition, Prentice Hall, 2014)

New Words and Expressions

irreversible *a.* 不能撤回的，不能取消的
elastomer *n.* 弹性体，人造橡胶
regain *v.* 收回，恢复
tire cord 轮胎帘布
polyethylene *n.* 聚乙烯
condensation *n.* 浓缩
elimination *n.* 排除，除去，消除，消灭
diamine *n.* 二（元）胺
diacid *n.* 二酸；*a.* 二价酸的，二酸的
formula *n.* 公式，规则
deceptive *a.* 欺骗性的
tetrahedral *a.* 有四面的，四面体的
depict *v.* 描述，描写
rotate *v.* （使）旋转
rigid *a.* 刚硬的，刚性的，严格的
flexible *a.* 柔韧性，易曲的，灵活的，柔软的，能变形的，可通融的
folding *a.* 可折叠的
macromolecule *n.* 巨大分子，高分子
cluster *n.* 串，丛；*v.* 丛生，成群
amorphous *a.* 无定形的，无组织的
drum *n.* 鼓，鼓声，鼓形圆桶；*v.* 击鼓，作鼓声，打鼓奏
versatile *a.* 通用的，万能的，多才多艺的，多面手的
degradation *n.* 降级，降格，退化
oxidation *n.* 氧化
plasticizer *n.* 塑化剂，塑解剂
pliable *a.* 易曲折的，柔软的，圆滑的，柔韧的
drainpipe *n.* 排水管
blend *v.* 混合；*n.* 混合
evaporation *n.* 蒸发（作用）
stiff *a.* 硬的，僵直的，拘谨的，呆板的，艰难的，费劲的，僵硬的
vulcanization *n.* （橡胶的）硫化（过程），硫化
isoprene *n.* 橡胶基质
orientation *n.* 方向，方位，定位，倾向性，向东方
extension *n.* 延长，扩充，范围；*a.* 外延的，客观现实的

susceptibility   *n*. 易感性，感受性，磁化系数
resilient   *a*. 弹回的，有回弹力的

Notes

① During the past 70 years or so, chemists have learned to form synthetic polymers by polymerizing monomers through controlled chemical reactions. or so：大约，表示时间不确定；monomer：单体。参考译文：在过去70年左右，化学家开始通过控制化学反应使单体聚合从而合成聚合物。

② For example, plastic milk containers are made from a polymer known as polyethylene that has a high molecular mass. known as：由于……而有名，众所周知；that 引导了一个定语从句，修饰前面的 polyethylene，即：聚乙烯具有很高的分子量。参考译文：例如，塑料牛奶盒是由一种被称为聚乙烯的聚合物材料制成的，该聚合物具有很高的分子质量。

③ Some polymers, such as nylon and polyesters, can also be formed into fibers that, like hair, are very long relative to their cross-sectional area and are not elastic. cross-sectional area：横截面积。are…are not…：是……，而不是……。参考译文：一些聚合物，例如尼龙和聚酯，可以加工成纤维，就像毛发一样，相对于它们的横截面积而言非常长，这一特点与弹性无关。

④ Only after many years of research were the right conditions identified for manufacturing this commercially useful polymer. Only 引导了一个倒装句，强调 only 后面的部分。参考译文：只有在多年的研究之后，人们才获得适当的条件来制造商业上广泛应用的聚合物。

⑤ When blended with a suitable substance of lower molecular mass, however, it forms a flexible polymer that can be used to make rain boots and doll parts. 本句的意思是：当它与合适的低分子量物质等混合后，就能形成柔韧性的聚合物，这种聚合物可用来制造雨靴和玩偶的零部件。

⑥ The greater the number of cross-links in a polymer, the more rigid the material will be. the more…the more… 句式，表示越……越……。参考译文：在聚合物中，交叉连接的数目越多，材料的刚性越强。

Exercises

1. Question for discussion

(1) Why do some synthetic polymers have a backbone of C—C bonds?

(2) What is an elastomer?

(3) When did Charles Goodyear discover a process of natural rubber?

(4) Why did the author say natural rubber is not a useful polymer?

(5) What is the main difference between thermoplastic and thermosetting materials?

(6) What is cross-linking?

(7) How would you expect the properties of vulcanized rubber to vary as the percentage of sulfur increases? Explain.

(8) Try to describe the process of addition polymerization.

2. Translate the following into Chinese

chemical reaction   amorphous materials
thermoplastic materials   physical properties
molecular mass   single bond

- A great many of these synthetic polymers have a backbone of carbon-carbon bonds because carbon atoms have an exceptional ability to form strong stable bonds with one another.
- Rather than exhibiting a well-defined crystalline phase with a sharp melting point, they soften over a range of temperatures.
- Depending on the conditions of formation, the molecular weights may be distributed over a wide range or be closely clustered around an average value.
- Goodyear accidentally discovered that adding sulfur to rubber and then heating the mixture makes the rubber harder and reduces its susceptibility to oxidation or other chemical attack.

3. Translate the following into English

热固性塑料   横截面积
聚合反应   双键
化学组成   羧酸
熔点   氧化降解

- 不同化学结构的聚合物具有不同的物理和化学性质。
- 热固性塑料成型后，由于不能取消化学过程，因此不能重新再成型。
- 天然橡胶不是一种有用的聚合物，因为它太软了，并且太容易发生化学反应。
- 我们可以在聚合物中加入各种不同的化合物，使聚合物具有抗日照和抗氧化降解的性质。

4. Reading Comprehension

(1) About plastics, which is TRUE?
(A) Materials that can be formed into various shapes, usually by the application of heat and pressure.
(B) Plastic materials can be reshaped.
(C) Plastic milk containers are made from a polymer known as polyethylene that has a very low molecular mass.
(D) Plastic is shaped through irreversible chemical processes and therefore cannot be reshaped readily.

(2) About elastomer, all the followings are true EXCEPT _____?
(A) An elastomer is a material that exhibits rubbery or elastic behavior.
(B) When subjected to stretching or bending, an elastomer cannot regain its original shape upon removal of the distorting force.
(C) An elastomer can be formed into fibers that, like hair.
(D) All of the above.

(3) In the polymerization reaction of the polyethylene formation, the double bond in

each ethylene molecule "opens up" and two of the electrons originally in this bond are used to form _____ with two other ethylene molecules.

(A) new C=C double bonds (B) new C—C single bonds
(C) a polymer   (D) monomers

(4) Depending on the conditions of formation, _____ may be distributed over a _____ range or be closely clustered around an average value.

(A) the molecular weight; narrow
(B) the molecular mass; narrow
(C) the molecular mass; wide
(D) the molecular weight; wide

(5) Because of the distribution in molecular weights, polymers are largely _____ materials.

(A) commonly crystalline
(B) amorphous
(C) a well-defined crystalline phase
(D) Not mentioned in the text

(6) Accidentally, Goodyear discovered that adding _____ to natural rubber and then heating the mixture makes the rubber harder and reduces its susceptibility to oxidation or other chemical attack.

(A) thermoplastic materials   (B) cross-linking of C=C double bonds
(C) sulfur   (D) a liquid resin

Reading Material

Smart Glass

Smart glass or switchable glass, also called smart windows or switchable windows in its application to windows or skylights, refers to electrically switchable glass or glazing which changes light transmission properties when voltage is applied.

Certain types of smart glass can allow users to control the amount of light and heat passing through: with the press of a button, it changes from transparent to opaque, partially blocking light while maintaining a clear view of what lies behind the window. Another type of smart glass can provide privacy at the turn of a switch.

Smart glass technologies are electrochromic devices, suspended particle devices, and liquid crystal devices. The use of smart glass can save costs for heating, air-conditioning and lighting and avoid the cost of installing and maintaining motorized light screens or blinds or curtains. When opaque, liquid crystal or electrochromic smart glass blocks most UV, thereby reducing fabric fading; for SPD-type smart glass, this is achieved when used in conjunction with low-e low emissivity coatings.

Critical aspects of smart glass include installation costs, the use of electricity, durability, as well as functional features such as the speed of control, possibilities for dimming, and the degree of transparency of the glass.

Electrically switchable smart glass

Electrochromic devices change light transmission properties in response to voltage and thus allow controlling the amount of light and heat passing through. In electrochromic windows, the electrochromic material changes its opacity: it changes between a colored, translucent state (usually blue) and a transparent state. A burst of electricity is required for changing its opacity, but once the change has been effectuated, no electricity is needed for maintaining the particular shade which has been reached. Darkening occurs from the edges, moving inward, and is a slow process, ranging from many seconds to several minutes depending on window size. Electrochromic glass provides visibility even in the darkened state and thus preserves visible contact with the outside environment. It has been used in small-scale applications such as rearview mirrors. Electrochromic technology also finds use in indoor applications, for example, for protection of objects under the glass of museum display cases and picture frame glass from the damaging effects of the UV and visible wavelengths of artificial light.

Recent advances in electrochromic materials pertaining to transition-metal hydride electrochromics have led to the development of reflective hydrides, which become reflective rather than absorbing, and thus switch states between transparent and mirror-like.

Suspended particle devices

In suspended particle devices (SPDs), a thin film laminate of rod-like particles suspended in a fluid is placed between two glass or plastic layers, or attached to one layer. When no voltage is applied, the suspended particles are arranged in random orientations and tend to absorb light, so that the glass panel looks dark (or opaque), blue or, in more recent developments, grey or black color. When voltage is applied, the suspended particles align and let light pass. SPDs can be dimmed, and allow instant control of the amount of light and heat passing through. A small but constant electrical current is required for keeping the SPD smart window in its transparent stage.

Polymer dispersed liquid crystal devices

In polymer dispersed liquid crystal devices (PDLCs), liquid crystal droplets are arranged in a sheet between two layers of glass. In the "off" state, they are randomly oriented and, when switched on, they align according to the electric field. The liquid crystals scatter light, without blocking it, thus the glass looks white even when in its transparent state. There is a possibility of controlling the amount of light and heat passing through, as discovered by SmartGlass International, when tints and special inner layers are used. It is also possible to create fire-rated and anti X-Ray versions for use in special applications. The device operates in on or off states only. This technology has been used in interior and exterior settings for privacy control (for example conference rooms, intensive-care areas, bathroom/shower doors) and as a temporary projection screen. SPD Systems manufactures and markets this glass under the name of "SmartScreen". A new (3rd) generation of switchable privacy film/glass, called 3G Privacy Film or NPD-LCD, is available now. NPD-LCD technology has greatly reduced haze level in clear state, lowered driving voltage from 80~100V to 20V and extended operational life-time many times.

Related areas of technology

The expression smart glass can be interpreted in a wider sense to include also glazings that change light transmission properties in response to an environmental signal such as light or temperature.

- Different types of glazing can show a variety of chromic phenomena, that is, based on photochemical effects the glazing changes its light transmission properties in response to an environmental signal such as light (photochromism), temperature (thermochromism), or voltage (electrochromism).

- Liquid crystals, when they are in a thermotropic state, can change light transmission properties in response to temperature.

- Tungsten doped Vanadium dioxide VO_2 coating reflects infrared light when the temperature rises over 29 degrees Celsius, to block out sunlight transmission through windows at high ambient temperatures.

These types of glazing cannot be controlled manually. In contrast, all electrically switched smart windows can be made to automatically adapt their light transmission properties in response to temperature or brightness by integration with a thermometer or photosensor, respectively.

The topic of smart windows in a wider sense includes also self-cleaning glass and the automatic opening or closing of windows for ventilation purposes, for example according to a timer or in response to a rain sensor.

Examples of Use

Smart Glass using one of the aforementioned technologies has been seen in a number of high profile applications in the past year. The technology is especially suited to the purpose, as the set was originally open to a public place, meaning that people could do obscene things behind the presenters. The new set with Smart Glass allows the street scene to be visible at times, or replaced with either opaque or transparent blue coloring, masking the view.

The new Boeing 787 Dreamliner features electrochromic windows which replace the pull down window shades on existing aircraft.

Kilwin's and Sloan's Ice Cream in Florida, USA are famous for having a bathroom whose door or walls are made of smart glass. When the door is unlocked, the glass in the bathroom is transparent, allowing a full view of the interior. When the door is locked, the glass becomes opaque, providing privacy for the occupant.

Smart glass was and is used for cars in small series. The Ferrari 575 M Superamerica had an electrochromic roof as standard and the Maybach has a PDLC roof as option.

(*Selected from http：//en.wikipedia.org/wiki/Smart_glass*，2014)

New Words and Expressions

switchable glass 开关玻璃
skylight   *n.* 天窗
glazing   *n.* 玻璃装配业，玻璃窗，上釉，上光
voltage   *n.* 电压，伏特数
button   *n.* 纽扣，按钮；*v.* 扣住，扣紧
opaque   *n.* 不透明物；*a.* 不透明的，不传热的，迟钝的
privacy   *n.* 独处而不受干扰，秘密
electrochromic   *a.* 电镀铬的
suspended   *a.* 暂停的，缓期的（宣判），悬浮的
emissivity   *n.* 发射率
hydride   *n.* 氢化物
dimming   减低亮度，变暗
translucent   *a.* 半透明的，透明的
opacity   *n.* 不透明性
effectuate   *v.* 实行，完成
rearview mirror   （车辆上的）后视镜
frame   *n.* 结构，体格；*v.* 构成，设计，制定
dispersed   *a.* 被驱散的，被分散的，散布的
temporary   *a.* 暂时的，临时的，临时性
laminate   *v.* 碾压
tungsten   *n.* 钨
doped   *a.* 掺杂质的
vanadium dioxide   二氧化钒 VO_2
ambient   *a.* 周围的；*n.* 周围环境
intensive-care areas   重病特别护理区，重症监护区
haze   *n.* 薄雾，疑惑，阴霾；*v.* 使变朦胧，变朦胧，变糊涂
aforementioned   *a.* 上述的，前述的
profile   *n.* 剖面，侧面，外形，轮廓
Ferrari   一种车名（法拉利）
Maybach   一种车名

Notes

① Smart glass or switchable glass，also called smart windows or switchable windows in its application to windows or skylights，refers to electrically switchable glass or glazing which changes light transmission properties when voltage is applied. light transmission：光

传导，光透射。参考译文：智能玻璃或开关玻璃，由于在应用中适应于窗户或天窗中，也被称为智能窗户或开关视窗，对这种玻璃施加电压时，可以改变其光透射性。

② Electrochromic devices change light transmission properties in response to voltage and thus allow controlling the amount of light and heat passing through. in response to：响应，适应。根据原文，这是一个原因在前，结果在后的句子，可以翻译成两个简单句。参考译文：由于电压可以使电镀铬的装置改变光透射性，因此可以根据这个响应来控制光和热透过的量。

③ Darkening occurs from the edges, moving inward, and is a slow process, ranging from many seconds to several minutes depending on window size. range from…to…：范围从……到……。参考译文：从边缘开始变暗，并向里移动，是一个很缓慢的过程。根据窗户的尺寸不同，这个过程可以持续几秒到几分钟的时间。

④ Recent advances in electrochromic materials pertaining to transition-metal hydride electrochromics have led to the development of reflective hydrides, which become reflective rather than absorbing, and thus switch states between transparent and mirror-like. pertaining to：与……有关系的，附属……的，为……固有的；transition-metal：过渡金属元素；reflective：反射的。这个句子比较复杂，有一个由which引导的定语从句，which修饰的是前面的句子。本句的意思是：电镀铬材料的优点与过渡金属氢化物有关，这导致了反射氢化物的发展，这种发展是反射的而不是吸收的，因此其状态介于透明的和像镜子似的之间。

⑤ In the "off" state, they are randomly oriented and, when switched on, they align according to the electric field. electric field，电场。they 指代上句的 liquid crystal droplets 本句的意思是：在关的状态，小的液晶滴是随意导向的，当开关合上的时候，它们则根据电场排列。

⑥ Smart glass was and is used for cars in small series. 这个句子看上去较简单，但它表示了过去和现在两层意思。参考译文：不论是过去还是现在，智能玻璃都应用到一小部分小汽车当中。

Reading Comprehension

(1) Which devices do not belong to smart glass technologies?

(A) Transparent devices (B) Electrochromic devices

(C) Suspended particle devices (D) Liquid crystal devices

(2) The electrochromic material changes its opacity between a _____ state and a _____ state in electrochromic windows.

(A) colorful; transparent (B) transparent; translucent

(C) colored; uncolored (D) uncolored; colored

(3) Electrochromic glass has been used in small-scale applications such as _____ .

(A) rearview mirrors (B) museum display glass

(C) picture frame glass (D) all of the above

(4) According to the passage, which of the following is NOT TRUE?

(A) When no voltage is applied, the suspended particles are arranged in random orientations.
(B) When no voltage is applied, the suspended particles are tend to absorb light.
(C) When voltage is applied, the glass panel looks dark (or opaque), blue or, in more recent developments, grey or black color.
(D) When voltage is applied, the suspended particles align and let light pass.

(5) According to the passage, which of the following is FALSE?
(A) Certain types of smart glass can allow users to control the amount of light and heat passing through.
(B) Electrochromic devices can not change light transmission properties in response to voltage and thus allow controlling the amount of light and heat passing through.
(C) Suspended particle devices can be dimmed, and allow instant control of the amount of light and heat passing through.
(D) When tints and special inner layers are used, there is a possibility of controlling the amount of light and heat passing through.

(6) which of the following word can replace the underlined word "expression", which is in the sentence "The expression smart glass can be interpreted in a wider sense to include also glazings that change light transmission properties in response to an environmental signal such as light or temperature."?

(A) meaning (B) interest
(C) showing (D) explain

Unit 14　Polymers for Food Packaging and Health Systems

The current global consumption of plastics is more than 200 million tonne, with an annual grow of approximately 5%, which represents the largest field of application for crude oil. It emphasizes how dependent the plastic industry is on oil and consequently how the increasing of crude oil and natural gas price can have an economical influence on the plastic market. It is becoming increasingly important to utilize alternative raw materials. Until now petrochemical-based plastics such as polyethylene terephthalate (PET), polyvinylchloride (PVC), polyethylene (PE), polypropylene (PP), polystyrene (PS) and polyamide (PA) have been increasingly used as packaging materials because their large availability at relatively low cost and because their good mechanical performance such as tensile and tear strength, good barrier to oxygen, carbon dioxide, anhydride and aroma compound, heat sealability, and so on. Plastic packaging materials are also often contaminated by foodstuff and biological substance, so recycling these material is impracticable and most of the times economically not convenient. The growing environmental awareness imposes to packaging films and process both user-friendly and eco-friendly attributes. As a consequence biodegradability is not only a functional requirement but also an important environmental attribute.

The compostability attribute is very important for biopolymer materials because while recycling is energy expensive, composting allows disposal of the packages in the soil. By biological degradation it produced only water, carbon dioxide and inorganic compounds without toxic residues.

Biopolymers made with manufactures renewable resources have to be biodegradable and especially compostable, so they can act as fertilizers and soil conditioners. Whereas plastics based on renewable resources do not necessary have to be biodegradable or compostable, the second ones, the bioplastic materials, do not necessary have to be based on renewable materials because the biodegradability is directly correlated to the chemical structure of the materials rather than the origin. In particular, the type of chemical bond defines whether and in which time the microbes can biodegrade the material. Several synthetic polymers are biodegradable and compostable such as starch, cellulose and lignin, which are naturally carbon-based polymers. Vice versa, same bioplast based on natural monomer, can loose the biodegradability property through chemical modification like polymerization, such as for example Nylon 9 types polymers obtained from polymerization of oleic acid monomer or Polyamid 11 obtained from the polymerization of castor oil monomer.

Plastics are compounds based on polymers and several other chemicals like additives, stabilizers, colorants, processing aids, etc., which quantity and type change from a polymer to another, because each final products have to be optimized with regard its processing and future application. For these reasons, manufacture a product using a 100% renewable resources is neither impossible in the early future and the tendency is to utilize the highest proportion of renewable resources possible. Bioplastics, like plastics, present a large spectrum of application such as collection bags for compost, agricultural foils, horticultures, nursery products, toys, fibers, textiles, etc. Other fields such as packaging and technical application are gaining importance. The performance expected from bioplastic materials used in food packaging application is containing the food and protecting it from the environment and maintaining food quality. It is obvious that to perform these functions is important to control and modify their mechanical and barrier properties, which consequently depend on the structure of the polymeric packaging material.

From our point of view, it is important to understand not only the physical and mechanical properties of such materials for the task but also the compatibility with the food, which has been recognized as a potential source of loss in food quality properties.

Chemistry of degradation

The bioplastic aim is to imitate the life cycle of biomass, which includes conservation of fossil resources, water and CO_2 production, as described in Figure 4.11.

Polymer-based products are required to biodegrade on a controlled way: natural polymer (like rubber, lignin, humus) and synthetic polymer like polyolefins biodegrade and cannot satisfy the rapid mineralization criteria requested for standard biodegradation. During the oxo-degradation of carboxylic acid, molecules of alcohols, aldehydes and

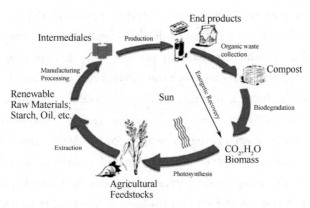

Figure 4.11 the life cycle of biomass

ketones biodegradable with low molar mass are produced by peroxidation, initiated by heat or light, which are the primary cause of the loss of mechanical properties of hydrocarbon polymers. Than bacteria, fungi, enzymes start the bioassimilation giving rise to biomass and CO_2 that finally form the humus. Generally synthetic polymers contain antioxidants and stabilizers added to protect the polymer against mechano-oxidation during the processing operation and to provide the required shelf-life. So, from one hand antioxidant is necessary to improve the performance of these materials but, on the other hand, for the biodegradation process it is better to not add these molecules during polymer processing.

Polyolefin were selected as a basis for the study of biodegradable polymer because they had already achieved a central position for packaging application, thanks to their combination of flexibility, toughness, excellent barrier properties, all at low cost because coming from low value oil fraction.

Synthetic and natural polymers stand at the opposite ends of a spectrum of properties: polyolefin are hydrocarbon hydrophobic polymers, resistant to peroxidation, biodegradation, highly resistant to hydrolysis, which is their main attribute in packaging, and not biodegradable. To make it biodegradable it is necessary to introduce prooxidant additives which promote the oxo-biodegradation by producing low molar mass oxidation compounds bioassimilate from the microorganisms. Natural compounds, like cellulose, starch and so on, are hydrophilic polymers, water wettable or swellable and consequently biodegradable. They are not technologically useful for food packaging where water resistant is required.

The use of long-lasting polymers as packaging materials for short application is not justified, also because physical recycling of these materials is often impractical because food contamination. While most of the commercialized biopolymer materials are biodegradable, these are not fully compostable in real composting conditions, which vary with temperature and relative humidity.

Conducting Polymers for drug delivery systems

Controlled delivery can improve the bioavailability of drugs by preventing degradation before the carriers arrive at the target site, thereby enhancing uptake and maintaining the concentration of drug. Therefore, the biomedical field has become more and more interested in finding and designing suitable biomaterials for safe and effective drug delivery. Currently, a wide range of drug delivery systems has been developed, including hydrogels, polymers, lipids, implants, and conducting polymers. CPs are excellent potential candidates for drug release systems because they can be easily synthesized on conductive surfaces on the nanoscale and have inherent electroactivity, which can be used to trigger molecule release. In the past few decades, many CPs have been investigated to determine if they could be used as effective drug carriers for stimuli-responsive drug delivery. Conducting polymers' unique redox properties, which involve the entry/expulsion of anions during oxidation or reduction, can control drug release (Figure. 4.12).

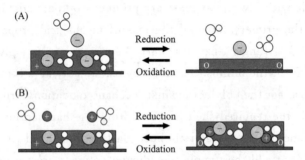

Figure 4.12. (A) PPY prepared with mobile anions contract and release anions when reduced (anion-driven actuation). (B) PPY prepared with immobilized anions swell and incorporate cations when reduced (cation driven actuation). Cations are later be released upon oxidation.

Nanostructured conducting polymer-based delivery systems have many advantages. They can tune the release profile by using different stimulation conditions and show enhanced drug loading capacities, easy loading, little influence on drug activity and well-controlled release rates. Nanostructured PEDOT has also been used for controlled drug release. Both in vitro and in vivo results demonstrated that the nanostructured PEDOT coatings reduced electrode impedance, improved charge delivery and increased local trophic factor release to cochlear fluids. In recent years, self-powered drug delivery systems based on nanostructured conducting polymers have also been developed. In addition, research on the application of polyaniline to drug release systems has been reported. Therefore, nanostructured conducting polymers have great potential in controlled drug delivery. Although nanostructured CPs have immense potential in drug-delivery applications, they also have some disadvantages that may limit their applications, including the occurrence of an initial burst release of the drug.

(*Selected from Valentina Siracusa, Pietro Rocculi, Santina Romani and Marco Dalla Rosa. Biodegradable polymers for food packaging: a review. Trends in Food Science & Technology, 2008, 634-643 and Http://www.aspbs.com/jnn/ Journal of Nanoscience & Nanotechnology, 2014; Figure 1 is reprinted from http://european-bioplastics.org and Figure 2 is reprinted from D. Svirskis, et al., J. Control. Release 146, 6 (2010). © 2010, Elsevier Science S.A.*)

New Words and Expressions

tonne　公吨（=1,000公斤或称 metric ton）
tons　*n.* 吨，容积单位，货物体积；大量，许多
alternative　　*n.* 二中择一，可供选择的办法，事物；*a.* 选择性的，二中择一的
petrochemical　*a.* 石化的；*n.* 石化产品
polyethylene terephthalate（PET）　*n.* 聚对苯二甲酸乙二醇酯
polyvinylchloride（PVC）　　*n.* 聚氯乙烯
polystyrene（PS）　*n.* 聚苯乙烯
polyamide（PA）　　*n.* 聚酰胺
carbon dioxide　*n.* 二氧化碳
anhydride　*n.* 酐
aroma compound　芳香族化合物
sealability　密封性能，胶黏性
foodstuff　*n.* 食品，粮食
impracticable　*a.* 不可行的
eco-friendly　*a.* 对生态环境友好的，不妨害生态环境的
biodegradability　生物降解能力
compostability　肥料稳定性；堆肥能力
bioplast　*n.* 原生质细胞，原生体
bioassimilate　*n.* 被生物同化物；*vt.* ［生理学］生物吸收（食物），生物消化，*vi.*（食物等）被生物吸收；被生物消化
biopolymer　*n.* 生物高聚物
toxic residue　残毒
microbe　*n.* 微生物，细菌
starch　*n.* 淀粉，浆粉
cellulose　*n.* 纤维素
lignin　*n.* 木质素
vice versa　*adv.* 反之亦然
nylon　*n.* 尼龙
oleic acid　*n.* 油酸，十八烯酸
castor oil　*n.* 蓖麻油
colorant　*n.* 着色剂
processing aid　加工助剂
additive　*a.* 附加的，加成的，添加的；*n.* 添加剂
horticulture　*n.* 园艺
imitate　*v.* 模仿，仿效，仿制，仿造
biomass　*n.*（单位面积或体积内）生物的数量；生物质
humus　*n.* 腐殖质
polyolefin　*n.* 聚烯烃

carboxylic acid 羧酸
aldehyde *n*. 醛，乙醛
ketone *n*. 酮
peroxidation *n*. 过氧化反应
fungi 真菌类（包括霉菌，食用伞菌，酵母菌等），似真菌的，由真菌引起的
enzyme *n*. 酶
bioassimilation *n*. 生物同化，生物同化作用，生物消化
prooxidant *n*. 氧化强化剂
swellable *a*. 可膨胀的
hydrogel *n*. [物化]水凝胶
lipid *n*. 脂肪，油脂；[生化]脂类
implant *n*. [医]植入物，植入管；*vt*. 种植，灌输，嵌入；*vi*. 被移植

Notes

① The current global consumption of plastics is more than 200 million tonnes, with an annual grow of approximately 5%, which represents the largest field of application for crude oil. crude oil：原油。with 引导了一个表示时间的状语从句，which 则引导了一个定语从句。参考译文：目前全球塑料的消费超过 2 亿公吨，并且以每年大约 5% 的速度增加，这代表了原油的最大应用领域。

② Until now petrochemical-based plastics such as polyethylene terephthalate (PET), polyvinylchloride (PVC), polyethylene (PE), polypropylene (PP), polystyrene (PS) and polyamide (PA) have been increasingly used as packaging materials because their large availability at relatively low cost and because their good mechanical performance such as tensile and tear strength, good barrier to oxygen, carbon dioxide, anhydride and aroma compound, heat sealability, and so on. 这个句子比较长，Until now 意为……。参考译文：由于它们的价格低和很好的力学性能，例如拉伸强度，对氧、二氧化碳、酐和芳香族化合物的阻碍性，热密封性等，直到现在以石化产品为基础的塑料诸如：PET, PVC, PE, PP, PS 和 PA 等才作为包装材料得到广泛的应用。

③ By biological degradation it produced only water, carbon dioxide and inorganic compounds without toxic residues. By…表示通过某种途径，it 是代词，指代的是上句中 biopolymer materials 的 recycling。参考译文：通过生物降解，它只生成水、二氧化碳和无机化合物，而没有残毒。

④ From our point of view, it is important to understand not only the physical and mechanical properties of such materials for the task but also the compatibility with the food, which has been recognized as a potential source of loss in food quality properties. 定语从句一般放在被修饰的词语之后，结构较长，起补充说明，分层叙述作用。可以翻译成并列分句。参考译文：从我们的观点来看，重要的是不仅要根据任务来理解这些材料的物理和力学性质，而且还要理解与食物的相容性。这在食品质量性质中作为潜在的资源是被人们所熟知的了。

⑤ So, from one hand antioxidant is necessary to improve the performance of these materials but, on the other hand, for the biodegradation process it is better to not add these molecules during polymer processing. from one hand…, on the other hand… 意为一方面……，另一方面……。it is better to not：最好不要作…。本句的意思是：一方面，为了改变这些材料的性能，加入抗氧化剂是必需的，另一方面，对生物降解过程来说，聚合过程中最好不要加入这些分子。

⑥ Natural compounds, like cellulose, starch and so on, are hydrophilic polymers, water wettable or swellable and consequently biodegradable. and so on：等等；consequently 表示结果，参考译文：纤维素、淀粉等天然化合物，是亲水性聚合物，是水可湿的或溶胀的，也因此是生物所能分解的。

Exercises

1. Question for discussion

(1) What are natural polymers?
(2) What are synthetic polymers?
(3) What are Conducting Polymers?
(4) How do we describe plastics property?
(5) Try to describe the life cycle of biomass.
(6) Why do we select polyolefin as a basis for the study of biodegradable polymer?
(7) What's the main difference between synthetic and natural polymers?
(8) Describe the advantages and disadvantages which nanostructured CPs have.

2. Translate the following into Chinese

crude oil   hydrophilic polymer
raw material   mechanical performance
eco-friendly   molar mass
chemical bond   toxic residue

• The growing environmental awareness imposes to packaging films and process both user-friendly and eco-friendly attributes.

• It is obvious that to perform these functions is important to control and modify their mechanical and barrier properties.

• During the oxo-degradation of carboxylic acid, molecules of alcohols, aldehydes and ketones biodegradable with low molar mass are produced by peroxidation, initiated by heat or light, which are the primary cause of the loss of mechanical properties of hydrocarbon polymers.

• The use of long-lasting polymers as packaging materials for short application is not justified, also because physical recycling of these materials is often impractical because food contamination.

• CPs are excellent potential candidates for drug release systems because they can be easily synthesized on conductive surfaces on the nanoscale and have inherent electroactivity, which can be used to trigger molecule release.

3. Translate the following into English

天然气   包装材料

芳香族化合物　　　　　　　　　生物高聚物材料
化学结构　　　　　　　　　　　生物的生命循环

• 细菌、真菌和酶的生物同化可以减少单位面积生物的数量和 CO_2 的量，但不能形成腐殖质。

• 生命物质的生命循环是指保持化石资源、水和 CO_2，而原生质细胞的目标是模仿这种生命循环过程。

• 在羧酸、醇、醛、酮的含氧生物降解过程中，由光或热引发的过氧化反应可以使之降解成低摩尔质量的物质。

• 大部分商业化的生物高聚物材料是可以被生物所能分解的，当然这与材料所处的条件如温度和湿度有很大关系。

• 目前科学家开发了一系列广泛的给药系统，包括水凝胶、聚合物、脂质、植入物以及导电聚合物。

4. Reading Comprehension

(1) According to the passage, which is a natural polymer?
(A) rubber　　　　　　　　　　(B) lignin
(C) humus　　　　　　　　　　(D) A, B and C

(2) Plastics are compounds based on polymers and several other chemicals like etc., which quantity and type change from a polymer to another. _____
(A) additives and stabilizers　　　(B) colorants and processing aids
(C) both A and B　　　　　　　(D) none of the above

(3) Polyolefin were selected as a basis for the study of biodegradable polymer because they had already achieved a central position for packaging application, thanks to their combination of ___, ___, ___.
(A) flexibility, additives and stabilizers
(B) toughness, colorants and processing aids
(C) excellent barrier properties, toughness, and colorants
(D) flexibility, toughness and excellent barrier properties

(4) Polyolefin's special properties are based on its _____.
(A) structure　　　　　　　　　(B) molecular
(C) functional group　　　　　　(D) not mentioned in the text

(5) About polyolefin, all the following properties are true EXCEPT _____.
(A) resistant to peroxidation
(B) highly resistant to hydrolysis
(C) promote the oxo-biodegradation
(D) resistant to biodegradation

(6) Bioplastics, like plastics, present a can be widely used in such as _____, large spectrum of application such as, agricultural foils, horticultures, and etc.
(A) collection bags for compost　(B) nursery products
(C) fibers and fuels　　　　　　(D) textiles and toys

(7) Which is disadvantage that nanostructured CPs have? _____

(A) Immense potential (B) Too expensive
(C) It's an initial burst release of the drug (D) Not mentioned in the text

Reading Material

Properties and Applications of Polymers for Food Packaging and Health Systems

Barrier properties

The determination of the barrier properties of a polymer is crucial to estimate and predict the product-package shelf life. The specific barrier requirement of the package system is related to the product characteristics and the intended end-use application. Generally plastics are relatively permeable to small molecules such as gases, water vapor, organic vapors and liquids and they provide a broad range of mass transfer characteristics, ranging from excellent to low barrier value, which is important in the case of food products. Water vapor and oxygen are two of the main permeations studied in packaging applications, because they may transfer from the internal or external environment through the polymer package wall, resulting in a continuous change in product quality and shelf-life. Carbon dioxide is now important for the packaging in modified atmosphere (MAP technology) because it can potentially reduce the problems associated with processed fresh product, leading a significantly longer shelf-life. For example, for fresh product respiration rate is of a great importance in MAP design so identify the best packaging is a crucial factor.

Mechanical properties

It is well-known that the polymer architecture plays an important role on the mechanical properties, and consequently on the process utilized to modeling the final product (injection moulding, sheet extrusion, blow moulding, thermoforming, and film forming). In addition, many packaging containers are commercially used below room temperature, so it is important to assess the mechanical performance under these conditions. Tensile test analyses are made to determine the tensile strength (MPa), the percent elongation at yield (%), the percent elongation at break (%) and the elastic modulus (GPa) of the food polymer packaging material.

Chemical resistance properties

Products that could be packaged in this kind of containers ay have weak or strong acid characteristics; so it is necessary to assess the performance and the suitability of biopolymers stored with common food packaging solution as a function of time. The interaction and absorption between chemical compounds and polymer may affect the final mechanical properties of a polymer. Normally the chemical resistance is tested measuring the tensile stress, elongation at break and modulus of elasticity of sample submerged in weak and strong acid solutions as a function of time, simulating real conditions, at ambient temperature (22℃) and at −18℃ etc. The weak acid solution is prepared with acetic acid while the strong acid solution is prepared with hydrochloric acid.

Biocompatibilities

The biocompatibility of conducting polymers is important for their use in neural probes. The usual assessment of cytocompatibility tends to focus on in vitro cell attachment and proliferation tests using neural-like cell lines. This cell line is robust and retains a number of neuronal characteristics, including the ability to sprout neurites in the presence of neuron growth factor.

The biocompatibility of PPy could examined by seeding primary cerebral cortical cells onto the PPy surface and implanting electrodes coated with PPy into the cerebral cortices of rats.

Some important production consideration

Currently, there are several types of bio-based polymers on the market: same coming from petrochemical monomer, like certain types of polyester, polyester amides and polyvinyl alcohol, produced by different manufacturer, used principally as films or moulding. Four other bio-based polymers are starch materials, cellulose materials, polylactic acid (Polyester, PLA), polyhydroxy acid (polyester, PHA). Until now, the PHA polymer is a very expensive polymer because it is commercially available in very limited quantities. PLA is becoming a growing alternative as a green food packaging materials because it was found that in many situations it performs better than synthetic ones, like oriented polystyrene (OPS) and PET materials. Different types of materials can be combined to form blend or compounds or semifinished products such as films.

The degradation of the materials is normally studied under real compost conditions and under ambient exposure by different techniques. The polymer degradation rate is determined by the nature of the functional groups and the polymer reactivity with water and catalysts. Any factor which affects the reactivity such as particle size and shape, temperature, moisture, isomer percentage, residual monomer concentration, molecular weight, molecular weight distribution, water diffusion, metal impurities from the catalyst, will affect the polymer degradation rate. In general high temperature and humidity will degrade more rapidly the polymer. By visual inspection the packages are observed for color, texture, shape and change in dimension. Generally a digital camera is used to take the pictures.

By gel permeation chromatography it is possible to determine the molecular weight of samples dissolved in the appropriate solvent. Molecular weight variations are an indication of the degradation rate of the polymers and give information about when the main fragmentation occurs in a polymer.

The determination of the pH of the sample surrounding is one of the most important factors of hydrolytic polymer degradation since pH variations can change hydrolysis rates by few orders of magnitude. The chemical resistance is normally determined exposing the materials to weak acid (pH=6, acetic acid solution) and strong acid (pH=2, hydrochloric acid solution) for a period of 0, 1, 3, 5 and 7 days.

Concerning the mechanical properties, the samples could be analyzed by Impact tests, tensile properties and Compression Test of Thermoformed Containers. Generally these parameters are studies at ambient temperature (22℃) and at frozen food storage temperatures of −18℃ etc., since fresh produce packaging and deli containers are generally used commercially at these conditions.

Biodegradable polymers applications in food packaging field

The field of application of biodegradable polymer in food-contact articles includes disposable cutlery, drinking cups, salad cups, plates, overwrap and lamination film, straws, stirrers, lids and cups, plates and containers for food dispensed at delicatessen and fast-food establishments. These articles will be in contact with aqueous, acidic and fatty foods that are dispensed or maintained at or below room temperature, or dispensed at temperatures as high as 60℃ and then allowed to cool to room temperature or below.

In the last few years, polymers that can be obtained from renewable resources and that can be recycled and composted, have garnered increasing attention. Also their optical, physical and mechanical properties can be tailored through polymer architecture so as a consequence, biodegradable polymers can be compared to the other synthetic polymers used in fresh food packaging field, like the most common oriented polystyrene (OPS) and polyethylene terephthalate (PET).

Depending on the production process and on the source, biopolymers can have properties similar to traditional ones. They are generally divided into three groups: polyesters; starch-based polymer; and others.

Others biomaterials not used in food application

Another natural plastic material, the casein formaldehyde, can be generated from a natural protein obtained from milk, horn, soy bean, wheat, etc. It is insoluble in water, inflammable and odorless. This material is used to make buttons, pins, cigarette-cases, umbrella handles and so on but not in food application.

The cellulose acetate (CA) is an amorphous tough thermoplastic obtained by introducing the acetyl radical of acetic acid into cellulose (cotton or wood). To decrease its inflammability it is used with additives, with self-extinguishing properties. Cellulose acetate is an insulator material with a little tendency to brittle under freezing point. Horn is an organic thermoplastic material containing 80% of keratin; it can be pressed in various objects and laminas, like buttons, combs, pens, and so on.

Linear Artificial Muscles or Actuators Based on Nanostructured Conducting Polymers

The simplest linear muscle-like actuators consist of freestanding conducting polymer

(CP) films that are connected at their ends. The actuators are based on the longitudinal expansion and contraction of the film when it is charged or discharged. Linear actuators produce greater force and are more easily preloaded and attached than layered actuators. Therefore, a variety of linear actuators have been fabricated. A polypyrrole (PPy) nanorod actuator was synthesized by electrochemically polymerizing pyrrole in the pores of an anodized aluminum oxide (AAO) template (Figure. 4.13).

The actuators produced a piston-like motion in the longitudinal direction by volume expansion and were activated in different liquid electrolytes containing various ion volumes. The PPy actuators achieved a 43% increase maximum; the increase was accompanied by increasing anion size in the liquid electrolytes. The actuators could potentially be used in nano-and micro-electromechanical systems or in the biomimetic or biomedical fields. The average diameter of the [poly (3,4-ethylenedioxythiophene)](PEDOT) /polystyrene-sulfonate (PSS) particles was 41 nm, and the film surface was entirely covered by large conductive regions, favoring current flow and leading to high electrical conductivity. Furthermore, leverage actuators (PolyMuscle) made of nanostructured PEDOT/PSS linear actuators were fabricated; the linear actuator produced enough leverage to cause the large displacement of a beam (Figure. 4.14). The results demonstrated that nanostructured conducting polymers may be good candidates for a new class of actuators or artificial muscles that work in air as a result of their electrical conductivity and hygroscopic nature.

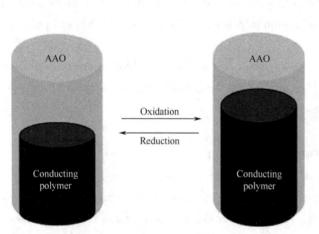

Figure 4.13 Schematic linear actuation of PPy nanorod.

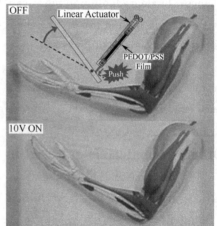

Figure 4.14 Photographs of leverage actuator 'PolyMuscle' using PEDOT/PSS linear actuators.

(*Selected from Valentina Siracusa, Pietro Rocculi, Santina Romani and Marco Dalla Rosa. Biodegradable polymers for food packaging: a review. Trends in Food Science & Technology, 2008, 634-643 and* <u>Http://www.aspbs.com/jnn/</u> *Journal of Nanoscience & Nanotechnology, 2014; Figure 1 is reprinted from S. Park, et al., Sens. Actuators B: Chem. 135, 592 (2009). © 2009, Elsevier Science S.A; Figure 2. Is reprinted from H. Okuzaki, et al., React. Funct. Polym. 73, 986 (2013). © 2013, Elsevier Science S.A*)

New Words and Expressions

barrier properties 防护性能，阻隔（水、气、光）性质
crucial *a*. 至关紧要的
shelf life *n*. （包装食品的）货架期，保存限期
permeable *a*. 有浸透性的，能透过的
respiration *n*. 呼吸，呼吸作用
cytocompatibility *n*. 细胞相容性
robust *a*. 强健的，健康的，粗野的，粗鲁的
moulding *n*. 模制，浇铸
permeation *n*. 渗入，透过
extrusion *n*. 挤出，推出，喷出的，突出的，赶出
thermoform *n*. （塑料等的）加热成形，热力塑型；*v*. 使加热成形，给……用热力塑型
assess *v*. 估定，评定
modulus of elasticity 弹性模量，弹性系数
hydrochloric *a*. 氯化氢的，盐酸的
ambient *a*. 周围的；*n*. 周围环境
isomer *n*. 异构体
residual *a*. 剩余的，残留的
gel *n*. 凝胶体；*v*. 成冻胶
fragmentation *n*. 分裂，破碎
hydrolytic *a*. 水解的，产生水解（作用）的
disposable *a*. 可任意使用的
cutlery *n*. 餐具
overwrap *n*. （香烟、面包等的）透明外包装纸
lamination *n*. 叠片结构
straw *n*. 稻草，麦秆
lids *n*. 盖子；*v*. 给……盖盖子
delicatessen *n*. 熟食店
garnered *v*. 储存
polyethylene terephthalate（PET） *n*. 聚对苯二甲酸乙二醇酯
starch *n*. 淀粉，浆粉
casein *n*. 干酪素，酪蛋白
formaldehyde *n*. 甲醛，蚁醛
cellulose *n*. 纤维素
keratin *n*. 角蛋白
leverage *n*. 手段，影响力，杠杆作用，杠杆效率；*v*. 利用，举债经营
actuator *n*. 促动器，驱动器，执行机构，螺线管
polypyrrole（PPy） 聚吡咯

anodized v. 阳极电镀，作阳极化处理
longitudinal a. 轻度的，纵的，经线的
expansion n. 扩充；膨胀；开展
contraction n. 收缩，传染，缩写式
biomimetic n. 生物测定学，生物统计学
hygroscopic a. 吸湿的，湿度器的

Notes

① Generally plastics are relatively permeable to small molecules such as gases, water vapor, organic vapors and liquids and they provide a broad range of mass transfer characteristics, ranging from excellent to low barrier value, which is important in the case of food products. 该句是定语从句，ranging from…to…，范围从……到……，修饰的是前面的 a broad range，而 which…引导的一个定语从句修饰的是前面的句子。参考译文：通常对于小分子例如气体、水蒸气、有机物蒸气和液体来讲，塑料具有相当好的渗透性，它提供了广泛的质量转移特征，范围从很好的到很低的障碍值，在食品生产中是非常重要的。

② The weak acid solution is prepared with acetic acid while the strong acid solution is prepared with hydrochloric acid. be prepared with 意为由……制备。参考译文：我们用乙酸制备弱酸溶液，而用盐酸制备强酸溶液。

③ Different types of materials can be combined to form blend or compounds or semifinished products such as films. be combined to form 表示结合起来形成……，blend 是指混合，semi-前缀，表示一半的或者1/2，semifinished 是半完成的；半成品的，参考译文：不同类型的材料可以结合形成混合物或化合物或者是半成品，例如胶卷。

④ The polymer degradation rate is determined by the nature of the functional groups and the polymer reactivity with water and catalysts. degradation rate：降解速率。参考译文：聚合物的降解速率可以通过功能团的种类和聚合物与水和催化剂的反应来确定。

⑤ By gel permeation chromatography it is possible to determine the molecular weight of samples dissolved in the appropriate solvent. gel permeation chromatography：凝胶渗透色谱法。本句的意思是：通过凝胶渗透色谱，可以确定溶解在适当溶剂中样品的分子量。

⑥ Another natural plastic material, the casein formaldehyde, can be generated from a natural protein obtained from milk, horn, soy bean, wheat, etc. It is insoluble in water, inflammable and odorless. 参考译文：另一种天然塑胶材料，干酪素甲醛，可以从天然的牛奶、触角、大豆、小麦等蛋白质中得到，它溶于水、易燃并且无味。

⑦ The results demonstrated that nanostructured conducting polymers may be good candidates for a new class of actuators or artificial muscles that work in air as a result of their electrical conductivity and hygroscopic nature. 参考译文：结果表明，纳米导电聚合物具有导电性和吸湿特性，可能适合作为新的驱动器或人工肌肉。

Reading Comprehension

(1) There are several types of bio-based polymers on the market, coming from_____,

like certain types of polyester, polyester amides and polyvinyl alcohol.

(A) polyhydroxy acid (B) polylactic acid
(C) starch materials (D) petrochemical monomer

(2) The degradation of the materials is normally studied under real compost conditions and under ambient exposure by_____.

(A) different microtechnics (B) different techniques
(C) advanced nanotechnology (D) complicated biological techniques

(3) Which is NOT TRUE about biodegradable polymers applications in food packaging field?

(A) The field of application of biodegradable polymer in food-contact articles includes ceramic cutlery, and fast-food establishments.
(B) Depending on the production process and on the source, biopolymers can have properties similar to traditional ones.
(C) In the last few years, polymers can be obtained from renewable resources and can be recycled and composted.
(D) Polymers have garnered increasing attention for the properties.

(4) There are many other biomaterials not used in food application, such as_____.

(A) cellulose acetate (B) horn
(C) casein formaldehyde (D) A, B and C

(5) Depending on the production process and on the source, biopolymers can be divided into three groups:_____.

(A) metals, ceramics, and polymers
(B) polyesters, starch-based polymer, and others
(C) plastics, polyesters, and rubbers
(D) polyolefin, polyesters, and others

(6) Which is NOT true according to the passage?

(A) It is necessary to make researches on the kind of material to enhance barrier properties.
(B) Biopolymers can have properties similar to traditional ones depending on the production process and on the source.
(C) Nanostructured conducting polymers may be good candidates for a new class of actuators or artificial muscles as a result of their electrical conductivity and hygroscopic nature.
(D) It is necessary to make researches on the kind of material to give to the consumer the impossibility to have more detailed product information than the current system.

Part V COMPOSITES

Unit 15 Introduction to Composites

A composite material is defined as a system made out of two or more phases, whose properties and performances are designed such as the result is greater than those of the constituent materials acting independently. Usually, one of the two phases is a discontinuous one, stiffer and stronger, and is known as the "strengthening", whereas the other is weaker, less stiff, and continuous, and is called the "matrix". In some cases, there can be an additional phase resulting from the chemical interactions or other effects, known as "interphase", occurring between the strengthening and the matrix. The term "composites" is usually used when the reinforcing component comprises long, or continuous, fibers and the term "compound" when the additive is in the form of discrete particles, such as powder, flakes, or short fibers. The properties of a composite result from the properties of its constituents, and from the geometry and distribution of the phases. One of the most relevant parameters is the volume (or weight) of the strengthening fraction or the volume ratio of the fibers. The distribution of the strengthening conveys the system its features. The less uniform the strengthening, the more heterogeneous the material and the higher the likeliness of failure in weaker portions, whereas the geometry and orientation of the strengthening impact on the anisotropy of the system. The composite phases play different roles and depend on the typology and application of the composite itself. In case of low-or medium-performance composites, the strengthening is usually made out of short fibers or particles, which allow for a certain stiffness and, at the same time, strengthen the material only locally. On the other hand, the matrix is the main member responsible for load bearing and for defining the mechanical features of the material. In case of high structural performance composites, they are usually made out of continuous fibers building the frame of the material and conveying it stiffness and resistance toward the fiber direction. The matrix phase conveys protection, support for fibers, and transfer of local strains from one fiber to the other. The interphase, though small in dimension, can play a very important role in controlling the failure mechanisms, the tensile strength, and, above all, the strains/stresses behavior of the material.

Classical examples of naturally occurring fibrous composites include wood and bone. It is well known that wood is a combination of cellulose fibers in a lignin polymer "matrix" and that bone is a combination of inorganic hydroxyapatite (calcium phosphate compound) and organic Type 1 collagen (protein) fiber, but the point here is that, for each of these materials, it is the specific combination and interaction of their constituent parts that together impart the observed desirable physical and mechanical properties. Lignin alone cannot carry the substantial physical load of mighty oak without the support of cellulose fibers and bones would be poorly adapted for their role in animal skeletal protection, support, and locomotion without their reinforcing collagen fibers. Likewise, fibers alone would be of little benefit without their matrix, which binds the fibers together, keeping them in place and providing a mechanism for load transfer to them from the outside physical environment.

The principles of fiber reinforcement are on composite materials but can be exemplified by considering a collection of parallel strings, held between the hands as a loose rope. In tension, the fibers making up the strings are capable of carrying load and it may take considerable force to break them. However, in compression, with no "matrix" to bind the fibers together, the separate strings easily buckle with almost negligible load.

Take the same set of strings and now impregnate and bond them together with a polymer adhesive resin and it becomes a different situation. The cured adhesive matrix fixes the strings together and provides a means of transferring load, so the "rope" is rigid in both tension and compression, although as one would expect, when placed under sufficient compressive load the rope will eventually fail by buckling as the strings separate and in all probability this will be at significantly lower load than when failure occurs under tension. There is a strong and direct correlation between the physical properties of the reinforcing fibers (making up the string in this example), the amount (volume fraction) of fibers, the length and orientation of the fibers, the nature of the polymeric matrix material, and the interface between matrix and fiber. As a demonstration of the latter point, imagine taking the same strings mentioned earlier, but this time coat. As a demonstration of the latter point, imagine taking the same strings mentioned earlier, but this time coat the strings in low-molecular-weight wax before applying the adhesive resin, such that the wax prevents the polymer matrix from penetrating the string and from effectively bonding the strings together as a unit. Now push along the axis of the rope and there will be a significant reduction in compressive strength compared with the previous case. This is as a result of the now very weak interfacial bond between the fibers and matrix. It is important, therefore, to have a strong and effective interfacial bond between fiber and matrix at the microscopic level to realize the full reinforcing potential of the fibers. In an engineering context, with the correct combination of fibers, matrix, and fiber orientation relative to the direction of applied load, the mechanical properties of the fabricated artifact can be significantly enhanced as the material of construction may be specifically tailored to meet the needs of the engineered design. These are the principles of fiber-reinforced composite materials. The same principles apply to compounds except that here the additive is either in the form of dispersed particles or short (mm and sub-mm length) fibers that in molded parts can be almost randomly oriented. The greater degree of randomness in the orientation of short fibers and the fact that the fibers are short in comparison with their diameter of a few microns limit the amount of property enhancement achieved compared with their continuous fiber counterparts. However, despite their limitations, short fiber reinforced polymers constitute an important class of materials, partly because of their relative ease of processing and partly because they present usefully enhanced mechanical or physical properties compared with unfilled materials; as such they have been the subject of significant research and application. In designing reinforced polymers, the objective is to attain desirable macroscopic material properties by combining materials at a microscopic level in the appropriate form, in optimized proportions, such that they operate in synergy whereby the resulting material can be processed by a convenient route to make artifacts that function according to the design requirements. The successful adoption of any material in any sphere of application depends on how it functions mechanically in comparison with other available materials and whether the material brings added benefits in terms of processing, design freedom, or specific functionality. For implantable materials, such functionality may include modulus matching to bone, or the ability to provide enhanced radiographic imaging.

(Selected from Steven M. Kurtz, PEEK Biomaterials Handbook, 1st Edition, Elsevier Inc., 2012)

New Words and Expressions

composite a. 混合成的，综合成的；n. 合成物，混合物，复合材料
matrix n. 基质
heterogeneous a. 多种多样的，混杂的，不均匀，非均匀，错杂
reinforce vt. 加固，使更结实，加强，充实；vi. 求援，得到增援，给予更多的支持；n. 加强加固物，加固材料
flake n. 小薄片，碎片；vi.（成小薄片）脱落，剥落；vt. 把（鱼、食物等）切成薄片
wood n. 木材，树林，木制品
bone n. 骨头，骨质物
cellulose n. 细胞膜质，纤维素
collagen n. 胶原蛋白，胶原质
protein n. 朊，蛋白（质）；a. 蛋白质的
lignin n. 木质素
oak n. 栎树；a. 栎树的，栎木制的
animal n. 动物，兽，牲畜；a. 动物的
locomotion n. 运动，移动，运动力，移动力
implantable a. 可植入的，可移植的
radiographic a. X光线照相术的
additive n. 添加剂，添加物；a. 附加的，加和的，加法的

Notes

① Each component making up the material contributes its unique physical property such that, when combined with the second material, there is some beneficial outcome. component, 成分, 零件; 要素, 组分; such that, 到这样的程度; outcome, 结果, 成果, 出路。参考译文: 构成一种材料的每种成分都有助于该材料独特的物理特性, 当与另外一种材料结合时将会获得一些有益的结果。

② It is well known that wood is a combination of cellulose fibers in a lignin polymer "matrix" and that bone is a combination of inorganic hydroxyapatite (calcium phosphate compound) and organic Type 1 collagen (protein) fiber, but the point here is that, for each of these materials, it is the specific combination and interaction of their constituent parts that together impart the observed desirable physical and mechanical properties. hydroxyapatite, 羟磷灰石; calcium phosphate, 磷酸钙; it is…that…, 该句型是强调句型, 将被强调的部分放在前面, 其他部分置于 that 之后。被强调部分可以是主语、宾语、表语或状语。强调的主语如果是人, that 可以由 who 换用。参考译文: 众所周知, 木材是由木质素聚合物基质中的纤维素纤维组合而成, 而骨头则是由无机羟基磷灰石(磷酸钙化合物)和有机1型胶原(蛋白)纤维结合而成, 但是这里关键的一点是, 对于这些材料中的每一种而言, 特定的组合和各种组分之间的相互作用赋予材料具有可见的理想物理和机械性能。

③ Likewise, fibers alone would be of little benefit without their matrix, which binds the fibers together, keeping them in place and providing a mechanism for load transfer to them from the outside physical environment. Likewise, 同样地, 也, 而且; 参考译文: 同样地, 如果没有基质材料存在纤维本身没有优点可言, 基质的作用可以把纤维结合到一起将其固定, 并为纤维提供从外部物理环境进行负荷传递的机制。

④ The greater degree of randomness in the orientation of short fibers and the fact that the fibers are short in comparison with their diameter of a few microns limit the amount of property enhancement achieved compared with their continuous fiber counterparts. 参考译文: 同连续长纤维相比, 短纤维取向性非常差; 与纤维几个微米的直径相比纤维长度是非常短的, 这些会限制短纤维复合材料性质的提高。

⑤ The cured adhesive matrix fixes the strings together and provides a means of transferring load, so the "rope" is rigid in both tension and compression, although as one would expect, when placed under sufficient compressive load the rope will eventually fail by buckling as the strings separate and in all probability this will be at significantly lower load than when failure occurs under tension. 参考译文: 这种固化的胶黏剂基质将植物纤维固定在一起, 提供了一种传输负载的途径, 这样绳子的伸张和压缩性是刚性的, 然而正如一个人所料想的那样, 当绳子承载足够多的压缩负荷时, 植物纤维将会分离而导致绳子断裂, 很可能, 在压缩情况下绳子所承受的最大负荷强度要低于受到拉伸作用断裂是所承受的负荷量。

⑥ In designing reinforced polymers, the objective is to attain desirable macroscopic material properties by combining materials at a microscopic level in the appropriate form, in optimized proportions, such that they operate in synergy whereby the resulting material can be processed by a convenient route to make artifacts that function according to the design requirements. Synergy, 协同, 配合, 企业合并后的协力优势或协合作用; such that, 这样, 以便, 如此; whereby, 然而, 反之, 鉴于, 尽管, 但是。参考译文: 在设计复合材料时,

主要目的是在微米水平上通过合适的方式选择合适的配比将不同材料相结合以得到理想宏观材料的性能，这样通过便利的加工方法根据设计要求用材料制造产品时，不同材料可以协同起作用。

Exercises

1. Question for discussion

(1) What is the composite? Can you give some examples of the basic composites?

(2) According to the text, can you give the differences between the composites and compound?

(3) What is the matrix? What is its function in the composite?

(4) How many kinds of phases do the composite materials include?

(5) What is the interphase? What is its function in the composite?

(6) What do the physical properties of the reinforcing fibers depend on?

2. Translate the following into Chinese

low-molecular-weight   the volume ratio of the fibers
high structural performance composites   mechanical properties of materials
fiber-reinforced composite materials   a means of transferring load
tensile strength   the length and orientation of the fibers

• Classical examples of naturally occurring fibrous composites include wood and bone.

• one of the two phases is a discontinuous one, stiffer and stronger, and is known as the "strengthening"

• The other is weaker, less stiff, and continuous, and is called the "matrix".

• The properties of a composite result from the properties of its constituents, and from the geometry and distribution of the phases.

• One of the most relevant parameters is the volume (or weight) of the strengthening fraction or the volume ratio of the fibers.

• This is as a result of the very weak interfacial bond between the fibers and matrix.

3. Translate the following into English

材料各向异性   低或中等性能的复合材料
连续纤维   短纤维增强的聚合物
聚合物基质   拉伸强度

• 复合材料一个两或多相系统。

• 基质是负责承载负荷和界定材料力学特征的主要成分。

• 在微观水平上纤维和基体之间一个强力有效的界面黏结对于充分实现纤维的加强功能是很重要的。

• 对高性能结构复合材料结构而言，他们通常是由连续纤维构成，这些连续纤维搭建成材料的框架。

• 界面相虽然尺寸小，但是在控制失效机制和拉伸强度方面发挥了非常重要的作用。

• 如果没有基质把纤维结合在一起，单独的植物纤维非常容易弯曲几乎无法承重。

4. Reading Comprehension

(1) The first paragraph is intended to _____ .
(A) explain what the composite materials are
(B) classify the composite materials
(C) describe the unique properties and performances of materials
(D) tell us that composite phases play different roles and depend on the typology and application of the composite itself.

(2) From the first paragraph, one can learn that _____ .
(A) In a historical perspective, the concept of fiber strengthening is quite an old one
(B) In case of high performance composites, the strengthening is usually made out of short fibers or particles
(C) The strengthening phase conveys protection, support for fibers, and transfer of local strains from one fiber to the other
(D) The strengthening become less uniform, thematerial will be more homogeneous

(3) About the composites, which of the following is true?
(A) The strengthening is a continuous phase while the matrix is a discontinuous one.
(B) The volume of the strengthening fraction or the volume ratio of the fibers might have little effect on the properties of a composite.
(C) Wood and bone are classical examples of naturally occurring fibrous composites.
(D) The properties of a composite material are not necessarily greater than those of the constituent materials acting independently.

(4) According to the text, which of the following is true?
(A) The properties of a composite result from the properties of its constituents, and have nothing to do with the geometry and distribution of the phases.
(B) The properties of short fiber reinforced polymers is similar to those of the continuous fiber counterparts.
(C) The implantable material in medical science is a kind of composites.
(D) The cellulose fibers can not be found in animal bones.

(5) What is the function of the strengthening in the composite?
(A) The strengthening allow for a certain stiffness.
(B) The strengthening is the main member responsible for load bearing and for defining the mechanical features of the material.
(C) The strengthening can control the failure mechanisms, the tensile strength of the material.
(D) The strengthening can protect the fibers from mechanical damage.

(6) Which of the following is the advantage of the short fiber reinforced polymers?
(A) They present usefully enhanced mechanical properties compared with unfilled materials.
(B) Their processing is relative ease.
(C) The physical properties exceed those of unfilled materials.
(D) The orientation of short fibers has greater degree of randomness.

Reading Material

Roles of the Matrix, Fiber and Fiber/Matrix Interface in Composites

Role of the Matrix

In polymer composite systems, the matrix is typically the component with the lowest tensile strength and stiffness (modulus of elasticity) compared with the reinforcing component. For example, some carbon fibers have a tensile strength of 5000MPa and modulus of elasticityof around 270GPa compared with <150MPa and <5GPa for the matrix, respectively. As in the string example described earlier, it is the fibers that take up the applied load and provide strength and stiffness, whereas the matrix holds the fibers in position relative to each other. The polymer matrix binds with the fibers to create a unified material, such that fibers and matrix function cooperatively to carry the applied load. The matrix may also serve to encapsulate the fibers to provide a barrier to chemical attack, protect the fibers from mechanical damage, or provide a mechanism for toughening the material system. This is achieved by providing a means of blunting any developing cracks, or deflecting cracks, or redirecting them along the fiber/matrix interface to absorb increasing amounts of energy, thereby increasing the work of fracture.

Role of the Fiber

The role of the fiber is to provide reinforcement. To achieve a material with enhanced strength and stiffness, the additive needs to be capable of carrying load. It must, therefore, be stronger and stiffer than the host polymer matrix and be of suitable geometry to enable efficient load transfer. Fibers fulfill these criteria extremely well and are remarkable in that their mechanical properties can be significantly better than the same generic material in bulk form. For example, bulk glass has a tensile strength of between 27 and 62MPa, whereas freshly drawn glass fibers can have strengths in excess of 3500MPa. This is as a result of there being far fewer flaws in glass fibers than otherwise are present in the bulk material. Under tensile stress, especially in brittle materials such as glass, flaws of sufficient size (which can be microscopically small) can quickly develop into cracks of fatal dimensions that can quickly propagate and result in brittle fracture. The strength of the material can be significantly increased by avoiding such flaws. Needless to say, there has been a lot of effort expended over the last 50+ years to develop engineered fibers and improve their mechanical strength and stiffness. This has resulted in a broad range of products that are now commercially available, including materials such as glass, carbon, boron, and a variety of organic synthetic fibers. More recent research has introduced nanofiber materials more especially based on carbon for commercial application in engineered products, although such materials, however remarkable, are not yet commercially significant for implantable devices and will not be considered further here. For implantable materials, the most significant fiber additive is carbon, because this class of material, above others, is considered more appropriate for introduction into living tissue.

Role of the Fiber/Matrix Interface

The interface enables load transfer between fibers and matrix. It is particularly important in determining the mechanical response of short fiber reinforced materials, because the discontinuous fibers exist as more or less isolated entities within the matrix that are disconnected with the outside world except via the matrix and interface. Loads applied from the outside environment must be "transferred" to the individual fibers by some mechanism and analysis shows that under tension this process occurs as a result of shear stresses at a microscopic scale in regions toward the ends of the fibers, particularly for those fibers that are more highly aligned parallel to the applied load. This applied load acts through the interface to load the fiber in tension. A weak fiber/matrix interface (with low shear strength) would mean that fibers would likely debond from the matrix at low applied stress and in this case the material would be relatively weakened and the fibers would be relatively inefficient at reinforcing the polymer. A strong interface between fiber and matrix allows for more efficient fiber utilization, meaning that a greater proportion of each fiber is capable of sustaining load. Figure 5.1 is an electron micrograph of a polyetheretherketone (PEEK) /short carbon fiber fracture surface showing PEEK polymer matrix adhering to carbon fibers after a tensile test. This clearly illustrates that in the case of carbon fibers and PEEK there is a strong interfacial bond between the two components, because a weak interface would have resulted in "clean fibers" without any adhering PEEK polymer. A low interfacial strength can be problematic with regard to materials' performance in the application. Indeed, the dangers of using materials that are substantially incompatible at the microscale of the interface can be il-

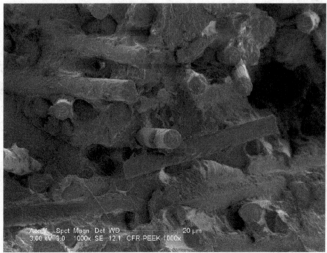

Figure 5.1 Electron micrograph of fractured short fiber reinforced PEEK compound illustrating adhered matrix on fibers and a strong fiber/matrix interfacial bond.

lustrated with reference to the ill-fated development of carbon fiber-filled ultrahigh-molecular-weight polyethylene (UHMWPE) in tibial bearing components. Carbon fiber-reinforced polyethylene, coupled with a smooth cobalt chrome alloy counterpart, was used in the development of tibial bearing components in a total knee arthroplasty device. Seventeen of 35 implants failed. These failures were categorized into three modes: breakout of mainly the posterior lips, delamination, and poor fiber/matrix adhesion. The latter point is important and it is worth comparing laboratory measurements of the interfacial strengths of PEEK and UHMWPE coupled with carbon under different conditions and by different methods. The strength of the fiber/matrix interface between carbon fibers and UHMWPE has been studied under both dry and wet (saline) conditions using single fiber pull-out tests. The results by this method indicate that the bond strength is extremely low (7.1 MPa) in the dry condition and even lower (4.5 MPa) in a saline environment. In comparison, the interfacial shear strength of CFRPEEK polymer has been measured to be 72.8 MPa using an identical fiber pull-out method. Further, it has been reported to be 85 ± 29 MPa using a more accepted transverse tensile test method, and between 74 and 112 MPa for CFRPEEK polymer quenched after annealing. Other studies report even higher interfacial shear strengths for CFRPEEK polymer (202 MPa) determined from the tensile stress/strain behavior of short CFRPEEK polymer. Taking the lesser of these values, the interfacial strength between carbon and PEEK polymer is, on average, at least an order of magnitude stronger than that between carbon fibers and UHMWPE. This is an important conclusion that supports the use of PEEK in preference to UHMWPE in combination with carbon fibers for applications such as bearing surfaces.

(*Selected from Steven M. Kurtz, PEEK Biomaterials Handbook, 1st Editon. Elsevier Inc.*, 2012)

New Words and Expressions

unified *a.* 统一的，统一标准的，一元化的
encapsulate *vt.* 封装，概述； *vi.* 形成囊状物
toughen *vt.* 使变坚韧，使变强硬，使变坚强；*vi.* 变坚韧，变强硬，变坚强
blunt *a.* 钝的，不锋利的，迟钝的，直率的，呆板的；*vt.* 使迟钝，使钝
flaw *n.* 瑕疵，缺点；裂缝，裂纹
generic *a.* 类的，属性的，一般的
boron *n.* 硼
polyetheretherketone 聚醚醚酮
crack *n.* 裂缝，缝隙，（可听到响声的）重击
deflect *vt.* & *vi.* 使歪斜，使弯曲，偏转，偏离
redirect *vt.* 使改寄，改变方向，改变线路
criterion. 标准，准则
shear stress 剪应力，切变应力，黏性摩擦应力
ill-fated *a.* 不幸的，噩运的

arthroplasty　　*n*. 关节造形术，关节形成术
saline　　*a*. 含盐的，咸的；*n*. 生理盐水，盐溶液

Notes

① Fibers fulfill these criteria extremely well and are remarkable in that their mechanical properties can be significantly better than the same generic material in bulk form. Criterion，标准，准则；generic，类的，属性的；in that，因为。参考译文：由于纤维具有比同种类型的块体材料更好的力学性能，因此纤维非常符合这些标准，也非常引人注目。

② This is as a result of there being far fewer flaws in glass fibers than otherwise are present in the bulk material. Under tensile stress, especially in brittle materials such as glass, flaws of sufficient size (which can be microscopically small) can quickly develop into cracks of fatal dimensions that can quickly propagate and result in brittle fracture. bulk *a*. 大批的，大量的，散装的，"as a result of there being far fewer flaws in glass fibers than otherwise are present in the bulk material."在此作为句子的宾语。参考译文：结果就是与散装材料相比，玻璃纤维有更少的缺陷。在拉应力作用下，特别是在玻璃等脆性材料中，足够小的缺陷（这种缺陷可以很微小）可以很快发展成致命尺寸大小的缺陷，然后可以迅速传播，从而导致裂纹的脆性断裂。

③ More recent research has introduced nanofiber materials more especially based on carbon for commercial application in engineered products, although such materials, however remarkable, are not yet commercially significant for implantable devices and will not be considered further here. implantable *a*. 可植入的，可移植的；however 用作副词表示让步，意为"无论如何""不管怎样"，用来修饰形容词或副词。参考译文：最近的研究介绍了基于碳基础上的纳米纤维材料在工程产品上的商业意义，不管这些材料怎么引人注目，但是这些材料对于移植设备没有的商业意义，在这里将不做进一步的考虑。

④ The interface enables load transfer between fibers and matrix. It is particularly important in determining the mechanical response of short fiber reinforced materials, because the discontinuous fibers exist as more or less isolated entities within the matrix that are disconnected with the outside world except via the matrix and interface. disconnect *vt*. 切断，断开，拆开，使中断。参考译文：界面可以在纤维和基体之间传递负载。它对于短纤维增强的材料的力学响应是特别重要的，因为在基质内不连续纤维或多或少存在单独的个体，除了通过基质和界面之外纤维与外部世界是没有联系的。

⑤ Loads applied from the outside environment must be "transferred" to the individual fibers by some mechanism and analysis shows that under tension this process occurs as a result of shear stresses at a microscopic scale in regions toward the ends of the fibers, particularly for those fibers that are more highly aligned parallel to the applied load. 参考译文：作用于外部环境的负载必须通过某种机理"转移"到单个纤维，分析表明在张力下这一过程的发生是由于在微观尺度区域内剪切应力对应纤维的端点，特别是那些与所施加的负载高度平行的纤维。

⑥ Carbon fiber-reinforced polyethylene, coupled with a smooth cobalt chrome alloy counterpart, was used in the development of tibial bearing components in a total knee arthroplasty device. tibial *a*. 胫骨的；bearing *n*. 轴承，支座；cobalt chrome alloy, 钴铬合金。参考译文：在全膝关节置换装置中，碳纤维增强的聚乙烯和光滑的钴铬合金，可用于胫骨轴承组件的开发应用。

Reading Comprehension

(1) In polymer composite systems, all of the following is the role of the martx EXCEPT _____ .

(A) The polymer matrix binds with the fibers to create a unified material

(B) The matrix may carry the applied load

(C) The matrix may serve to encapsulate the fibers to provide a barrier to chemical attack

(D) The matrix may protect the fibers from mechanical damage

(2) The freshly drawn glass fibers can have strengths in excess of 3500MPa, which is much greater than those of bulk glass, which of the following is real reason? _____

(A) The very small flaws can lead to cracks of fatal dimensions in the bulk glass.

(B) The glass fibers improve their mechanical strength and stiffness.

(C) The fibers can redirect crack along the fiber/matrix interface to absorb increasing amounts of energy.

(D) There are far fewer flaws in glass fibers than in the bulk material.

(3) About the role of the fiber, which of the following is wrong? _____

(A) The carbon nanofiber materials are commercially significant for implantable devices

(B) For implantable materials, carbon fiber is considered more appropriate for introduction into living tissue.

(C) The fiber has suitable geometry to enable efficient load transfer.

(D) The strength of the material can be significantly increased by avoiding such flaws

(4) Loads from the outside environment must be transferred to the individual fibers, under what circumstances is this process more likely to occur? _____

(A) A weak interface exists between fiber and matrix.

(B) Discontinuous fibers exist as more or less isolated entities within the matrix.

(C) When the fibers are more highly aligned parallel to the applied load.

(D) The shear stresses at a microscopic scale in regions work toward the ends of the fibers.

(5) When a strong interface exists between fiber and matrix, which of the following is wrong? _____

(A) A greater proportion of each fiber is capable of sustaining load

(B) This allows for more efficient fiber utilization

(C) The material would be relatively strengthened and the fibers would be relatively efficient at reinforcing the polymer

(D) Fibers would likely fall off the matrix at high applied stress

Unit 16　Properties of Composite Materials

Electrical and/or thermal conductivity

Among the most important non-structural functions that a structure may need are electrical and thermal conductivity, but the most widely used composites have polymer matrix materials, which are typically poor conductors. One very important application of polymer composites where electrical conductivity is required is in aircraft structures, where non-conducting structures may be damaged by lightning strikes. Here, conductive polymer composites are being investigated as possible replacements for non-conducting polymer matrix materials. This would eliminate the need for add-on metallic conductors, which are too heavy and may be difficult to repair. Enhanced thermal conductivity of composites is important for cooling of electronic circuits and propulsion systems. The structural advantages of composites have already been summarized in the previous section, and there is abundant evidence in the literature of simultaneous improvements in mechanical and electrical properties of composites. It turns out that very small concentrations of carbon nanotubes or other conducting nanoreinforcements in polymers lead to disproportionately large improvements in the electrical conductivity of the composite. The "percolation threshold", φ_c, which is the CNT concentration in the polymer that characterizes the insulator-conductor transition, is only 0.04 wt. % in this case. The percolation threshold for CNTs in polymer matrix materials is so low because the extremely high aspect ratios of CNTs make it relatively easy for a contiguous conducting path or percolation network to form along the tangled CNTs in the insulating polymer matrix. Since processing typically breaks up CNTs into shorter lengths, it is important to develop processes which preserve the high aspect ratios of CNTs, thus insuring the desired low percolation thresholds.

Although the thermal conductivity of CNT/polymer composites increases with the increasing CNT concentration, the increase is gradual and there is no sharp insulator-conductor transition or percolation threshold as in electrical conductivity. Although there is a lack of a percolation threshold for thermal conductivity in CNT/polymer composites, small amounts of CNTs still lead to disproportionate increases in composite thermal conductivity. For example, Biercuk et al. found that 1 wt. % SWNTs in epoxy resulted in a 125% increase in thermal conductivity at room temperature, Bonnet et al. measured a 55% increase in thermal conductivity for a 7wt. % SWNT/PMMA composite, and Kim et al. reported a 57% increase in thermal conductivity by adding 7wt. % MWNTs in phenolic resin. However, since higher filler loadings are required to create significant improvements in thermal conductivity of polymers, this may lead to processing issues. For example, Ganguli et al. were able to achieve a 28-fold increase in thermal conductivity of epoxy by adding 20 wt. % chemically functionalized and exfoliated graphite flakes, but graphite loading levels greater than 4 wt. % were found to increase the viscosity of the mixture beyond the desirable processing window for the vacuum-assisted-resin-transfer molding (VARTM) process. In some applications, only small amounts of CNTs are needed to produce acceptable thermal conductivity. For example, Sihn et al. found that the through-thickness thermal conductivity of epoxy adhesive joints can be increased by several orders of magnitude when aligned MWNT "nanograss" is incorporated in the epoxy adhesive.

Advantages of Composite Materials

Composites offer outstanding advantages compared to monolithic materials, such as high resistance, high stiffness, long duration under fatigue, low density, and great adaptability to different functions pursued for the structure. Further improvements can also be achieved for corrosion resistance, wear and tear, esthetics, behavior at different temperatures, thermal stability, thermal insulation and conductivity, and sound insulation. The fundamental features of the structural performances of composites are the high specific resistance (resistance/density ratio) and high specific stiffness (modulus/density ratio), and the anisotropic and heterogeneous nature of the material. These last features convey the composite system several "degrees of freedom" allowing for an optimization of the material configuration. Yet, composites also show some limits that conventional monolithic material do not imply. As for the fiber dimensions, composites offer the advantage of high stiffness and high fiber resistance. The usual low breaking strength of fibers is counterbalanced by the energy dissipation of the fiber/matrix interface and by the matrix ductility. The capacity to transfer matrix strengths allows for the development of diffused tensile mechanisms. Besides, fibers show a relatively high resistance dispersion. The concentration of local stresses around fibers substantially reduces the cross tensile strength.

Conventional materials are more sensitive to their microstructure and to local imperfections impacting the brittle and fragile behavior of material. Regarding the macromechanics perspective, assuming the material to be almost uniform, its anisotropy can be exploited as an advantage. The average behavior of the material can be predicted and controlled by knowing the properties of its constituents. Nevertheless, the anisotropic analysis is more complex and more dependent on the measurement procedures, whereas the analysis of conventional materials is easier due to their isotropy and uniformity.

Analyzing a composite structure requires the entry of data related to the average properties of the materials. These can even be predicted on the basis of the properties and the configuration of their constituents. In any case, the experimental testing of the analysis or an independent characterization requires a complete and comprehensive program/software to identify the parameters of a great number of basic materials. For conventional materials, the mechanical characterization is easier, since only two elastic constants and two values of resistance are required. Composites can even endure longer periods of time in aggressive environments. They show great endurance under fatigue and, in many applications, they can be easily fixed. As a contra, they are very sensitive to hygrothermal shocks. The increase of damage caused by wear and tear can occur inside the composite, thus requiring sophisticated and noninvasive detection and monitoring techniques. It can also be necessary to use protective coats against erosion, surface damages, and lightning strikes. Conventional materials, mainly metals, are usually subjected to corrosion in aggressive environments. Wear and tear can lead to the formation of defects and cracks, which grow and expand to the point of engendering disastrous failures. Even if detecting these defects can be easy, fixing conventional materials is not as easy. The following are the main advantages conveyed by the use of composite materials:

- No additional loads are put on the structure
- "Adhoc" design can be performed according to different directions of stresses
- Speedy and easy application
- Reversibility of reinforcement application
- Noninvasive esthetic application
- No change to the original geometry
- Increase of structural ductility

Composite materials can even be more resistant and—particularly in the case of carbon fiber composites—stiffer than conventional materials used for construction. It follows that, when, for certain specific projects, the weight of the structure is a relevant factor, composites can become a very attractive solution thanks to their lower density. The specific density (resistance/density) of composites can even attain values four times greater than those shown by traditional materials; their normal specific elasticity modulus (modulus/density) can even be two times greater. This means, that, with equal stiffness, a structure made out of composite materials can weigh half the weight of one built with a traditional material. The nature of the phases comprising the composite dramatically impacts the final properties conveyed to the material. Nevertheless, in order to obtain a composite with high mechanical strength, using "resistant" fibers is not enough: a good bonding between the matrix and the strengthening is of utmost importance. Bonding is usually enhanced by way of a third component applied in a very thin layer on the fiber surface in order to harmonize with the organic matrix. The fibers most commonly used for the production of composite materials are glass, carbon, and aramid fibers. Their special filamentous geometry, though extremely flexible for composite production, enhances the material stiffness and strength significantly more than those shown by the same materials when used in a three-dimensional configuration. This is due to the lower percentage of imperfections compared to the monodimensional configuration. Alongside the several advantages listed above, when designing a strengthening of a structural member, it is very useful to review all possible and feasible alternatives. The fact that a special type of intervention may be performed using fiber strengthened materials does not necessarily represent a condition sufficient by itself to make this the most suitable solution. The advantages and disadvantages of these applications should be reviewed one by one according to the specific conditions of the structure, according to other possible strengthening solutions available, and according to an accurate technical and economic evaluation.

(Selected from D. Brigante, *New Composite Materials: Selection, Design and Application*, Springer International Publishing Switzerland, 2014)

New Words and Expressions

lightning strikes　雷击
electronic circuit　电子电路
propulsion　*n*. 推进，推进力
disproportionately　*adv*. 不匀称，不相称
percolation　*n*. 过滤，浸透，渗滤，渗漏
threshold　*n*. 阈值，临界值
phenolic　*a*. 酚的，石碳酸的
epoxy　*adj*. 环氧的；*n*. 环氧树脂
adhesive　*n*. 黏合剂，黏着剂
esthetics　*n*. 美学
comprehensive　*a*. 广泛的，综合的，有理解力的
hygrothermal　*a*. 湿热的
shock　*n*. 震惊，震动，打击，冲击
noninvasive　*a*. 非侵害的，非侵袭的
wear and tear　损坏，损耗；消损；磨损
bonding　*n*. 黏结；连［搭，焊，胶，粘］接
harmonize　*vt*. 使和谐；为（旋律）配和声；*vi*. 和谐；以和声演奏或歌唱
filamentous　*a*. 细丝状的，纤维所成的，如丝的
elasticity modulus　弹性模量

Notes

① One very important application of polymer composites where electrical conductivity is required is in aircraft structures, where non-conducting structures may be damaged by lightning strikes. "One very important application of polymer composites where electrical conductivity is required" 在句子中作为主语，两个 "where" 都是引导地点状语从句，第一个 "where" 修饰 "in the application"，第二个 "where" 修饰 "in aircraft structures"。参考译文：具有导电性的高分子复合材料一个非常重要的应用是用于飞机部件，在飞机部件上非导电结构可能会遭受雷击而损坏。

② The percolation threshold for CNTs in polymer matrix materials is so low because the extremely high aspect ratios of CNTs make it relatively easy for a contiguous conducting path or percolation network to form along the tangled CNTs in the insulating polymer matrix. contiguous *a*. 接触的，邻近的，共同的；tangled *a*. 纠缠的，紊乱的，混乱的，杂乱的。参考译文：在聚合物基体材料中的碳纳米管的渗滤阈值是很低，这是因为碳纳米管极高的轴径比使它在导电聚合物基质中很容易沿着杂乱的碳纳米管形成连续的导电路径或者渗透网络。

③ Composites offer outstanding advantages compared to monolithic materials, such as high resistance, high stiffness, long duration under fatigue, low density, and great adaptability to different functions pursued for the structure. adaptability *n*. 适应性，合用性。参考译文：与块体材料相比，复合材料具有明显的优势，如高性能，高硬度，长时间抗疲劳性，

低密度，对不同功能结构而言具有很强的适应性。

④ It follows that, when, for certain specific projects, the weight of the structure is a relevant factor, composites can become a very attractive solution thanks to their lower density. it follows that… 由此得出结论……，因而断定，when 引导"the weight of the structure is a relevant factor"作为状语从句。参考译文：因此断定，对某些特定的项目而言，当结构的重量是一个相关因素，复合材料由于其较低的密度可以成为一个很有吸引力的解决途径。

⑤ Their special filamentous geometry, though extremely flexible for composite production, enhances the material stiffness and strength significantly more than those shown by the same materials when used in a three-dimensional configuration. 参考译文：尽管复合材料的生产极为灵活，但是这种特有的纤维结构提高了材料的硬度和强度，其硬度和强度要远远高于具有三维结构的同种材料。

⑥ The fact that a special type of intervention may be performed using fiber strengthened materials does not necessarily represent a condition sufficient by itself to make this the most suitable solution. intervention n. 介入，干涉，干预；调解，排解。"a special type of intervention may be performed using fiber strengthened materials"在此作为句子的主语。参考译文：事实上，仅仅采用纤维增强的材料进行专门介入并不一定是最合适的解决途径

Exercises

1. Question for discussion

(1) Why can metal conductors be gradually replaced by conductive polymer composites in aircraft structures?

(2) What are the fundamental features of the structural performances of composites?

(3) Why may the analysis and mechanical characterization of conventional materials be easier than composites?

(4) What are the main advantages conveyed by the use of composite materials?

2. Translate the following into Chinese

insulator-conductor transition　　　　contiguous conducting path
percolation threshold　　　　　　　　conductive polymer composites
thermal conductivity　　　　　　　　higher filler loading

• As for the fiber dimensions, composites offer the advantage of high stiffness and high fiber resistance.

• Analyzing a composite structure requires the entry of data related to the average properties of the materials.

• Composites can even endure longer periods of time in aggressive environments.

• Conventional materials, mainly metals, are usually subjected to corrosion in aggressive environments.

• The specific density (resistance/density) of composites can even attain values four times greater than those shown by traditional materials.

- In order to obtain a composite with high mechanical strength, using "resistant" fibers is not enough

3. Translate the following into English

非导电高分子基质材料　　　　　　　隔音

提高几个数量级　　　　　　　　　　复合材料的结构性能

高比电阻　　　　　　　　　　　　　导热性提高 20 倍

- 最常见的用于制造复合材料的纤维是玻璃纤维、碳纤维和芳族聚酰胺纤维。
- 传统材料力学性能的表征是很容易的，因为只需要两个弹性常数和两个电阻值。
- 传统的材料对于其微观结构和局部缺陷更敏感，局部缺陷影响材料的脆性和易碎行为。
- 导电聚合物复合材料正在被研究用来作为非导电聚合物基体材料可能的替代品。
- 由于需要更高的填料量来改善聚合物的热导率，这可能会导致处理问题。

4. Reading Comprehension

(1) About the electrical and thermal conductivity of the materials, which of the following is true? _____

(A) They are the important non-structural functions

(B) It is important to increase electrical conductivity of composites for cooling of electronic circuits and propulsion systems.

(C) aircraft structures are made up of non-conducting polymer matrix materials

(D) The electrical and thermal conductivity of CNT/polymer composites have percolation threshold

(2) Biercuk et al. found that 1 wt.% SWNTs in epoxy resulted in a _____ increase in thermal conductivity at room temperature.

(A) 125%　　　(B) 55%　　　(C) 57%　　　(D) 20%

(3) The mechanical characterization of composites is more difficult than conventional materials, which of the following is not a reason?

(A) A composite structure requires the entry of data related to the average properties of the materials.

(B) Their characterization requires a complete and comprehensive program/software to identify the parameters of a great number of basic materials.

(C) They require sophisticated and noninvasive detection and monitoring techniques.

(D) They are isotropy and uniformity

(4) The following are the main advantages conveyed by the use of composite materials EXCEPT _____ .

(A) Speedy and easy application

(B) No change to the original geometry

(C) Invasive esthetic application

(D) Increase of structural ductility

(5) According the last paragraph, one can learn that _____ .

(A) With equal stiffness, a structure made out of composite materials can weigh half the weight of one built with a traditional material.

(B) In order to obtain a composite with high mechanical strength, using "resistant" fibers is enough.
(C) The specific density of composites can even attain a quarter less than those shown by traditional materials
(D) The special filamentous geometry of the fibers decrease the material stiffness and strength significantly.

Reading Material

Manufacture of Composite Materials

Several technologies can be used to produce composite materials: materials with very high physical and mechanical properties can be obtained, as well as very high volumetric percentages of fibers, and it is also possible to obtain members with lower properties but dramatically reduced production costs. Manufacturing technologies of members made with composite materials vary according to the shape, size, and properties required for the finished part.

There are several production processes of composite materials, among which the most widespread are the following:

Hand Impregnation Without Pressure or Vacuum

This is still a largely common process for works on wide surfaces, such as swimming pools and boat hulls, which are typically produced in small lots and it is the most employed process in civil engineering. Reinforcements in the form of mats or fabric, in a percentage as per the design, are spread inside the mold, which, for applications in civil engineering, is the masonry or reinforced concrete support. Afterwards, the fibers are impregnated with catalyzed resin and then laid up by hand and strengthened by using metal or plastic rolls in order to eliminate the excess resin. Polymerization usually occurs at room temperature. The typical values of V_f, being the volume fraction of the fibers (ratio between the volume of the fibers and the overall volume of the composite), that can be obtained with this technology are $25\% \sim 30\%$. In a few cases, in order to improve the quality of the printed laminate, the impregnation of the fabrics is performed before laying them up, with ad hoc equipment so as to use the right quantity of resin for each foil, which allows to reach V_f values of $35\% \sim 38\%$.

Filament Winding

Even though this technique has been known for more than 30 years now, it has been profitably used only recently thanks to the introduction of reliable materials and devices which facilitated production and made it less expensive. Together with pultrusion, it is undoubtedly the production process which has seen major developments in high-quality series at relatively low costs. The process mainly consists in the winding of continuous filaments coated with resin on a rotating body, called a mandrel, whose shape corresponds to the geometry of the part to be produced. Resin solidification is obtained by placing the component in an oven or autoclave. The fundamental factors underlying this production technology which strongly impact the properties conveyed to the final composite product are:

(a) The type of winding
(b) The type of impregnation
(c) The type of mandrel
(d) The type of machine
(e) The type of polymerization process

Pultrusion

The meaning of the term "pultrusion" becomes extremely clear if we think about the technological model on which the process is based. Actually, while the extrusion of aluminum or of thermoplastics results from exerting a thrust on the material such as to force it to pass through the mold, in the case of strengthened plastics, the same shape can be obtained by pulling the fibers, forcing them, once wet with resins, to pass through the mold. That is, the thrust action of the extrusion process is replaced by a pulling action, thus the origin of the term "pultrusion". This technology is characterized by a continuous production; when the system is equipped with an automated "flying" cutting saw, production only requires a reduced human presence, limited to system startup and control of possible power interruptions to reinforcement or to the level of resin in the impregnation basin. Only recently has this technology found relevant industrial applications, but, actually, its first application dates back to 1948 and the first patent goes back to 1951. The first products manufactured by pultrusion were high-precision bars, which are still the most popular product today. The high tensile strength and percentage of reinforcement that can be manufactured, alongside other meaningful properties, such as electrical insulation, corrosion resistance, and low weight, lead to an extension of the pultruded products' palette to applications such as cable-carrying columns, insulator bars, spillways for sewage treatment plants, gangways, decks and parapets, scales, connector sockets and fused isolators, guardrails, Citizens' Bands (CB) aerials, structural beams, and much more. The process requires a mainly continuous fiber strengthening and a low-viscosity resin, usually a thermosetting liquid. The most popular reinforcement is glass roving; only recently, due to economic reasons, and in specific cases, have carbon and aramid fiber reinforcements been applied. These kinds of reinforcements are also used for hybrid composites together with glass. The basic scheme of the process is:

(a) Reinforcement feeding
(b) Preforming
(c) Forming and polymerization
(d) Pulling mechanism
(e) Chopping

(f) Postforming

Resin Transfer Molding

Resin transfer molding (RTM) refers to a special technique used to produce polymer matrix composites by injecting catalyzed resin into a mold impression having the shape of the section to be realized and previously inserted with the dry reinforcement. The chamber is obtained matching the two parts of the mold. There can be different types of mold; the most common are those made from fiberglass or metal. The RTM process can be summarized as follows:

- Mold cleaning
- Seconding coating
- Gel-coat application
- Strengthening
- Mold closing and blocking
- Resin injection and polymerization
- Mold opening and extraction of the section
- Finishing

The first two steps are common to any kind of technique, so here, it is not appropriate to deal with them further. For the remaining steps, they are mainly: strengthening application following the direction and the desired sequence, mold closing, and resin injection. This is mainly a cold process, although the mold can also be preheated to speed up the proceedings. Pressure exerted by a liquid resin is uniformly spread out on the sheet to be produced, allowing for an even thickness and excellent product quality. Usually, the pressures exerted for injection range between 0.5 and 4 bar, and the injection delays range between 20 s and 2 min. The resin transfer molding forming technique is particularly interesting for the opportunity of automation it offers and, therefore, large-scale production. Moreover, very large members can be thus molded. The use of autoclave technology to produce composite members allows for the manufacturing of sheets with very high mechanical properties compared to the more traditional and cost-effective technologies described herein The use of an autoclave allows for an enhancement of compaction with an increase of pressure during the cycle of up to nearly 7~10 atm and temperatures up to 2,000 ℃. The most up-to-date autoclaves offer different possibilities to adjust the pressure and temperature during the polymerization cycle in compliance with the most suitable law for each type of resin used. A higher pressure prevents the formation of vacuum between the layers beyond a percentage of 65 %, which is the maximum limit allowed for composite production. This kind of manufacturing process is usually chosen when specific mechanical properties are pursued, such as those required for aeronautics, the space industry, or medical devices. The autoclave process basically represents one of the most up-to-date technologies in the production of composite members.

(*Selected from D. Brigante, New Composite Materials: Selection, Design and Application, Springer International Publishing Switzerland, 2014*)

New Words and Expressions

impregnation   n. 注入
civil engineering   土木工程
mat   n. 席子, 垫子, 团, 簇
fabric   n. 织物, 布, 构造, 质地
masonry   n. 石工工程, 砖瓦工程, 砖石建筑
resin   n. 树脂, 合成树脂, 松香
volume fraction   体积分数, 体积分率, 容积率
laminate   n. 层压材料, 叠层, 层压
foil   n. 箔, 金属薄片, 陪衬, 陪衬物
filament windin   纤维缠绕
pultrusion   n. 拉挤成型
saw   n. 锯
palette   n. 调色板, 颜料
spillway   n. 溢洪道, 泄洪道, 溢口
sewage   n. (下水道里的) 污物, 下水道, 污水
thermosetting   a. 热硬化性的, 热固
aramid   n. (用以制造子午线轮胎及防弹背心等轻质高强度合成纤维) 芳族聚酰胺

Notes

① Several technologies can be used to produce composite materials: materials with very high physical and mechanical properties can be obtained, as well as very high volumetric percentages of fibers, and it is also possible to obtain members with lower properties but dramatically reduced production costs. volumetric percentages, 体积分数。参考译文: 几种技术可以用来生产复合材料: 可以生产具有很高的物理和机械性能的材料, 也可以得到高的体积百分比的纤维, 也可以获得具有较低的性能材料, 但明显降低了材料的生产成本。

② In a few cases, in order to improve the quality of the printed laminate, the impregnation of the fabrics is performed before laying them up, with ad hoc equipment so as to use the right quantity of resin for each foil, which allows to reach V_f values of 35%～38%. Impregnation   n. 注入, 浸渍, ad hoc   a. 特别的, 临时的, 特设的; adv. 特别地。参考译文: 在有些情况下, 为了提高质量的印刷板, 在储存之前需要通过专门的设备对织物进行浸渍, 以便使每一片衬底上树脂的体积分数 V_f 保持在 35%～38%。

③ Actually, while the extrusion of aluminum or of thermoplastics results from exerting a thrust on the material such as to force it to pass through the mold, in the case of strengthened plastics, the same shape can be obtained by pulling the fibers, forcing them, once wet with resins, to pass through the mold. thermoplastic   n. 热塑性塑料, 热塑性塑料; thrust   n. 推力。参考译文: 实际上, 铝或热塑性塑料的挤压导致对材料产生推力这样迫使材料通过模具而喷出, 对于增强塑料而言, 一旦湿树脂通过模具, 具有与模具相同的形状材料可以通过拉纤维迫使他们喷出而获得。

④ This technology is characterized by a continuous production; when the system is equipped with an automated "flying" cutting saw, production only requires a reduced human presence, limited to system startup and control of possible power interruptions to reinforcement or to the level of resin in the impregnation basin. 参考译文：该技术的特点是连续生产；当系统配备了自动的"飞"切割锯，生产减少了工人在岗时间，工人只需要将系统启动和电力中断时进行强化控制或在电力中断时对浸渍池中树脂液位进行控制。

⑤ The high tensile strength and percentage of reinforcement that can be manufactured, alongside other meaningful properties, such as electrical insulation, corrosion resistance, and low weight, lead to an extension of the pultruded products' palette to applications such as cable-carrying columns, insulator bars, spillways for sewage treatment plants, gangways, decks and parapets, scales, connector sockets and fused isolators, guardrails, Citizens' Bands (CB) aerials, structural beams, and much more. 参考译文：可以生产具有高拉伸强度和高加固性能的材料，以及具有其他一些有意义的性能的材料，如电绝缘性、耐腐蚀性和低质量百分比，材料的这些性能导致拉挤产品应用可以拓展到很多领域，如电缆承载柱、绝缘棒、污水处理厂的泄洪道、舷梯、甲板和护栏、体重秤、连接器插座和融合隔离、护栏、CB天线、结构梁，等等。

⑥ The most up-to-date autoclaves offer different possibilities to adjust the pressure and temperature during the polymerization cycle in compliance with the most suitable law for each type of resin used. up-to-date a. 现代的，最新的，最近的，新式的；in compliance with 顺从，符合，根据。参考译文：在聚合反应周期最新的高压反应器提供不同的可能性来调节压力和温度以便为所用的每一种树脂提供最合适条件。

Reading Comprehension

(1) The first patent of pultrusion goes back to _____ .
(A) 1948   (B) 1951   (C) 30 years ago   (D) 1960

(2) Combined with _____, pultrusion has seen major developments in high-quality series at relatively low costs.
(A) hand impregnation   (B) pultrusion
(C) resin transfer molding   (D) autoclave forming

(3) The use of filament winding should thank to _____ .
(A) the combination with pultrusion
(B) the progress of science and technology
(C) the introduction of reliable materials and devices
(D) acilitated production and less expensive

(4) According to the text, what two kinds of technology do require the use of autoclaves?
(A) hand impregnation and pultrusion
(B) resin transfer molding and filament winding
(C) resin transfer molding and pultrusion

(D) hand impregnation and resin transfer molding

(5) According to resin transfer molding, which of the following is wrong?

(A) It is a special technique used to produce polymer matrix composites.

(B) Mold cleaning and seconding coating are common to any kind of technique.

(C) The autoclave process represents ordinary technologies in the production of composite members.

(D) The resin transfer molding forming technique is particularly interesting for the opportunity of automation.

Unit 17　Polymer Nanotechnology: Nanocomposites

The general idea of polymer nanocomposites is based on the concept of creating a very large interface between the nano-sized heterogeneities and the polymer matrix. This large interface and the corresponding interphase are supposed to result in exceptional properties not possible to reach with traditional particulate filled polymers. Advantages offered by nanocomposites are claimed to be large reinforcement at very small nanoparticle content, but functional properties like decreased flammability or increased conductivity are often mentioned as well. Unfortunately nanocomposites often do not meet the expectations, they possess much worse properties than expected, not exceeding much those of traditional microcomposites. The main reason for the inferior properties is that the basic idea of nanocomposites is often not fulfilled; the large interface cannot be created. The main problems arise mostly from the fact that the homogeneous distribution of the particles in the polymer matrix is extremely difficult to achieve, the structure is not controlled or even known, and interfacial interactions are undefined. The limited degree of exfoliation, i.e. the number of individual platelets produced, is a major problem in composites containing plate-like reinforcement that leads to the formation of a complicated structure with several structural units. Aggregation is very difficult to avoid in composites containing fibers, tubes or spherical particles. Even more surprising is that compared to the basic idea behind nanocomposites, interfacial interactions are treated rather superficially, and the available information is limited and very often contradictory.

Nanocomposites can be classified in many ways; in this article we discuss them according to the dimensionality of the nanosized heterogeneity. The size is in the nanometre range in all three dimensions for particles like silica (SiO_2), TiO_2, calcium carbonate ($CaCO_3$) or polyhedral oligomeric silsesquioxane (POSS). Nanotubes and fibers (carbon nanotubes, CNTs; halloysite) are small in two dimensions, but can be micrometre long, while the individual platelets of layered minerals (montmorillonite, MMT; layered double hydroxide, LDH) are approximately 1nm thick, but their other two dimensions are usually much larger. Unlike many others, we assume that in spite of particular differences, the general rules of heterogeneous materials apply also for nanocomposites and their properties are determined by the same four factors, i.e. component properties, composition, structure and interactions. The properties of both the matrix and the filler or reinforcement influence composite properties strongly. Larger reinforcement is achieved in a soft matrix than in a stiff polymer, while particle size, size distribution, aspect ratio, specific surface area and surface energy are the most important particle characteristics to be considered. All properties depend on composition and amount of filler added to the polymer. Several structure related phenomena must be considered in nanocomposites, aggregation and orientation of anisotropic particles may occur in all systems, but the structure is much more complex in the case of layered reinforcements. Interactions can be divided into matrix/particle and particle/particle interactions, but they are more complex again in layered silicate or double hydroxide composites because of the presence of surfactants, coupling agents and occasionally other additives. Because of their increased importance in nanocomposites we focus our attention mainly on structure and interfacial interactions. The structure is not characterized properly in a large number of publications, e. g. the formation of an intercalated/exfoliated structure is claimed in layered mineral nanocomposites without defining the extent of exfoliation or looking for other structural units. Similarly, interactions are treated in very general terms using expressions like compatibility, miscibility, hydrophobicity, polarity, etc. without their definition or quantitative characterization. We also mention some factors, which are largely neglected during the discussion of nanocomposite preparation, structure and properties. Our views occasionally do not agree with generally accepted beliefs, but we find it important to point out contradictions, to raise doubt, and call attention to questions, which are neglected or not studied in sufficient detail.

Stiffness of the nanocomposites

Stiffness is the most often measured, modeled and discussed property of nanocomposites. The percentage increase in modulus is often used to prove the exceptional properties of this class of materials and also the high degree of exfoliation in nanocomposites prepared with layered reinforcements. The large increase in stiffness is observed in elastomers, indeed, but much more moderate in glassy or crystalline polymers. Polyamide (PA) is one of the exceptions in which a considerable increase of stiffness can be achieved by silicate modification. Based on data taken from the literature they argue that layered silicates offer exceptional reinforcement at very small filler content. Even larger reinforcement can be achieved by carbon nanotubes with large aspect ratio in PA59. However, often serious doubts arise on seeing such results because of the important effect of orientation, which is usually not known, on the one hand, and because sometimes basic values like the stiffness of the matrix do not seem to be correct. Because of its assumed importance, the stiffness of nanocomposites is modeled quite frequently. Usually the composition dependence of stiffness is modeled by continuum mechanical models developed for traditional composites. The Halpin-Tsai and the Mori-Tanaka models are used the most frequently, but other micromechanical models are also applied or developed occasionally. Although the papers usually claim good agreement between measured and predicted properties, the general validity of the conclusions is limited for several reasons. Various assumptions are used during the development of these models, like the linear elasticity of the components, homogeneous distribution of the reinforcement in the matrix, its unidirectional alignment, as well as the perfect adhesion of the phases. However, many of the polymers (PA, PP) deform plastically especially around the particles, the distribution of the reinforcement is never as regular as assumed (random close or cubic centered packing), unidirectional alignment cannot be achieved and orientation is difficult to characterize quantitatively, and the adhesion of the phases is never perfect due to the weak adhesion caused by surface modification. Obviously, most of the assumptions applied are not realistic and the conditions are difficult to satisfy in nanocomposites, thus the validity of the models is questionable. One encounters enhanced difficulties during modeling in layered silicate nanocomposites because of their complicated structure. Many of the models use various assumptions for the structure and try to account for the structural diversity of layered silicate nanocomposites. The structure is usually simplified in the calculations, i.e. particles and the silicate network are neglected and only individual layers and tactoids are considered. In spite of such simplifications the proper accommodation of the varying degree of exfoliation and changing orientation within the composite into the model present serious difficulties. Fornes and Paul proved that very tedious and meticulous procedure is needed to obtain acceptable data for model calculations. Accordingly, most of the modeling efforts are focused around assumptions concerning the structure of the composite and most output information is related to the structure as well. The resulting characteristics are, for example, the number of platelets per stack or the aspect ratio of the dispersed clay units. However, Osman et al. expressed their doubts about the validity of such estimates based on the argument that the composite modulus depends also on the particle orientation and on the Poisson's ratio of the matrix, and they came to the conclusion that the aspect ratio of the inclusions cannot be estimated from the Halpin-Tsai equation for layered silicate nanocomposites.

(*Selected from Gergely Keledi, József Hári and Béla Pukánszky, Polymer nanocomposites: Structure, Interaction, and Functionality, Nanoscale, 2012, 4, 1919-1938*)

New Words and Expressions

heterogeneity   *n.* 异质性，不均匀性，不纯一性
inferior   *a.* （质量等）低劣的，下级的，下等的
interfacial   *a.* （晶体或其他固体）面间的，面际的，界面的，形成界面的
exfoliation   *n.* 脱落，脱落物，表皮剥脱，页状剥落
superficially   *adv.* 浅薄地，肤浅地，表面地
contradictory   *a.* 矛盾的，反驳的；*n.* 对立物，矛盾因
dimensionality   *n.* 维度，度数
polyhedral   *a.* 多面的，多面体的
oligomeric   *a.* 低聚物的
silsesquioxane   *n.* 硅倍半氧烷
montmorillonite   *n.* 蒙脱石，胶岭石，高岭石
compatibility   *n.* 适合，互换性，通用性，和睦相处

miscibility *n.* 可混合性，易混合性
hydrophobicity *n.* 疏水性
polarity *n.* 极性，反向性
quantitative *a.* 定量的，数量（上）的
stiffness *n.* 强度，硬度，僵硬
modulus *n.* 系数，模数
polyamide *n.* 聚酰胺

Notes

① Advantages offered by nanocomposites are claimed to be large reinforcement at very small nanoparticle content, but functional properties like decreased flammability or increased conductivity are often mentioned as well. flammability *n.* 易燃，可燃性；as well 也，还有。参考译文：在颗粒含量非常小的情况下，纳米复合材料就能具有很大的加固性，通常文献中也经常提到其他功能性的改善，如易燃性降低或导电性的增加。

② Interactions can be divided into matrix/particle and particle/particle interactions, but they are more complex again in layered silicate or double hydroxide composites because of the presence of surfactants, coupling agents and occasionally other additives. be divided into 划分为，分为；coupling agent 偶联剂。参考译文：在复合材料中相互作用可分为基质和粒子之间和粒子与粒子间的相互作用，但在层状硅酸盐或双氢氧化物复合材料中由于表面活性剂的存在下，偶联剂或偶尔还有其他添加剂的存在时，这些复合材料中基质和粒子之间和粒子与粒子间的相互作用更复杂。

③ However, often serious doubts arise on seeing such results because of the important effect of orientation, which is usually not known, on the one hand, and because sometimes basic values like the stiffness of the matrix do not seem to be correct. 参考译文：然而，看到这样的结果通常会提出严重质疑，这是因为复合材料的取向影响是非常重要的，但经常在文章中并没有提及，另一方面，一些基本参数像基质的强度似乎并不正确。

④ Various assumptions are used during the development of these models, like the linear elasticity of the components, homogeneous distribution of the reinforcement in the matrix, its unidirectional alignment, as well as the perfect adhesion of the phases. elasticity *n.* 弹性，弹力，伸缩性；unidirectional *a.* 单向的，单向性的。参考译文：这些模型的发展过程中不同的假设被提出，比如像各组分的线性弹性，在基体中加固性的均匀分布，基体中加固性单向性排列，以及各相极好的附着性。

⑤ However, many of the polymers (PA, PP) deform plastically especially around the particles, the distribution of the reinforcement is never as regular as assumed (random close or cubic centered packing), unidirectional alignment cannot be achieved and orientation is difficult to characterize quantitatively, and the adhesion of the phases is never perfect due to the weak adhesion caused by surface modification. 参考译文：然而，许多聚合物（PA，PP）尤其是在颗粒的周围容易发生塑性变形，加固性分布是从来没有所假想的那么规则（假设为随机关闭或立方为中心的包装），单向排列无法实现，定位难以定量描述，由于表面改性导致弱黏附力使各体相黏附是不完美的。

⑥ The structure is usually simplified in the calculations, i. e. particles and the silicate network are neglected and only individual layers and tactoids are considered. In spite of such simplifications, the proper accommodation of the varying degree of exfoliation and changing orientation within the composite into the model present serious difficulties. tactoid   n. 触液取向胶，类晶团聚体；exfoliation n. 脱落，脱落物，表皮剥脱。参考译文：（层状硅酸盐复合材料的）结构通常在计算时进行简化，即颗粒和硅酸盐所形成的网络被忽略，只有单层结构和类晶团聚体被考虑在内。尽管已经做了这样的简化，要想恰当地调节脱落的不同程度和改变复合材料的取向性满足模型需求仍然存在严重困难。

Exercises

1. Question for discussion
(1) What is the general idea of polymer nanocomposites?
(2) What are advantages offered by nanocomposites?
(3) What difficulties do nanocomposites meet?
(4) What models are mentioned to explain the stiffness of the nanocomposites in the text?

2. Translate the following into Chinese
surface modification　　　　　　　polymer matrix
interfacial interaction　　　　　　　aggregation and orientation of anisotropic particles
an intercalated/exfoliated structure　quantitative characterization

- The general idea of polymer nanocomposites is based on the concept of creating a very large interface between the nano-sized heterogeneities and the polymer matrix.
- Aggregation is very difficult to avoid in composites containing fibers, tubes or spherical particles.
- The main reason for the inferior properties is that the basic idea of nanocomposites is often not fulfilled; the large interface cannot be created.
- Nanocomposites can be classified in many ways.
- Stiffness is the most often measured, modeled and discussed property of nanocomposites.
- The properties of both the matrix and the filler or reinforcement influence composite properties strongly.

3. Translate the following into English
高分子纳米复合材料　　　　　　传统颗粒填充的聚合物
单一分布　　　　　　　　　　　纳米颗粒的团聚
结晶聚合物　　　　　　　　　　表面改性

- 在PA59聚合材料中更大的加固性可以通过具有高轴径比的碳纳米管来实现。
- Halpin-Tsai模型和Mori-Tanaka模型是使用最频繁的，但其他的微机械模型也偶尔会被运用和发展。
- 由于层状硅酸盐纳米复合材料结构的复杂性，在建模过程中会遇到很多困难。
- 对于性能较差的主要原因使纳米复合材料的基本思想往往不能满足。

- 不幸的是，纳米复合材料往往不能满足期望，它们拥有比预期更糟糕的性能。

4. Reading Comprehension

(1) Which of the following are not main problems in the polymer matrix?

(A) The structure is not controlled or even known

(B) The homogeneous distribution of the particles in the polymer matrix is extremely difficult to achieve

(C) Aggregation is very difficult to avoid

(D) The interfacial interactions are undefined

(2) About POSS, which of the following is wrong?

(A) POSS is the shortened form of polyhedral oligomeric silsesquioxane.

(B) Their size is in the nanometre range in two dimensions.

(C) They are a new kind of organic-inorganic hybrid materials.

(D) They are composed of a robust silicon-oxygen frame work that can be easily functionalized with a variety of organic sub-stituents.

(3) Which of the following has the effect on the properties of nanocomposites?

(A) component properties (B) composition (C) structure (D) crystallinity

(4) In layered silicate or double hydroxide composites, matrix/particle and particle/particle interactions are more complex because of the presence of the following EXCEPT _____

(A) surfactants (B) coupling agents (C) filler (D) other additives

(5) About the stiffness, which of the following is wrong?

(A) Even larger reinforcement can be achieved by carbon nanotubes.

(B) Polyamide has a considerable increase of stiffness achieved by silicate modification.

(C) The large increase in stiffness is observed in glassy or crystalline polymers.

(D) Layered silicate nanocomposites have complicated structures.

Reading Material

Application of Polymer Nanocomposites

Nanocomposites can be used as structural elements in certain areas, but the real potential of these materials is in special, niche application utilizing their functional properties. In previous sections we mentioned already their use as additives in flame retardant packages, or as conductive fillers to render plastics antistatic or conductive. We mention several potential areas in this section like gas permeation and membrane technology, electronics, as well as biomedical and environmental applications. Gas barrier properties of polymers are claimed to be modified significantly by layered silicates. The general idea is that individual silicate layers with large aspect ratio increase the diffusion path of gases considerably especially if they are oriented parallel to each other. Several groups observed significant decrease in the oxygen permeability of PET/layered silicate nanocomposites produced by in situ polymerization. Brule et al. prepared blown films from PA6/polyolefin/silicate nanocomposites and found that their permeability for styrene decreased in the presence of the silicate. The main field of application for these materials is packaging where the targeted combination of properties is achieved by the preparation of co-extruded films. One solution already introduced into practice is the PA6 based Imperm nanocomposite offered by Nanocor for the production of multilayer films, and bottles for packaging of soft drinks. The same principles are used in graphene composites. Although the approach seems to work also in this case, practical applications are not known for graphene at the moment. In the last decades significant progress was made in the production of polymer based membranes. One limiting factor in improving the performance of these membranes is that selectivity decreases with increasing permeation, while productivity decreases with increasing temperature. One way to circumvent these problems is the preparation of nanocomposite membranes, which show improved permeation and selectivity at the same time. Nanocomposite membranes are used already in fuel cells as well. In these cells oxygen is reduced on electrodes containing carbon black and nano-sized platinum particles. The performance of the electrodes could be improved, when carbon nanotubes were used instead of carbon black. The diffusion of methanol is one of the main problems in methanol fuel cells decreasing efficiency considerably. Nanocomposite membranes decrease methanol permeation thus improving the performance of these cells. Another area discussed here is electronics where size reduction requires the use of nanotechnology. The size of active electronic parts is already in the nanometre range in most devices. Both the type and the specific application of nanocomposites are very diverse in this field. Light sensors, photodiodes, super condensers, other sensors, LEDs and transistors are produced from composites containing carbon nanotubes. The electric conductivity of nanotubes is used in various shielding applications as well as in diverse transparent conductive coatings, e. g. electronic displays are prepared from transparent conductive films containing carbon nanotubes. Sensors are prepared from conjugated polymers and nanoparticles, but metal oxide nanofibers, carbon nanotubes, gold, silver, platinum and palladium nanoparticles are also used in various electronic applications. Nanotechnology and nanocomposites play an increasing role in many biomedical applications. One important application is the production of networks from nanofibers for cell and tissue growth. Antibacterial effects are achieved with nano-sized silver, silver oxide, or other silver salt containing composites for dendrimer based drugs. Gelatin containing hydroxyapatite particles as well as other nanocomposites prepared with this filler are used as prostheses. Controlled drug release and targeted drug delivery are other promising fields in which nanocomposites may play a role in the future. Nanoparticles are used in increasing quantities also in various drug formulations, the particles and tubes are thought to slow down and regulate drug release. Iron oxide particles were used in several experiments targeting controlled drug release, and they were used as MR contrast or immuno-assay materials as well. The number of potential applications is probably unlimited also in this field Large efforts are done to explore the possible use of nanocomposites in environmental applications, in fact environmental nanotechnology is expected to play an important role in environmental engineering and science in the near future. Possible applications include catalytic and redox degradation of contaminants like phenol, trichlorobenzene, nitrobenzene and other compounds, biocatalysis, adsorption of pollutants like arsenic and other metallic contaminants (Pb^{2+}, Cu^{2+}, Zn^{2+}), but other applications like pollutant sensing and detection are also envisaged in this field. Although the potential of nanocomposites in environmental protection is great, several outstanding issues (interaction, optimum properties, effect of pollutants on composite properties) need resolution in the future. Moreover, the majority of recent ideasare based on laboratory tests thus industrial production and field application must be solved, which needs further efforts. The potentials of nanocomposites are extremely large in many fields, but progress towards practical applications is slower than expected. Nevertheless, nanocomposites found functional application in several areas.

(*Gergely Keledi, József Hári and Béla Pukánszky, Polymer nanocomposites: structure, interaction, and functionality, Nanoscale, 2012, 4, 1919-1938.*)

New Words and Expressions

antistatic   *a.* 抗静电的
permeability   *n.* 渗透性；磁导率；可渗透性
styrene   *n.* 苯乙烯
productivity   *n.* 生产率，生产力
selectivity   *n.* 选择性，专一性
circumvent   *vt.* 防止，避免
platinum   *n.* 铂金
membrane   *n.* 薄膜，隔膜，膜状物
sensor   *n.* 传感器，灵敏元件
photodiode   *n.* 光敏二极管，光电二极管
super condenser   超级电容器
transistor   *n.* 晶体管
conjugated   *a.* 共轭的，成对的
palladium   *n.* 钯
antibacterial   *a.* 抗菌的
dendrimer   *n.* 聚合物，树形分子，树状聚物
prosthesis   *n.* 假体，人体修复（术）
immuno assay   免疫测定法，免疫化验

Notes

① Composites offer outstanding advantages compared to monolithic materials, such as high resistance, high stiffness, long duration under fatigue, low density, and great adaptability to different functions pursued for the structure. monolithic *a.* 块体的，整体的，庞大的；resistance, 电阻；fatigue, 疲劳，疲乏，*vt.* 使疲劳，使疲乏；adaptability, 适应性，合用性。参考译文：与块体材料相比，复合材料具有明显的优势，如高阻抗，高强度，长时

间的抗疲劳性，低密度，针对不同的结构功能性具有很强的适应性。

② The fundamental features of the structural performances of composites are the high specific resistance (resistance/density ratio) and high specific stiffness (modulus/density ratio), and the anisotropic and heterogeneous nature of the material. anisotropic a. 各向异性的；heterogeneous a. 混杂的，不均匀的，非均匀的。参考译文：复合材料的结构性能的基本特征是高的电阻率（电阻/密度比）和高的比强度（模/密度比），以及材料各向异性和非均质性。

③ The electric conductivity of nanotubes is used in various shielding applications as well as in diverse transparent conductive coatings, e.g. electronic displays are prepared from transparent conductive films containing carbon nanotubes. shielding a. 防护的，屏蔽的；transparent a. 透明的，可为（X光等）透射的。参考译文：碳纳米管的导电性用于各种屏蔽应用以及各种不同的透明导电涂层，例如电子显示器就是用含有碳纳米管的透明导电薄膜制备。

④ Large efforts are done to explore the possible use of nanocomposites in environmental applications, in fact environmental nanotechnology is expected to play an important role in environmental engineering and science in the near future. play an important role in 在……中起重要作用。参考译文：人们做了很多的努力来探索纳米复合材料在环境保护中的应用，事实上环境纳米技术有望在不久的将来，在环境工程与科学中扮演着重要的角色。

⑤ Possible applications include catalytic and redox degradation of contaminants like phenol, trichlorobenzene, nitrobenzene and other compounds, biocatalysis, adsorption of pollutants like arsenic and other metallic contaminants (Pb^{2+}, Cu^{2+}, Zn^{2+}), but other applications like pollutant sensing and detection are also envisaged in this field. trichlorobenzene n. 三氯（代）苯；nitrobenzene n. 硝基苯；arsenic n. 砷，三氧化二砷。参考译文：可能的应用包括催化和污染物如苯酚，降解氯苯，硝基苯等其他化合物的氧化还原降解，生物催化，如砷和其他金属污染物（Pb^{2+}，Cu^{2+}，Zn^{2+}）的吸附，但也可以用于其他领域比如污染物的传感和检测。

⑥ Moreover, the majority of recent ideas are based on laboratory tests thus industrial production and field application must be solved, which needs further efforts. majority n. 多数。参考译文：此外，（关于纳米复合材料）最近的观点大部分都是基于实验室测试，这样工业生产和现场应用必须解决，这需要进一步的努力。

Reading Comprehension

(1) According to the text, nanocomposites can be used as structural elements in certain areas EXCEPT _____.
(A) additives in flame retardant package
(B) biomedical and environmental applications
(C) fuel cells
(D) information domain

(2) Gas barrier properties of polymers are claimed to be modified significantly by

layered silicates, please give possible explanation?
(A) Layered silicates are oriented parallel to each other
(B) Layered silicates show improved permeation and selectivity
(C) Silicate layers with large aspect ratio increase the diffusion path of gases
(D) Silicate layers have the large surface area

(3) About the nanocomposite membrane, which of the following is ture?
(A) One limiting factor in improving the performance of membranes is that selectivity increases with decreasing permeation
(B) Nanocomposite membranes are used already in fuel cells, where the performance of the electrodes could be improved by the use of carbon black.
(C) The preparation of nanocomposites can improve permeation and selectivity of the membranes
(D) Nanocomposite membranes increase methanol permeation thus improving the performance of these cells.

(4) About the application of nanocomposite in the electronics, which of the following is ture?
(A) The size of active electronic parts is mainly in the micrometre range in most devices.
(B) Carbon nanotubes have a wide range of applications in the electronics.
(C) LEDs and transistors are produced from composites containing carbon black.
(D) Silver nanoparticles are rarely used in various electronic applications.

(5) In many biomedical applications, which of the following is ture?
(A) Gelatin containing hydroxyapatite particles were used in several experiments targeting controlled drug release due to their antibacterial effects.
(B) Iron oxide particles were used as MR contrast or immunoassay materials as well.
(C) silver oxide, or other silver salt containing composites are used as prostheses
(D) Nanoparticles and nanotubes are thought to speed up and regulate drug release.

Part VI NANOSTRUCTURED MATERIALS

Unit 18 Nanotechnology and Nanostructured Materials

Nanoscience and nanotechnology are based on the manipulation of individual atoms and molecules to produce materials from them for applications well below the sub-microscopic level. They involve physical, chemical and biological knowledge at scales ranging between individual atoms and molecules below the nanometer, up to ca 100nm. The subject also concerns the integration of the resulting structures into larger systems. Many definitions of nanotechnology refer to dimensions; according to the National Nanotechnology Initiative (NNI) in the United States, for instance, "nanotechnology is the understanding and control of matter at dimensions between approximately 1 and 100 nanometres, where unique phenomena enable novel applications". Nanotechnology is associated with at least three distinct advantages:

1. It offers the possibility of creating materials with novel combinations of properties.

2. Devices in the nanoscale need less material to make them, use less energy and other consumables, their function may be enhanced by reducing the characteristic dimensions, and they may have an extended range of accessibility.

3. It offers a universal fabrication technology, the apotheosis of which is the personal nanofactory.

What is nanomaterial?

Nanoscale materials are defined as a set of substances where at least one dimension is less than 100 nanometres (nm). The nanometre is a metric unit of length, and denotes one billionth of a metre or 10^{-9} m; "nano" is also used as an adjective to describe objects, systems or phenomena with characteristics arising from nanometre-scale structure. While "micro" has come to mean anything small, "nano" emphasizes the atomic granularity that produces the unique phenomena observed in nanoscience. Often only one or two dimensions are in the nanoregime, as in quantum wells and nanowires but sometimes all three dimensions are nanoscale, as in quantum dots and nanocrystals. A challenge is to make every dimension as small as possible, as in nanoelectronics, but other times the aim is to make at least one dimension as large as possible, as in carbon nanotubes. A material consisting of a nanolayer surface, as for instance ultrathin coatings, is not necessarily considered as such as a nano-material. If only one of the dimensions is restricted, we have a layered shape or 2-D material; if two dimensions are limited in size, we will have a wired or 1-D material; if all dimensions are in the range of a few nanometers, we have 0-D materials. Many aspects of nanotechnology are based on the fact that the nanoscale world is different from the macroscopic world that we are so well accustomed to deal with in life and in applications.

Unique properties of nanomaterials

At the micron size level and above, materials have conventional properties that obey the laws of classical science, while submicroscopic objects—mesoscopic between $1\mu m$ and 100nm and nanoscopic below this size range—have properties that are affected by fluctuations around the average and become subject to the strange and unpredictable laws of quantum mechanics. In this way, many exciting new tools and functionalities are opening up in this new technological field. And this leads also to a plethora of new economic challenges and opportunities in the scientific realm too. As length scales of materials decrease, surface-area effects become extremely important and quantum effects appear that lead to profound changes in the properties of materials and devices. One effect of the small size of the materials is the increasing percentage of atoms that are situated on the surface of the objects. There is a famous quote from Wolfgang Pauli that was expressed long ago, it says: "God made the bulk, the surface was invented by the Devil".

With this logic, in nano-sized materials the Devil's realm has been extended enormously. In nanoscience and technology surface physics and chemistry start dominating the materials properties and this must be duly taken into account. The large percentage of atoms on the surface for small entities, and the reactivity that this gives rise to, concerns one of the principal factors that differentiate properties of nanostructures from those of the bulk material. One important result of the high surface area per unit mass is the reactivity of nano-size materials. If, for instance, the surface of nanoparticles is not protected through surface passivation, interactions between the particles will readily occur. Thus, in nanotechnology common concepts of chemistry lose their validity: an insulator can become conductor, stable material can become combustible, and a relatively inert material like gold might become an efficient and selective catalyst when reduced to the size of a few nanometers.

The property changes resulting from the size effects lead to both advantages and drawbacks. For example, on one side, there is the ability of quantum particles to tunnel through barriers that repel classical particles; this, for instance, underpins the operation of the scanning tunneling microscope, a revolutionary new way of the observation of nature. On the other side, the same tunnelling effect can be a source of serious problems in ultra small-scale nano-electronic devices. One other aspect to consider is that as structures enter the nanoscale regime, the van der Waals force increases. For example, it is this force that clamps graphene samples to substrates, and also holds together individual graphene sheets in multi-layer samples. Microstructures, electronics, nanotechnology are large fields of research and development. Increasingly they are now growing together. Recently, newly commercialized products indicate the innovative potential and future applications. Essential for future developments is to keep track of the composition and the structure. For that, the pursuit of chemical analysis at extremely small size levels is necessary. We cannot go here into any detail on the vastly expanding research on nanotechnology and nanoscience. There is a wide variety of analytical techniques that may provide elemental and molecular information with high spatial resolution and that are currently used for atomic scale observation, determination of structure and for the quantification of the chemical composition. Analytical techniques in the field of nano-analyses benefited of the enormous progress made in the digital realm, which allowed the high speed of signal acquisition, and on the other side, in the development in nano-sized materials and tools which are mostly used as analytical probes. The synergy created by this combination allowed the development of sophisticated analytical imaging tools that combine high sensitivity with unrivalled spatial discrimination potential.

(Selected from Freddy. C. Adams, Carlo Barbante, *Nanoscience*, *nanotechnology and spectrometry*, Spectrochimica Acta Part B, 2013, 86: 3-13.)

New Words and Expressions

manipulation　*n.* 操作，操纵
dimension　*n.* 尺度，维度
quantum dots　*n.* 量子点
nanoelectronics　*n.* 纳米电子学
classical　*a.* 古典的，经典的，传统的
fluctuation　*n.* 波动，涨落，起伏
be subject to　受支配，从属于，可以……的，常遭受
inert　*adj.* 迟钝的，不活泼的，惰性的
granularity　*n.* 间隔尺寸，粒度
as in　作为，就像，如
quantum well　量子阱
as for instance　例如，比如
submicroscopic　*a.* 亚微观的
surface passivation　表面钝化
scanning tunneling microscope　扫描隧道显微镜
van der Waals force　范德华力
tunnelling effect　隧道效应

Notes

① Nanotechnology is the understanding and control of matter at dimensions between approximately 1 and 100 nanometres, where unique phenomena enable novel applications. where 关系副词，引导定语从句主要用于修饰表示地点的名词，同时它在定语从句中用作地点状语，在这里用以修饰"at dimensions"。参考译文：纳米科学是理解和控制尺寸大小在 1 到 100nm 之间的物质，在 1 到 100nm 的尺寸上，物质所展现的独特现象可以赋予其新的用途。

② At the micron size level and above, materials have conventional properties that obey the laws of classical science, while submicroscopic objects—mesoscopic between 1μm and 100nm and nanoscopic below this size range—have properties that are affected by fluctuations around the average and become subject to the strange and unpredictable laws of quantum mechanics. unpredictable a. 不可预知的，变幻莫测的。mesoscopic a. 介观的。参考译文：在微米及微米级以上，材料遵循经典科学的法则表现出常规性质；而当材料的尺寸大小处于 1μm 和 100nm 之间的介观尺寸甚至低于 100nm 的更小尺寸时，材料的性质将会受平均波动性影响，遵循量子力学的法则而表现出异常性质。

③ Devices in the nanoscale need less material to make them, use less energy and other consumables, their function may be enhanced by reducing the characteristic dimensions, and they may have an extended range of accessibility. accessibility n. 易接近，可到达。参考译文：制造纳米级的器件需要更少的材料，更少的能源以及其他材料，纳米器件的功能可通过降低特征尺寸而得以提高，它们还有很广阔的拓展空间。

④ It is this force that clamps graphene samples to substrates, and also holds together individual graphene sheets in multi-layer samples. 这是一个强调句 it is…that…。参考译文：正是这种作用力可以将石墨样品固定在基片上，也可以将单个石墨片层组合成多层物质。

⑤ Organic functional nanoparticles created by different methods including self-assembling show remarkable molecular recognition, adhesion, optical, ionic, and molecular transport properties. molecular recognition 分子识别。参考译文：通过不同合成方法包括自组装制备的有机功能纳米颗粒展现出非凡的功能性，包括分子识别，附着力，光学性质，离子性以及分子传输性质。

⑥ Insulator can become conductor, stable material can become combustible, and a relatively inert material like gold might become an efficient and selective catalyst when reduced to the size of a few nanometers. insulator n. 绝缘体；conductor n. 导体；combustible a. 易燃的。参考译文：当材料的尺寸降低到几个纳米时，材料的性质将会发生明显变化；绝缘体可以变成导体，而原本稳定的材料可以变成易燃物质，像金这样惰性的材料也可以成为一种有效的选择性催化剂。

Exercises

1. Question for discussion
（1）What is nanotechnology?
（2）Take examples to illustrate the unique properties of nanomaterials compared to bulk materials?
（3）How many types do nanostructured materials have based on their number of dimension?
（4）Please explain why nanomaterials reveal exciting properties according to the third section in the text?
（5）What dose the small size of the materials cause according to the text?

2. Translate the following into Chinese
National Nanotechnology Initiative   ultrathin coatings

surface-area effect   nano-electronic devices
per unit mass   spatial discrimination
individual atoms   surface passivation

• Many aspects of nanotechnology are based on the fact that the nanoscale world is different from the macroscopic world that we are so well accustomed to deal with in life and in applications.

• They involve physical, chemical and biological knowledge at scales ranging between individual atoms and molecules below the nanometer, up to ca 100nm.

• While 'micro' has come to mean anything small, 'nano' emphasizes the atomic granularity that produces the unique phenomena observed in nanoscience.

• A material consisting of a nanolayer surface, as for instance ultrathin coatings, is not necessarily considered as such as a nano-material.

• As length scales of materials decrease, surface-area effects become extremely important and quantum effects appear that lead to profound changes in the properties of materials and devices.

3. Translate the following into English

纳米科学与技术   块体材料
经典粒子   量子效应
宏观世界   空间分辨率

• 仅有一维尺寸在纳米范围内，像量子线和纳米线，但有时三个维度都是纳米级的，像量子点和纳米晶。

• 纳米材料是一类至少有一个维度尺寸小于100nm的物质。

• 材料的小尺寸所产生的效应之一就是位于物质表面原子比例提高。

• 单位质量的高表面积的一个重要结果是纳米材料的反应活性。

• 尺寸效应所产生的性质的变化既有优点也有缺点。

• 微观结构、电子学及纳米技术都是很广阔的研究和发展领域。

4. Reading Comprehension

(1) According to the text, which of the following discipline is not related to the nanotechnology?

(A) physical   (B) chemical   (C) biological   (D) Mathematics

(2) Thus, common concepts of chemistry in nanotechnology lose their validity: which of the following is not given in the text?

(A) Gold nanoparticles are very reactive

(B) Ultra-high-strength steel of up to 1.5GPa is obtained owing to the inclusion of nanoparticles of nickel, titanium, and molybdenum

(C) Stable material can become combustible

(D) Insulator can become conductor

(3) Which of the following factor is related to unique properties of nanomaterials?

(A) high surface area (B) quantum effect   (C) the size effect   (D) A, B and C

(4) One can learn from the text EXCEPT _____.

(A) A single atom of a metal such as gold, although chemically gold, has a different optical absorption spectrum from that of bulk gold

(B) As structures enter the nanoscale regime, the van der Waals force increases.

(C) The tunnelling effect can be a source of serious problems in ultra small-scale nano-electronic devices.

(D) The property changes resulting from the size effects lead to both advantages and drawbacks.

(5) About the nanotechnology, which of the following is wrong?

(A) Nanotechnology offers the possibility of creating materials with novel combinations of properties

(B) Nanotechnology is the understanding and control of matter at dimensions below 1nm.

(C) The essence of nanotechnology is the ability to work at the molecular level, atom-by-atom, to create large structures with fundamentally new molecular organization

(D) Nanotechnology is concerned with materials and systems whose structures and components exhibit novel and significantly improved physical, chemical, and biological properties due to their nanoscale size

(6) The property changes resulting from the size effects lead to both advantages and drawbacks, which of the following is the drawbacks resulting from the size effects?

(A) There is the ability of quantum particles to tunnel through barriers that repel classical particles

(B) The tunnelling effect can be a source of serious problems in ultra small-scale nano-electronic devices

(C) As structures enter the nanoscale regime, the van der Waals force increases

(D) The van der Waals force can clamp graphene samples to substrates

Reading Materials

Characterization of Nanomaterials: Physicochemical Approaches

Advances in nanotechnology and nanomaterials are brought about by enhanced techniques for characterization of these materials. Techniques are required that are sensitive to nanoscale dimensions. Many characterization techniques are available for all types of materials because they respond to chemical structures, element analysis, or other general characteristics that are independent of physical size scale. Size, shape, molecular structure, electron distributions, supramolecular structures, and organization are important determinants of nanomaterial properties. Techniques available must be those that can resolve features, properties, or chemistry at the nanoscale.

X-ray diffraction

X-ray diffraction (XRD) is a technique used in structural characterization of materials, commonly at solid state (powder mixtures). X-rays have wavelengths appropriate for scattering from nanoscale structures in reciprocal space. In the process of X-ray diffraction, the crystal diffracts an X-ray beam that passes through it and yields beams at particular angles depending on the wavelength of X-ray irradiation, the orientation, and the structure of the crystal. Soon afterwards, the X-rays are significantly diffracted through electron density, and analysis of the angles in diffraction yields an electron density map of the crystal, which is used to analyze the crystalline of materials. Analysis of the diffraction pattern allows obtaining information such as lattice parameter, crystal structure, sample orientation, and particle size.

We will only mention that lattice parameters are obtained from the Bragg formula: $2d\sin\theta = n\lambda$, where d is the lattice spacing. In a typical setup, a collimated beam of X-rays is incident on the sample. The intensity of the diffracted X-rays is measured as a function of the diffraction angle 2θ. The intensities of the spots provide information about the atomic basis. The sharpness and shape of the spots relates to the perfection of the crystal. The two basic procedures involve either a single crystal or a powder. With single crystals, a lot of information about the structure can be obtained. On the other hand, single crystals might not be readily available and orientation of the crystal is not straightforward. One disadvantage of XRD is the low intensity of the diffracted beam for low-Z materials.

Optical spectroscopy

Optical spectroscopy uses the interaction of light with matter as a function of wavelength or energy in order to obtain information about the material. For example, absorption or emission (photoluminescence or PL) experiments with visible and UV light tend to reveal the electronic structure. Vibrational properties of the lattice (i.e. phonons) are usually in the IR and studied using either IR absorption or Raman spectroscopy. Raman is an example of an inelastic process whereby the energy of the incoming light is changed. The others are elastic processes whereby the intensity is changed. Typical penetration depth is of the order of 50nm. IR spectrum of a given compound is a sort of fingerprint of a compound: it is able to identify functional groups, polar molecules, and chemical bonds. These properties allow this technique to be used extensively to characterize a wide range of materials, including nanocomposites. UV-vis spectroscopy addresses electronic transitions. UV-vis spectroscopy is useful to characterize the absorption, transmission, and reflectivity of a variety of technologically important materials, coatings, thin films, and solutions. Particularly intriguing is, for example, the intense scattering and absorption of light from noble metal nanoparticles, which confer beautiful colors in stained-glass windows. These nanoparticles exhibit a strong UV-vis absorption band that is not present in the spectrum of the bulk metal, but depends on size, shape, and local dielectric environment. Optical spectroscopy is attractive for materials characterization because it is fast, nondestructive, and of high resolution.

TEM and SEM

Electron beams can be used to produce images. The basic operation in a transmission electron microscope (TEM) is for electrons to be generated from an electron gun, which are then scattered by the sample, focused using electrostatic lenses, and finally form images. A typical accelerating voltage is 100kV for which the electrons have mean free paths of the order of a few tens of nm for light elements and a few hundreds of nm for heavy elements. These would be the ideal nm thicknesses since much thinner films would lead to too little scattering and much thicker ones would lead to too much scattering of the same electron resulting in a blurred image of low resolution. The imaging mode can be controlled by the use of an aperture. If most of the unscattered electrons are allowed through, the resulting image is called a bright-field image. If specific scattered beams are selected, the image is known as a dark-field image. In addition to forming images, a TEM can be used for chemical analysis and melting-point determination. A problem with techniques such as TEM is that a small area is examined that may not be representative of the whole material. Particle dispersion and separation may be suggested by viewing a few such particles in a small region of material. A percolation network may be suggested by TEM examination, however it can be confirmed by measurements such as conductivity, modulus, or other bulk properties sensitive to a network formation.

If the TEM is operated in scanning mode, it is known as a scanning electron microscope or SEM. (SEM) instruments can resolve to 1nm and magnify to 400000X. An SEM is similar to an optical microscope operated in reflection mode. The accelerating voltage for the electron beam in SEM is smaller than for TEM since the SEM beam does not penetrate the specimen. Specimen preparation is much easier and some materials can be observed directly, though it is preferable to apply a conductive coating to insulating materials to conduct the current from the electron beam to the stage. compared to TEM-produced images, SEM images have a better depth of field. The image reveals surface contours that may reflect the material or its method of preparation or damage done to it. Surface etching, extraction, or other physical treatments that distinguish surface components assist in revealing the nature of materials surfaces.

(*Selected from Narendra Kumar and Rajiv Kumar, Nanotechnology and Nanomaterials in the Treatment of Life-Threatening Diseases, Elsevier Inc.* 2013)

New Words and Expressions

reciprocal space   *n.* 倒易空间
characterization   *n.* 表征，表述
electron distribution   *n.* 电子分布
lattice parameter   层状参数
Bragg formula   布拉格公式
lattice spacing   晶格间距，点阵间距
wavelength   *n.* 波长，波段

photoluminescence　*n*. 光致发光，光激发光
Raman spectroscopy　拉曼光谱学，喇曼光谱学
elastic　*a*. 有弹力的，可伸缩的，灵活的
fingerprint　*n*. 指纹，指印；　*vt*. 采指纹
polar　*a*. 极地的，两极的，正好相反的，磁极的，有磁性的
free path　自由程
collimated beam　平行光束，准直光束
electronic structure　电子结构
incoming light　入射光

Notes

① Size, shape, molecular structure, electron distributions, supramolecular structures, and organization are important determinants of nanomaterial properties. supramolecular　*a*. 超分子的。参考译文：材料的尺寸，形貌，分子结构，电子分布，超分子结构以及组织结构对于纳米材料的性质而言，都是非常重要的决定性因素。

② In the process of X-ray diffraction, the crystal diffracts an X-ray beam that passes through it and yields beams at particular angles depending on the wavelength of X-ray irradiation, the orientation, and the structure of the crystal. orientation　*n*. 方向，定位，取向，排列方向。参考译文：在 X 射线衍射过程中，晶体衍射的 X 射线束穿过晶体并在特定的角度产生光束，所产生光束的角度取决于 X 射线辐射的波长大小，晶体取向及晶体结构。

③ Optical spectroscopy is attractive for materials characterization because it is fast, nondestructive, and of high resolution. nondestructive　*a*. 非破坏性的。参考译文：光谱技术对材料表征而言是非常有吸引力的，因为它快速、无损，并具有较高的分辨率。

④ The basic operation in a transmission electron microscope (TEM) is for electrons to be generated from an electron gun, which are then scattered by the sample, focused using electrostatic lenses, and finally form images. 参考译文：透射电子显微镜（TEM）的基本操作是电子从电子枪产生，然后由样品散射，利用静电透镜的聚焦，并最终形成图像。

⑤ These would be the ideal nm thicknesses since much thinner films would lead to too little scattering and much thicker ones would lead to too much scattering of the same electron resulting in a blurred image of low resolution. scattering　*n*. 散射，散乱，分散。参考译文：这将是理想的纳米厚度，因为薄膜太薄将会导致散射强度过小，然而对同一电子束而言，薄膜太厚导致散射过强从而使得图像低分辨率低而显像模糊。

⑥ Surface etching, extraction, or other physical treatments that distinguish surface components assist in revealing the nature of materials surfaces. etching　*n*. 蚀刻版画；extraction *n*. 提取（法），萃取（法），回收物，提出物；assist in 在……上给予协助。参考译文：扫描电镜可以反映材料表面蚀刻状况，是否经过提取，或用于区分表面成分的其他物理处理，这些都有助于揭示材料的表面性质。

Reading Comprehension

(1) X-ray diffraction (XRD) is an important technique used in structural characteriza-

tion of materials, the analysis of diffraction pattern allows obtaining much information except _____.

 (A) lattice parameter   (B) crystal structure

 (C) particle size   (D) the dispersion and the orientation of the nanomaterials

(2) About the XRD, which of the following is wrong _____.

(A) XRD can be used to analyze the crystalline of materials

(B) One advantage of XRD is low intensity of diffracted beam for low-Z materials.

(C) XRD is generally used to provide information concerning the microstructure of composites

(D) The intensity of diffracted X-rays is measured as a function of the diffraction angle 2θ.

(3) X-ray diffraction (XRD) is a technique used in structural characterization of materials, commonly _____.

 (A) at solid state   (B) at liquid state

 (C) at solid or liquid state   (D) at gas state

(4) From the text, one can learn that _____.

(A) a small area examined by TEM is completely representative of the whole material.

(B) A percolation network may not be suggested by TEM examination

(C) Raman is an example of an inelastic process whereby the energy of the incoming light is constant

(D) The accelerating voltage for the electron beam in SEM is smaller than for TEM

(5) What is the difference between the scanning electron microscopy and transmission electron microscopy _____.

(A) Compared to SEM-produced images, TEM images have a better depth of field.

(B) Compared to TEM, the SEM beam can penetrate the specimen

(C) Compared to SEM, TEM can achieve a higher magnification.

(D) Specimen preparation of TEM is much easier and some materials can be observed directly

(6) From the Optical spectroscopy, one can learn that _____.

(A) UV-vis spectroscopy is able to identify functional groups, polar molecules, and chemical bonds.

(B) IR spectroscopy can characterize the absorption, transmission, and reflectivity of materials.

(C) Similar to IR spectroscopy, UV-vis spectroscopy addresses electronic transitions

(D) Raman is an example of an elastic process whereby the intensity is changed.

Unit 19 Creation of Nanomaterials

Several hundreds of nanomaterials belonging to inorganic, organic, or polymeric or composite categories have now been obtained by the following general approaches, i. e.

 (a) A top-down approach.

(b) A bottom-up approach.

The main objectives for applying a particular technique were as follows: (I) the synthetic method should be reproducible, (II) the method should produce monodispersed nanomaterials, (III) the surface of the nanomaterials should be defect free, and (IV) the method should be economical, scalable, and environment friendly.

Top-down methods

The top-down approach involves the breaking down of the bulk material into nanosized structure and particle. These approaches are inherently an extension of those that have been used for producing micron-sized products. They involve the slicing or successive cutting of a bulk material to get nanosized particles or to produce their desired structure with appropriate properties. This technique is quite useful to produce nanosized particles on a large scale by using mechanical force. However, the biggest problems associated with this are their imperfection of surface structure, surface dislocation, and clustering together with difficulty in controlling morphology of the particles. The main advantages are universality (i. e., applicability to virtually any material) and low cost. Even soft organic matter (e. g., leaves of grass) can be ground by first freezing it in liquid nitrogen to make it brittle. The main disadvantages are polydispersity of the final particles, the introduction of many defects and the impossibility of achieving nanoscale comminution, depending on the material.

Bottom-up methods

While nanomaterials have been generated by top-down or in other words physical methods such as arc discharged, laser aviation, chemical vapor deposition, etc., the bottom-up or in other words, the chemical approach is found to be more useful. It involves more effective build-up of a material from the bottom: atom by atom, molecule by molecule, or cluster by cluster. Though the bottom-up approach has often been referred to in nanotechnology, it is not a new concept. All the living beings in the nature only undergo growth by this approach and it has been in industrial use for the production of a variety of chemicals. Examples include the production of soap etc. The major advantages of the bottom-up approach lie in the production of nanostructures with less defects, more homogeneous chemical composition, better control of size and shape, etc. Some of the common methods belonging to bottom-up approaches are: (I) precipitation/wet chemical/soft chemical methods, (II) reduction of metal salt/solution method, (III) hydrothermal/Solvothermal, (IV) hot thermolysis/colloidal synthesis, (V) flame synthesis, (VI) photochemical synthesis, (VII) sol-gel methods, (VIII) self-assembly, (IX) biometic, etc.

Chemical method: details and procedure

(a) Precipitation/wet chemical method/soft chemical method

Precipitation is the most common technique to grow the desire sized nanoparticles. Traditionally, both aqueous and organic solvents are used.

(b) Hydrothermal/solvothermal

This is another solution-based method to prepare a wide range of nanomaterials having diverse shapes and sizes. Hydrothermal synthesis can be defined as a method of synthesis of single crystals that depends on the solubility of minerals in hot water under high pressure. The crystal growth is performed in an apparatus consisting of a steel pressure vessel called an autoclave. A gradient of temperature is maintained at the opposite ends of the growth chamber, so that the hotter end dissolves the nutrient and the cooler end causes seeds to grow.

The solvothermal method is very much similar to the hydrothermal route (where the synthesis is conducted in a stainless steel autoclave), the only difference being that the precursor solution is usually not aqueous. Using the solvothermal route one gains the benefits of both the sol-gel and hydrothermal routes. Thus solvothermal synthesis allows for the precise control over the size, shape distribution, and crystallinity of metal oxide nanoparticles or nanostructures. These characteristics can be altered by changing certain experimental parameters, including reaction temperature, reaction time, solvent type, surfactant type, and precursor type.

(c) Reverse micelle method

Reverse micelles are water-in-oil droplets stabilized by a surfactant. The surfactant most often used is sodium salt of bis (2-ethylhexyl) sulfosuccinate, usually called Na (AOT). These droplets are displayed randomly and subjected to Brownian motion. They exchange their water content and re-form two distinct micelles. Furthermore, the size of the water-in-oil droplets increases linearly, i.e. the micellar concentration decreases, with increasing water content, defined as $w=[H_2O]/[AOT]$. This involves the preparation of two separate microemulsions, incorporating the different reactants. Upon mixing, nucleation occurs on the micelle edges as the water inside them becomes supersaturated with reactants. Growth then occurs around this nucleation point, with the arrival of more reactants fed via intermicellar exchange.

The reverse micelle permits the synthesis of a very wide range of nanomaterials such as II-VI semiconductors, metals, etc., with good control of size and shape. These are formed by adding a small amount of water to a surfactant in a hydrocarbon solvent, e.g. precipitation of CdS by adding sulfide to a solution of a cadmium salt. The size is determined by the size of the droplet (controlled by the water/surfactant ratio).

(d) Sol-gel process

The sol-gel process, as the name implies, involves the evolution of inorganic networks through the formation of a colloidal suspension (sol) and gelation of the sol to form a network in a continuous liquid phase (gel). The precursors for synthesizing these colloids usually consist of a metal or metalloid element surrounded by various reactive ligands. The starting material is processed to form a dispersible oxide and forms a sol in contact with water or dilute acid. Removal of the liquid from the sol yields the gel, and the sol/gel transition controls the particle size and shape. Calcination of the gel produces the oxide.

Sol-gel processing refers to the hydrolysis and condensation of alkoxide-based precursors such as $Si(OEt)_4$ (tetraethyl orthosilicate, or TEOS). The reactions involved in the sol-gel chemistry based on the hydrolysis and condensation of metal alkoxides $M(OR)_z$ can be described as follows:

MOR + H_2O ⟶ MOH + ROH (hydrolysis),
MOH + ROM ⟶ MOM + ROH (condensation).

The sol-gel method of synthesizing nanomaterials is very popular among chemists and is widely employed to prepare oxide materials.

(*Selected from Narendra Kumar and Rajiv Kumar, Nanotechnology and Nanomaterials in the Treatment of Life-Threatening Diseases, Elsevier Inc., 2013*)

New Words and Expressions

reproducible *a.* 能繁殖的，可再生的，可复写的
aggregate *n.* 合计，聚集体；*a.* 总数的，聚合的；*vt.* 使聚集，使积聚，总计达
laser aviation 激光溅射
chemical vapor deposition 化学气相沉积
living beings 生物
homogeneous *a.* 同性质的，同类的；均匀的
precursor *n.* 前驱体，初期形式
crystallinity *n.* 结晶性，结晶度
bis (2-ethylhexyl) sulfosuccinate *n.* 双（2-乙基己基）磺基琥珀酸钠
brownian motion 布朗运动
micellar *n.* 胶束的，微胞的，微团的
microemulsion *n.* 微乳液
semiconductors *n.* 半导体
sol-gel method 溶胶-凝胶法
reproducible *a.* 能繁殖的，可再生的，可复写的
monodispersed *a.* 单分散的
polydispersion *n.* 多分散性，多分散体
surface dislocation 表面位错
homogeneous *a.* 同性质的，同类的，均匀的
gradient *n.* 梯度，陡度，变化率，梯度变化曲线
aqueous *a.* 水的，水成的
construct *vt.* 修建，建造，构成，创立

Notes

① The main objectives for applying a particular technique were as follows: (Ⅰ) the synthetic method should be reproducible, (Ⅱ) the method should produce monodispersed nanomaterials, (Ⅲ) the surface of the nanomaterials should be defect free, and (Ⅳ) the method should be economical, scalable, and environment friendly. as follows 列举如下。参考译文：对于纳米材料合成而言采用一种特定技术应该达到以下目标：（Ⅰ）合成方法具有可重复性（Ⅱ）这种方法可以得到单分散的纳米材料，（Ⅲ）所合成的纳米材料表面没有缺陷，（Ⅳ）该法经济，可以拓展，并和环境友好。

② However, the biggest problems associated with this are their imperfection of surface structure, surface dislocation, and clustering together with difficulty in controlling morphology of the particles. 参考译文：然而，自下而上方法的最大问题在于制备的产物表面结构存在缺陷，表面存在位错，颗粒容易团聚，形貌难于控制。

③ The major advantages of the bottom-up approach lie in the production of nanostructures with less defects, more homogeneous chemical composition, better control of size and shape, etc. bottom-up 自下而上；lie in 在于，位于。参考译文：这种自下而上的方法的主要优点在于得到的纳米材料缺陷少，化学成分更均一，尺寸和形貌更具有可控性等优点。

④ A gradient of temperature is maintained at the opposite ends of the growth chamber, so that the hotter end dissolves the nutrient and the cooler end causes seeds to grow. so that 以便，结果，以致。参考译文：在反应容器的两端形成温度梯度，这样较热的一端使物质溶解，较冷的一端导致晶核生长。

⑤ The solvothermal method is very much similar to the hydrothermal route (where the synthesis is conducted in a stainless steel autoclave), the only difference being that the precursor solution is usually not aqueous. be similar to…，与……相似。参考译文：溶剂热方法与水热法非常类似（合成过程都是在不锈钢反应釜中进行），唯一不同的是溶剂热的前驱体溶液是非水体系。

⑥ Our ability to create nanostructures improves as we gain understanding of biological self-assembly, develop new molecular structures, and construct new tools. as *conj.* 同时，当……时候；像，像……一样；由于，尽管。参考译文：当我们理解了生物自组装，发展出新的分子结构并构建出新的工具时我们合成纳米结构材料的能力将会提高。

Exercises

1. Questions for discussion

(1) What are the two methods for preparing nanostructured materials?
(2) Give some examples of top-down and bottom-up, respectively.
(3) Give the advantages and disadvantages of the top-down method, respectively.
(4) Give the advantages and disadvantages of the bottom-up method, respectively.
(5) Please elaborate the approach of sol-gel process according to the text.

2. Translate the following into Chinese

polydispersion   surface dislocation
hydrothermal/solvothermal   surfactant
water-in-oil   cluster by cluster
chemical composition   self-assembly

- Several hundreds of nanomaterials belonging to inorganic, organic, or polymeric or composite categories have now been obtained by the following general approaches.

- They involve the slicing or successive cutting of a bulk material to get nanosized particles or to produce their desired structure with appropriate properties.
- Even soft organic matter (e. g., leaves of grass) can be ground by first freezing it in liquid nitrogen to make it brittle.
- While nanomaterials have been generated by top-down or in other words physical methods such as arc discharged, laser aviation, chemical vapor deposition, etc., the bottom-up or in other words, the chemical approach is found to be more useful.
- Hydrothermal synthesis can be defined as a method of synthesis of single crystals that depends on the solubility of minerals in hot water under high pressure.
- Self-assembly means setting up an environment such that atoms assemble or grow automatically on prepared surfaces.

3. Translate the following into English

光化学合成   微米材料
化学气相沉积   纳米颗粒团聚
反应温度   单晶
细胞膜   不锈钢反应釜

- 自上而下的方法就是把块体材料粉碎成纳米尺寸的颗粒。
- 沉淀法是合成纳米材料最常用的方法。
- 溶剂热合成可以精确地控制材料的尺寸大小，形貌以及结晶度。
- 自组装就意味建立一个环境，在那里原子可以在准备好的表面上自动组装或生长。
- 它们相互交换含水量重新形成两种不同的胶束。

4. Reading Comprehension

(1) About the top-down methods, which of the following is true?
(A) The top-down approach is a chemical process.
(B) The top-down approach is more effective to controlle morphology of the particles
(C) Nanomaterials generated by top-down have less defects
(D) This technique is useful to produce nanosized particles on a large scale
(2) About the bottom-up methods, which of the following is true?
(A) Discharged, laser aviation and chemical vapor deposition are attributed to the bottom-up approachs.
(B) The bottom-up approach has often been referred to in nanotechnology, it is a new concept.
(C) It involves more effective build-up of a material from the bottom.
(D) The major advantages of the bottom-up approach lie in universality and low cost.
(3) According to the text, hydrothermal synthesis is _____ .
(A) a top-down approach
(B) a solution-based method which can gains the benefits of both the sol-gel and solvothermal routes
(C) defined as a method of synthesis of single crystals that depends on the solubility of

minerals in nonaqueous system under nonaqueous sysnonaqueous systnonmnohigh pressure

(D) is very much similar to the solvothermal route

(4) According to the reverse micelle method, which of the following is wrong?

(A) The size nanomaterials is controlled by the water/surfactant ratio.

(B) The size of the water-in-oil droplets increases linearly, i. e. the micellar concentration increase, with decreasing water content.

(C) These droplets are displayed randomly and subjected to Brownian motion.

(D) The reverse micelle permits the synthesis of a very wide range of nanomaterials such as II-VI semiconductors, metals, etc.

(5) About the sol-gel process, one can learn that _____.

(A) The sol/gel transition can control the particle size and shape

(B) Calcination of the sol produces the oxide

(C) Removal of the liquid from the gel yields the sol

(D) The sol is a network in a continuous liquid phase

(6) According to the text, surfactant must be used in the following method?

(A) Precipitation.

(B) Reverse micelle method.

(C) Hydrothermal/solvothermal.

(D) Sol-gel process.

Reading Material

Nanomaterials Developments for Higher-Performance Lithium Ion Batteries

Lithium ion batteries (LIBs) provide portable power for a variety of applications, ranging from personal electronic devices to electric vehicles. They are fully rechargeable, have high energy density, high operating voltage, and low self discharge, and require little maintenance; yet, future applications require more advanced batteries. Electric vehicles and large-scale utility energy storage applications need batteries that can operate safely under widely varying environmental conditions with significantly higher energy density than is currently possible. Future needs, as in the integration of electronic devices with living systems (i. e., humans), require entirely new battery concepts: batteries must be very lightweight, mechanically flexible, conformable, and even stretchable, to enable seamless integration with active components, such as sensors and delivery devices, and those that harvest energy, such as microsolar cells or piezoelectric devices. The LIB consists of two electrodes, the cathode and the anode, each hosting the Li that cycles reversibly between these materials. The charge storage capacity of the battery depends on the amount of Li that each electrode can hold in the charged and discharged state, and there is an intense search for electrode materials that can hold more Li. The cathode is a Li metal oxide, such as $LiCoO_2$, and the anode is graphite, with charge storage capacities of 137 (for $LiCoO_2$) and 372 mA/(h·g). To advance LIB capability, new cathode and anode materials are needed. On the anode side, there are several alternatives to graphite that have significantly higher charge storage capacity, and of these, silicon has the highest possible charge storage capacity of 3579 mA/(h·g). Cathode replacements with extremely high storage capacity are harder to find, but there is an active search for more advanced cathodes as well. One paper by Song, Hu, and Paik highlights the creation of Si nanostructures with unique morphologies that can improve performance (especially, cycle stability) in LIBs. Another paper by Seung-Taek Myung, Hyung-Joo Noh, and co-workers focuses on advanced cathode materials with increased storage capacity combined with improved safety, which is a major challenge. Myung et al. describe their research group's progress over the past 10 years as they have advanced toward higher-capacity cathode materials with improved safety. Their approach is to combine the positive attributes of higher storage materials (which turn out to be more dangerous) with lower storage materials that are safer. Their first generation of cathode materials with these attributes were core-shell particles with high capacity [200 mA/(h·g)] $Li[Ni_{0.8}Co_{0.1}Mn_{0.1}]O_2$ in the core coated with a protective shell of lower capacity [140mA/(h·g)], $Li[Ni_{0.5}Mn_{0.5}]O_2$. The core material has poor thermal stability associated with exothermic oxygen evolution at temperatures above 200℃, whereas the shell material is much more stable. The problem with these materials was that the core and shell exhibited different levels of expansion and contraction during lithiation/delithiation that eventually led to degradation. The next generation of materials involved the creation of particles with a controlled composition gradient, thus alleviating the abrupt interface between materials with different amounts of expansion and contraction. Further improvements in the cathode material were obtained by creating rod-shaped particles instead of spheres. Each of these impressive advances in materials synthesis led to improvements in capacity, cycle stability, and safety. On the anode side, Si is closing in on commercial viability as an alternative to graphite as a LIB electrode material. Si has nearly 10 times the charge storage capacity of graphite, and advances in Si materials chemistry and battery formulation have enabled many demonstrations now of exceptional capacities, greater than 1000 mA/(h·g) for more than hundreds of cycles. Still, there are many challenges facing commercial use of Si anodes in LIBs, including current matching between the cathode and anode, as well as making Si materials costs competitive with graphite. Perhaps the most significant challenge, however, remains in attaining long-term, stable battery performance at reasonably fast charge/discharge rates. To fully lithiate Si to the saturated Li-Si phase, $Li_{15}Si_4$, Si must expand by nearly 300%; it is like a sponge for Li. The Si "crystal" must itself tolerate this expansion and not fall to pieces; furthermore, the entire battery must be designed to accommodate these volume changes. Many of the advances in Si nanomaterials design for LIBs have focused on creating structures that are mechanically robust under strenuous conditions of large volume expansions and contractions, and many very creative concepts have emerged. As described by Song, et al., these include the creation of porous nanostructures and nanostructures with mechanically strengthening and chemically protective coatings. Many of these nanomaterials design criteria have evolved from the combination of new synthetic capability with new understanding due especially to powerful in situ electron microscopy techniques that allow direct visualization of individual nanostructures as they undergo lithiation and delithiation. New phenomena have been observed, such as reversible mesoscopic pore formation and unanticipated degradation pathways, like those arising from spatially anisotropic expansion and contraction. Similar to the approach taken for cathodes described by Myung, et al. of integrating materials with complementary positive attributes to make up for their shortcomings, anode materials have been made with combinations of carbon, Si, and germanium (Ge). Si has the highest Li storage capacity of these three materials but has the poorest electrical conductivity. Battery cycling occurs by electrochemical oxidation and reduction, and electrical current needs to move through the electrodes. Intrinsic Si has such poor electrical conductivity that it can only cycle at very slow rates or when it is in intimate contact with the current collector. The addition of much more electrically conductive carbon and Ge to the Si nanostructures greatly improves performance of the nanowire electrodes by speeding the charge/discharge rate capability. The addition of coatings, such as graphene, can also mechanically stabilize the materials while improving other aspects in the electrode like the electrical conductivity. These developments, however, must be implemented in electrode layers with sufficient loading or "areal density" to provide useful amounts of current to power devices. Very thin electrode layers are not sufficient for real applications, and large amounts of Si nanomaterials are needed at a cost that is reasonably competitive with that of graphite. Thicker electrode films composed of nanoparticles or nanowires require a polymeric binder to hold the electrode material intact during electrode layer deposition and processing. The binder also keeps the anode layer intact as the Si expands and contracts, and the binder chemistry can dramatically influence the capacity and cycle stability. The other important factor in the battery is the electrolyte. Graphite undergoes a surface reaction with the electrolyte to form a chemically passivating solid-electrolyte interphase (SEI) layer, which is crucial to the performance of the LIB. Reactions involved in SEI layer formation on Si are different than those for graphite, and new electrolyte formulations are needed; for example, small additions of fluoroethylene carbonate (FEC) to the typical carbonate electrolyte formulation provides significant stability to Si anodes. Clearly, the future use of Si anodes in LIBs will rely on morphologically and compositionally advanced nanostructures as the active storage material formulated into electrode layers using subtle, yet distinct, modifications of the chemistry that has been so well developed for graphite. As new cathode and anode materials are developed, ultimately, the two materials must be combined into the same battery. This is not a trivial exercise. Si anodes have an order of magnitude larger charge storage capacity than the most advanced cathode materials. This means that batteries must be formulated using either very little anode material or massive amounts of cathode material. Neither approach is adequate at the moment, although progress is being made toward prelithiation of

Si nanomaterials to help alleviate this problem. The batteries must also be extremely stable with long calendar life and operate safely. For applications like electric vehicles, safety is of the utmost importance and is a major challenge facing very high energy density LIBs. Perhaps one of the application areas most suited for next generation ultrahigh energy density lightweight LIBs is in medicine, where there is no current technology that can satisfy the need for portable power seamlessly integrated with medical devices interfaced with the human body.

(Brian A. Korgel, *Physical Chemistry Letters*, 2014, 5, 749-750.)

New Words and Expressions

electric vehicles　电动汽车
rechargeable　*a.* 可再充电的
maintenance　*n.* 维持，保持，保养，保管，维护，维修
lightweight　*a.* 轻量的，不重要的
conformable　*a.* 适合的，一致的
stretchable　*a.* 有弹性的
capacity　*n.* 容量，性能，生产能力
seamless　*a.* 无缝的；无漏洞的
integration　*n.* 结合，整合，一体化
sensor　*n.* 传感器，灵敏元件
piezoelectric　*a.* 压电的
cathode　*n.* 阴极，负极
anode　*n.* 阳极
charge　*vt.* 使充电；*vi.* 充电
perspective　*n.* 透视，观点，全景
alleviate　*v.* 减轻，缓解，缓和
lithiation　*n.* 锂化，潜锂
delithiation　*n.* 脱锂
degradation　*n.* 退化，堕落，降级
expansion　*n.* 扩大，扩张，扩张物，膨胀物
contraction　*n.* 收缩，缩减
viability　*n.* 生存能力，发育能力，生活力
tolerate　*vt.* 容许，承认，忍受，容忍
strenuous　*a.* 费力的，艰苦的
electrolyte　*n.* 电解液，电解质
fluoroethylene carbonate　氟代碳酸乙烯酯
an order of magnitude　一个数量级

Notes

① Lithium ion batteries (LIBs) provide portable power for a variety of applications, ranging from personal electronic devices to electric vehicles. They are fully rechargeable, have high energy density, high operating voltage, and low self discharge, and require little maintenance; yet, future applications require more advanced batteries. self discharge 自动放电, 自放电; maintenance *n.* 维持, 保持; 保养, 保管; 维护; 维修。参考译文: 锂离子电池 (LIB) 为各种应用提供便携式电源, 从个人电子设备到电动车辆。它们完全充电, 能量密度高, 工作电压高, 低自放电, 并且需要很少的维护; 然而, 未来的应用需要更先进的电池。

② Future needs, as in the integration of electronic devices with living systems (i.e., humans), require entirely new battery concepts: batteries must be very lightweight, mechanically flexible, conformable, and even stretchable, to enable seamless integration with active components, such as sensors and delivery devices, and those that harvest energy, such as microsolar cells or piezoelectric devices. as *adv.* 同样地, 一样地, 例如; *conj.* 像, 像……一样; 由于; 同时, 当……时, 在这里翻译为"像" solar cells 太阳能电池。参考译文: 未来 (对于锂电池的) 需求, 像在电子设备的与生物系统 (即, 人类) 的结合, 需要全新的电池概念: 电池必须很轻, 机械柔性, 舒适, 甚至可拉伸, 使电池能够与活动组件完美结合, 这些组件如传感器和输送装置, 和那些获取能源装置, 如微型太阳能电池或压电器件。

③ The charge storage capacity of the battery depends on the amount of Li that each electrode can hold in the charged and discharged state, and there is an intense search for electrode materials that can hold more Li. 参考译文: 电池的电荷存储容量取决于每个电极在充电和放电状态可以容纳的锂的数量, 对此人们做了很多研究来寻找能够储存更多锂的材料。

④ Many of these nanomaterials design criteria have evolved from the combination of new synthetic capability with new understanding due especially to powerful in situ electron microscopy techniques that allow direct visualization of individual nanostructures as they undergo lithiation and delithiation. evolve from 从……逐渐形 [发展] 成, in situ electron microscopy 原位电子显微镜, visualization *n.* 想像, 目测。参考译文: 由于原位电子显微镜这种强有力的技的发展, 许多用于锂电池电极的纳米材料的设计标准已经发展为将新的合成能力与对纳米材料新的理解相结合, 通过原位电子显微镜可以在潜锂和脱锂的过程中对单个纳米结构直接进行观察。

⑤ Clearly, the future use of Si anodes in LIBs will rely on morphologically and compositionally advanced nanostructures as the active storage material formulated into electrode layers using subtle, yet distinct, modifications of the chemistry that has been so well developed for graphite. morphologically *adv.* 形态, 形态学, 词法; compositionally *adv.* 成分; formulate *vt.* 构想出, 规划, 制定; subtle *a.* 微妙的, 巧妙的。参考译文: 显然, 通过使用巧妙的, 但效果明显的化学改性, 硅阳极在未来锂电池上的使用将依靠于形貌和成分上先进的纳米结构作为有效存储材料来制成电极层, 这些化学改性在石墨材料上已经得到很大的发展。

⑥ Perhaps one of the application areas most suited for next generation ultrahigh energy density lightweight LIBs is in medicine, where there is no current technology that can satisfy the need for portable power seamlessly integrated with medical devices interfaced with the human body. 参考译文：很可能医学是最适合使用于下一代超高能量密度轻量级锂离子电池的一个应用领域，但目前医学上还么有相关技术能够满足便携式电池的需要，使它能够与医疗设备完美结合以满足于与人体的直接接触。

Reading Comprehension

(1) Future applications require more advanced batteries, which of the following is the reason?
  (A) The power-battery's high security bring out higher requirements
  (B) Future need may the batteries that must be very lightweight, mechanically flexible, conformable.
  (C) Large-scale utility energy storage applications need batteries with significantly higher energy density than is currently possible.
  (D) Most of electrode materials suffer low electronic conductivity and slow lithium ion diffusion due to their intrinsic character.

(2) About the Lithium ion batteries, which of the following is wrong?
  (A) $LiCoO_2$ is a type of anode material.
  (B) The LIB consists of two electrodes, the cathode and the anode.
  (C) The binder chemistry can dramatically influence the capacity and cycle stability of the electrode.
  (D) Si has the highest Li storage capacity among carbon, Si, and germanium (Ge).

(3) There is the most significant challenge facing commercial use of Si anodes in LIBs, what is it?
  (A) There is no good matching between the cathode and anode.
  (B) Making Si materials costs is high, can not be competitive with graphite.
  (C) It is difficult to attain long-term, stable battery performance at reasonably fast charge/discharge rates.
  (D) To fully lithiate Si to the saturated Li-Si phase, Si must expand by nearly 300%.

(4) Which of the following measurecan can not effectively improve the performances of the electrode as the Si is used to as the anode in LIBs?
  (A) The carbon or Ge can be added into the Si nanostructures.
  (B) The core-shell particles are prepared to improve the performances of the electrode.
  (C) Grapheme used as the coatings can also mechanically stabilize the materials.
  (D) The fluoroethylene carbonate is added into the electrolyte.

(5) According to the text, which one is not mentioned in the cell structure?
  (A) cathode (B) anode (C) electrolyte (D) separator

(6) According to the text, which of the following is true?
  (A) Si has nearly 10 times the charge storage capacity of graphite
  (B) For applications like electric vehicles, high capacity is of the utmost importance.
  (C) Reactions involved in SEI layer formation on Si are similar to those for graphite

(D) Si anodes have an order of magnitude larger charge storage capacity than the most advanced anode materials

Unit 20 Applications of Nanostructured Materials

The unique features in nanostructures, such as large surface area, energy level discretization due to quantum confinement, novel density of states and phonon coupling, and capability of exciting surface plasmonic modes, have given nanostructures distinctive properties that are usually absent in their bulk counterparts. More importantly, many of those unique properties can be fine-tuned through structural design, providing flexibility in tailoring specific properties for target applications. The potential application areas for nanostructures are extremely broad, from the microelectronics industry to bioengineering, because nanostructures are truly a multidisciplinary topic. Some of those applications are already seen in commercial products, while others remain in the lab. Due to the maturity of top-down fabrication techniques, lithographically defined nanostructures have been widely used in nanoelectronics for achieving better device, circuit, and system performance, as demonstrated in modern day CPUs and memory devices. For optoelectronic devices, quantum dots and quantum wells grown by molecular beam epitaxy (MBE) or metal organic chemical vapor deposition (MOCVD) techniques have led to a series of breakthroughs in solid-state lasers, photodetectors, and high-frequency resonant tunneling devices. Other areas, such as high density magnetic information storage, are being hotly pursued, with the main focus on the perfection of fabricating large area and high-density bit-patterned media with extremely low defect density and high fabrication throughput. Photonic nanostructures also show great potential in practical applications. Surface-enhanced Raman scattering (SERS) based on metallic nanostructures are becoming a standard technique for detecting trace level molecules. The field enhancement and spatial confinement of optical energy are promising for nonlinear optics, high-resolution imaging, deep subwavelength optical lithography, and energy focusing. In additional to fundamental research, current efforts in these areas include developing an easy-to-use plasmonic platform for commercial applications. Nanoparticles and nanowires synthesized in solution or deposited by vapor deposition have attracted great interest for their easy processing, low cost, and high throughput. Those carbon-based and compound semiconductor nanomaterials are currently being explored for energy harvesting, biomedical engineering, catalysts, and new nanocomposite materials. However, other issues, such as the limitations informing higher order nanostructures, have seriously limited their real potential. Particularly for electronic applications, there exist several prominent challenges: the need for the alignment and placement of the nanomaterials for integrated circuit fabrication, the practical performance deterioration introduced by large density of defects, surface states and impurities, and the interference of charge transport by the often-needed surface passivation groups. There have been high hopes for those semiconducting nanostructures, but then the practical issues outlined above kill their chances, such as in the case of

CNTs. Although there is a strong resurgence in another carbon-based nanomaterial—graphene—its real potential in the microelectronic industry may be very limited due to many practical issues. It is interesting to investigate the new science in nanostructures, but the limitations of nanostructures in engineering applications should not be overlooked. Often it is not enough to just show that nanostructures can be made into certain devices or can achieve certain functionalities; we also need to compare holistically between nanostructures and conventional techniques in terms of functionality and cost. For engineering applications, a superior material property is often not enough to deliver its success in commercial applications. Also, in recent years, the health and environmental impact of some nanomaterials have raised concerns. Thus, a candid and objective evaluation of the value of some nanostructures in practical applications should be followed, to make the best out of research efforts and resources. A summary of the nanoproducts and applications for the three industrial sectors is given below.

Agrifood

Nanotechnology applications are expected to bring a range of benefits to the food sector, including new tastes, textures and sensations, a decrease in the use of fat, enhanced absorption of nutrients and improved packaging, traceability and security of food products. The agrifood sector can be divided into three main subsectors:

i) agricultural production (production of materials from raising domesticated animals and cultivation of plants);

ii) food processing and functional food (turning agricultural produce into consumer products); and food packaging and distribution (materials designed to preserve or protect fresh or processed foods).

iii) Nanoclays are the most commonly utilized type of nanomaterial in agricultural production, with gold nanoparticles and carbon nanotubes being used predominantly in food processing and titanium and silver used in particular in food packaging. Currently, only a limited number of nanotechnology applications within the agrifood sector are on the market, for example nanoemulsions in pesticides, equipment coatings for disinfection and delivery systems for nutrients.

Construction

Material innovations are continuously finding their way into modern building structure, including innovations based on nanotechnology. Applications of nanotechnology in the construction industry include cement-based materials (e.g., cement additives and ultra-high-performance concrete), coatings (e.g., self-cleaning glass, antireflective coatings), living comfort and building safety applications (e.g., flame-retardant coatings and antibacterial surfaces) and sustainability and environmental applications (e.g., thermal insulation). Some applications have been brought to the market, such as selfcleaning windows and roof tiles that utilize titanium dioxide (TiO_2) or nano-enhanced cement that uses silica or carbon nanotubes (CNT), but use is not widespread mainly due to expense. Titanium dioxide and silicon dioxide (SiO_2) are currently the most commonly used nanomaterials in the construction industry. Other nanomaterials such as CNTs are being discussed intensively as potential candidates for future construction materials but have no significant influence at present. It is likely that the potential for exposure will be high in the construction industry if the use of nanomaterials becomes widespread, in particular for those applications where nanomaterials are likely to be incorporated into production in powder or slurry form.

Energy

Nanotechnology has the potential to provide a multitude of improvements and new solutions in the energy sector, enabling a reduction in the amount of material required, the introduction of new properties to existing materials, and thus the development of alternative and more efficient energy solutions. Potential nanotechnology-based applications within this sector include photovoltaics, thermoelectricity, fuel cells, batteries and super-capacitors, fossil fuel, nuclear energy and energy harvesting. Types of nanomaterials that are being investigated for use within these applications include CNTs and other carbon-based nanomaterials (e.g., fullerenes, graphene, diamond), metal oxide nanoparticles and nanowires (e.g., oxides of zinc, titanium, yttrium, silicon, etc.) and, primarily for batteries, lithium-based nanoparticles (e.g., $LiFePO_4$). In general, it is considered that as nanomaterials are bound to a substrate and fully confined, human or environmental exposure is unlikely during normal use of the final application. However, many nanomaterial-based applications within the energy sector are still at an early stage of development, and in some cases there is still a wide gap between industrial specifications and the state-of-the-art. One of the main nanotechnology-enabled products to have emerged onto the marketplace in this area is batteries, using nanostructured or nanoparticle-coated anodes or cathodes to increase battery capacity. In some areas the application of nanotechnology is anticipated to be of little value for the foreseeable future, for example in nuclear energy, fossil fuel or high-temperature fuel cells, mainly because the high temperature destroys the nano-scale structure of materials.

(*Selected from Ulla Vogel Msc, Kai Savolainen, Qinglan Wu, et al., Handbook of Nanosafety Measurement, Exposure and Toxicology, 1st Edition, Academic Press*, 2014)

New Words and Expressions

discretization   *n.* 离散化

quantum confinement   量子限域

phonon coupling   声子耦合

counterpart   *n.* 配对物，副本，相对物，极相似的人或物

fine-tune   *v.* 调整，使有规则

multidisciplinary   *a.* 包括各种学科的，有关各种学问的，多学科，多部门，多科目

molecular beam epitaxy 分子束外延生长
thermoelectricity *n*. 热电，温差电
fossil fuel 化石燃料
passivation *n*. 钝化
foreseeable 可预见到的
state-of-the-art 最先进的，最高级的，最新型的，顶尖水准的，使用了最先进技术的
nanoclay *n*. 纳米黏土
pesticide *n*. 农药
disinfection *n*. 消毒，灭菌
maturity *n*. 成熟
nonlinear optics 非线性光
lithography *n*. 光刻
holistically *adv*. 整体地，全盘地
cement *n*. 水泥
concrete *n*. 混凝土，钢筋混凝土
antireflective *a*. 抗反射，抗反光
flame-retardant *n*. 阻燃
fat *n*. 脂肪
nutrient *n*. 养分

Notes

① Due to the maturity of top-down fabrication techniques, lithographically defined nanostructures have been widely used in nanoelectronics for achieving better device, circuit, and system performance, as demonstrated in modern day CPUs and memory devices. 参考译文：由于成熟的自上而下的制造技术，光刻定义的纳米结构已被广泛应用于纳米电子学以获得更好的器件、电路和系统性能，如现代的 CPU 和存储器装置。

② The field enhancement and spatial confinement of optical energy are promising for nonlinear optics, high-resolution imaging, deep subwavelength optical lithography, and energy focusing. 参考译文：光能场增强效应和空间限域效应有望用于非线性光学、高分辨率成像、深亚波长光刻和能量聚焦。

③ Often it is not enough to just show that nanostructures can be made into certain devices or can achieve certain functionalities; we also need to compare holistically between nanostructures and conventional techniques in terms of functionality and cost. in terms of in terms of 根据，用……的话，就……而言，以……为单位。参考译文：通常，仅仅显示纳米结构材料可以制造某种器件或者获得了某种功能性，这是远远不够的；我们也需要针对功能性和价格对纳米结构和传统技术进行全面的比较，做出权衡。

④ Applications of nanotechnology in the construction industry include cement-based materials (e. g. , cement additives and ultra-high-performance concrete), coatings (e. g. , self-cleaning glass, antireflective coatings), living comfort and building safety applications (e. g. , flame-retardant coatings and antibacterial surfaces) and sustainability and environmental applications (e.g., thermal insulation). 参考译文：纳米科技在建筑领域的应用包括水泥基材料（比如水泥添加剂和高能混凝土），涂料（比如，自洁净玻璃，反光图层），用于改善生活和提供建筑安全的材料（阻燃涂层和抗菌表面）以及有利于环境可持续发展的环境材料（比如保温材料）。

⑤ Nanotechnology applications are expected to bring a range of benefits to the food sector, including new tastes, textures and sensations, a decrease in the use of fat, enhanced absorption of nutrients and improved packaging, traceability and security of food products. 参考译文：纳米科技的应用在食品领域将会带来很多的便利，这包括给食品带来新口味，新的质感和新的触感，减少脂肪的利用，提高营养物质的吸收，改进食品包装，以及提高食品可追溯性和安全性。

⑥ Nanotechnology has the potential to provide a multitude of improvements and new solutions in the energy sector, enabling a reduction in the amount of material required, the introduction of new properties to existing materials, and thus the development of alternative and more efficient energy solutions. a multitude of 大量的；solution 解决，答案。参考译文：纳米技术在能源领域有潜力给出改进并提供新的解决方案，它能减少所需材料的量，并能赋予现有材料新的特性，从而为发展更有效的可替代能源提出解决途径。

Exercises

1. Questions for discussion

(1) What field does the application of nanotechnology is anticipated to be of little value, Why?

(2) What kinds of nanomaterials are commonly used in the construction industry in the text?

(3) According to the text, how should one understand the value of the nanostructures in practical applications?

(4) What are the main problems in the practical applications of electronic devices?

(5) Please give examples to show the nanotechnology applications within the agrifood sector on the market

2. Translate the following into Chinese

high-frequency resonant tunneling devices from microelectronics industry to bioengineering
Surface-enhanced Raman scattering easy-to-use plasmonic platform
high throughput biomedical engineering
nuclear energy fuel cells

- Surface-enhanced Raman scattering (SERS) based on metallic nanostructures are becoming a standard technique for detecting trace level molecules.
- In additional to fundamental research, current efforts in these areas include developing an easy-to-use plasmonic platform for commercial applications.
- There have been high hopes for those semiconducting nanostructures, but then the practical issues outlined above kill their chances, such as in the case of CNTs.

- It is interesting to investigate the new science in nanostructures, but the limitations of nanostructures in engineering applications should not be overlooked.

3. Translate the following into English

纳米线　　　　　　　　　　量子限域
电荷传输　　　　　　　　　超级电容器
金属有机化学气相沉积　　　工程应用
将农产品转变成消费品　　　食品包装

- 纳米材料的应用有些已经进入商业市场，有一些仅停留在实验室。
- 通过液相合成或者气相沉积合成的纳米颗粒和纳米线由于制备过程简单，成本低廉且产量高而引起人们极大的兴趣。
- 近年来，有些纳米材料对人类健康问题和环境问题影响已经引起人们的关注。
- 在实际的应用中对于一些纳米材料的价值应该给予公正客观的评价。
- 纳米材料所具有的新奇性能很多可以通过结构设计进行微调。
- 金纳米粒子主要用于食品加工而银纳米颗粒主要用于食品包装。

4. Reading Comprehension

(1) There exist several prominent challenges for electronic applications of nanomaterials, which of the following is not given in the text?
   (A) The alignment and placement of the nanomaterials are need for integrated circuit fabrication
   (B) The large density of defects, surface states and impurities lead to the practical performance deterioration
   (C) The interference of charge transport is disturbed by the often-needed surface passivation groups.
   (D) The high temperature destroys the nano-scale structure of materials.

(2) What does have emerged onto the marketplace in the field of energy?
   (A) fossil fuel (B) batteries (C) super-capacitors (D) nuclear energy

(3) According to the text, which of the following is true _____ .
   (A) The superior properties of namomaterials is the main factor to deliver its success in commercial applications
   (B) The health and environmental impact of some nanomaterials have raised concerns
   (C) Titanium dioxide and silicon dioxide (SiO_2) are is widespread as additive in self-cleaning windows and roof tiles.
   (D) Grapheme has realized their real potential in the microelectronic industry

(4) Which types of nanomaterials are mentioned in the text and can be used within the construction and energy?
   (A) carbon nanotubes and titanium dioxide　　(B) $LiFePO_4$
   (C) yttrium oxide　　　　　　　　　　　　　(D) zinc oxide

(5) Compared to bulk materials, nanostructures have the unique features, which of the following is mentioned in the text?
   (A) large surface area　　　　　　　　　　　(B) novel density of states
   (C) energy level discretization　　　　　　　(D) high reaction activity

(6) According to the text, what are used for detecting trace level molecules?
(A) CNTs　　(B) SERS　　(C) quantum dots　　(D) quantum wells

Reading Materials

Nanomaterials for (Nano) medicine

The expectations are high for the next generation of nanomedicines: a personalized and efficient therapy with lower side effects. In tissue engineering, nanomaterial-based scaffolds will offer a biodegradable support for cell growth and infiltration to be naturally replaced with time by new biological tissue. In drug delivery, smart nanodevices will target the disease site; there, an external trigger will prompt the controlled release of multiple agents for sensing, high-resolution imaging, and therapy. The nanomaterial landscape is vast. The medicinal chemist will see all of the well-characterized polymers, proteins, sugars, and surfactants that can be engineered into novel nanoformulations. Dendrimers and nanogels have been used for both controlled drug delivery and cell growth scaffolds. They are present in many nanomedicines that made it to the clinic, and most likely, they will appear to some extent also in the nanomedicines of the future. Which way does a medicinal chemist have to go for the best ingredients for the next generation nanomedicines? Many chemists would make their bet on mesoporous silica NPs. These are among the best-characterized NPs in vivo and indeed offer a number of advantages. Their synthesis can be fine-tuned to a variety of shapes and sizes (down to a few nanometers). The use of silane mixtures in their preparation allows for convenient incorporation of functional groups of choice (e.g., amino, carboxylic, thiol, etc.) for incorporation of therapeutic or imaging agents. Their porosity allows for high drug loading (up to 35 wt %). Remarkably, the "Cornell dots" are the first silica-based multimodal (optical/PET) diagnostic NPs recently approved for human clinical trials; their PEG coating and small size (<10nm) allow for good biodistribution in a melanoma model, and fluorescent dye encapsulation in the NP core gives them notable brightness. However, despite these very encouraging advances, concerns still exist on the nanomaterial landscape about the coating stability of mesoporous silica NPs, since it has been shown that uncoated silica NPs are hemolytic. Magnetic NPs offer different advantages. They are wellknown in medicine as MRI agents; in addition, their ability to respond to external magnetic fields gives an opportunity to develop cutting edge applications in protein and cell manipulation. In particular, superparamagnetic iron oxide NPs (SPIONs) have attracted a lot of attention for drug delivery applications in theranostics (i.e., combined therapy and diagnosis). One of the promises of SPIONs is targeted delivery to the disease site following an external magnetic force. In fact, their directional movement is usually hampered by blood flow, and their sensitivity to magnets can be notably reduced by the presence of a polymer coating (e.g., dextran). However, this organic "shell" is essential to reduce NPs undesired interaction with proteins and their subsequent opsonization. Therefore, SPIONs design needs careful fine-tuning of the "shell" for optimal performance. To date, opportunities exist to improve SPIONs colloidal stability in biological fluids (i. e., loss of the polymer coating) and to control drug delivery, avoiding undesired burst release from the polymer component. Another class that is drawing a lot of attention is gold NPs (AuNPs). Besides spherical NPs, the literature is rich with nanorods, nanocages, nanostars, and gold shells used to coat other NPs (e. g., SPION cores). Gold has been known in medicine for a very long time, but the attentive reader will note that the behavior of nanosized gold objects is a different matter, due to the high surface area and unique physicochemical properties. The shape of AuNPs has a big impact on their properties: spheres absorb visible light, and rods, cages, and shells absorb light in the near-infrared (NIR) region, where the human body is mostly transparent. NIR absorption is very useful, since it is employed in photothermal therapy (i. e., for heat generation to damage diseased tissue) and in highresolution photoacoustic imaging (i. e., for the generation of ultrasound waves). AuNPs, modified with both a strong Raman scatter and an antibody, enhance the Raman response (surface enhanced Raman scattering, SERS), whereas the antibody imparts antigenic specificity. There is an increasing number of studies on the matter, but the heterogeneity of gold NP formulations makes it difficult to generalize important aspects such as biosafety assessments. In addition, despite the vast number of studies on gold nanomaterials, the functionalization chemistry of gold NPs usually revolves around the use of either thiols or amines, somewhat limiting the choice of triggers for drug loading and release. Nevertheless, imaginative variations have been found, such as the photothermal release of DNA cargos upon laser irradiation. QDs are yet another class of which we hear more and more in nanomedicine, especially in applications of multimodal imaging. The battle against cancer needs weapons of increasing sophistication, including tools to locate micrometastasis with exquisite spatiotemporal resolution. To this end, we may rely on multimodal imaging, because it is only with the combination of different techniques that we can go beyond the limitations of each modality, especially for imaging of deep tissues. QDs could be useful components of sophisticated nanodevices due to their very small size (typically of only a few nanometers), remarkable brightness, photostability, and ample offering of emission light colors for optical detection. Nevertheless, major limitations are posed by their chemical nature, since they are typically composed of heavy metals (e. g., cadmium, lead), for which QDs stability and safe excretion from the human body is a must. In the field of theranostics, CNTs are excellent candidates, as they exhibit many properties relevant to these objectives. For instance, CNTs possess relatively strong NIR absorption, which can be used for both high-resolution imaging (e. g., photoacoustic modality) and photothermal therapy. Although biocompatibility and safety of CNTs are still an open issue, it is important to note that CNTs comprise a highly heterogeneous class of materials, for which biocompatibility data cannot, and should not, be generalized. There is a growing body of work that shows that CNT in vivo is highly dependent on their purity, physical properties (i. e., length, diameter, etc.), and chemical nature (i. e., functionalization). Importantly, there is increasing evidence that biodegradation of CNTs can be achieved by appropriate chemical modification. Derivatization of CNTs offers a variety of options for the imaginative medicinal chemist, who can covalently attach the polymer of choice for favorable interactions with biological entities. In addition to their high external surface, their hollow nature might permit loading with drugs or other bioactive cargoes, for their safe delivery in a cellular environment bypassing biological barriers. For instance, data exist on the ability of certain tubes to act as "cell membrane needles" and avoid the endocytic pathway. Another unique property is their ability to increase electrical activity of multilayered neuronal networks and cultured cardiac myocytes: the mechanisms of this phenomenon are still unclear and obviously need further investigation. Clearly, mastering such properties would pave the way to innovative tissue engineering that, until a few years back, was simply unthinkable. In our point of view, their unique properties offer ample opportunity for unprecedented performance in the field of "smart" nanomedicines; however, their application in the field is still in its infancy. In conclusion, the landscape of nanomaterials for medicines of the next generation is rich with options, and innovative solutions will likely be found in the wise combination of different components. It is clear that the examples reported in this viewpoint are only a few, representative of a class of materials that is continuously expanding and that includes an exceedingly high number of examples and ideas. The medicinal chemists who venture into this field should not impose limits on their imagination; instead, they should reach out to and partner with physicists, biologists, and clinicians to find creative solutions to these complex, multidisciplinary problems. We believe that hybrid, multifunctional nanomaterials will be the key components of the next generation of nanomedicines, and the brave medicinal chemists shall venture into the field to make them a reality.

(*Silvia Marchesan and Maurizio Prato*, *Nanomaterials for Nanomedicine*, *Medicinal Chemistry Letters*, 2013, 4, 147-149.)

New Words and Expressions

Therapy　*n.* 治疗，疗法，疗效，心理治疗，治疗力
scaffold　*n.* 支架
biodegradable　*a.* 能进行生物降解的，能起生物递解分解作用的
infiltration　*n.* 渗透，下渗，渗滤，入渗
conceive　*vt.* 构思，想像，*vi.* 设想，考虑
landscape　*n.* 风景；风景画，乡村风景画，地形
formulation　*n.* 配方，构想，规划，公式化
dendrimer　*n.* 聚合物，树形分子，树状聚合物
clinic　*n.* 诊所，门诊部，特殊病例分析，临床讲授，临床实习课
ingredient　*n.* （混合物的）组成部分，（烹调的）原料，（构成）要素，因素
bet bet　*n.* 打赌，赌博，赌注，被下赌注的对象，可能性
in vivo　在活的有机体内
therapeutic　*a.* 治疗（学）的，疗法的，有益于健康的

hemolytic　*a*.［医］溶血的
theranostics　*n*.治疗诊断学
dextran　*n*.右旋糖酐
photothermal therapy　光热疗法
micrometastasis　*n*.（残留癌肿的）微小转移
spatiotemporal　*a*.空间与时间的，时空的
covalently　*adv*.共有原子价，共价键
neuronal　*n*.神经元，二乙基溴乙酰胺
cardiac myocytes　心肌细胞

Notes

① Their synthesis can be fine-tuned to a variety of shapes and sizes (down to a few nanometers). The use of silane mixtures in their preparation allows for convenient incorporation of functional groups of choice (e.g., amino, carboxylic, thiol, etc.) for incorporation of therapeutic or imaging agents. silane *n*.硅烷；amino *a*.氨基的；carboxylic *a*.羧基的；thiol *n*.硫醇，巯基。参考译文：纳米颗粒的形貌和尺寸大小（小到几纳米）可以通过合成手段进行调整。在制备过程中硅烷混合物的使用非常便于引入各种官能团（例如，氨基酸、羧基、巯基等）用于治疗剂或显像剂。

② Remarkably, the "Cornell dots" are the first silica-based multimodal (optical/PET) diagnostic NPs recently approved for human clinical trials; their PEG coating and small size (<10nm) allow for good biodistribution in a melanoma model, and fluorescent dye encapsulation in the NP core gives them notable brightness. multimodal *a*.多种方式的，多峰；clinical trial 临床试验；melanoma *n*.（恶性）黑素瘤，（良性）胎记瘤；fluorescent *a*.荧光的，发荧光的，（颜色、材料等）强烈反光的；发亮的。参考译文：很明显，Cornell dots 是第一类可用于多模式诊断（光/高分子聚合物）的硅基纳米颗粒，近来被批准用于人体临床试验；它们的聚乙二醇包覆层和小尺寸（<10nm）使得它们在黑色素瘤中有很好的生物分布特性，在纳米颗粒核内包覆的荧光染料使得它们具有明显的亮度。

③ AuNPs, modified with both a strong Raman scatter and an antibody, enhance the Raman response (surface enhanced Raman scattering, SERS), whereas the antibody imparts antigenic specificity. antibody *n*.抗体；antigenic *a*.抗原的；specificity *n*.特异性，特征，种别性；种特性；whereas *conj*.鉴于；然而；反之。参考译文：通过强拉曼散射和抗体改性的金纳米颗粒，提高了拉曼光谱反应（表面增强拉曼光谱），因此抗体具有抗原特异性。

④ To this end, we may rely on multimodal imaging, because it is only with the combination of different techniques that we can go beyond the limitations of each modality, especially for imaging of deep tissues. To this end 为此；rely on 信赖，依赖，依靠，信任；go beyond 超出，超载，逾；tissue *n*.组织。参考译文：为此，我们可能需要多模式成像，因为只有通过不同技术的结合，我们才能超越每种方法的局限性，特别是对于深层组织成像。

⑤ Although biocompatibility and safety of CNTs are still an open issue, it is important to note that CNTs comprise a highly heterogeneous class of materials, for which biocompatibility data cannot, and should not, be generalized. biocompatibility n. 生物相容性；heterogeneous adj. 多种多样的，混杂的，不均匀，非均匀；for which 为此，对于那些，为其，为某种。参考译文：尽管碳纳米管的生物相容性和安全性仍存在争议，但是值得关注的是碳纳米管是一类高度异质性的材料，所以它的生物相容性不能也不应该普及。

⑥ The medicinal chemists who venture into this field should not impose limits on their imagination; instead, they should reach out to and partner with physicists, biologists, and clinicians to find creative solutions to these complex, multidisciplinary problems. venture into 冒险进入；partner vt. 使合作，与……合伙；multidisciplinary a. 包括各种学科的，有关各种学问的，多学科。参考译文：进入这个领域药物化学家不应该限制他们的想象力；相反，他们应该与物理学家、生物学家和临床医生合作以寻找方案来解决这些复杂的、多学科的问题。

Reading Comprehension

(1) According to the text, which type of nanoparticles is not mentioned?
(A) AuNPs   (B) iron oxide NPs   (C) silica NPs   (D) TiO_2 NPs

(2) From the text, one can learn that the application of nanomaterial in the nanomedicines is _____ .
(A) futureless   (B) vast   (C) disputable   (D) unthinkable

(3) Mesoporous silica NPs are among the best-characterized NPs in vivo and indeed offer a number of advantages. Which of the following is menetioned in the text?
(A) Their synthesis can be fine-tuned to a variety of shapes and sizes.
(B) The use of silane mixtures allows for the incorporation of functional groups.
(C) Mesoporous silica NPs havethe high surface area and unique physicochemical properties.
(D) Their porosity allows for high drug loading.

(4) About the gold NPs (AuNPs), which of the follow is true?
(A) The chemical modification of gold NPs revolves around the use of either thiols or amines, which limits the choice of triggers for drug loading and release.
(B) AuNPs, modified with both a strong Raman scatter and an antibody can decrease the Raman response.
(C) The homogeneity of gold NP formulations makes it difficult to generalize important aspects such as biosafety assessments.
(D) The shape of AuNPs has a little impact on their properties.

(5) CNTs are excellent candidates in the nanomedicine, all of the following are relevant to these objectives, EXCEPT _____ .
(A) CNTs possess relatively strong NIR absorption.
(B) CNTs comprise a highly heterogeneous class of materials.
(C) Another unique property is their ability to increase electrical activity of multilayered neuronal networks.
(D) Their hollow nature might permit loading with drugs or other bioactive cargoes.

(6) Which of the following is not conducive to the application of the QDs in nanomedicine?

(A) Their small size and ample offering of emission light colors for optical detection make QDs as excellent candidates.

(B) QDs could be useful components of sophisticated nanodevices.

(C) they are typically composed of heavy metals.

(D) QDs have remarkable brightness and photostability.

PART Ⅶ BIOMATERIALS

Unit 21 Biomaterial: An Introduction

A *biomaterial* can be defined as any material used to make devices to replace a part or a function of the body in a safe, reliable, economic, and physiologically acceptable manner. A variety of devices and materials is used in the treatment of disease or injury. Commonplace examples include sutures, tooth fillings, needles, catheters, bone plates, etc. A biomaterial is a synthetic material used to replace part of a living system or to function in intimate contact with living tissue. The Clemson University Advisory Board for Biomaterials has formally defined a biomaterial to be "a systemically and pharmacologically inert substance designed for implantation within or incorporation with living systems." These descriptions add to the many ways of looking at the same concept but expressing it in different ways. By contrast, a *biological material* is a material such as bone, skin, or artery produced by a biological system. Artificial materials that simply are in contact with the skin, such as hearing aids and wearable artificial limbs, are not included in the definition of biomaterials since the skin acts as a barrier with the external world.

Because the ultimate goal of using biomaterials is to improve human health by restoring the function of natural living tissues and organs in the body, it is essential to understand relationships among the properties, functions, and structures of biological materials. Thus, three aspects of study on the subject of biomaterials can be envisioned: biological materials, implant materials, and interaction between the two in the body.

The success of a biomaterial or an implant is highly dependent on three major factors: the properties and biocompatibility of the implant, the health condition of the recipient, and the competency of the surgeon who implants and monitors its progress. It is easy to understand the requirements for an implant by examining the characteristics that a bone plate must satisfy for stabilizing a fractured femur after an accident. These are: (1) acceptance of the plate to the tissue surface, i. e., biocompatibility (this is a broad term and includes points 2 and 3); (2) pharmacological acceptability (nontoxic, nonallergenic, nonimmunogenic, noncarcinogenic, etc.); (3) chemically inert and stable (no time-dependent degradation); (4) adequate mechanical strength; (5) adequate fatigue life; (6) sound engineering design; (7) proper weight and density; (8) relatively inexpensive, reproducible, and easy to fabricate and process for large-scale production.

The materials to be used in vivo have to be approved by the FDA (United States Food and Drug Administration). If a proposed material is substantially equivalent to one used before the FDA legislation of 1976, then the FDA may approve its use on a Premarket Approval (PMA) basis. This process, justified by experience with a similar material, reduces the time and expense for the use of the proposed material. Otherwise, the material has to go through a series of "biocompatibility" tests. In general biocompatibility requirements include: (1) Acute systemic toxicity, (2) Cytotoxicity, (3) Hemolysis, (4) Intravenous toxicity, (5) Mutagenicity, (6) Oral toxicity, (7) Pyrogenicity, and (8) Sensitization.

The guidelines on biocompatibility assessment are given in Table 7.1. The data and documentation requirements for all tests demonstrate the importance of good recordkeeping. It is also important to keep all documents created in the production of materials and devices to be used in vivo within the boundaries of Good Manufacturing Practices (GMP), requiring completely isolated clean rooms for production of implants and devices. The final products are usually sterilized after packaging. The packaged item is normally mass sterilized by γ-radiation or ETO (ethylene oxide gas).

Table 7.1 Guidelines on Biocompatibility Assessment

A. Data required to assess suitability
  1. Material characterization. Identify the chemical structure of a material and any potential toxicological hazards. Residue levels. Degradation products. Cumulative effects of each process.
  2. Information on prior use. Documented proof of prior use, which would indicate the material(s) suitability.
  3. Toxicological data. Results of known biological tests that would aid in assessing potential reaction (adverse or not) during clinical use.

B. Supporting documents
  1. Details of application: shape, size, form, plus time in contact and use.
  2. Chemical breakdown of all materials involved in the product.
  3. A review of all toxicity data on those materials in direct contact with the body tissues.
  4. Prior use and details of effects.
  5. Toxicity tests [FDA or ISO(International Standard Organization guides)]
  6. Final assessment of all information including toxicological significance.

One can classify biomaterials into permanent and transient, depending on the time intended to be in the body. Sometimes a temporary implant becomes permanent if one does not remove it, such as a bone plate after a fractured bone is completely healed.

Another important area of study is that of the mechanics and dynamics of tissues and the resultant interactions between them. Generally, this study, known as *biomechanics*, is incorporated into the design and insertion of implants. More sophisticated analysis can be made using computer methods, such as FEM and FEA (finite-element modeling/analysis). These approaches help to design a better prosthesis or even custom make them for individual application.

Nanotechnology is a rapidly evolving field that involves material structures on a size scale typically 100nm or less. New areas of biomaterials applications may develop using nanoscale materials or devices. For example, drug delivery methods have made use of a microsphere encapsulation technique. Nanotechnology may help in the design of drugs with more precise dosage, oriented to specific targets or with timed interactions. Nanotechnology may also help to reduce the size of diagnostic sensors and probes.

Transplantation of organs can restore some functions that cannot be carried out by artificial materials, or that are better done by a natural organ. For example, in the case of kidney failure many patients can expect to derive benefit from transplantation because an artificial kidney has many disadvantages, including high cost, immobility of the device, maintenance of the dialyzer, and illness due to imperfect filtration. The functions of the liver cannot be assumed by any artificial device or material. Liver transplants have extended the lives of people with liver failure. Organ transplants are widely performed, but their success has been hindered due to social, ethical, and immunological problems.

Since artificial materials are limited in the functions they can perform, and transplants are limited by the availability of organs and problems of immune compatibility, there is current interest in the regeneration or regrowth of diseased or damaged tissue. *Tissue engineering* refers to the growth of a new tissue using living cells guided by the structure of a substrate made of synthetic material. This substrate is called a scaffold. The scaffold materials are important since they must be compatible with the cells and guide their growth. Most scaffold materials are biodegradable or resorbable as the cells grow. Most scaffolds are made from natural or synthetic polymers, but for hard tissues such as bone and teeth ceramics such as calcium phosphate compounds can be utilized. The tissue is grown in vitro and implanted in vivo. There have been some clinical successes in repair of injuries to large areas of skin, or small defects in cartilage.

It is imperative that we should know the fundamentals of materials before we can utilize them properly and efficiently. Meanwhile, we also have to know some fundamental properties and functions of tissues and organs. The interactions between tissues and organs with manmade materials have to be more fully elucidated. Fundamentals-based scientific knowledge can be a great help in exploring many avenues of biomaterials research and development.

(*Selected from Joon Park, R. S. Lakes, Biomaterials: An Introduction, Springer, 2007*)

New Words and Expressions

inert   *a.* 惰性的，迟钝的
recipient   *n.* 接受者
competency   *n.* 能力
surgeon   *n.* 外科医生
pharmacological   *a.* 药物学的，药理学的
sound   *a.* 健全的，可靠的，合理的
in vivo   在体内
in vitro   在体外，在试管内
cytotoxicity   细胞毒性
hemolysis   溶血
intravenous   *a.* 静脉的，静脉注射的

mutagenicity *n*. 诱变（性）

sterilized *v*. 杀菌（消除，冻结）； *a*. 无菌的（消毒的）

dosage *n*. 药量

sensor *n*. 检测计

probe *n*. 探针，调查，探测针； *v*. 用探针测，详细调查

kidney *n*. 肾，腰子

filtration *n*. 过滤

liver *n*. 肝脏

substrate *n*. 基片（基层，真晶格，基质）

cartilage *n*. 软骨

elucidate *v*. 阐明，说明

Notes

① It is easy to understand the requirements for an implant by examining the characteristics that a bone plate must satisfy for stabilizing a fractured femur after an accident. stabilizing，稳定化处理；femur，大腿骨，股骨。参考译文：对于事故后固定断裂大腿骨的手术，必须检测骨板的特性是否满足手术的需求，这一点是很容易理解的。

② One can classify biomaterials into permanent and transient, depending on the time intended to be in the body. classify，归类，分类。参考译文：根据在身体里存在时间的长短，我们可以将生物材料分成永久性材料和暂时性材料。

③ Another important area of study is that of the mechanics and dynamics of tissues and the resultant interactions between them. that，代指 study。参考译文：另一个重要的研究领域是组织的力学与动力学性能以及它们之间的相互作用。

④ Nanotechnology may help in the design of drugs with more precise dosage, oriented to specific targets or with timed interactions. precise dosage，oriented to specific targets，timed interactions 在句中的关系是并列的，此句为一个简单句。

⑤ Transplantation of organs can restore some functions that cannot be carried out by artificial materials, or that are better done by a natural organ. 两个 that 引导两个并列的定语从句，修饰 functions。artificial materials，人工材料；natural organ，正常器官。

⑥ It is imperative that we should know the fundamentals of materials before we can utilize them properly and efficiently. imperative，需要的。it 为形式主语，that 后面的句子才是真正的主语。参考译文：在我们合理有效地应用这些材料之前，有必要先知道这些材料的基本应用原则。

Exercises

1. Question for discussion

(1) What are biological materials? Please give some examples?

(2) Give the basic classification of biological materials and artificial materials.

(3) What is the success of a biomaterial or an implant highly dependent on?

(4) Which characteristics are needed for a bone plate stabilizing a fractured femur after an accident?

(5) Please describe the nanotechnology in the biomaterials applications.

(6) Why is current interest in the regeneration or regrowth of diseased or damaged tissue?

2. Translate the following into Chinese

intimate contact   inert substance
artificial materials   pharmacological acceptability
the mechanics and dynamics of tissues   individual application
microsphere encapsulation technique

- A biomaterial is a synthetic material used to replace part of a living system or to function in intimate contact with living tissue.

- By contrast, a *biological material* is a material such as bone, skin, or artery produced by a biological system.

- Sometimes a temporary implant becomes permanent if one does not remove it, such as a bone plate after a fractured bone is completely healed.

- Transplantation of organs can restore some functions that cannot be carried out by artificial materials, or that are better done by a natural organ.

- Fundamentals-based scientific knowledge can be a great help in exploring many avenues of biomaterials research and development.

3. Translate the following into English

生物材料   生物相容性
助听器   环氧乙烷
组织工程   器官移植

- 根据在身体里存在时间的长短，我们可以将生物材料分成永久性材料和暂时性材料。
- 通常，众所周知的生物力学的研究是设计与移植物嵌入的结合。
- 一些生物材料应用的新领域可能会采用纳米级材料或装置。
- 因为采用的支架必须与细胞相容，并且还要指引细胞的生长，所以支架材料的选择非常重要。

4. Reading comprehension

(1) How dose the author introduce the biomaterials?

(A) Justifying an assumption

(B) Explaining a phenomenon

(C) Making a comparison

(D) Taking an example

(2) Which of the following is NOT the success of a biomaterial or an implant highly depending on? _____.

(A) The properties and biocompatibility of the implant

(B) Acceptance of the plate to the tissue surface

(C) The health condition of the recipient

(D) The competency of the surgeon who implants and monitors its progress

(3) The FDA may approve the use of a proposed material on a Premarket Approval (PMA) basis which is substantially equivalent to one used before the FDA legislation of 1976 because _____.

    (A) the process justified by experience with a similar material, reduces the time and expense for the use of the proposed material

    (B) the material has to go through a series of "biocompatibility" tests

    (C) the materials to be used in vivo have to be approved by the FDA

    (D) the success of a biomaterial or an implant is highly dependent on three major factors

(4) Which of the following is NOT true according to the nanotechnology applications? _____.

    (A) The size scale of nanomaterial structures is 100nm or less

    (B) All areas of biomaterials applications use nanoscale materials or devices

    (C) Nanotechnology may help in the design of drugs with timed interactions

    (D) Nanotechnology may also help to reduce the size of diagnostic sensors and probes

(5) Organ transplants are widely performed, but their success has been hindered because of all of the following factors EXCEPT _____.

    (A) social problem   (B) ethical problem

    (C) technological problem   (D) immunological problem

Reading Material

Biomaterials and Health

Life expectancy over the years has increased significantly. During the last five decades alone, life expectancy has risen by 15% (from 69 to 80 years) in North America, and we see similar trends across the globe except for Sub-Saharan Africa. More importantly, not only are we living longer but our quality of life has dramatically improved thanks to the many advances in medicine, biology, and MSE.

We have seen tremendous advances in biomaterials; Biomaterial is defined to be "a structural material, derived from synthetic or natural sources, that interacts with tissue for medical therapeutic or diagnostic purposes." The market potential for structural tissue engineering is $90~100 billion, and for the biomaterials industry R&D growth spending is about 24% a year. Recent advances and developments include: cornea tissue regeneration, artificial skin, caticel implantation in the perosteal flap, and so on. Devices such as artificial heart valves (e.g., mitral valve), coronary stents, and particularly drug eluting stents have seen significant utilization for the benefit of society (see Figure 7.1). These developments are critically dependent on the advances that have been made and continue to be made in MSE.

Implantable medical devices have seen a huge growth during the last decade (see Table

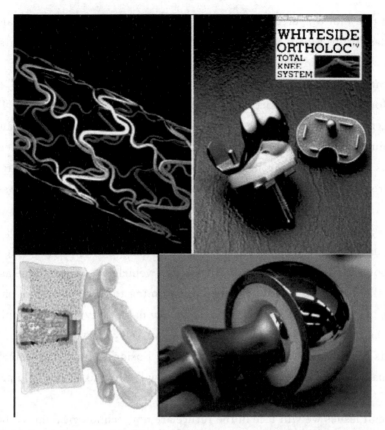

Figure 7.1 Innovative materials for medical applications; clockwise from top right corner:
knee implant; hip joint; Medtronic's Sofamor Danek INFUSE® bone graft and
cage lumber fusion device; and coronary stent.

7.2). 49 Hip joints, artificial knees, spinal cord fusion devices, and many other parts are now being replaced on almost routine basis. Thus, in the last two decades alone we have witnessed medical advances that have profoundly improved quality of life; the unfortunate part is that many parts of the globe cannot afford these advances nor do they have access to such medical services.

Table 7.2 Demand for Implantable Medical Devices (for U.S.)

Implantable Devices	1997	2002	2007
Cardiac Implants	3620	7080	13740
Orthopedic Implants	4460	6410	8730
Other Implants	640	1120	1880
Total	8720	14610	24350

In the future we will see major developments in the area of surface modification of biomaterials to better control blood and tissue compatibility; biomaterials can be modified by plasma treatment or by chemical grafting. Through surface modification, we will be able to manipulate material attributes such as resistance to infection, resistance to clot formation, lubricity, and wear resistance. A good example is how heparin (an anticoagulant) is covalently coupled to a multi-layered base coat of a biomaterial surface. Implants and devices that are also vehicles for drug delivery will be another area for future developments. Examples of such devices are steroid-releasing pacing electrodes and drug-eluting stents. Tissue engineering coupled with innovative materials for the manufacture of "smart" heart valves is another area for growth and opportunity for future developments. The whole field of biomaterials for regenerative medicine is a fertile area for the materials science and engineering (MSE) community; one example is how we might use biomaterials to regenerate insulin-producing cells of the pancreas from stem cells. Technologies that will be critical for the development of regenerative medicine will be supramolecular chemistry and self-assembly of atoms to create the necessary bio-active architecture. In brief, biomaterials of the future will not solely serve mechanical functions, rather they will be regulators of biological activity.

In the future we will see major advances in bio-organic-inorganic composites; at present, bio-erodable polyanhydrides are being synthesized as vehicles to release large as well as small molecules. In the future we will see this field blossoming to carry out "local chemotherapy." The approach of synthesis and application of bio-erodable polymers for implantable tissue scaffolds will be used to create liver tissue, blood vessels, nerves, and heart muscle, and "InfoTech plus biotech will transform health care." Fusion of information technology, biotechnology, nanotechnology, and neural networks will allow us to not only prevent but also cure disease.

The difficult issues we will face in the future are not technological ones, but rather ethical ones. Imagine what will be the consequence of being able to know the prognosis for disease and especially a life-threatening disease in a newborn. In less than a decade when the genome project is completed, we will be able to have such information. How will insurance companies assess risk and how will society cope with these issues? The future is bright for medical advances as a result of the developments in the materials science and engineering (MSE); what we have seen in the recent past is only the beginning. The difficult questions will be societal ones: will health care only benefit those that can afford it? How do we cope with inequalities across the globe? Lastly, we will need to address the ethical issues that will arise by knowing a-priori a person's propensity for disease and poor health. We hope that future advances will enable us to cure diseases and mitigate the difficult ethical issues.

(*Selected from Looking Beyond the Last* 50 *Years*: *The Future of Materials Science and Engineering*, *by Diran Apelian*, 2007)

New Words and Expressions

life expectancy   平均寿命
therapeutic   *a*. 治疗（学）的，疗法的
cornea   *n*. 角膜
artificial heart valves   人工心脏瓣膜
coronary stents   冠状动脉支架
drug eluting stents   药物涂层支架

spinal cord fusion devices 脊髓融合装置
orthopedic *a.* 整形外科的，矫形术的
plasma *n.* 等离子体，血浆，等离子
grafting 嫁接，移植（术）
clot *n.* 凝块；*v.* 凝结，使……凝结
lubricity *n.* 润滑性，润滑能力
wear resistance 耐磨性
steroid *n.* 类固醇，拟脂醇
pacing electrodes 起搏电极
insulin-producing cells 胰岛素分泌细胞
pancreas *n.* 胰腺，胰，胰脏
stem cells 干细胞
mitigate *v.* 缓解，减轻，缓和

Notes

① More importantly, not only are we living longer but our quality of life has dramatically improved thanks to the many advances in medicine, biology, and MSE. 本句为 not only… but (also) 结构，因为 not only 在句首，所以用倒装。参考译文：更重要的是，由于医学、生物学和材料科学工程的进步，不仅我们的寿命更长，而且我们的生活质量也在飞速提高。

② Biomaterial is defined to be "a structural material, derived from synthetic or natural sources, that interacts with tissue for medical therapeutic or diagnostic purposes." …be defined to…，……定义为……。参考译文：生物材料定义为一种与组织相互作用从而达到医学治疗或诊断目的的合成或天然结构材料。

③ The unfortunate part is that many parts of the globe cannot afford these advances nor do they have access to such medical services. that 引导两个并列的表语从句。参考译文：令人遗憾的是世界上许多地方负担不起高昂的费用或者他们没有权利使用这样的医疗设施。

④ Technologies that will be critical for the development of regenerative medicine will be supramolecular chemistry and self-assembly of atoms to create the necessary bio-active architecture. supramolecular chemistry，超分子化学；self-assembly，自组装。that 引导一个定语从句。参考译文：对再生医学的发展有重要作用的超分子化学和原子自组装技术可以制造出所需要的生物活性结构体系。

⑤ In brief, biomaterials of the future will not solely serve mechanical functions, rather they will be regulators of biological activity. solely，独自地，单独地。参考译文：简而言之，未来生物材料不仅仅单纯发挥其机械性能，它们还将是生物活性的调节器。

⑥ Imagine what will be the consequence of being able to know the prognosis for disease and especially a life-threatening disease in a newborn. 本句为以动词 imagine 开头的祈使句。参考译文：想像一下，能够在婴儿时提前预知疾病，尤其是威胁生命的疾病，会是一种什么结果？

Reading Comprehension

(1) From the first paragraph we learn that _____.
(A) life expectancy has risen by 15% in the whole globe during the last five decades alone
(B) life expectancy over the years has decreased in Sub-Saharan Africa
(C) our quality of life has dramatically improved attribute to the many advances in medicine, biology, and MSE
(D) we living longer is more important than our quality of life

(2) According to the passage, the developments of biomaterials are critically dependent on _____.
(A) the advances in the materials science and engineering
(B) the increase of life expectancy
(C) medical advances
(D) the improvements of our quality of life

(3) Which of the following is NOT mentioned in the developments of biomaterials? _____.
(A) We will see major developments in the area of surface modification of biomaterials to better control blood and tissue compatibility in the future
(B) Another important area of study is that of the mechanics and dynamics of tissues and the resultant interactions between them.
(C) Implants and devices that are also vehicles for drug delivery will be another area for future developments
(D) Tissue engineering coupled with innovative materials for the manufacture of "smart" heart valves is another area for growth and opportunity for future developments

(4) The author uses the example of using biomaterials to regenerate insulin-producing cells of the pancreas from stem cells to show that _____.
(A) we will be able to manipulate material attributes through surface modification
(B) implants and devices also vehicles for drug delivery
(C) the whole field of biomaterials for regenerative medicine is a fertile area for the materials science and engineering community
(D) biomaterials of the future will be regulators of biological activity

(5) What can we learn from the last paragraph? _____.
(A) Technology and ethic are difficult issues we will face in the future
(B) The materials science and engineering has developed rapidly as a result to medical advances
(C) Future advances can certainly enable us to cure diseases and mitigate the difficult ethical issues
(D) Not all people can afford health care because of the existing inequalities across the globe

Unit 22　Applications of Biocomposites

The use of biofibre reinforced composites has extended to almost all fields. Recently three-layer particleboards were produced from a mixture of sunflower stalks and poplar wood at certain ratios utilizing urea-formaldehyde (UF) adhesives. Panels with a density of 0.7 g/cm^3 were manufactured with the ratios of 25, 50, and 75 percent particles from sunflower stalks or poplar. Panels were subjected to various tests for physical properties. Results show that all the panels provide properties required by the normal standards for general purpose-use particleboards.

Bio-based composite roof structures were successfully fabricated from soy oil-based resin and cellulose fibers in the form of paper sheets made from recycled cardboard boxes. This recycled paper was previously tested in composite sheets and structural unit beams and was found to give the required stiffness and strength required for roof construction.

In a study encompassing many applications, the flame retardancy of biodegradable polymers and biocomposites was investigated. For the comparison, flame retarded lignocellulosic filler reinforced biocomposites were prepared using polypropylene (PP), polyurethane (PUR) and fully biodegradable starch matrices. The compatibility of wood flake with PP was improved by application of an alkoxy silane based reactive surfactant. The silylation improved not only the compatibility but also the thermal stability of the wood flake according to TG measurements. Raman spectroscopic analysis of the silylated product showed that the improved thermal stability is the result of reduced ratio of the amorphous phase of cellulose. The phosphorus additives in flame retarded PUR biocomposites, comprising waste bio fillers and recycled polyol, proved to be very effective because both the matrix and the filler components participate in mechanism of flame retardancy.

Researchers developed a new low dielectric constant material suited to electronic materials applications using hollow keratin fibers and chemically modified soybean oil. The unusual low value of dielectric constant was due to the air present in the hollow microcrystalline keratin fibers and the triglyceride molecules. It is suggested that the low cost composite made from avian sources and plant oil has the potential to replace the dielectrics in microchips and circuit boards in the ever growing electronics materials field. And the coefficient of thermal expansion (CTE) of the composite was low enough for electronic applications and similar to the value of silicon materials or polyimides used in printed circuit boards.

Plastic/wood fiber composites are being used in a large number of applications in decks, docks, window frames and molded panel components. It has been reported that 460 million pounds of plastic/wood fiber composites were produced in 1999. Statistics show that the production of these composites in 2001 has increased to 700 million pounds. Over the last three decades considerable research has been committed to finding an alternative fiber to replace asbestos in fiber cement products. Australian research was centered on natural fibers and ultimately it was a natural fiber, wood pulp fiber, which was responsible for the greatest replacement of asbestos in the beleaguered global fiber cement industry. As these fibers are cheap and readily available, the energy required for the processing of these composites is low; also the incorporation of random vegetable fibers in cement matrices requires only a small number of trained personnel in the construction industry. Recently, the use of bamboo fiber as reinforcement in structural concrete elements has been explored. Pulp from eucalyptus waste and residual sisal and coir fibers have also been studied as a replacement for asbestos in roofing components. The use of cactus pulp as a stabilizing agent to improve the behavior of the sisal fiber reinforced soil has been studied. Chopped barley straw has also been used as a suitable reinforcement for composite soil.

Biocomposites also offer immense opportunities for an increasing role as alternate material, especially as wood substitutes in the furniture market. Yet biofiber as construction material for buildings were known long before. For centuries, mixtures of straw and loam, dried in the sun, were employed as construction composite in Egypt. Pipes, pultruded profiles and panels with polyester matrices are also quite popular. Large projects have been promoted where jute-reinforced polyester resins are used for buildings, e. g. the Madras House and grain elevators. Today, a renaissance in the use of natural fibers as reinforcement in technical applications is taking place, mainly in the automobile and packaging industries (e. g. , egg boxes).

In the automotive industry, cotton fibers embedded in polyester matrix was used in the body of the East German "Trabant" car. The use of flax fibers in car disk brakes to replace asbestos fibers is also another example. Daimler - Benz has been exploring the idea of replacing glass fibers with natural fibers in automotive components since 1991. A subsidiary of the company, Mercedes Benz pioneered this concept with the "Beleem project" based in Sao Paolo, Brazil. In this case, coconut fibers were used in the commercial vehicles over a 9-year period. Mercedes also used jute-based door panels in its E-class vehicles in 1996. In September 2000, Daimler Chrysler began using natural fibers for their vehicle production. The bast fibers are primarily used in automotive applications because they exhibit greatest strength.

The other advantages of using bast fibers in the automotive industry include weight savings of between 10% and 30% and corresponding cost savings. Recent studies have also indicated that hemp-based natural fiber mat thermoplastics are promising candidates in automotive applications where high specific stiffness is required.

Virtually all the major car manufacturers in Germany (Daimler Chrysler, Mercedes, Volkswagen, Audi Group, BMW, Ford and Opel) now use biocomposites in various applications. Interior trim components such as dashboards and door panels using polypropylene and natural fibers are produced by Johnson Controls, Inc. for Daimler Chrysler. In 2000 Audi launched the A2 midrange car in which door trim panels were made of polyurethane reinforced with mixed flax/sisal mat. DaimlerChrysler has now increased its research and development in flax reinforced polyester composites for exterior applications.

It should be pointed out the importance of biofibers and biocomposites in the automotive industry. The end of life vehicle (ELV) directive in Europe states that by 2015, vehicles must be constructed of 95% recyclable materials, with 85% recoverable through reuse or mechanical recycling and 10% through energy recovery or thermal recycling. This will definitely lead to an increased use of biofibers.

The diverse range of products utilizing biofibers and biobased resins derived from soy beans is giving life to a new generation of composites for a number of applications like hurricane-resistant housing and structures.

(*Selected from Maya Jacob John, Sabu Thomas: fibres and biocomposites, Carbohydrate Polymers* 71 (2008) 343-364)

New Words and Expressions

particleboard *n.* 芯板材，刨花板
urea-formaldehyde 尿素甲醛
cellulose *n.* 纤维素
retardancy *n.* 阻滞性（阻……能力）
flame retardancy 阻燃性
lignocellulosic *a.* 木质纤维的
starch *n.* 淀粉
polyurethane *n.* 聚氨酯，聚氨基甲酸酯
silylation *n.* 甲硅烷基化作用，硅烷化（作用）
Raman spectroscopic analysis 拉曼光谱分析
amorphous *a.* 无定形的，非晶质，非结晶的
phosphorus *n.* 磷
polyol *n.* 多羟基化合物
dielectric constant 介电常数
keratin *n.* 角质素，角蛋白
triglyceride *n.* 甘油三酸酯
polyimide *n.* 聚酰亚胺
pulp *n.* 浆
eucalyptus *n.* 桉树
sisal *n.* 剑麻（波罗麻）
coir *n.* 椰子壳的纤维
cactus *n.* 仙人掌
renaissance *n.* 复兴

Notes

① This recycled paper was previously tested in composite sheets and structural unit beams and was found to give the required stiffness and strength required for roof construction. 这是由 and 连接的两个并列句。参考译文：这种可回收的纸在先前的复合板和结构单元横梁中被测试过，发现这种纸具有屋顶建设所需要的硬度和强度。

② The silylation improved not only the compatibility but also the thermal stability of the wood flake according to TG measurements. 宾语中含一个 not only…but also…结构，意为不仅……而且……。参考译文：通过 TG 测试，硅烷化不仅可以改善木薄片的兼容性，并且可以改善它的热稳定性。

③ It is suggested that the low cost composite made from avian sources and plant oil has the potential to replace the dielectrics in microchips and circuit boards in the ever growing electronics materials field. microchips，微芯片；circuit boards，电路板。参考译文：在不断进步的电子材料领域中，由禽类和植物油制成的低成本复合材料具有代替微芯片和电路板中的电解质的潜能。

④ Australian research was centered on natural fibers and ultimately it was a natural fiber, wood pulp fiber, which was responsible for the greatest replacement of asbestos in the beleaguered global fiber cement industry. 本句为 and 连接的两个并列句，其中在第二个句子中含有一个由 which 引导的定语从句，natural，在这里的意思是"天然的"，be responsible for，对……负责。

⑤ Recent studies have also indicated that hemp-based natural fiber mat thermoplastics are promising candidates in automotive applications where high specific stiffness is required. specific stiffness，比刚度；本句中 where 引导一个状语从句来修饰"in automotive applications"。参考译文：最近研究表明在需要高比刚度的汽车应用中，天然大麻纤维垫片热塑性塑料是很有潜力的候选材料。

⑥ The end of life vehicle (ELV) directive in Europe states that by 2015, vehicles must be constructed of 95% recyclable materials, with 85% recoverable through reuse or mechanical recycling and 10% through energy recovery or thermal recycling. state，陈述，规定。参考译文：欧洲《关于报废汽车的技术指令》规定：到 2015 年，可循环的材料占汽车材料的 95%，其中通过再利用或机械回收的可回收材料占 85%，通过能量或热量回收的占 10%。

Exercises

1. Question for discussion

(1) Why the paper sheets made from recycled cardboard boxes can be used in the bio-based composite roof structures?

(2) Why the composite made from hollow keratin fibers and chemically modified soybean oil has low dielectric constant?

(3) Briefly state the applications of plastic/wood fiber composites.

(4) Why are the bast fibers primarily used in automotive applications?

(5) Please describe the natural fibers applications in the automotive industry.

2. Translate the following into Chinese

alkoxy silane   Raman spectroscopic analysis
circuit boards   residual sisal
alternate material   natural fibers

• Recently three-layer particleboards were produced from a mixture of sunflower stalks and poplar wood at certain ratios utilizing urea-formaldehyde (UF) adhesives.

• The coefficient of thermal expansion (CTE) of the composite was low enough for electronic applications and similar to the value of silicon materials or polyimides used in printed circuit boards.

• Recently, the use of bamboo fiber as reinforcement in structural concrete elements has been explored.

• The bast fibers are primarily used in automotive applications because they exhibit greatest strength.

3. Translate the following into English

表面活性剂　　　　　　　　　介电常数
热膨胀系数　　　　　　　　　稳定剂
韧皮纤维　　　　　　　　　　比刚度

•最近三十年，在纤维水泥产品方面存在大量的研究，致力于发现一种可替代的纤维来代替石棉。

•研究人员运用中空角蛋白纤维和化学修饰豆油，发明了一种新的适合电子材料应用的低介电常数材料。

•作为替代材料，生物复合材料发挥着越来越重要的作用，尤其是在家具市场中作为木材代用品。

•今天，在技术应用中作为加强剂的天然纤维的应用正在复兴，主要在汽车与包装工业（如鸡蛋盒）。

4. Reading comprehension

(1) From the first paragraph we learn that _____ .

(A) three-layer particleboards were produced from a mixture of sunflower stalks and polar wood with a ratio of 25 percent.

(B) three-layer particleboards were produced only using a mixture of sunflower stalks and polar wood.

(C) three-layer particleboards were produced using two kinds of adhesives—a mixture of sunflower stalks and polar wood and urea-formaldehyde.

(D) Different panels were manufactured with different ratios particles from sunflower stalks or polar wood.

(2) The biocomposite can be used in the electronics materials field because of _____ .

(A) low dielectric constant and low coefficient of thermal expansion of materials

(B) the flame retardancy of biocomposite

(C) its biodegradable property

(D) the low cost of biocomposite

(3) Which of the following is TRUE according to paragraph 5.

(A) Plastic/wood fiber composites were firstly applied in 1999.

(B) Natural fiber was responsible for the greatest replacement of asbestos in the fiber cement industry.

    (C) Cactus pulp has been studied as a replacement for asbestos in roofing components.

    (D) The use of chopped barley straw as a stabilizing agent to improve the behavior of the sisal fiber reinforced soil has been studied.

(4) All of the following are advantages of using bast fibers in the automotive industry except _____.

    (A) greatest strength   (B) weight savings   (C) cost savings   (D) flame retardancy

(5) The author's attitude towards applications of biocomposites seems to be _____.

    (A) biased   (B) indifferent   (C) approving   (D) puzzling

Reading Material

Examples of Biomaterial Applications

    Biomaterials are used in joint replacements, bone plates, bone cement, artificial ligaments and tendons, dental implants for tooth fixation, blood vessel prostheses, heart valves, skin repair devices, cochlear replacements, and contact lenses. Biomaterials must be compatible with the body, and there are often issues of biocompatibility which must be resolved before a product can be placed on the market and used in a clinical setting. Because of this, biomaterials are usually subjected to the same requirements of those suffered by new drug therapies. All manufacturing companies are also required to ensure traceability of all of their products so that if a defective product is discovered, others in the same batch may be traced.

Heart Replacement and Repairs

    The term cardiovascular pertains to the heart, blood, and blood vessels. The heart is, of course, an absolutely essential organ. A heart that fails completely may be replaced by a donor organ. About 60 000 people suffer terminal heart failure each year in the United States, yet only about 2500 donor hearts become available for transplant. Many attempts have been made—and continue to be made—to produce an artificial heart that can serve over a long period of time as a replacement for the natural organ. We will not devote attention to these efforts, except to note that recent results are quite promising.

    It often happens that only a part of the heart, such as the aortic valve, fails and needs replacement. Repair could be made by using foreign tissue (for example, a pig heart valve) or a mechanical heart valve implant to replace a diseased one. About 250000 valve replacement procedures are performed annually worldwide. In the United States about 45% of the procedures involve a mechanical valve.

    It is vital to minimize fluid disturbance as the blood passes through artificial devices. Surface roughness in a device causes hemolysis, the breakdown of red blood cells. Furthermore, surface roughness can serve as a site for invading bacteria to adhere and colonize. Finally, rough surfaces also promote coagulation of the blood, which forms a thrombus, or blood clot. Thus, even though we may have a perfectly fine piece of machinery from a mechanical point of view, the heart valve may not be suitable as a long-term implant. To minimize blood clots, the discs in the heart valve must have a smooth, chemically inert surface.

A second challenge in the use of a heart valve implant is to fix it in place. The retainer ring that forms the body of the valve is covered with a mesh of woven fabric. The material of choice is the fiber formed from polyethylene terephthalate (PET, a polyester). The mesh acts as a lattice on which the body's tissues can grow, so that the valve becomes incorporated into its surroundings. Tissue grows through the polyester mesh, whereas it does not do so on many other plastics. Apparently the polar, oxygen-containing functional groups along the polyester chain afford attractive interactions to facilitate tissue growth.

Vascular Grafts

A vascular graft is a replacement for a segment of diseased arteries. Where possible, diseased blood vessels are replaced with vessels taken from the patient's own body. When this is not feasible, artificial materials must be used. Dacron is used as replacement for large-diameter arteries around the heart. For this purpose, it is fabricated into a crimped, woven, tubular form. The tubing is crimped to enable it to bend without serious decrease in its cross-sectional area. The graft must integrate with surrounding tissue after it has been put in place. It must therefore have an open structure, with pores on the order of 10/zm in diameter. During the healing process blood capillaries grow into the graft and new tissues form throughout it. Similarly, polytetrafiuoroethylene $[-\!(CF_2CF_2)_{\!\overline{n}}\,]$ is used for the smaller diameter vascular grafts in the limbs.

Ideally, the inside surface of the graft would become lined with the same sorts of cells that line the native artery, but this process does not occur with materials currently available. Instead, the inside surface of the tubing is recognized as being foreign to the blood. Platelets, which are circulating components of the blood, normally serve the function of sealing up wounds in the blood vessel walls. Unfortunately, they attach to foreign surfaces and cause blood coagulation. The search for a more biocompatible lining for grafts is an area of active research, but at present there is a continuing risk of blood clots. Excess tissue growth at the intersection of the graft with the native artery is also a frequent problem. Because of the possibility of blood clot formation, patients who have received artificial heart valves or vascular grafts are generally required to take anticoagulation drugs on a continuing basis.

Artificial Tissue

The treatment of patients who have lost extensive skin tissue—for example, burn patients or those with skin ulcers—is one of the most difficult problems in therapeutic medicine. Today, laboratory-grown skin can be employed to replace grafts in such patients. Ideally, the "artificial" tissue would be grown from cells taken from the patient. When this is not possible, for example, with burn victims, the tissue cells come from another source. When the graft skin is not formed from the patient's own cells, drugs that suppress the body's natural immune defense system must be used or steps must be taken to modify the new cell line to prevent rejection of the tissue.

The challenge in growing artificial tissue is to get the cells to organize themselves as they would in a living system. The first step in accomplishing this objective is to provide a suitable scaffold for the cells to grow on, one that will keep them in contact with each other and allow them to organize. Such a scaffold must be biocompatible; cells must adhere to the scaffold and differentiate (that is, develop into cells of different types) as the culture grows. The scaffolding must also be mechanically strong and biodegradable.

The most successful scaffolds have been lactic acid—glycolicmers. The copolymer has an abundance of polar carbon-oxygen bonds along the chain, affording many opportunities for hydrogen-bonding interactions. The ester linkages formed in the condensation reaction are susceptible to hydrolysis, which is just the reverse reaction. When the artificial tissue is deployed in the body, the underlying copolymer scaffold slowly hydrolyzes away as the tissue cells continue to develop and merge with adjacent tissue.

"Smart" Sutures

Until the 1970s, if you had to go to the doctor to get stitches, you later had to go back to get the stitches removed. Stitches that are used to hold living tissue together are called sutures. Since the 1970s, biodegradable sutures have been available. After the sutures have been applied to the tissue, they slowly dissolve away and do not release any harmful byproducts.

Today's biodegradable sutures are made out of lactic acid-glycolic acid copolymers, similar to those just described, that slowly hydrolyze over time.

More recently, scientists have developed what are colloquially called "smart" materials for biological applications. In this context, "smart" means a material that will reversibly change its behavior in response to an external stimulus. For example, smart eyeglasses turn dark when you go outside in the sun, then turn light again when you go inside. In the case of smart sutures, scientists have developed a thermoplastic polymer that organizes itself reversibly, via intermolecular forces, as a function of temperature. The material shrinks if it is heated to body temperature or higher. Thus, sutures made from this material can be tied loosely by the surgeon, and then after warming up to body temperature, the sutures tighten up to provide the optimum force. This polymer was first made in 2002, and it is not on the market at the time of this writing. It is expected, however, that it will be very useful to doctors performing surgery in very small spaces (for example, through an endoscope).

(*Selected from Theodore L. Brom, H. Eugene LeMay, Jr., and Bruce E. Bursten, Chemistry: The Central Science, 13th Edition, 2014*)

New Words and Expressions

biocompatibility   *n*. 生物相容性，生物适合性
traceability   *n*. 跟踪能力，可追溯性
defective   *a*. 有缺陷的
batch   *n*. 组，批，成批
cardiovascular   *a*. 心脏血管的，心血管的
donor organ   捐献器官
terminal   *a*. 致死的
hemolysis   *n*. 溶血，溶血作用
coagulation   *n*. 凝结，凝聚，凝固
thrombus   *n*. 血栓，血块
polyethylene terephthalate   聚对苯二甲酸乙二醇酯
vascular   *a*. 血管的，脉管的
arteries   *n*. 动脉
anticoagulation   *n*. 抗凝血作用
ulcers   *n*. 溃疡
scaffold   *n*. 脚手架，支架
lactic acid   乳酸
ester linkage   酯键
condensation reaction   缩合反应
stitches   缝线
endoscope   *n*. 内诊镜，内窥镜

Notes

① Biomaterials must be compatible with the body, and there are often issues of biocompatibility which must be resolved before a product can be placed on the market and used in a clinical setting. which 引导一个定语从句修饰 issues of biocompatibility。参考译文：生物材料必须与身体相容，并且在产品放到市场临床应用之前，生物兼容性问题必须解决。

② Because of this, biomaterials are usually subjected to the same requirements of those suffered by new drug therapies. be subjected to, 经历，遭受；those 代指 requirements。参考译文：因为这个原因，所有生物材料必须要经过新药物疗法。

③ About 60 000 people suffer terminal heart failure each year in the United States, yet only about 2500 donor hearts become available for transplant. terminal, 致死的；heart failure, 心力衰竭。参考译文：在美国每年大约有60000人忍受致死的心力衰竭疾病，然而只有大约2500捐献心脏可用作器官移植。

④ Platelets, which are circulating components of the blood, normally serve the function of sealing up wounds in the blood vessel walls. platelets, 血小板；seal up, 密封，愈合。参考译文：通常，作为血液循环成分的血小板在血管壁上起到愈合伤口的功能。

⑤ The first step in accomplishing this objective is to provide a suitable scaffold for the cells to grow on, one that will keep them in contact with each other and allow them to organize. this objective 是指上文中提到的 "get the cells to organize themselves", 后面的分句中的 that 引导一个定语从句, 是对 "scaffold" 的解释说明。参考译文：要达到这个目标首先要做的是提供一个合适的利于细胞生长的支架, 这个支架可以使细胞互相联系, 从而将它们组织起来。

⑥ The copolymer has an abundance of polar carbon-oxygen bonds along the chain, affording many opportunities for hydrogen-bonding interactions. polar, 极性的; carbon-oxygen bonds, 碳氧键; hydrogen-bonding, 氢键。参考译文：这种共聚物链上有足够的极性碳氧键, 为氢键结合提供了许多机会。

Reading Comprehension

(1) From the first paragraph we learn that _____.
(A) biomaterials can be used in all sides of medicine.
(B) biomaterials which are used in joint replacements, bone plates and bone cement are not suffered new drug therapies.
(C) biomaterials are usually subjected to new drug therapies because of issues of biocompatibility.
(D) issues of biocompatibility must be resolved after a product can be placed on the market and used in a clinical setting.

(2) According to Heart Replacement and Repairs, which of the following is TRUE? _____.
(A) All hearts that fail completely can be replaced by donor organs.
(B) It often happens that the whole heart fails and needs replacement.
(C) Repair could be made by using a pig heart valve to replace a diseased one.
(D) In the United States about 45% of the procedures involve a foreign tissue.

(3) All of the following are reasons to minimize fluid disturbance as the blood passes through artificial devices EXCEPT _____.
(A) having a perfectly fine piece of machinery from a mechanical point of view
(B) surface roughness in a device causing hemolysis, the breakdown of red blood cells
(C) surface roughness serving as a site for invading bacteria to adhere and colonize
(D) rough surfaces promoting coagulation of the blood, which forms a thrombus, or blood clot

(4) Patients who have received artificial heart valves or vascular grafts are generally required to take anticoagulation drugs on a continuing basis because _____.
(A) the inside surface of the graft would become lined with the same sorts of cells that line the native artery
(B) the inside surface of the tubing is recognized as being foreign to the blood
(C) platelets normally serve the function of sealing up wounds in the blood vessel walls
(D) platelets attach to foreign surfaces and cause blood coagulation

(5) Which of the following is NOT a description of scaffolds?
(A) The scaffolding must also be mechanically strong and biodegradable.
(B) The most successful scaffolds have been lactic acid—glycolicmers.
(C) Polar carbon-oxygen bonds can afford opportunity for hydrogen-bonding interactions.
(D) When the artificial tissue is deployed in the body, the underlying copolymer scaffold slowly hydrolyzes away.

(6) It can be learned from the last paragraph that _____ .
(A) since the 1970s, smart sutures have been available
(B) if you had to go to the doctor to get smart sutures, you later had to go back to get the stitches removed.
(C) smart eyeglasses turn light when you go outside in the sun, then turn light again when you go inside.
(D) smart sutures polymer is not on the market at the time of this writing.

Unit 23   Biocompatible Dental Materials

It is important to determine dental material biological compatibility (biocompatibility). There are three different levels of biocompatibility to consider: general, immunological, and bio-energetic.

1. General biocompatibility—On this most basic level, we have to look at how the material reacts generally with human tissue. In other words, how toxic the material is at a cellular level. Does it poison cells? This toxicity tends to be an inherent property of the material, and all people will react to it in a similar manner. Using a toxic material such as mercury or nickel would always be a mistake.

2. Immunological biocompatibility—This level looks at materials from a standpoint of how an individual reacts to the material. The problem is analogous to what happens when someone with an allergy to mushrooms consumes an edible mushroom. The adverse reaction is due to an immunological and/or allergic type response based on the patient's biochemical makeup.

3. Bio-energetic biocompatibility—For thousands of years, Eastern medicine has studied the flow of energy through the human body and applied this to such healing arts as acupuncture. If energetically incompatible materials are used, interferences are created on the meridians associated with the teeth being restored. According to Eastern medicine, each tooth correlates with and potentially influences different organ systems.

To select a restorative material of the highest levels of compatibility, start with materials that exhibit low toxicity to cells, then eliminate the ones that elicit an immunological response, and then, to further narrow down the choice, select from the remaining materials. Using such a multi-step approach should give you the highest probability of selecting a non-reactive, compatible material. Of course, many patients will skip the testing and simply ask to have a material used that has been found to generally biocompatible.

Once the final restorative material has been selected, it is important to understand that other materials are used in order to get a finished product. In the case of a metal restoration, this usually involves only the dental cement used to adhere the crown to the tooth (unless the tooth is so broken down that it requires a build-up, in which case all of the following steps also apply). If the restoration is a ceramic or composite, a number of steps are required to complete the bonding process.

Composite Fillings

These materials consist of tiny glass particles suspended in a *resin* (plastic) matrix. The size and amount of the glass particles give the composite filling materials different characteristics, such as strength and polishability. Composites are used in areas where the fillings are relatively small and there is plenty of tooth structure for support.

Composite fillings are less durable than amalgam if the filling is large, but comparable in durability if the filling is small to average size. Composite fillings in back teeth are significantly more difficult and time-consuming to place than amalgam fillings, therefore more expensive. Composite materials are most commonly placed directly into the tooth (like amalgam fillings), but can also be prefabricated and bonded into place indirectly (like a crown).

However, they are more natural-looking, require less tooth reduction to place, and are bonded in place for a better seal. Composites are not totally compatible either. Most are made of the petro-chemical bis-phenol, which some research indicates leaches out estrogen-like substances. Some composites are less biocompatible than others because of the amount of iron oxide, aluminum oxide, barium, and other materials in them.

Direct composites can cause hairline cracks in the tooth from the hardening process, whereas indirect composites do not because they are hardened in the lab. Porcelain is more natural-looking than composites, but because it is harder and more brittle, it causes a wearing away of everything it contacts with and can crack instead of flex from stress.

All porcelains contain aluminum oxide. The one exception is unshaped decor, which is weaker and not very natural-looking (over a period of $3 \sim 4$ months, unshaped decor will pick up the shade of the tooth under it). If metal is not used in a crown or bridge, it is significantly weaker and has an increased risk of breakage during normal function. Gold fillings, porcelain fillings, indirect composite fillings, and crowns require more tooth structure to be trimmed away than for amalgam and direct composites, and take two appointments rather than one. Most "gold" crowns placed today contain from 1% to 40% gold and have nickel in them, which is inappropriate for those with a compromised immune system. Special order higher content gold will obviously cost more due to the cost of gold.

Studies of gallium alloys have reported problems with corrosion, durability, tooth fracture, and tooth sensitivity. More research and development is needed, but for now, it is recommended for use in baby teeth only. Some experts consider all metals, even non-allergenic or non-toxic metals, to be disruptive and therefore believe they should never be used in the body. Since nearly all composites and porcelains contain iron and aluminum oxides, some experts limit their choice of materials to only a few.

Still others think the use of high quality metals like high content gold or titanium is acceptable, but only if one brand and formulation is used for the entire mouth. One must weigh biocompatibility against function and durability. Because of contractual language and statistics, use of titanium, high content gold, and composite for crowns, bridges, or fillings will probably result in lessened insurance benefits, even though the time, cost, and effort in doing them is the same or more as for standard gold alloy and porcelain materials. Cadmium is used for color stabilization, so cadmium-free materials may lose some color over time.

Filling Materials

Amalgam is the most commonly used material for back teeth. It contains approximately 50% mercury and varying amounts of silver (30%), tin, zinc, and copper. It is the least costly and least time-consuming to place. It does not hold its shape over time, corrodes easily, and is expected to last 5~10 years. The controversy is that it contains mercury, a known neurotoxin (poison to the nervous system).

Galloy is a brand new material containing silver, tin, copper, indium, and gallium. It is meant to be mercury-free alternative to amalgam. Why is the American Dental Association developing & patenting this substitute for mercury amalgam if mercury amalgam is safe?

A direct composite is a special plastic material that bonds to tooth structure, is tooth colored, is more easily repairable, and requires less tooth structure to be trimmed away than any other material. It is expected to last 5~7 years, although small to moderate size fillings may last longer. Research has shown that it reinforces the tooth and makes it stronger. Cost and time to perform is about 50%~75% more than amalgam. Composites are a petrochemical derivative and, as such, are a possible problem for the environmentally sensitive.

This type of restoration is used when ideal fit and durability is desired, which is seldom achieved with a direct composite filling. Cost is approximately 2~3 times that of an amalgam filling and takes two visits.

Dental ceramics (sometimes referred to as dental porcelains) have come a long way! Until a few years ago, these materials were relatively weak (that's why they required support from a metal substructure) and abrasive (causing wear on the opposing teeth). Today there are many different types of ceramic systems: Feldspathic, Leucite-reinforced, Polymer-reinforced, Zirconium-based-each with unique properties. From rebuilding broken teeth to replacing missing teeth (even in the back of the mouth), there is a ceramic to do the job. However, they are more difficult to use than conventionally cemented (non-bonded) crowns.

Picking the right ceramic for the job, proper tooth preparation, quality laboratory work, and meticulous cementation technique are all needed for a successful tooth restoration. It costs about the same as an indirect composite inlay/onlay and takes two visits. Most ceramic and resin-based materials contain metals in the form of oxides (such as aluminum) or even heavy metals (such as cobalt, barium or cadmium). These are usually added to give the materials strength and improve their appearance. Sometimes they are added to make the restoration show up on X-rays. The number of materials that do not contain any of these products is very limited. However, the advantage of being oxide-free is lost when these are bonded to the tooth using an oxide-containing luting agent.

Because of gold's long history, it is the standard against which other materials are judged. This type of restoration is used when maximum strength is desired and appearance is not a factor. Gold is almost never used in its pure form; rather gold is used as an alloy with other metal elements. It costs approximately three to four times more than an amalgam and takes 2 visits. There are many formulations of gold, varying from 1% to 99%. The other metals are added in order to give the gold strength and the ability to bond to porcelain (in the case of porcelain veneer fused to cover a gold crown). The most commonly added metals are palladium, silver, copper, and platinum.

The composition and amount of each metal in the alloy determines whether it is classified as a "high noble," "noble," or "base" metal. "Noble" metals are defined as gold, platinum and palladium. The most expensive gold alloys are "high noble" and they are defined as having at least 60% noble metals and at least 40% gold. An alloy can still be called "noble" if it has at least 25% noble metal content. The cheapest materials fail even that test and are called "base" alloys—they have less than 25% noble metals. It is especially important for patients with metal sensitivities to avoid the base alloys since these usually contain toxic metals such as nickel and chromium. But even the high noble materials can be incompatible for patients and even toxic; palladium, for example, is toxic.

Titanium is used when a gold alloy is not biocompatible; otherwise, the benefits, cost, and time to perform are the same as for a gold alloy, even though it is not a precious metal. It takes two visits.

(*Selected from http://tuberose.com/Biocompatible_Dental_Materials.html*, 2014)

New Words and Expressions

accumulation　*n.* 积累
dissimilar　*a.* 不同的
erythema　*n.* 红斑
endocrine　*a.* 内分泌的
bis-phenol　双酚
allergy　*n.* 敏感症,反感; *a.* 过敏性的
edible　*a.* 可食用的
corrosion　*n.* 侵蚀,腐蚀状态
estrogen-like　雌激素一样的(东西)
stabilization　*n.* 稳定性
porcelain　*n.* 瓷器,瓷; *a.* 瓷制的,精美的,脆的

mercury *n*. 水银
mercury-free 无汞
trim *a*. 整齐的，整洁的；*v*. 整理，修整，装饰
petrochemical *a*. 石化的；*n*. 石化产品
biocompatible *a*. 生物相适应性的
toxicity *n*. 毒性
meticulous *a*. 小心翼翼的，一丝不苟的
acrylic *a*. 丙烯酸的
resin-based materials 树脂物质
immunological *a*. 免疫学
exhibit *v*. 展出，陈列，展示；*n*. 展览品，陈列品，展品
acupuncture *n*. 针刺疗法；*v*. 施行针刺疗法
organ *n*. 元件，机构，机关，机关报，嗓音，器官
durability *n*. 耐久性
noble *a*. 高尚的，贵族的，高贵的；*n*. 贵族

Notes

① This toxicity tends to be an inherent property of the material… tends to be，倾向于，inherent property of the material 材料的固有性质。参考译文：这种毒性是材料固有的性质……

② The adverse reaction is due to an immunological and/or allergic type response based on the patient's biochemical makeup. biochemical makeup 生物化学组成，参考译文：这种逆反应是根据患者的生物化学组成而导致的免疫学和/或过敏性的响应。

③ Using such a multi-step approach should give you the highest probability of selecting a non-reactive, compatible material. multi-step，多步的，多级的。参考译文：使用这种多步方法，你可以最大限度地选择不反应的、兼容的材料。

④ Once the final restorative material has been selected, it is important to understand that other materials are used in order to get a finished product. 本句的意思是：为了获得成品，在修复材料确定后，还需了解其他材料的性能。

⑤ If the restoration is a ceramic or composite, a number of steps are required to complete the bonding process. a number of ＋可数名词的复数形式，表示很多的，数量多的。本句的意思是：如果修复物是陶瓷或复合物，那么就需要很多步骤来完成结合过程。

⑥ Composite fillings are less durable than amalgam if the filling is large, but comparable in durability if the filling is small to average size. 如果填补物尺寸比较大，复合物的填补物要比汞合金的耐用性差一些，如果填补物比较小，那么它们的耐用性就差不多大了。

Exercises

1. Question for discussion

（1）What may be used to determine sensitivity to corrosion by-products of components?

(2) How we can differ direct composites from indirect composites?
(3) Why does no-precious alloy cost less than gold alloy?
(4) Which materials could called "base" alloy?
(5) Why composite filling in back teaches is more expensive than amalgams fillings?
(6) Why does the author say "Dental ceramics have come a long way?"

2. Translate the following into Chinese

polish ability   stainless steel
biochemical makeup   zirconium oxide
indirect composite fillings   liquid form
biocompatibility   inlay and onlay

- Except in rare situations, currently used dental materials are sale in the mouth.
- Because some people have sensitivity to certain substances, the choice of dental materials may have to be limited.
- Studies of gallium alloys have reported problems with corrosion, durability, tooth fracture and tooth sensitivity.
- Some composites are less biocompatible than others because of amount of iron oxide, aluminum oxide, barium, and other materials in them.
- These are not quite as wear-resistant or esthetic as porcelain but very acceptable from normal situation.
- Indirect composites are used when appearance is an important factor but when the risk of porcelain fractures and wearing down the other teeth is to be avoided.
- Picking the right ceramic for the job, proper tooth preparation, quality laboratory work, and meticulous cementation technique are all needed for a successful tooth restoration.
- Titanium is used when a gold alloy is not biocompatible, otherwise, the benefits, cost and time to perform are the same as for a gold alloy, even though it is not a precious metal.
- The size and amount of the glass particles give the composite filling materials different characteristics, such as strength and polish ability.

3. Translate the following into English

生物适应性   副产品
光化学反应   不会引起过敏反应的金属
临床试验   低毒性

- 我们已经知道有三种不同的生物适应性：常规，免疫和生物能生物配伍。
- 氧化锆的优势是它有很高的抗腐蚀性和稳定的水解性，而且与其他陶瓷材料相比，它具有较高的生物适应性。
- 假牙材料的突破性发展，是技术发展的基础。
- 氧化锆陶瓷与其他陶瓷相比具有一个不寻常的特点，就是晶体结构的高压表面是可以转化的。
- 当我们期望得到最大的浓度时就用钛合金，金合金则会引起排斥反应。

- 所有的陶瓷都包括氧化铝。金填充物、陶瓷填充物、复合物填充物都需要用氧化铝来平衡牙齿结构。

4. Reading Comprehension

(1) According to the author, micro amps of current could cause _____.
(A) ablepsia　　　　(B) deafness　　　　(C) erythema　　　　(D) calculus

(2) According to the passage, which of the following is TRUE?
(A) Composites are totally compatible.
(B) The unshaped decor contains aluminum oxide.
(C) Porcelain is harder and more brittle.
(D) Excepts believe that the non-allergenic or non-toxic metals can be used in body.

(3) Which material has overcome most of the pitfalls of present day products?
(A) Porcelain　　　(B) Indirect composite　(C) Zirconium oxide　(D) Titanium

(4) The function of in ceramic and resin-based materials exclude _____.
(A) improving strength
(B) improving appearance
(C) making the restoration show up on X-rays
(D) improving weight

(5) Which one of the materials below may be a mistake if be used for the dental materials?
(A) silver　　　　(B) ceramic　　　　(C) gold　　　　(D) nickel

(6) Someone has an allergy to edible mushroom and what's the most possible cause?
(A) he's ill
(B) immune reaction
(C) the mushroom's poisonous
(D) because of the weather

Reading Material

Dental Material Philosophies and Denture Materials

Dental Material Philosophies

Except in rare situations, currently used dental materials are safe in the mouth. The important criteria are how durable, natural looking, inexpensive, and practical they are for the dentist and dental laboratory to use. Concerns therefore are economics and aesthetics. Because some people have sensitivity to certain substances, the choice of dental materials may have to be limited. A special blood test may be used to determine sensitivity to corrosion by-products of components.

Some dental materials contain toxic substances that, depending on exposure and other factors, may impact total toxic body load. Non-toxic alternatives should be used to decrease exposure to and accumulation of scientifically confirmed environmental toxins. Some dental treatment and materials can be disruptive to the normal flow of energy through the acupuncture meridians. Eastern philosophy believes chronic disruption of energy flow causes dysfunction and resultant health problems on the associated meridian; therefore, the choice of dental materials and treatments is limited.

Dissimilar metals in the mouth, including different formulations of the "same" metal, create microamps of current which could cause oral pain, corrosion of the metal (black mercury amalgam fillings), dry mouth, metallic taste, erythema (red & swollen gums), and possible dysfunction of other organ systems, endocrine glands, etc. on that meridian.

Crown and Bridge Materials

A gold alloy is used when maximum strength is desired and appearance is not a factor. There are many formulations of gold, varying from 1% to 99%.

Titanium is used when maximum strength is desired, appearance is not a factor, and a gold alloy is not biocompatible. There are different purities of titanium, with grade-1 being the purest. This is used in joint replacement, dental implants, and bone pins. Cost is the same as for gold alloy.

Non-precious alloys are used when maximum strength is desired, appearance is not a factor, but cost is most important. Since it does not contain any gold, cost is less. There are two basic formulations, one that contains nickel and one that is nickel-free. The controversial issue is that nickel, beryllium, cobalt, chromium, and palladium may cause immune problems and/or toxicity.

Porcelain is used when appearance and wear resistance is the most important factor. It is much more fragile than metal and may break easily. Porcelain alone is not normally recommended for bridges.

Indirect composites are used when appearance is an important factor but when the risk of porcelain fractures and wearing down the other teeth is to be avoided. These are not quite as wear-resistant or esthetic as porcelain but very acceptable for normal situations.

One of the most difficult areas in dentistry today is the restoration of dental structures with biocompatible materials that are strong enough to withstand the forces of chewing (500~1000lbs pressure on molar teeth). Recent technology from Germany now offers a material that has overcome most of the pitfalls of present day products. Patients now have a choice of a material that is esthetic, strong, pure, biocompatible and capable of being used for single and long span dental bridgework. That material is called Zirconium oxide.

Zirconium oxide has the following superior characteristics that make it the most ideal material available:
- Excellent biological compatibility: absolutely bio-inert.
- Outstanding physical and mechanical qualities:
  Hardness (Vickers) 1200 HV
  Compressive Strength 2000 MPa
  Bending Strength 1000 MPa
  Modulus of Elasticity 210 GPa
  Tensile Strength 7 Mpavm

Wear characteristics (Ring on disc) <0.002 mm^3/h

Absolute corrosion resistance: Ringer's solution 370C <0.01mg/m$^2 \times 24$h

Very small particle size: <0.6ym

No glass phase for particle binding

Extremely high density

Porosity: 0%

Purity (Zr/Hf/Y): 99.9%

Translucence of the framework material makes excellent cosmetic results possible

Equivalent fit to precision gold castings: edge opening 20~50 yr. Preclude the need to use adhesive cements.

Zirconium oxide is manufactured and optimized industrially so that the material qualities remain unchanged through the complete production chain.

Optimal material for crowns: tasteless, radiopaque, no pulp irritation because there is no need to use adhesive cements and minimal invasive preparation by dentist.

Zirconium oxide forms the core of each crown and provides the cross-link that bridges the gap of missing teeth. The precision fit of the Zirconium core is derived from computer guided Swiss lathes that cut the form out of a solid Zirconium oxide block. The cutting instructions are obtained from a laser beam that reads 120 points per millimeter from the anatomy of a model of the prepared teeth. Once formed, new synthetic porcelain (99.9% pure) is baked on to the Zirconium core and then shaped like a tooth. Because of the extreme accuracy of the crown fit, the crowns can be cemented with biocompatible dental luting material. This avoids the use of an invasive procedure of etching the tooth with acid and injuring the pulp or nerve of the tooth. This latter procedure often times results in the pulp dying and necessitating root canal therapy.

Zirconium oxide ceramic primarily stands out due to its high crack resistance. Crack resistance is the resistance with which the material counteracts the spreading of cracks. If a material is stressed, it usually comes to excessively high tension within a defect area (pores, surface deficiencies, cavities) or it cracks. While with metals under high tension in the area of cracks, plastic deformation appears and the top of the tension can be reduced by rounding the cracks; in ceramics due to missing plastic deformation possibility the cracks continue to grow. The unusual feature of zirconium oxide ceramic in comparison with other ceramics is that at the appearance of a high-tension area a transformation of the crystal structure can take place. This process is also accompanied by a volume expansion. By this volume increase it builds wedges in the crack and therefore it reduces the continuation of the crack.

In connection with the tensile strength there also stands the characteristic of bending strengths. While conventional glass ceramics show results of 100~200 MPa and aluminum oxide ceramics lie in the area of 400~600 MPa, zirconium oxide reaches a bending strength of over 1000MPa.

Because of the high tensile strengths exhibited in test results, it is now possible to fabricate posterior bridges with zirconium oxide. Further decisive advantages of zirconium oxide are its high resistance to corrosion; stability to hydrolysis and its high biocompatibility in comparison with other ceramics makes this material ideal for restorative dentistry.

In medicine, zirconium oxide is being used more and more as the material of choice especially for hip prosthesis. For years there have existed substantial clinical tests and examinations which confirm the high quality of zirconium oxide.

Denture Materials

Dentures are usually made from acrylic, stainless steel, and chromium-cobalt, but can be made of nylon, a gold alloy, or titanium. Most pink-colored acrylics and vinyls contain cadmium, which is considered toxic and/or immune reactive. The alternative is to use cadmium-free pink or clear materials. Metals are used to increase rigidity and increase retention of the prosthesis in the mouth during function. If metals are not used, the opposite is true, which is not desirable from a functional perspective.

Since all direct fillings (composites) and most indirect restorations (inlays, onlays, and crowns) being placed today use a process called bonding, it's good to have a basic knowledge of how this process works. While there are a myriad of variations in this process, here are the basic steps:

Step 1—Prepare the tooth surface using a mild acid solution. This creates a "honeycomb" in the top layer of tooth.

Step 2—Paint a liquid resin-bonding agent on the tooth. It flows and "locks" into the honeycomb created in Step 1 (technically forming a hybrid layer that is part-tooth and part dental-resin). This layer is "cured" (hardened using a photo-chemical reaction) with a visible light source.

Step 3—Place luting cement if an indirect restoration (e.g., crown) is being used. Essentially, this material is a more liquid form of white filling material. It bonds to both the tooth and the pre-fabricated ceramic restoration and fills the gaps between them. The surface of the first layer of cured bonding agent is highly reactive and is easily bonded to with today's composite filling materials.

There are a number of advantages to using bonding. Besides allowing the placement of non-metal restorations, less removal of healthy tooth structure is required. The dentist needs to remove only the unhealthy tooth structure and a precisely fitted piece can be bonded into place to replace it. In the case of fillings, bonded restorations have other physical advantages over amalgam.

Breakthroughs in the development of dental materials and techniques are occurring on a regular basis. We have yet to find one single material that is compatible for everyone. Debate continues about how to best restore a patient's mouth to optimal health and no perfect solution has yet presented itself. The best we can do is to keep an open mind and keep searching for answers. Only by thorough testing can it be determined which is most compatible for any one person.

(*Selected from http://tuberose.com/Biocompatible_Dental_Materials.html*, 2014)

New Words and Expressions

philosophies＝philosophize　*v.* 进行哲学探讨，使哲学化
aesthetics　*n.* 美学，美术理论，审美学，美的哲学
toxin　*n.* 毒素
disruptive　*a.* 使破裂的，分裂性的
acupuncture　*n.* 刺疗法；*v.* 施行针刺疗法
chronic　*a.* 慢性的，延续很长的
swollen　*a.* 肿胀的
dysfunction　*n.* 机能不良，功能紊乱，官能障碍
meridian　*n.* 子午线，正午，顶点；*a.* 子午线的，正午的，顶点的
erythema　*n.* 红斑，非冻疮
endocrine　*n.* 内分泌
gland　*n.* 腺，密封管
formulation　*n.* 用公式表示，明确地表达，作简洁陈述
titanium　*n.* 钛
controversial　*a.* 争论的，争议的
beryllium　*n.* 铍
palladium　*n.* 钯
immune　*a.* 免疫的
fragile　*a.* 易碎的，脆的
fracture　*n.* 破裂，骨折；*v.* （使）破碎，（使）破裂
pitfall　*n.* 缺陷
esthetic　*a.* 感觉的
zirconium oxide　氧化锆
inert　*a.* 无活动的，惰性的，迟钝的
compressive　*a.* 有压缩力的
bending　弯曲（度），挠度
modulus of elasticity　弹性模量，弹性系数
tensile　*a.* 可拉长的，可伸长的，张力的，拉力的
porosity　*n.* 多孔性，有孔性
translucence　*n.* 半透明
cosmetic　*n.* 化妆品；*a.* 化妆用的
preclude　*n.* 排除
optimal　*a.* 最佳的，最理想的
tasteless　*a.* 没味道的，无鉴赏力的
radiopaque　*a.* 辐射透不过的
pulp　*n.* 纸浆；*vt.* 使化成纸浆，变成纸浆
therapy　*n.* 治疗
honeycomb　*n.* 蜂房，蜂巢，蜂脾

Notes

① There are many formulations of gold, varying from 1% to 99%. 是个定语从句，省略了 which，应为…which varying from…。vary from …to…从……到……不同，参考译文：含量从1%到99%有很多种不同的金合金。

② Cost is the same as for gold alloy. the same as：与……同样的，相同的。参考译文：对于金合金来说，价格是相同的。

③ It is much more fragile than metal and may break easily. 代词 It 指的是上句所提到的 Porcelain。参考译文：比起金属来说，陶瓷更脆，因此更易被打碎。

④ Since all direct fillings (composites) and most indirect restorations (inlays, onlays, and crowns) being placed today use a process called bonding, it's good to have a basic knowledge of how this process works. 直接填充物是指复合物；间接填充物是指镶嵌，镶上的和冠状的填充物。

⑤ There are a number of advantages to using bonding. a number of+可数名词的复数形式，表示很多的，数量多的。这里是指很多优点。

⑥ Only by thorough testing can it be determined which is most compatible for any one person. 这是一个由 only 引起的倒装句，因此后面用到了 can it be，为的是强调 only 后面的句子。正常语序为 It can be determined only by thorough testing which is most compatible for any one person. 参考译文：只有通过实验才能确定哪种才是最适合人们的。

Reading Comprehension

(1) According to the author, what does Eastern philosophy believe?
(A) Some dental materials contain toxic substances that, depending on exposure and other factors, may impact total toxic body load.
(B) Some dental treatment and materials can be disruptive to the normal flow of energy through the acupuncture meridians.
(C) The choice of dental materials and treatments is unlimited.
(D) Chronic disruption of energy flow causes dysfunction and resultant health problems on the associated meridian

(2) Which characteristics does zirconium oxide have?
(A) No glass phase for particle binding
(B) Outstanding physical and mechanical qualities
(C) Very small particle size: <0.6ym
(D) All of the above

(3) What can make the crowns be cemented with biocompatible dental luting material?
(A) Extreme accuracy of the crown　　　　(B) Porcelain
(C) Zirconium oxide　　　　(D) Titanium

(4) Which character may be for the optimal material crowns?
(A) Taste　　(B) Radiopaque　　(C) Pulp irritation　　(D) Invasive

(5) According to the in the process of all direct fillings and most indirect restorations being placed, which of the following is TRUE?

(A) There are 3 steps in this process.

(B) It creates a "honeycomb" in the top layer of tooth in step 1.

(C) Paint liquid and gas resin-bonding agents on the tooth in step 2.

(D) Place luting cement if a crown is being used in step 3

(6) Why does zirconium oxide ceramic primarily stand out?

(A) Because of its low crack resistance

(B) Because of its high-tension area

(C) Because of its high crack resistance

(D) Not mentioned in the text

APPENDIXES

Main Journals of Materials Science and Technology

Journal Full Title	Journal Abbreviated
1. Aatcc Review	Aatcc Rev
2. Aci Materials Journal	Aci Mater J
3. Acta Materialia	Acta Mater
4. Acta Metallurgica Sinica	Acta Metall Sin
5. Advances in Applied Ceramics	Adv Appl Ceram
6. Advanced Cement Based Materials	Adv Cem Based Mater
7. Advances in Cement Research	Adv Cem Res
8. Advanced Composites Letters	Adv Compos Lett
9. Advanced Composite Materials	Adv Compos Mater
10. Advanced Engineering Materials	Adv Eng Mater
11. Advanced Functional Materials	Adv Funct Mater
12. Advanced Materials For Optics And Electronics	Adv Mater Opt Electron
13. Advanced Performance Materials	Adv Perform Mater
14. Advanced Materials	Advan Mater
15. Advanced Materials & Processes	Advan Mater Process
16. American Ceramic Society Bulletin	Amer Ceram Soc Bull
17. Annual Review Of Materials Research	Ann Rev Mater Res
18. Annual Review Of Materials Research	Annu Rev Mater Res
19. Annual Review Of Materials Science	Annu Rev Mater Sci
20. Anti-Corrosion Methods And Materials	Anti-Corros Method Mater
21. Appita Journal	Appita J
22. Applied Composite Materials	Appl Compos Mater
23. Applied Surface Science	Appl Surf Sci
24. Archives Of Metallurgy	Arch Metall
25. Archives Of Metallurgy And Materials	Arch Metall Mater
26. Biointerphases	Biointerphases
27. Biomaterials	Biomaterials
28. Biomedical Materials	Biomed Mater
29. Boletin De La Sociedad Espanola De Ceramica Y Vidrio	Bol Soc Esp Ceram Vidr
30. British Ceramic Transactions	Brit Ceram T
31. British Corrosion Journal	Brit Corros J
32. Bulletin Of Materials Science	Bull Mater Sci
33. Canadian Ceramics	Can Ceram
34. Canadian Metallurgical Quarterly	Can Metall Quart
35. Cellulose Chemistry And Technology	Cell Chem Technol
36. Cellular Polymers	Cell Polym
37. Cellulose	Cellulose
38. Cement And Concrete Research	Cem Concr Res

Journal Full Title	Journal Abbreviated
39. Cement Concrete And Aggregates	Cement Concrete Aggregates
40. Cement & Concrete Composites	Cement Concrete Composites
41. Ceramics International	Ceram Int
42. Ceramics-Technical	Ceram Tech
43. Ceramics-Silikaty	Ceramics-Silikaty
44. Cfi-Ceramic Forum International	Cfi-Ceram Forum Int
45. Chemistry Of Materials	Chem Mater
46. Chemical Vapor Deposition	Chem Vapor Deposition
47. Coal Preparation	Coal Prep
48. Composite Interfaces	Compos Interface
49. Composites Part A-Applied Science And Manufacturing	Compos Part A-Appl Sci Manuf
50. Composites Part B-Engineering	Compos Part B-Eng
51. Composite Structures	Compos Struct
52. Composites Science And Technology	Composites Sci Technol
53. Computational Materials Science	Comput Mater Sci
54. Construction And Building Materials	Constr Build Mater
55. Corrosion Engineering Science And Technology	Corros Eng Sci Technol
56. Corrosion Prevention & Control	Corros Prevent Control
57. Corrosion Reviews	Corros Rev
58. Corrosion Science	Corros Sci
59. Corrosion	Corrosion
60. Current Nanoscience	Curr Nanosci
61. Current Opinion in Solid State & Materials Science	Curr Opin Solid State Mat Sci
62. Diamond And Related Materials	Diam Relat Mater
63. Diamond Films And Technology	Diamond Film Technol
64. Die Casting Engineer	Die Cast Eng
65. Digest Journal Of Nanomaterials And Biostructures	Dig J Nanomater Biostruct
66. Drevarsky Vyskum	Drev Vysk
67. Electronic Materials Letters	Electron Mater Lett
68. European Cells & Materials	Eur Cells Mater
69. Fatigue & Fracture Of Engineering Materials & Structures	Fatigue Fract Eng Mater Struc
70. Fibers And Polymers	Fiber Polym
71. Fibres & Textiles in Eastern Europe	Fibres Text East Eur
72. Fire And Materials	Fire Mater
73. Fire Technology	Fire Technol
74. Fizika Metallov I Metallovedenie	Fiz Metal Metalloved
75. Glass And Ceramics	Glass Ceram-Engl Tr
76. Glass Physics And Chemistry	Glass Phys Chem-Engl Tr
77. Glass Science And Technology	Glass Sci Technol
78. Glass Science And Technology-Glastechnische Berichte	Glass Sci Technol-Glastec Ber
79. Glass Technology	Glass Technol
80. Glastechnische Berichte-Glass Science And Technology	Glastech Ber-Glass Sci Techn
81. Gold Bulletin	Gold Bull
82. Granular Matter	Granul Matter
83. Heat Treatment Of Metals	Heat Treat Metal
84. High Temperature And Materials Science	High Temp Mat Sci
85. High Temperature Materials And Processes	High Temp Mater Process
86. High Temperature Material Processes	High Temp Mater Process-Us
87. Holz Als Roh-Und Werkstoff	Holz Roh Werkst
88. Hydrometallurgy	Hydrometallurgy
89. Ieee Transactions On Components Packaging And Manufacturing Technology Part A	Ieee Trans Compon Pack Man A

Journal Full Title	Journal Abbreviated
90. Ieee Transactions On Components Packaging And Manufacturing Technology Part B-Advanced Packaging	Ieee Trans Compon Pack Man B
91. Industrial Ceramics	Ind Ceramics
92. Industrial Diamond Review	Ind Diamond Rev
93. Industria Textila	Ind Textila
94. Indian Journal Of Fibre & Textile Research	Indian J Fibre Text Res
95. Inorganic Materials	Inorg Mater-Engl Tr
96. International Journal Of Adhesion And Adhesives	Int J Adhes Adhes
97. International Journal Of Applied Ceramic Technology	Int J Appl Ceram Technol
98. International Journal Of Cast Metals Research	Int J Cast Metals Res
99. International Journal Of Clothing Science And Technology	Int J Cloth Sci Technol
100. International Journal Of Fatigue	Int J Fatigue
101. International Journal Of Materials & Product Technology	Int J Mater Prod Technol
102. International Journal Of Materials Research	Int J Mater Res
103. International Journal Of Nanotechnology	Int J Nanotechnol
104. International Journal Of Non-Equilibrium Processing	Int J Non-Equilib Process
105. International Journal Of Powder Metallurgy	Int J Powder Metall
106. International Journal Of Refractory Metals & Hard Materials	Int J Refract Met Hard Mater
107. International Materials Reviews	Int Mater Rev
108. International Polymer Processing	Int Polym Proc
109. Intermetallics	Intermetallics
110. Ironmaking & Steelmaking	Ironmaking Steelmaking
111. Isij International	Isij Int
112. Journal Of Adhesion	J Adhes
113. Journal Of Adhesion Science And Technology	J Adhes Sci Technol
114. Journal Of Advanced Concrete Technology	J Adv Concr Technol
115. Journal Of Advanced Materials	J Adv Mater
116. Journal Of Alloys And Compounds	J Alloys Compounds
117. Journal Of The American Ceramic Society	J Amer Ceram Soc
118. Journal Of The American Leather Chemists Association	J Amer Leather Chem Assn
119. Journal Of Applied Biomaterials & Biomechanics	J Appl Biomater Biomech
120. Journal Of Biobased Materials And Bioenergy	J Biobased Mater Bioenergy
121. Journal Of Biomedical Materials Research	J Biomed Mater Res
122. Journal Of Biomedical Materials Research Part A	J Biomed Mater Res Part A
123. Journal Of Biomedical Materials Research Part B-Applied Biomaterials	J Biomed Mater Res Part B
124. Journal Of Central South University Of Technology	J Cent South Univ Technol
125. Journal Of Ceramic Processing Research	J Ceram Process Res
126. Journal Of The Ceramic Society Of Japan	J Ceramic Soc Jpn
127. Journal Of Coatings Technology And Research	J Coat Technol Res
128. Journal Of Coatings Technology	J Coating Technol
129. Journal Of Composites For Construction	J Compos Constr
130. Journal Of Composite Materials	J Compos Mater
131. Journal Of Composites Technology & Research	J Compos Tech Res
132. Journal Of Computational And Theoretical Nanoscience	J Comput Theor Nanosci
133. Journal Of Computer-Aided Materials Design	J Comput-Aided Mater Des
134. Journal Of Elastomers And Plastics	J Elastom Plast
135. Journal Of Electroceramics	J Electroceram
136. Journal Of Electronic Materials	J Electron Mater
137. Journal Of Energetic Materials	J Energ Mater

Journal Full Title	Journal Abbreviated
138. Journal Of Engineering Materials And Technology-Transactions Of The Asme	J Eng Mater Technol
139. Journal Of The European Ceramic Society	J Eur Ceram Soc
140. Journal Of Fire Sciences	J Fire Sci
141. Journal Of Inorganic Materials	J Inorg Mater
142. Journal Of Intelligent Material Systems And Structures	J Intel Mat Syst Struct
143. Journal Of Iron And Steel Research International	J Iron Steel Res Int
144. Journal Of The Japan Institute Of Metals	J Jpn Inst Metal
145. Journal Of The Korean Institute Of Metals And Materials	J Korean Inst Met Mater
146. Journal Of Materials Chemistry	J Mater Chem
147. Journal Of Materials Engineering And Performance	J Mater Eng Perform
148. Journal Of Materials Processing & Manufacturing Science	J Mater Process Manuf Sci
149. Journal Of Materials Processing Technology	J Mater Process Technol
150. Journal Of Materials Research	J Mater Res
151. Journal Of Materials Science	J Mater Sci
152. Journal Of Materials Science Letters	J Mater Sci Lett
153. Journal Of Materials Science & Technology	J Mater Sci Technol
154. Journal Of Materials Science-Materials in Electronics	J Mater Sci-Mater Electron
155. Journal Of Materials Science-Materials in Medicine	J Mater Sci-Mater Med
156. Journal Of Materials Synthesis And Processing	J Mater Synth Process
157. Journal Of Nanoparticle Research	J Nanopart Res
158. Journal Of Nanoscience And Nanotechnology	J Nanosci Nanotechnol
159. Journal Of Nondestructive Evaluation	J Nondestruct Eval
160. Journal Of Optoelectronics And Advanced Materials	J Optoelectron Adv Mater
161. Journal Of Plastic Film & Sheeting	J Plast Film Sheeting
162. Journal Of Polymer Engineering	J Polym Eng
163. Journal Of Porous Materials	J Porous Mat
164. Journal Of Pulp And Paper Science	J Pulp Pap Sci
165. Journal Of Reinforced Plastics And Composites	J Reinf Plast Composite
166. Journal Of Rubber Research	J Rubber Res
167. Journal Of Sandwich Structures & Materials	J Sandw Struct Mater
168. Journal Of The Society Of Leather Technologists And Chemists	J Soc Leather Technol Chem
169. Journal Of Sol-Gel Science And Technology	J Sol-Gel Sci Technol
170. Journal Of Testing And Evaluation	J Test Eval
171. Journal Of The Textile Institute	J Text Inst
172. Journal Of Thermal Spray Technology	J Therm Spray Technol
173. Journal Of Thermoplastic Composite Materials	J Thermoplast Compos Mater
174. Journal Of University Of Science And Technology Beijing	J Univ Sci Technol Beijing
175. Journal Of Vacuum Science & Technology A	J Vac Sci Technol A
176. Journal Of Vacuum Science & Technology B	J Vac Sci Technol B
177. Journal Of Wood Chemistry And Technology	J Wood Chem Technol
178. Journal Of Wuhan University Of Technology-Materials Science Edition	J Wuhan Univ Technol-Mat Sci
179. Jct Coatingstech	Jct Coatingstech
180. Jct Research	Jct Res
181. Jom	Jom
182. Jom-Journal Of The Minerals Metals & Materials Society	Jom-J Min Met Mat Soc
183. Kautschuk Gummi Kunststoffe	Kaut Gummi Kunstst

Journal Full Title	Journal Abbreviated
184. Key Engineering Materials	Key Eng Mat
185. Kovove Materialy-Metallic Materials	Kovove Mater-Metal Mater
186. Kunststoffe-Plast Europe	Kunstst-Plast Eur
187. Maderas-Ciencia Y Tecnologia	Maderas-Cienc Tecnol
188. Magazine Of Concrete Research	Mag Concr Res
189. Materials Science & Engineering C-Biomimetic And Supramolecular Systems	Mat Sci Eng C-Biomim Supram S
190. Materials Science & Engineering R-Reports	Mat Sci Eng R
191. Materials Characterization	Mater Charact
192. Materials Chemistry And Physics	Mater Chem Phys
193. Materiales De Construccion	Mater Constr
194. Materials And Corrosion-Werkstoffe Und Korrosion	Mater Corros
195. Materials & Design	Mater Design
196. Materials Evaluation	Mater Eval
197. Materials At High Temperatures	Mater High Temp
198. Materials Letters	Mater Lett
199. Materials And Manufacturing Processes	Mater Manuf Process
200. Materials Performance	Mater Perform
201. Materiale Plastice	Mater Plast
202. Materials Research Bulletin	Mater Res Bull
203. Materials Research Innovations	Mater Res Innov
204. Materials Science And Engineering A-Structural Materials Properties Microstructure And Processing	Mater Sci Eng A-Struct Mater
205. Materials Science And Engineering B-Advanced Functional Solid-State Materials	Mater Sci Eng B-Adv Funct Sol
206. Materials Science And Engineering B-Solid State Materials For Advanced Technology	Mater Sci Eng B-Solid State M
207. Materials Science Forum	Mater Sci Forum
208. Materials Science Research International	Mater Sci Res Int
209. Materials Science In Semiconductor Processing	Mater Sci Semicond Process
210. Materials Science And Technology	Mater Sci Technol
211. Materials Science	Mater Sci-Engl Tr
212. Materials Science-Poland	Mater Sci-Poland
213. Materials And Structures	Mater Struct
214. Materials Technology	Mater Technol
215. Materiali in Tehnologije	Mater Tehnol
216. Materials Today	Mater Today
217. Materials Transactions	Mater Trans
218. Materials Transactions Jim	Mater Trans Jim
219. Materials World	Mater World
220. Materialprufung	Materialprufung
221. Materialwissenschaft Und Werkstofftechnik	Materialwiss Werkstofftech
222. Mecanique Industrielle Et Materiaux	Mec Ind Mater
223. Mechanics Of Advanced Materials And Structures	Mech Adv Mater Struct
224. Mechanics Of Cohesive-Frictional Materials	Mech Cohesive-Frict Mater
225. Mechanics Of Composite Materials And Structures	Mech Compos Mater Struct
226. Mechanics Of Composite Materials	Mech Composite Mater-Engl Tr
227. Mechanics Of Materials	Mech Mater
228. Mechanics Of Time-Dependent Materials	Mech Time-Depend Mater

Journal Full Title	Journal Abbreviated
229. Metals And Materials International	Met Mater Int
230. Metals Materials And Processes	Met Mater Processes
231. Metals And Materials-Korea	Met Mater-Korea
232. Metalurgia International	Metal Int
233. Metal Science And Heat Treatment	Metal Sci Heat Treat-Engl Tr
234. Metall	Metall
235. Metallurgical And Materials Transactions A-Physical Metallurgy And Materials Science	Metall Mater Trans A
236. Metallurgical And Materials Transactions B-Process Metallurgy And Materials Processing Science	Metall Mater Trans B
237. Metallofizika I Noveishie Tekhnologii	Metallofiz Noveish Tekhnol
238. Metallurgist	Metallurgist-Engl Tr
239. Metalurgija	Metalurgija
240. Microporous Materials	Microporous Mater
241. Microporous And Mesoporous Materials	Microporous Mesoporous Mat
242. Modern Plastics	Mod Plast
243. Modelling And Simulation in Materials Science And Engineering	Model Simul Mater Sci Eng
244. Mokuzai Gakkaishi	Mokuzai Gakkaishi
245. MP Materials Testing-Materials And Components Technology And Application	Mp Mater Test
246. Mrs Bulletin	Mrs Bull
247. Mrs Internet Journal Of Nitride Semiconductor Research	Mrs Internet J Nitride Semi R
248. Nanostructured Materials	Nanostruct Mater
249. Nanotechnology	Nanotechnol
250. Nature Materials	Nat Mater
251. Ndt & E International	Ndt E Int
252. New Carbon Materials	New Carbon Mater
253. New Diamond And Frontier Carbon Technology	New Diam Front Carbon Technol
254. New Polymeric Materials	New Polym Mat
255. Nondestructive Testing And Evaluation	Nondestruct Test Eval
256. Nordic Pulp & Paper Research Journal	Nord Pulp Paper Res J
257. Optical Materials	Opt Mater
258. Optoelectronics And Advanced Materials-Rapid Communications	Optoelectron Adv Mater-Rapid
259. Oxidation Of Metals	Oxidat Metal
260. Paperi Ja Puu-Paper And Timber	Pap Puu-Pap Tim
261. Papier	Papier
262. Particuology	Particuology
263. Philosophical Magazine	Philos Mag
264. Physics And Chemistry Of Glasses	Phys Chem Glasses
265. Physics And Chemistry Of Glasses-European Journal Of Glass Science And Technology Part B	Phys Chem Glass-Eur J Glass-B
266. Physics Of Metals And Metallography	Phys Metals Metallogr Engl Tr
267. Pigment & Resin Technology	Pigm Resin Technol
268. Plastics Engineering	Plast Eng
269. Plastics Rubber And Composites Processing And Applications	Plast Rub Compos Process Appl
270. Plastics Rubber And Composites	Plast Rubber Compos
271. Plating And Surface Finishing	Plat Surf Finish
272. Polymer Composites	Polym Composite
273. Polymer Engineering And Science	Polym Eng Sci

Journal Full Title	Journal Abbreviated
274. Polymer Gels And Networks	Polym Gels Networks
275. Polymers & Polymer Composites	Polym Polym Composites
276. Polymer Testing	Polym Test
277. Polymer-Plastics Technology And Engineering	Polym-Plast Technol Eng
278. Powder Metallurgy And Metal Ceramics	Powd Metall Met Ceram Engl-Tr
279. Powder Metallurgy	Powder Met
280. Praktische Metallographie-Practical Metallography	Prakt Metallogr-Pract Metallo
281. Progress in Materials Science	Prog Mater Sci
282. Progress in Organic Coatings	Prog Org Coating
283. Protection Of Metals	Prot Met-Engl Tr
284. Pulp & Paper-Canada	Pulp Pap Can
285. Rare Metal Materials And Engineering	Rare Metal Mat Eng
286. Rare Metals	Rare Metals
287. Refractories And Industrial Ceramics	Refract Ind Ceram
288. Research in Nondestructive Evaluation	Res Nondestruct Eval
289. Reviews On Advanced Materials Science	Rev Adv Mater Sci
290. Revue De Metallurgie-Cahiers D Informations Techniques	Rev Metall-Cah Inf Tech
291. Revista De Metalurgia	Rev Metalurgia
292. Revista Romana De Materiale-Romanian Journal Of Materials	Rev Rom Mat
293. Russian Journal Of Nondestructive Testing	Russ J Nondestruct T-Engl Tr
294. Russian Metallurgy	Russ Met-Engl Tr
295. Sampe Journal	Sampe J
296. Scandinavian Journal Of Metallurgy	Scand J Metall
297. Science And Engineering Of Composite Materials	Sci Eng Compos Mater
298. Science Of Sintering	Sci Sinter
299. Science And Technology Of Advanced Materials	Sci Technol Adv Mater
300. Science And Technology Of Welding And Joining	Sci Technol Weld Join
301. Scripta Materialia	Scripta Mater
302. Sensors And Materials	Sensor Mater
303. Silicates Industriels	Silic Industriels
304. Small	Small
305. Smart Materials & Structures	Smart Mater Struct
306. Soft Materials	Soft Mater
307. Soft Matter	Soft Matter
308. Solar Energy Materials And Solar Cells	Solar Energ Mater Solar Cells
309. Stahl Und Eisen	Stahl Eisen
310. Steel Research	Steel Res
311. Steel Research International	Steel Res Int
312. Steel In Translation	Steel Transl
313. Surface & Coatings Technology	Surf Coat Tech
314. Svensk Papperstidning-Nordisk Cellulosa	Svensk Papperstidn
315. Tappi Journal	Tappi J
316. Tekstil	Tekstil
317. Tetsu To Hagane-Journal Of The Iron And Steel Institute Of Japan	Tetsu To Hagane
318. Textile Chemist And Colorist	Text Chem Color
319. Textile Chemist And Colorist & American Dyestuff Reporter	Text Chem Color Am Dyest Repo
320. Textile Research Journal	Text Res J
321. Thin Solid Films	Thin Solid Films

Journal Full Title	Journal Abbreviated
322. Transactions Of The Indian Ceramic Society	Trans Indian Ceram Soc
323. Transactions Of The Indian Institute Of Metals	Trans Indian Inst Met
324. Transactions Of The Institute Of Metal Finishing	Trans Inst Met Finish
325. Transactions Of The Metal Finishers Association Of India	Trans Met Finish Assoc India
326. Transactions Of Nonferrous Metals Society Of China	Trans Nonferrous Metal Soc Ch
327. Vacuum	Vacuum
328. Vide-Science Technique Et Applications	Vide
329. Wear	Wear
330. Welding Journal	Weld J
331. Wochenblatt Fur Papierfabrikation	Wochenbl Papierfabr
332. Wood Research	Wood Res
333. Zeitschrift Fur Metallkunde	Z Metallk
334. Zkg International	Zkg Int

Answer to Reading Comprehension

	For the Text	For Reading Material
Unit 1	ADBDCD	BAADCB
Unit 2	CCDDBD	DDCBBC
Unit 3	DBDABD	ABDCDB
Unit 4	BBCCAB	CBACDC
Unit 5	BBBAAC	ABCBCD
Unit 6	CBADA	CDACC
Unit 7	CDDABA	ADBDCD
Unit 8	ACABDBD	DBADCC
Unit 9	BCDBBA	BCDCBAA
Unit 10	CBBAD	ABDBAC
Unit 11	CBCDB	CBDCCB
Unit 12	CDCBAD	AABAADDD
Unit 13	AABDBC	ABDCBA
Unit 14	DCDDDAC	DBADBD
Unit 15	AACCAD	BDACD
Unit 16	AADCA	BBCBC
Unit 17	CBDCC	DCCBB
Unit 18	DBDABB	DAADCD
Unit 19	DCDBAB	DACBDA
Unit 20	DBBADB	DBCABC
Unit 21	CBABC	CABCD
Unit 22	DABDC	CCADCD
Unit 23	BCCDDA	DDABBA

Glossary

A

abrade　　$v.$ 磨损，摩擦，折磨
abrasion resistance　　抗磨损性
abrasive　　$n.$ 研磨剂
abrasives　　研磨剂，研磨材料
accumulation　　$n.$ 积累
acicular　　$a.$ 针状的
acronym　　$n.$ 缩写字，字头语
acronyms　　$n.$ 首字母缩略词（acronym 的名词复数）
acrylic　　$a.$ 丙烯酸的
activator　　$n.$ 催化剂，触媒
actuator　　$n.$ 促动器，驱动器，执行机构，螺线管
acupuncture　　$n.$ 针刺疗法；$v.$ 施行针刺疗法
additive　　$a.$ 附加的，加成的，添加的；$n.$ 添加剂，添加物；$adj.$ 附加的，加和的，加法的
additives　　$n.$ 添加剂，助剂
adhesive　　$n.$ 黏合剂，黏着剂
aerodynamic　　$a.$ 空气动力学的
aerospace　　$n.$ 大气圈及其以外的宇宙空间；$a.$ 宇宙空间的，宇宙航行的
aesthetics　　$n.$ 美学，美术理论，审美学，美的哲学
aforementioned　　$a.$ 上述的，前述的
agglomerate　　$n.$ 大团，大块；$a.$ 成块的，凝聚的
aggregate　　$n.$ 合计，聚集体；$a.$ 总数的，聚合的；$vt.$ 使聚集，使积聚，总计达
alchemy　　$n.$ 炼金术
aldehyde　　$n.$ 醛，乙醛

alignment　　$n.$ 调整（成直线，准线，定向，直线性），对准，校直，对齐
allergy　　$n.$ 敏感症，反感；$a.$ 过敏性的
alleviate　　$v.$ 减轻，缓解，缓和
alternative　　$n.$ 二中择一，可供选择的办法，事物；$a.$ 选择性的，二中择一的
aluminium　　$n.$ 铝；$a.$ 铝的
aluminosilicate　　$n.$ 铝硅酸盐（硅酸铝）
Alzheimer　　老年痴呆症，阿兹海默氏症
amber　　$n.$ 琥珀；琥珀色；$a.$ 琥珀色的，琥珀制的 $v.$ 使成琥珀色，钙铝榴石
ambient　　$a.$ 周围的；$n.$ 周围环境
amorphous　　$a.$ 无定形的，非晶质，非结晶的
amplitude　　$n.$ 振幅
an order of magnitude　　一个数量级
angstrom　　$n.$ 埃（长度单位）
anhydride　　$n.$ 酐
animal　　$n.$ 动物，兽，牲畜；$a.$ 动物的
anion　　$n.$ 阴离子
anisotropic　　$a.$ 各向异性的（非均质）
anneal　　$n.$ 退火，焖火，锻炼，磨练（意志）
anode　　$n.$ 阳极，正极
anodising　　阳极处理
anodized　　$v.$ 阳极电镀；作阳极化处理
antibacterial　　$a.$ 抗菌的
anticoagulation　　$n.$ 抗凝血作用
antinoise　　$a.$ 抗噪音的，减少噪音的
antireflective　　$a.$ 抗反射，抗反光
antistatic　　$a.$ 抗静电的
apatite　　$n.$ 磷灰石
aqueous　　$a.$ 水的，水成的
aqueous chemistry　　液相化学

aramid n.（用以制造子午线轮胎及防弹背心等轻质高强度合成纤维）芳族聚酰胺

arithmetic n. 算术，计算，演算，估算；a. 算术（上）的，运算的，根据算术法则的

aroma compound 芳香族化合物

arteries n. 动脉

arthroplasty n. 关节造形术，关节形成术

artificial heart valves 人工心脏瓣膜

as for instance 例如，比如

as in 作为，就像，如

assess v. 估定，评定

astronomy n. 天文学

astrophysics n. 天体物理学

atomic force microscopy 原子力显微镜

atomic structure 原子结构

attributable a. 可归功于……的

austenitic a. 奥氏体的

austenitic alloy steel 奥氏合金钢（高锰钢）

autologous a. 自体的，自身的

B

backbone n. 脊椎，中枢

bakelite n. 酚醛树脂，电木，酚醛塑料，电胶木

bakeware n. 烘焙用具，烘烤器皿

ballast n. 压舱物，沙囊

barrier properties 防护性能，阻隔（水、气、光）性质

basin n. 盆，脸盆

batch n. 组，批，成批

be calculated for 为适合……而设计的，适合于

be subject to 受支配，从属于，可以……的，常遭受

bearing n. 轴承

bending 弯曲（度），挠度

beryllium n. 铍

bet n. 打赌，赌博，赌注，被下赌注的对象，可能性

bioassimilate n. 被生物同化物；vt.〔生理学〕生物吸收（食物），生物消化；vi.（食物等）被生物吸收，被生物消化

bioassimilation n. 生物同化，生物同化作用，生物消化

bioceramics 生物陶瓷

biocompatibility n. 生物相容性，生物适合性

biocompatible a. 生物相适应性的

biodegradability 生物降解能力

biodegradable a. 能进行生物降解的，能起生物递解分解作用的；

biomass n.（单位面积或体积内）生物的数量，生物质

biomaterial a. 生物材料的；n. 生物材料

biomaterial n. 生物材料

biomimetic n. 生物测定学，生物统计学

bioplast n. 原生质细胞，原生体

biopolymer n. 生物高聚物

bis（2-ethylhexyl）sulfosuccinate n. 双（2-乙基己基）磺基琥珀酸钠

bis-phenol 双酚

blade n. 刀刃，刀片

blend v. 混合；n. 混合

blunt a. 钝的，不锋利的，迟钝的，直率的，呆板的；vt. 使迟钝，使钝

blur vt. & vi. 涂污，弄脏，（使）变模糊，（使）难以区分，疾驰残影，模糊，污点，污迹；n. 污迹，污斑，模糊不清的事物，暧昧不明

body fluids 体液

bonding n. 黏结，连〔搭，焊，胶，粘〕接

bone n. 骨头，骨质物

boron n. 硼

Bragg formula 布拉格公式

brass n. 黄铜

bridge bearings 桥梁支座

brittle a. 易脆的，易碎的

brownian motion 布朗运动

button n. 纽扣，按钮；v. 扣住，扣紧

by virtue of 依靠（……力量），凭借，由于，因为

C

cactus n. 仙人掌
calcium carbonate 碳酸钙
calcium hydroxyapatite 羟基磷灰石
cancellous a. 多孔的，网眼状的，网状骨质的
capacitor n. 电容器
capacity n. 容量，性能，生产能力
carbide n. 碳化物
carbon dioxide n. 二氧化碳
carbon fibres 碳纤维
carbon nanotube 碳纳米管
carboxylic acid 羧酸
cardiac myocytes 心肌细胞
cardiovascular a. 心脏血管的，心血管的
cartilage n. 软骨
casein n. 干酪素，酪蛋白
cast n. 投掷，铸件，脱落物；v. 投，抛，投射，浇铸
casting n. 铸造，铸件，投掷，角色分配；v. 铸造，投掷，投向，选派演员，扔掉（cast 的 ing 形式）
castor oil n. 蓖麻油
catalyst n. 催化剂，触媒
cathode n. 阴极，负极
cation n. 正离子，阳离子
cellulose n. 细胞膜质，纤维素
cement n. 水泥
cementation n. 黏固
ceramic n. 陶瓷，陶瓷制品；制陶术，制陶业；a. 陶器的
ceramic-matrix composites 陶瓷基复合材料
Characterization n. 表征，表述
charge vt. 使充电；vi. 充电
chemical makeup 化学组成
chemical vapor deposition 化学气相沉积

chemical/mechanical polishing 化学机械抛光
chlorine n. 氯
chromium n. 铬
chronic a. 慢性的，延续很长的
circumvent vt. 防止，避免
civil engineering 土木工程
classical a. 古典的，经典的，传统的
classification n. 分类，类别
cleave v. 劈，劈开，裂开；v. 黏着，坚持
cleaving 劈开，裂开
clinic n. 诊所，门诊部，特殊病例分析，临床讲授，临床实习课
close tolerance 紧公差，严格的容限
clot n. 凝块；v. 凝结，使……凝结
cluster n. 串，丛；v. 丛生，成群
coagulate vt.&vi. 凝固，使结块，使变稠；a. [废语] 凝固的，凝结的，凝聚的
coagulation n. 凝结，凝聚，凝固
coarse-grained a. 纹理粗糙的，粗鲁的，粗鄙的
cobalt n. 钴
coefficient n. 系数
coir n. 椰子壳的纤维
collagen n. 胶原，骨胶原，胶原蛋白，胶原质
collide v. 碰撞，互撞，抵触
collimated beam 平行光束，准直光束
colorant n. 着色剂
combustion n. 燃烧
compatibility n. 适合，互换性，通用性，和睦相处
competency n. 能力
composite a. 合成的，复合的；n. 合成物，复合材料
composite a. 混合成的，综合成的；n. 合成物，混合物，复合材料，复合物，复合体
composition gradient 成分梯度

compostability 肥料稳定性；堆肥能力
comprehensive a. 广泛的，综合的，有理解力的
compression n. 压缩，缩小
compressive a. 有压缩力的
conceive vt.&vi. 构思；想像；设想；考虑
concrete n. 混凝土，钢筋混凝土
condensation n. 浓缩
condensation reaction 缩合反应
condense v. 升华
configuration n. 结构，布局，形态
conformable a. 适合的，一致的
conjugated a. 共轭的，成对的
conservative values 守恒值
consortium n. 联合，合伙
constant a. 经常的，不变的；n. 常数，恒量
construct vt. 修建，建造，构成，创立
contamination n. 玷污，污染，污染物
continual a. 连续的，频繁的，持续不断的
contract v. 缩短，缩小，收缩
contraction n. 收缩，缩减，传染，缩写式
contradictory a. 矛盾的，反驳的；n. 对立物，矛盾因
controversial a. 争论的，争议的
conveyor belts 输送带
coolant n. 冷冻剂
copolymer n. 共聚物，共多聚体
copper n. 铜
cornea n. 角膜
coronary stents 冠状动脉支架
corrode v. 使腐蚀，侵蚀
corrosion n. 侵蚀，腐蚀（锈），腐蚀状态
corrosion resistance ［化学］耐蚀性，抗腐蚀性
corrosive a. 腐蚀的，蚀坏的，腐蚀性的；n. 腐蚀物，腐蚀剂
cortical a. 皮层的，皮质的，有关脑皮层的
cosmetic n. 化妆品；a. 化妆用的

counterpart n. 配对物，副本，相对物，极相似的人或物
covalent a. 共有原子价的，共价的
covalently adv.（共有原子价，共价键）的变形
crack n. 裂缝，缝隙，（可听到响声的）重击
craft n. 工艺，手艺
creep corrosion 裂隙腐蚀
creep resistance 蠕变阻力，蠕滑阻力，抗蠕变力，蠕变强度，蠕爬极限
crevice n.（墙壁，岩石等的）裂缝
criterion n.（pl. criteria）标准，准则，尺度
crucial a. 至关紧要的
crucible n. 坩埚
crush v. 压碎，碾碎，压服，压垮，粉碎，（使）变形
cryogenic a. 低温学的
crystalline a. 晶体的，结晶的
crystallinity n. 结晶性，结晶度
cupro-nickel alloys 铜镍合金
currency n. 货币
cutlery n. 餐具
cylindrical a. 呈圆筒形的，圆柱体的［亦作 cylindric］
cytocompatibility n. 细胞相容性
cytotoxicity 细胞毒性

D

dacron 涤纶，聚酯纤维，涤纶织物
dealloying 脱合金成分腐蚀
deceptive a. 欺骗性的
decompose v. 分解，腐烂
defective a. 有缺陷的
deflect vt. 使歪斜，使弯曲；vi. 偏转，偏离
deform v.（使）变形
degradation n. 降级，降格，退化
delicatessen n. 熟食店

delithiation n. 脱锂
dendrimer n. 聚合物，树形分子，树状聚物
density n. 密度
depict v. 描述，描写
deposition n. 沉积作用（沉积物，矿床）
deteriorate v. （使）恶化
dextran n. 右旋糖苷
dezincification 脱锌
diacid n. 二酸；a. 二价酸的，二酸的
diamagnetic a. 反磁性的；n. 反磁性体
diamine n. 二（元）胺
dielectric constant 介电常数
diesel n. 柴油机，内燃机
dilute v. 冲淡，稀释
dimension n. 尺度，维度
dimensionality n. 维度，度数
dimming 减低亮度，变暗
directionality n. 方向，方向性
discrete a. 不连续的，离散的
discretization n. 离散化
disinfection n. 消毒，灭菌
dislocation n. 混乱，断层，脱臼
dislocation n. 位错，错位，断层
persistent slip bands（PSB） 稳定滑移带
dispersed a. 被驱散的，被分散的，散布的
disposable a. 可任意使用的
disposable a. 一次性的，可任意处理的，用后就抛弃的，免洗的，可供使用的；n. 使用后随即抛掉的东西（尤指容器等），一次性用品，一次性，一次性手套
disproportionately adv. 不匀称，不相称
disrupt v. 使……分裂，使……分散
disruptive a. 使破裂的，分裂性的
dissimilar a. 不同的
dissolve v. 溶解，解散
distinguished by 以……为特征
domain n. 领土，领地，范围，领域
donor organ 捐献器官

doped 掺杂质的
dosage n. 药量
drainpipe n. 排水管
drug eluting stents 药物涂层支架
drum n. 鼓，鼓声，鼓形圆桶；v. 击鼓，作鼓声，打鼓奏
ductility n. 可延展性，延伸度，可锻性，韧性，柔软性，顺从
durability n. 耐久性
durability test 耐久性试验，施工测量，寿命试验，疲劳试验
dysfunction n. 机能不良，功能紊乱，官能障碍

E

eco-friendly a. 对生态环境友好的，不妨害生态环境的
edible a. 可食用的
effectuate v. 实行，完成
elaboration n. 详尽的细节，解释，阐述
elastic a. 有弹力的，可伸缩的，灵活的
elasticity modulus 弹性模量
elastomer n. 弹性体，人造橡胶
electric vehicles 电动汽车
electrical conductivity 电导率，导电率，导电性
electrochromic a. 电镀铬的
electrode n. 电极
electrolyte n. 电解液，电解质
electrolytic a. 电解的，由电解产生的
electromotive a. 电测的
electromotive force 电动势
electron distribution n. 电子分布
electronic circuit 电子电路
electronic structure 电子结构
electrooptical a. 电光的
elimination n. 排除，除去，消除，消灭
elucidate v. 阐明，说明
emissivity n. 发射率
empower v. 授权，准许，使能够

empower sb. to do sth. 授权某人做某事
enamel n. 珐琅，瓷釉
encapsulate v. 装入胶囊，压缩，形成胶囊
encapsulate vt. 封装，概述；vi. 形成囊状物
encapsulation n. 封装，封装性，密封
encase v. 包围，包住，包裹
encountered n. 遇到
endocrine a. 内分泌的；n. 内分泌
endoscope n. 内诊镜，内窥镜
enrich v. 使富足，使肥沃，装饰，加料于，浓缩
entanglement n. 纠缠
environmental degradation 环境退化
enzyme n. 酶
epoxy a. 环氧的；n. 环氧树脂
erythema n. 红斑，非冻疮
ester linkage 酯键
esthetic a. 感觉的
esthetics n. 美学
estrogen-like 雌激素一样的（东西）
ethane n. 乙烷
eucalyptus n. 桉树
evaporation n. 蒸发（作用）
exclusively adv. 排外地，专有地
exfoliation n. 脱落，脱落物，表皮剥脱；页状剥落；
exhibit v. 展出，陈列，展示；n. 展览品，陈列品，展品
expansion n. 扩大；扩张；扩张物；膨胀物
extension n. 延长，扩充，范围；a. 外延的，客观现实的
extraction n. 抽出，取出，抽出物
extractive a. 引得出的，抽取的，萃取的；n. 抽出物，精，熬汁
extrusion n. 挤出，推出，喷出的，突出的，赶出

F

fabric n. 织物，布，构造，质地
fat n. 脂肪
fatigue n. 疲乏，疲劳，累活；v. 使疲劳，使心智衰弱，疲劳
felspathic a. 长石质的
femoral-head 股骨头
Ferrari 一种车名（法拉利）
ferrites n. 陶铁磁体
ferromagnetic a. 铁磁的，铁磁体的；n. 铁磁体
ferrous a. 含铁的
fiberglass n. 纤维玻璃
fiber-optic a. 光纤的，光纤材料的
filament windin 纤维缠绕
filamentous a. 细丝状的，纤维所成的，如丝的
filiform a. 丝状的，纤维状的
filtration n. 过滤
fine-tune v. 调整，使有规则
fingerprint n. 指纹，指印；vt. 采指纹
flake n. 小薄片，碎片；vi.（成小薄片）脱落，剥落；vt. 把（鱼、食物等）切成薄片
flame retardancy 阻燃性
flame-retardant n. 阻燃
flammability n. 易燃的，可燃性的
flaw n. 瑕疵，缺点，裂缝，裂纹
flexibility n. 灵活性，柔韧性
flexible a. 柔韧性，易曲的，灵活的，柔软的，能变形的，可通融的
flexible a. 灵活的，易弯曲的，柔韧的，易被说服的，柔性，灵活，弹性的，多变的
fluctuate v. 波动，变动，起伏
fluctuation n. 波动，涨落，起伏
fluorescence n. 发荧光，荧光
fluorescent n. 荧光灯；a. 荧光的
fluoroethylene carbonate 氟代碳酸乙烯酯
foil n. 箔，金属薄片，陪衬，陪衬物
folding a. 可折叠的
foodstuff n. 食品，粮食

forerunner n. 先驱（者），预兆
foreseeable 可预见到的
forge v. 稳步前进，铸造，伪造
forging n. 锻件，锻造（法）
formaldehyde n. 甲醛，蚁醛
formation n. 形成，构成
formula n. 公式，规则
formulation n. 配方，构想，规划，公式化
formulation n. 用公式表示，明确地表达，作简洁陈述
fossil fuel 化石燃料
foundry n. 铸造，铸造场，铸造类
Fourier transform infrared spectroscopy 傅里叶变换红外光谱
fracture n. 破裂，骨折，龟裂；v. （使）破碎，（使）破裂
fracture toughness 断裂韧度
fragile a. 易碎的，脆的
fragmentation n. 分裂，破碎
frame n. 结构，体格；v. 构成，设计，制定
free path 自由程
free radicals 自由基
fuel efficiency 燃烧效率
fungi 真菌类（包括霉菌，食用伞菌，酵母菌等），似真菌的，由真菌引起的

G

galvanic a. 流电的，抽搐的，以流电所产的
garnered v. 储存
gas turbine n. 燃气涡轮
gaskets n. 垫圈，衬垫（gasket 的名词复数）密合垫，材料垫片
gel n. 凝胶体；v. 成冻胶
generic a. 属性的，一般的
get rid of v. 摆脱，除去
getter n. 吸气剂
giant a. 庞大的，巨大的；n. 巨人，大力士，巨大的动物或植物

gland n. 腺，密封管
glass fibres 玻璃纤维
glassceramic 微晶玻璃
glazing n. 玻璃装配业，玻璃窗，上釉，上光
goggles n. 护目镜，眼罩
gradient n. 倾斜度，梯度，陡度，变化率，梯度变化曲线
grafting 嫁接，移植（术）
grain boundary [晶体学] 晶界
granularity n. 间隔尺寸，粒度
grapheme n. 石墨
grind v. 磨（碎），碾（碎），折磨
guillotine n. 断头台，（切纸的）闸刀；v. 处斩刑，切（纸）

H

HA 透明质酸
hafnium n. 铪
hardness n. 硬度，硬性
harmonize vt. 使和谐；为（旋律）配和声；vi. 和谐，以和声演奏或歌唱
Hastelloy 哈司特镍合金，镍基合金（耐盐酸，耐蚀，耐热）
Haynes alloys 海恩斯（姓氏）合金
haze n. 薄雾，疑惑，阴霾；v. 使变朦胧，变朦胧，变糊涂
heat capacity 热容
hematite n. 赤铁矿
hemolysis n. 溶血，溶血作用
hemolysis 溶血
hemolytic a. [医] 溶血的
heterogeneity n. 异质性，不均匀性，不纯一性
heterogeneous a. 多种多样的，混杂的，不均匀，非均匀，错杂
hevea Brasiliensis trees 巴西橡胶树
high resilience 高弹性
histogram n. [统计] 直方图，柱状图，频率曲线

hitherto *adv.* 到目前为止，迄今，至今
holistically *adv.* 整体地，全盘地
homogeneous *a.* 均质的
homogeneous *a.* 同性质的，同类的；均匀的
honeycomb *n.* 蜂房，蜂巢，蜂脾
horticulture *n.* 园艺
humus *n.* 腐殖质
hydride *n.* 氢化物
hydrochloric *a.* 氯化氢的，盐酸的
hydrogel *n.* ［物化］水凝胶
hydrogen fuel cell 氢燃料电池
hydrolytic *a.* 水解的；产生水解（作用）的
hydrophobicity *n.* 疏水性
hydrostatic weighing 流体静力称重，水下皮脂测定法
hydroxyapatite *n.* 羟磷灰石
hygroscopic *a.* 吸湿的，湿度器的
hygrothermal *a.* 湿热的

I

ill-fated *a.* 不幸的，噩运的
imitate *v.* 模仿，仿效，仿制，仿造
immune *a.* 免疫的
immuno assay 免疫测定法，免疫化验
immunological *a.* 免疫学
impetus *n.* 动力，促进，势头，声势
implant *n.* ［医］移植，植入，植入物，植入管；*vt.* 种植，灌输，嵌入；*vi.* 被移植
implantable *a.* 可植入的，可移植的
impracticable *a.* 不可行的
impregnate *v.* 浸渍，饱和
impregnation *n.* 注入
impurity *n.* 不纯，杂质
in vitro 在体外，在试管内
in vivo 在体内
inclusive *a.* 包括的，包含的
incoming light 入射光
indicator *n.* 指示器，指示剂

inductance *n.* 感应系数，自感应
inert *a.* 惰性的，迟钝的，不活泼的
inferior *a.* （质量等）低劣的，下级的，下等的
infiltration *n.* 渗透，下渗，渗滤，入渗
inflammation *n.* 发炎，红肿，炎症
ingredient *n.* （混合物的）组成部分；（烹调的）原料；（构成）要素；因素
inhale *v.* 吸入
inhibitor *n.* 抑止剂
injurious *a.* 有害的，伤害的
In-situ synthesis 原位合成
inspect *v.* 检查，调查，监查，检阅
insulative *a.* 绝缘的
insulator *n.* 绝缘体，绝热器
insulin-producing cells 胰岛素分泌细胞
integration *n.* 结合，整合，一体化
intensive-care areas 重病特别护理区，重症监护区
interdisciplinary *a.* 交叉学科的
interfacial *a.* （晶体或其他固体）面间的，面际的，界面的，形成界面的
interferometer *n.* 干涉计，干涉仪
intergranular 晶粒间的，粒间的
intermediary *a.* 中间人的，调解的，居间的，媒介的；*n.* 中间人，媒介，调解人，中间阶段，中介，仲裁者
intravenous *a.* 静脉的，静脉注射的
intricate *a.* 复杂的，错综的
intrusion *n.* 凹陷
iodide method 碘化法
irradiation *n.* 照射，辐射
irrespective *a.* 不考虑的，不顾的，无关的，不论，不考虑的
irreversible *a.* 不能撤回的，不能取消的
isomer *n.* 异构体
isoprene *n.* 橡胶基质

J

judicious *a.* 明智的

K

keratin *n*. 角质素，角蛋白
ketone *n*. 酮
kidney *n*. 肾，腰子

L

lactic acid 乳酸
laminate *n*. 层压材料，叠层，层压；*v*. 碾压
lamination *n*. 叠片结构
landscape *n*. 风景，风景画，乡村风景画，地形
laser aviation 激光溅射
latex *n*. 胶乳，（尤指橡胶树的）橡浆，人工合成胶乳（用以制作油漆、黏合剂和织物）
lathe *n*. 车床；*v*. 用车床加工
latter *a*. 后者的，末了的，较后的，后者，次序或时间在后，后面的
lattice *n*. 晶格
lattice parameter 层状参数
lattice spacing 晶格间距，点阵间距
leach *v*. 滤去
leverage *n*. 手段，影响力，杠杆作用，杠杆效率；*v*. 利用；举债经营
lids *n*. 盖子；*v*. 给……盖盖子
life expectancy 平均寿命
ligaments *n*. 韧带
lightning strikes 雷击
lightweight *a*. 轻量的，不重要的
lignin *n*. 木质素
lignocellulosic *a*. 木质纤维的
lipid *n*. 脂肪，油脂，[生化]脂类
lithiation *n*. 锂化，潜锂
lithium-aluminosilicate 锂铝硅酸盐
lithography *n*. 光刻
liver *n*. 肝脏
living beings 生物
locomotion *n*. 运动，移动，运动力，移动力

longitudinal *a*. 轻度的，纵的，经线的
low damping 弱阻尼
lubricity *n*. 润滑性，润滑能力
luster *n*. 光泽；*v*. 有光泽，发亮，使……发光
lustrous *a*. 有光泽的，光辉的

M

macromolecule *n*. 巨大分子，高分子
macrostructure *n*. 宏观结构
magnesium *n*. 镁
magnetic *a*. 磁的，有磁性的，有吸引力的
magnetic levitation 磁悬浮
magnitude *n*. 大小，数量，巨大，广大，量级
maintenance *n*. 维持，保持，保养，保管，维护，维修
malignant *a*. 恶性的，有害的
malleability *n*. 可锻性，延展性，柔韧性
malleable *a*. 有延展性的，可锻的
manipulation *n*. 操作，操纵
marine turbine 船用汽轮机
masonry *n*. 石工工程，砖瓦工工程，砖石建筑
mass fraction *n*. 质量分数
mat *n*. 席子，垫子，团，簇
matrix *n*. 基质
maturity *n*. 成熟
maxillofacial *a*. 颌面部的
Maybach 一种车名
mechanical behavior 力学行为
melts *n*. [冶]熔体（melt 的复数）；*v*. 熔化（melt 的第三人称单数形式）
membrane *n*. 薄膜，隔膜，膜状物
mercury *n*. 汞，水银
mercury-free 无汞
meridian *n*. 子午线，正午，顶点；*a*. 子午线的，正午的，顶点的
metalloid *n*. 非金属；*a*. 非金属的

metallurgical　*a*. 冶金的，冶金学的
metallurgist　*n*. 冶金家，冶金学者
metallurgy　*n*. 冶金，冶金术；冶金学
metalworking　*n*. 金属加工术，金属工
methodology　*n*. 方法学，方法论
meticulous　*a*. 小心翼翼的，一丝不苟的
micellar　*n*. 胶束的，微胞的，微团的
microbe　*n*. 微生物，细菌
microelectromechanical systems　微机电系统
microemulsion　*n*. 微乳液
micrometastasis　*n*.（残留癌肿的）微小转移
microstructure　*n*. 微观结构，显微结构
microwave　*n*. 微波
mimic　*v*. 模仿
miscibility　*n*. 可混合性，易混合性
mitigate　*v*. 缓解，减轻，缓和
modulus　*n*. 模数，模量，系数
modulus of elasticity　弹性模量，弹性系数
moieties　*n*. 基团
molecular beam epitaxy　分子束外延生长
molten　*v*. 熔化；*a*. 熔铸的
molybdenum　*n*. 钼
Monel　*n*. 蒙乃尔铜-镍合金
monoclinic　*a*. 单斜的
monodispersed　*a*. 单分散的
monolithic　*n*. 单片电路，单块集成电路
monomer　*n*. 单体
montmorillonite　*n*. 蒙脱石，胶岭石，高岭石
mould　*n*.［亦作 mold］霉，模具；*v*. 用土覆盖，发霉，铸造
moulding　*n*. 模制，浇铸
multidisciplinary　*a*. 包括各种学科的，有关各种学问的，多学科，多部门，多科目
mutagenicity　*n*. 诱变（性）

N

nanoclay　*n*. 纳米黏土
nanocrystalline　*n*. 纳米晶体，奈米晶
nanoelectronics　*n*. 纳米电子学
nanoengineered　*a*. 纳米工程的
nanomaterial　*n*. 纳米材料；*a*. 纳米材料的
nanotube　*n*. 纳米管
nebulous　*a*. 星云的，云雾状的，模糊的，朦胧的
neoprene rubber　*n*. 氯丁（二烯）橡胶，氯丁橡胶，药水糊，氯丁胶
neuronal　*n*. 神经元，二乙基溴乙酰胺
nickel　*n*. 镍
niobium　*n*. 铌
nitride　*n*. 氮化物
noble　*a*. 高尚的，贵族的，高贵的；*n*. 贵族
noninvasive　*a*. 非侵害的，非侵袭的
nonlinear optics　非线性光
nonlocalized electrons　游离电子
nonrenewable　*a*. 不可再生的
nonrenewable resource　不可再生资源
normal axis　垂直轴，法线轴
notch　*n*. 刻痕
nozzle　*n*. 喷嘴，接管
nuclear　*a*. 核子的，原子能的，核的，中心的［复数 nucleus］*n*. 核子
nucleate　*v*. 成核，形成晶核
nucleosynthesis　*n*. 核合成，核聚变
numismatics　*n*. 货币学，古币
nutrient　*n*. 养分
nylon　*n*. 尼龙

O

oak　*n*. 栎树；*a*. 栎树的，栎木制的
oleic acid　*n*. 油酸，十八烯酸
oligomeric　*a*. 低聚物的
opacity　*n*. 不透明性
opaque　*n*. 不透明物；*a*. 不透明的，不传热的，迟钝的

oppositely *adv.* 相对地，对立地
optical *a.* 眼的，视力的，光学的
optimal *a.* 最佳的，最理想的
optimize *v.* 优化，使……完善
orbital *a.* 眼窝的
ore *n.* 矿石，含有金属的岩石
organ *n.* 元件，机构，机关，机关报，嗓音，器官
orientation *n.* 方向，方位，定位，倾向性，向东方
orthopedic *a.* 整形外科的，矫形术的
ossicle *n.* 听小骨
outermost *a.* 最外面的，最远的
overriding *a.* 最重要的，高于一切的
overwrap *n.* （香烟、面包等的）透明外包装纸
oxidation *n.* 氧化，氧化作用，生锈
oxide *n.* 氧化物
oxidize *v.* 氧化，生锈
ozone oxidation 臭氧氧化，臭氧氧化法，臭氧法，臭氧的氧化

P

pacing electrodes 起搏电极
pail *n.* 桶，提桶
palette *n.* 调色板，颜料
palladium *n.* 钯
pancreas *n.* 胰腺，胰，胰脏
paralysis *n.* 瘫痪
paramagnetic *a.* 顺磁性的；*n.* 顺磁性体
particleboard *n.* 芯板材，刨花板
passivation *n.* 钝化
peak *n.* 高峰，峰值
percolation *n.* 过滤，浸透，渗滤，渗漏
performance *n.* （材料的）性能
periodontal *a.* 牙周的
permeability *n.* 渗透性，磁导率，渗透率
permeable *a.* 有浸透性的，能透过的
permeation *n.* 渗入，透过
peroxidation *n.* 过氧化反应

perpendicular *n.* 垂直线，垂直的位置
perspective *n.* 透视，观点，全景
pesticide *n.* 农药
petrochemical *a.* 石化的；*n.* 石化产品
pharmaceutical *a.* 药物的（医药的）
pharmacological *a.* 药物学的，药理学的
phase *n.* 相，相位，时期，阶段
phenolic *a.* 酚的，石碳酸的
philosophies＝philosophize *v.* 进行哲学探讨，使哲学化
phonon coupling 声子耦合
phosphorus *n.* 磷
photodiode *n.* 光敏二极管，光电二极管
photodynamic therapy 光动力学疗法
photoluminescence *n.* 光致发光，光激发光
photoresists *n.* 光阻剂；光产酸剂；碱溶性聚酯
photothermal therapy 光热疗法
physiological *a.* 生理的，生理学的
piezoelectric *a.* 压电的
piezoelectric ceramics 压电陶瓷
pin *v.* 将……用针别住，钉住，压住
pitfall *n.* 缺陷
pitting *n.* 金属点状腐蚀（小孔，烧熔边缘，软化），蚀损斑
plantations *n.* 种植园，大农场（plantation的名词复数）
plasma *n.* 等离子体，血浆，等离子
plastic *a.* 塑料的；*n.* 塑料，（外科）整形的
plasticizer *n.* 可塑剂
plating *n.* 电镀，被覆金属；*v.* 镀
platinum *n.* 铂金
pliable *a.* 易曲折的，柔软的，圆滑的，柔韧的
polar *a.* 极地的，两极的，正好相反的，磁极的，有磁性的
polarity *n.* 极性，反向性
polished *a.* 抛光的，擦亮的
polyamide（PA） *n.* 聚酰胺

polychloroprene n. 聚氯丁烯,氯丁橡胶; 聚氯丁二烯
polycrystalline a. [晶体]多晶的
polydispersion n. 多分散性,多分散体
polyetheretherketone 聚醚醚酮
polyethylene (PE) n. 聚乙烯
polyethylene terephthalate (PET) n. 聚对苯二甲酸乙二醇酯
polyhedra n. 多面体
polyhedral a. 多面的,多面体的
polyimide n. 聚酰亚胺
polymer n. 聚合物,聚合体,聚合材料
polymeric a. 聚合的,聚合体的
polyol n. 多羟基化合物
polyolefin n. 聚烯烃
polypropylene (PP) n. 聚丙烯
polypyrrole (PPy) n. 聚吡咯
polystyrene (PS) n. 聚苯乙烯
polyurethane n. 聚氨酯,聚氨基甲酸酯
polyvinylchloride (PVC) n. 聚氯乙烯
porcelain n. 瓷器,瓷; a. 瓷制的,精美的,脆的
porosity n. 多孔性,有孔性
possess v. 持有,占有,拥有
pottery n. 陶瓷,陶器
precaution n. 注意事项,预防措施
precipitate n. 沉淀物; v. 猛抛,使陷入,促成,使沉淀,猛地落下
precipitation n. 沉淀,凝结,析出
preclude n. 排除
precursor n. 前驱体,初期形式
preferential a. 先取的,优先的,特惠的
prefix n. 前缀,词首,前加成分
previously adv. 先前,以前
principal a. 主要的,最重要的
privacy n. 独处而不受干扰,秘密
probabilistic n. 概率的,概率性的
probe n. 探针,调查,探测针; v. 用探针测,详细调查
processing v. (材料的)加工,处理

processing aid 加工助剂
productivity n. 生产率,生产力
profile n. 剖面,侧面,外形,轮廓
prohibitive a. 禁止的,抑制的
prone a. 倾向于
prooxidant n. 氧化强化剂
propagate v. 传播,传送,传输
propensity n. 倾向,习性,倾向性
property n. (材料的)特征,性质
propulsion n. 推进,推进力
prosthesis n. 假体,人体修复(术)
protein n. 朊,蛋白(质); a. 蛋白质的
proton n. 质子
pulp n. 纸浆; vt. 使化成纸浆,变成纸浆
pultrusion n. 拉挤成型
purification n. 净化,纯化,提纯
pyrex n. 耐热玻璃
pyrolytic a. 热解的(高温分解的)
pyrolytic a. 热解的(高温分解的)
pyrometallurgy n. 火法冶金学(热冶学,火冶学)

Q

quantitative a. 定量的,数量(上)的
quantum confinement 量子限域
quantum dots n. 量子点
quantum well 量子阱
quench v. 结束,熄灭,淬火,熄灭,平息

R

radar n. 雷达
radiator hose 散热器软管,水箱橡皮管,水箱软管,侧散热器软管
radioactive waste 放射性废弃物
radiographic a. X光线照相术的
radiolysis n. 射解(作用),辐解(作用)
radiopaque a. 辐射透不过的
Raman spectroscopic analysis 拉曼光谱分析

Raman spectroscopy 拉曼光谱学，喇曼光谱学
rare earth *n*. 稀土元素，稀土
rarity *n*. 稀薄（稀有，珍品）
rearview mirror （车辆上的）后视镜
recession *n*. 经济衰退，不景气，后退，撤退，凹处，退场
rechargeable *a*. 可再充电的
recipient *n*. 接受者
reciprocal *n*. 倒数
reciprocal space *n*. 倒易空间
redirect *vt*. 使改寄，改变方向，改变线路
reduction factor 换算系数，简缩因数
reflectivity *n*. 反射
refraction *n*. 折射
refractories 耐火材料
regain *v*. 收回，恢复
reinforce *vt*. 加固，使更结实，加强，充实；*vi*. 求援，得到增援，给予更多的支持；*n*. 加固物，加固材料
remelt *v*. 再融化，再熔化
renaissance *n*. 复兴
Rene alloys 雷内（男子名）合金
repel *v*. 击退，抵制
reproducible *a*. 能繁殖的，可再生的，可复写的
residual *a*. 剩余的，残留的
resilience *n*. 弹力，弹性，弹性变形
resilient *a*. 弹回的，有回弹力的
resilient mounts *a*. 能复原的，弹回的，有弹性的，能立刻恢复精神；*n*. 坚韧，弹性
resin *n*. 树脂，合成树脂，松香
resin-based materials 树脂物质
resistivity *n*. 抵抗力，电阻系数
resolution *n*. 分辨率，清晰度
resonator *n*. 共鸣器，共振器
respiration *n*. 呼吸，呼吸作用
retardancy *n*. 阻滞性（阻……能力）
rhenium *n*. 铼

rigid *a*. 刚硬的，刚性的，严格的
robust *a*. 强健的，健康的，粗野的，粗鲁的
roll *a*. 滚动，滚转，（使）摇摆，（使）摇晃，卷起，卷拢；*v*. 辗，轧
rotate *v*. （使）旋转
rotation *n*. 旋转
rupture *v*. 破裂，裂开，断绝（关系等），割裂；*n*. 破裂，决裂，割裂
rupture strength 断裂强度
rust *n*. 铁锈；*v*. （使）生锈
ruthenium *n*. 钌

S

sacrifice *n*. 牺牲，献身，祭品，供奉；*v*. 牺牲，献出，献祭，供奉
saline *a*. 含盐的，咸的；*n*. 生理盐水，盐溶液
sanitaryware *n*. 卫生洁具，卫生陶器
sanskrit *n*. 梵文，梵语
sapphire *n*. 蓝宝石，宝石蓝；*a*. 蓝宝石色的
saw *n*. 锯
scaffold *n*. 脚手架，支架
scanning probe microscope 扫描探针显微镜
scanning tunneling microscope 扫描隧道显微镜
scatter *n*. 散布，分散
schematic *a*. 示意性的
sealability 密封性能，胶黏性
seals *n*. 密封件；*v*. 密封（seal 的第三人称单数），决定，确定，封上（信封）
seamless *a*. 无缝的，无漏洞的
segregate *a*. 分离的，被隔离的；*v*. 分离，隔离，分凝
selectivity *n*. 选择性；专一性
semiconductor *n*. 半导体，半导体材料
semiconductors *n*. 半导体
sensor *n*. 传感器，传感材料，灵敏元件

sensor n. 检测计
sewage n. （下水道里的）污物，下水道，污水
sewer n. 下水道，污水管
shattering 破碎，震动，震裂
shear n. 剪切，切变，扭曲
shear stress 剪切应力，剪应力，切变应力，黏性摩擦应力
shelf life n. （包装食品的）货架期，保存限期
shock n. 震惊，震动，打击，冲击
silicosis n. 矽肺病（硅肺）
silsesquioxane n. 硅倍半氧烷
silylation n. 甲硅烷基化作用，硅烷化（作用）
sinter n. 烧结物，熔渣；v. 使烧结
sintered v. 烧结；a. 烧结的（熔结的，黏结的）
sisal n. 剑麻（波罗麻）
skeleton n. 骨架，骨骼
skylight n. 天窗
slurry n. 浆体，研磨液
sodium n. 钠
soft ferrites 软性铁氧体
solar cell 太阳能电池
sol-gel method 溶胶-凝胶法
solidification n. 凝固
sound a. 健全的，可靠的，合理的
spatiotemporal a. 空间与时间的，时空的
speciality n. 专业，专长，特性，特制品，同specialty
specific strength [力]比强度，强度系数
specimen n. 样本，标本，试样，样品
spectrum n. 光，光谱，型谱，频谱
spillway n. 溢洪道，泄洪道，溢口
spinal cord fusion devices 脊髓融合装置
stabilization n. 稳定性
starch n. 淀粉，浆粉
state-of-the-art 最先进的，最高级的，最新型的，顶尖水准的，使用了最先进技术的
stem cells 干细胞
stepwise a. 逐步地，分阶段地
sterilized v. 杀菌（消除，冻结）；a. 无菌的（消毒的）
steroid n. 类固醇，拟脂醇
stiff a. 硬的，僵直的，拘谨的，呆板的，艰难的，费劲的，僵硬的
stiffness n. 强度，刚度，硬度，僵硬
stitches 缝线
stoichiometric number 化学计算（数）值
strain n. 应变，拉紧
straw n. 稻草，麦秆
strength n. 强度
strenuous a. 费力的，艰苦的
stress n. 应力，压力
stretchable a. 有弹性的
structure n. （材料的）结构，构造
styrene n. 苯乙烯
sublattice n. 子格
submicroscopic a. 亚微观的
substrate n. 基片（基层，真晶格，基质）
succeeding a. 接连的（随后的）
sunscreen n. （防晒油中的）遮光剂
super condenser 超级电容器
superalloy n. 超耐热合金
superficially adv. 浅薄地，肤浅地，表面地
surface dislocation 表面位错
surface passivation 表面钝化
surgeon n. 外科医生
susceptibility n. 易感性，感受性，磁化系数
susceptible a. 易受影响的，易感动的，容许……的；n. （因缺乏免疫力而）易得病的人
suspended a. 暂停的，缓期的（宣判），悬浮的
swellable a. 可膨胀的
switchable glass 开关玻璃
swollen a. 肿胀的

T

tableware n. 餐具
tailing n. 残渣，尾料，屑
tangle n. 混乱状态；v. 处于混乱状态
tantalum n. 钽
tasteless a. 没味道的，无鉴赏力的
temperature gradient 温度梯度
temporary a. 暂时的，临时的，临时性
tendon n. 腱，肌腱
tensile a. 可拉长的，可伸长的，张力的，拉力的
tension n. 张力，拉力
terminal a. 致死的
terminate v. 结束，终止
terminator n. 终结者，终结器
terpolymer n. 三元共聚物
terylene n. 涤纶
tetragonal a. 四角形的，正方晶系的，四方的
tetrahedral a. 有四面的，四面体的
the Far East n. 远东地区；远东
the fatigue threshold 疲劳极限
theranostics n. 治疗诊断学
therapeutic a. 治疗（学）的，疗法的，有益于健康的
therapy n. 治疗，疗法，疗效，心理治疗，治疗力
thermal conductivity 热导性，热导率
thermal cycling 热循环，热交变
thermodynamics n. 热力学
thermoelectricity n. 热电，温差电
thermoform n.（塑料等的）加热成形，热力塑型；v. 使加热成形，给……用热力塑型
thermoplastic a. 热塑性的；n. 热塑性塑料
thermoset a. 热固的；n. 热固性树脂，热固性塑料
thermosetting n. 热固性树脂，热固性塑料；a. 热固的
thermostat n. 恒温器
threshold n. 阈值，临界值
thrombus n. 血栓，血块
tiles n. 瓷砖
tire cord 轮胎帘布
titanium n. [化学] 钛（金属元素）
tolerate vt. 容许，承认，忍受，容忍
tomography n. 断层摄影术
tonne 公吨（＝1,000 公斤或称 metric ton）
tonnes n. 吨，公吨（tonne 的名词复数）
tons n. 吨，容积单位，货物体积，大量，许多
torsion n. 扭力，扭转，扭曲
toughen vt. 使变坚韧，使变强硬，使变坚强；vi. 变坚韧，变强硬，变坚强
toughness n. 强硬，韧性，黏性
toughness test 韧性试验，韧度试验
toxic residue 残毒
toxicity n. 毒性
toxin n. 毒素
trabeculae n. 骨小梁
traceability n. 跟踪能力，可追溯性
transistor n. 晶体管
translucence n. 半透明
translucent a. 半透明的，透明的
transmutation n. 变形，变化
transparent a. 透明的，显然的，明晰的
transportation vehicle 交通工具
triglyceride n. 甘油三酸酯
trim a. 整齐的，整洁的；v. 整理，修整，装饰
tumor n. 肿块，肿瘤
tungsten n. 钨
tunnelling effect 隧道效应
turbocharger n. 涡轮增压器
tyre sidewalls 轮胎侧壁

U

ulcers n. 溃疡

ultrapure *a.* 超高纯的
ultraviolet *a.* 紫外线的
unified *a.* 统一的，统一标准的，一元化的
unit mass 单位质量，质量单位
unpainted *a.* 无复层的，未上漆的
unsealed *a.* 未密封的，打开的
uppermost *a.* 最高的，至上的；*adv.* 最初，首先
urea-formaldehyde 尿素甲醛

V

vacuum *n.* 真空，空间
valence bands 价带
van der Waals force 范德华力
vanadium dioxide 二氧化钒 VO_2
varistor *n.* 压敏电阻
vascular *a.* 血管的，脉管的
ventilation *n.* 通风，换气
versatile *a.* 通用的，万能的，多才多艺的，多面手的
viability *n.* 生存能力，发育能力；生活力
vibrating *n.* 振动，振荡
vice versa *adv.* 反之亦然
viscous *a.* 黏的，有黏性的，黏性的
visible light 可见光

vocal cords 声带
voltage *n.* 电压，伏特数
volume fraction 体积分数，体积分率，容积率
vulcanization *n.* （橡胶的）硫化（过程），硫化
vulcanized rubbers 硫化橡胶，橡皮，硬橡皮

W

Waspaloy 沃斯帕洛伊合金，一种耐高热镍基合金
wavelength *n.* 波长，波段
wax *n.* 蜡，蜡状物，增加，月亮由亏转盈；*v.* 变大，增大，月亮渐满，上蜡于
wear and tear 损坏，损耗，消损，磨损
wear resistance 耐磨性
wood *n.* 木材，树林，木制品

Y

yield stress 屈服应力，屈服点
yoke *n.* 轭，轭状物

Z

zirconium *n.* 锆
zirconium oxide 氧化锆

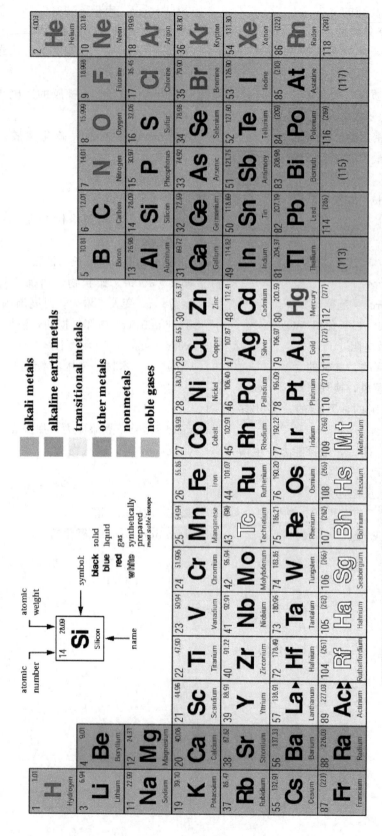